Hypno Annihilating Anxiety!

Penetrating confessions of a Rogue Hypnotist.

By the Rogue Hypnotist.

Disclaimer: the Rogue Hypnotist accepts no legal liability for the use or misuse of the information contained in this book. People who are not qualified professionals use the information at their own risk. This book is intended for entertainment and educational purposes only. **Nothing in this book is to be taken as being medical advice. This book represents a lifetime of research by the Rogue Hypnotist into hypnotherapeutic approaches to anxiety treatment that work!** Only the 20+ hypnosis scripts, assorted techniques, the diagram etc. contained within are for your personal or public use copyright free. They may not be resold.

Note: British English spelling and punctuation conventions are used throughout. What appears as 'bad grammar' is often hypnotic language. I use repetition throughout to ram various points home; this also occurs as each reader may want to read a particular section on a particular problem – everything is there that you need to know.

Also in this internationally bestselling series...

- *How to Hypnotise Anyone - Confessions of a Rogue Hypnotist.*
- *Mastering Hypnotic Language - Further Confessions of a Rogue Hypnotist.*
- *Powerful Hypnosis - Revealing Confessions of a Rogue Hypnotist.*
- *Forbidden hypnotic secrets! - Incredible confessions of the Rogue Hypnotist.*
- *Wizards of trance - Influential confessions of a Rogue Hypnotist.*
- *Crafting hypnotic spells! - Casebook confessions of a Rogue Hypnotist.*
- *Hypnotically deprogramming addiction - Strategic confessions of a Rogue Hypnotist.*

And finally...

- *Weirdnosis! - Astounding confessions of a Rogue Hypnotist.*

CONTENTS

8

Acknowledgements

Dedicated to scared people everywhere...

<u>Introduction: all anxiety is 'CURABLE'!</u>

*In this book you will learn how to do real therapy without the bullsh*t!*

This book, your book, starts off with a bold but banal statement: **<u>hypnotic interventions can cure ALL known anxiety disorders.</u>** If you know what you're doing obviously. The aim of this book is to teach you, step by step the 'know what you're doing' bit. Sound like a good deal sugar puff? By the way, I keep having to say, 'curable' in quotes for legal reasons. Even though the things I show and tell you how to do in this book <u>will</u> 99.9% of the time annihilate anxiety in all motivated clients, so it never comes back as a problem again, ever. I can't say that; even though it's true. Ho-hum! I should probably say, as the old UK Carlsberg lager ad did, 'This is the best set of methods to 'annihilate' anxiety...Probably.'

<u>Why anxiety problems are eminently 'curable'.</u>

Because **anxiety is a feeling** and ALL feelings originate and are controlled by what we call for convenience the subconscious or unconscious mind. Hypnosis is the best way to communicate with the 'other than conscious processes' that generate what we call, for convenience's sake, 'anxiety'. Anxiety or 'anxious responses' are also upheld by –

- **Beliefs.**

- **Thoughts.**

- **Behaviours.**

- **Perceptions.**

- **Pattern matching.**

All controlled by 'unconscious mechanisms'. BINGO! Hypnosis can influence them all. Psycho-physiologically the sympathetic part of the nervous system (the 'arousal' phase) is modulated in function by the unconscious matrix of mind; and it causes all anxiety. We can ask it to calm down and by doing so trigger the parasympathetic phase (calming down) of the nervous system. We'll be doing much more than that but that's just to let you know the basics. And I mean the basics. In short anxious people need to relearn how to be calm and how to solve problems calmly

13

with minimum internal fuss or bother.
Hypnosis can teach anyone how to do this,
after all it's natural – you, the hypnotist, are
merely revivifying its latent expression: this is
what we call 'cure'. Everyone has 'calmness
potential': deep down, underneath the
tension.

Oh by the way, as most books on anxiety are
so very serious and so make it all sound very
dramatic and fearful I wrote a book that deals
with this 'scary' subject in a very humorous
way. When you can laugh at fear you have
mastered it. Remember the line from 'Dune':
Fear is the mind killer. You'd better
believe it babe.

<u>Unmet needs and anxious responses.</u>

Anxiety is also treatable because it is
ultimately caused by **unmet needs**: once
needs are met the anxiety signal has no need
to keep communicating. It is replaced by a
feeling of genuine satisfaction. More on this
soon.

Why read this book?

Prepare to read a book on anxiety unlike any other you've ever read!

Do you really want to help people who are suffering and get THE CLIENT results! Or are you here to prove 'your' indoctrination right? Or worse do you want to be a 'therapist' because you want to feel smug at dinner parties? Well? You should read this book for 1 of two reasons – One: you are interested in the reality of the book's topic. Two: you want to 'CURE' people of anxiety disorders just with words. If you answered 'YES!' to either, Bucko you are in the right place.

I lied! There's a third reason: you are suffering from an anxiety disorder and want to understand it and perhaps seek the right professional help for it or use the knowledge you gained in this book to treat yourself. The latter is doable *but at your own risk.* If you aren't a qualified hypnotherapist and you use the stuff in this little treasure trove and balls it all up because you lacked experience then don't say I didn't warn you. However that doesn't mean it's an impossibility. I take NO responsibility for what you do with this information. I am trusting the reader to use their best judgement.

This book is divided into two parts:

Part 1: The ABCs of anxiety. This is the theory bit. It tells you all you really need to know to know how to help someone. This is the why, when, what, who part.

Part 2: The anxiety annihilation scripts. This is the HOW part. The how to get rid of specific anxiety problems bit. In technique and script form. The scripts are easy to 'perform'; they'll help you get your clients results now. They will see immediate improvement. By the session's ends they'll feel better. That's my promise to you. But before we move on, I've forgotten my manners; why, I haven't even introduced myself!

Who is the Rogue Hypnotist?

My credentials madam and monsieur, if you're new: very quickly, here are my hypnotic vital statistics if you will...

- 8 soon to be 9 internationally bestselling hypnosis books on Amazon globally!

- I run a pretty successful hypnotherapy practise in London, UK.

- I have helped people from all walks of life: multimillionaires, TV celebrities, journalists, teachers, police officers, nurses, construction industry workers, catering assistants – people aged from 8 to people in their eighties, people from all around the world, people who practise all global religions and none at all. My experience is great and varied.

- A 1, 1 hour hypnotic session success rate with 99.9% of hypnotherapy clients even for problems like O.C.D, depression etc.

- Over 20 years spent studying hypnosis, NLP (the bits that work), persuasion, 'mind control', symbology and human needs etc.

- A fully qualified clinical hypnotherapist, stage hypnotist and Master Practitioner of NLP. So the 6 accredited certificates on my wall tell me...

- I have a 100% success rate now with all motivated clients.

- My books are informal, fun, funny and accessible to hypnotic professionals and the enthusiastically interested!

- I am totally irreverent and love it! Yeah baby!

- I can 100% promise you that your hypnotic ability will increase from reading my books.

- I can promise you that you will understand yourself and others as never before.

- I can promise you that your conscious mind's analytical abilities will be enhanced and rebooted! The protective firewall of your mind will become powerful; you will not remain the impressionable dummy you once were.

- I know more about the human mind than 99% of therapists, quacks, head shrinkers etc. because my approach to hypnotic interventions is that the mind needs deprogramming not more harmful programming or reprogramming.

- I have covered aspects of hypnosis that no other author on the subject has ever done. Hopefully these books will change this past shortfall by inspiring others to be more adventurous in future.

- I even get good reviews from Goodread readers: a notoriously hard to please bunch, unless they're reviewing some world classic like the Twilight vampire series!

- Oh and my books really piss of humourless, weird people and those threatened by the Western European tradition of individualism and freedom. A good thing.

None of this is 'boasting': they're just the facts.

May I make a confession?

This is the 9th and penultimate Rogue Hypnotist book. Here's the thing, probably my strangest, surprising confession: I never wanted to be a hypnotist – it just kind of

happened!...I was working as a TV writer. I had created a children's TV show. Had it optioned by THE top UK and EU animation company. Then the whole deal collapsed. I was left penniless and worse than that three more TV companies stole two of my ideas without paying me a penny. I was 32, flat broke. I needed cash, fast. Hold on I thought, you know a lot about hypnosis dummy; become a professional hypnotherapist. Got my certificates. Set up my business. 3 clients in my first year. The British aren't known for being adventurous! But I was learning: therapy is mainly about YOU and how well you can get on with people. It's also easy. Next year I see one client – she had my first crappy no clue leaflet/flyer for about 2 years before calling! I cured her or rather she self-cured in one session from smoking addiction. She was so shocked and pleased she referred pretty much anyone she knew to me for help. I had a business. I started realising that what I had been taught was not enough. The systems that professed to cure everything: NLP, authoritarian, permissive etc. etc. didn't always work. Sometimes the techniques failed out right! I needed to develop a system that worked every time. That was 100% solid. My clients were paying me their hard earned cash – they deserved results. I needed the money to eat! It took me 3 more years of trial and error.

Anxiety annihilation is the key to ALL successful therapy.

I learnt the key to all therapy is cracking anxiety. If you can do that, everything else will follow. Part of the 'anxiety code' is: **Anxiety is brain pain** – it's the signal saying, *'Hey STOOPID! Something is wrong! I am scared about the way things are going! Change course or I'll make you feel worse!'*

But 99% of my clients don't listen; they don't even know they SHOULD listen: and so they end up seeing me. Learning about anxiety treatment is about learning what it is that fundamentally makes us human. No one is born anxious. ANXIETY IS A WARNING SIGNAL. If you heed the warning anxiety goes away. It's actually trying to help you. It's

21

nature's feedback signal to let us know if we are headed on the right path in life or not.

This book will give the enthusiastically interested and the professional in any therapeutic field the keys to the 'anxiety code' and specifically how to crack it and all for a bit over £1 or $1; in kindle book version at least.

Why so cheap? ***It is more important that you heal others than it is that I make lots of cash. I don't want to become rich from the suffering of others.*** I want this info out there doing good: I learnt and formulated this stuff and now it's time to pass it on; what's the point of learning anything if you don't share your discoveries?

This is a professional level technique book that anyone can understand and use. Now class, are you ready to calm people all - the – way - down!? Then young Padawan, we shall begin. And yes the thieving bastard psychopath TV companies did make multi millions from my ideas – what ya gonna do!? Shall we dance?

Part 1: The ABCs of anxiety.

Anxiety and hypnosis: why hypnosis is THE best treatment for anxiety.

Apart from the stuff I mentioned above I'll tell you: NO DRUGS ARE INVOLVED OR NEEDED. Although I will tell you more about how disastrous so-called 'anti-anxiety' or worse 'anti-depressant' drugs are for you, you can know now that whatever brain/emotion suppressing/damaging qualities they have they do not in any way shape or form address the underlying problems that caused the anxiety in the first place; in fact they mask it and potentially worsen it. Think of it this way. You tread on glass and slice your big toe wide open. You need to phone a hospital and get stitches. That's what will solve that problem. It is bleeding a lot and it f***ing hurts like hell too. So what do you do? You take a pain killer which makes you high and forget about your injured foot. You are so high you bleed to death. The essential warning signal saying SOMETHING IS WRONG DO SOMETHING TO RECTIFY THIS NOW is for all intents and purposes simply ignored.

Does that sound wise? Sane? No. Does it make billions for 'Big Pharma' Corporations etc. every year? Oh yeah baby. And that's what that is all about. You get addicted to the 'treatment'/suppressant and it can be really hard getting off those drugs once you're hooked. With hypnosis you work with the mind's signals. With hypnosis you can alter unconscious information processing that led to the problem. With hypnosis you can learn essential life skills that banish anxiety. With hypnosis you can relearn to effortlessly relax and get that creative brain working for you instead of against you, if at all! With hypnosis you can relearn to satisfy those essential needs whose deficit made you 'unwell' to begin with. With hypnosis you can do all this and more, as you'll soon see. With NO side effects. Sound like a very good deal?

No one with anxiety is 'unwell' in the medical/disease model sense. No matter how seemingly odd the unhealthy responses. One of the keys to the 'anxiety code' of which you will be hearing much in this book is, **All behaviour is positively intended. No matter how odd it appears.***

More on this later. Unlike drugs hypnosis won't just make you viable enough to return to the system that made you unhealthy in the first place: it can give you your life back and in fact leave you behaving, feeling, thinking and living in ways superior to your 'functioning' before the anxiety even began in earnest. Sound like a good deal? I thought you looked smart Padawan.

(*Unless we are talking about the behaviour of psychopaths.)

Permissive hypnosis is vastly superior to authoritarian hypnosis when treating anxiety – why?

When I first started using hypnosis therapeutically I had a dumb idea that authoritarian direct hypnosis could be used for everything. When it came to treating and helping people with anxiety problems I was to find out how wrong I was. Now don't get me wrong; with low level anxiety issues you can use quite to very direct hypnosis – both bog-standard confidence and phobias can be hypnotised away in such a fashion. It's when you come to problems like severe and complex OCD (Obsessive Compulsive Disorders), GAD (General Anxiety Disorder) and Depression that you quickly come unstuck. I'm not saying you can NEVER use authoritarian tools; it's just that Ericksonian approaches have, in my considerable experience now, led to far greater success in fewer sessions.

Take an example: depression. A client comes to see you. Let's imagine you use a stage hypnotic induction and whack them into trance! Zoom – they're under. You quickly say, 'You feel happy! You are not depressed at all!' You wake them up. They feel a bit relaxed, they feel a bit better. The only problem is clinical depression has nothing to do with someone's mood. People who know nothing about depression think it means that someone is sad. In everyday life we say, 'I'm depressed,' when we feel fed up or down in the dumps. 'Depression' is something the subconscious does. It is a series of patterns, programmes if you like that are being run simultaneously outside of any conscious awareness.

In my 3rd book 'Powerful Hypnosis', I said you need to tell people to do the opposite of what the problem is. With something like clinical depression that 'something' is rather complex. Not complicated or hard but the problem matrix of a set of patterns that we call 'depression' needs a wide set of very specific solution modules (the solution matrix) tailored to the individual to get rid of it forever. You have to teach someone how to stop doing depression and start doing relaxed problem solving unconsciously. *That* is the solution to depression. In the depression section I'll show you how precisely.

In my private practise I learned that all my alcoholism, OCD, nervous twitch and stammer/stuttering clients had experienced

27

trauma as children. Often chronic – taking place repeatedly over years and acute, involving specific dramatic events. This had left a 'trauma residue'. An intertwined matrix or constellation of emotions caused by the initial trauma stimulus. You cannot get rid of this by saying, 'You feel really calm and relaxed now.' It won't even get near to working. You need to have a specific process for getting rid of the troubling emotions that exist as a trace, an emotional ghost, a stain, a scar on the psyche. If you listen to traumatised clients or read transcripts with therapists they all say the same thing at some point – 'I DON'T WANT TO *FEEL* LIKE THIS!!!!' An NLPer would respond, 'Like what specifically?' sending the traumatised client back into those feelings he or she so wants to avoid. Worse still psychodynamically trained 'therapists' (unconscious Gnostic priests) would say, 'Let's talk about what happened at that time...' BANG! That person is hypnotised back into the trauma state. WRONG! Your client told you they don't want to feel that way; so do something to change the way they feel NOWWWWWW! *Lesson 1: Listen to your clients!*

As you will see in the scripts that follow later on, permissive processes in hypnosis, that *respect the subjectivity* of the client and *their own* unconscious symbolism will affect 'cure'. You see, people who become anxious can often be rebels too: those who go along to get along, who have no balls or spirit are often broken by their experiences and conform to all manner of mental and physical bullying just to survive. The ones who get 'neurotic' problems are the fighters. They are unconsciously trying to 'mature' but don't know how. They are trying to re-organise their own psychic process but don't know how: your job is to show them, guide them through the how and leave the unique expression of the solution to them. Rebels don't like know it alls or control freaks: they've been fighting against them their whole lives. Not all anxious people are rebels and you can help the conformists too. We'll get to all that.

The question is: do we live in times, now, at this point in history that lead people to be more prone to anxiety disorders than ever before? YES! Ever so slightly. To this reality we turn our attention next. Prepare for a potted history lesson my cuddly Padawan.

Do we live in the 'Age of anxiety'!?

The establishment biased media are addicted to passing on buzz words and phrases. They don't have the brains to create them but they love short-circuiting the public's thinking capacities by downloading them with slogans. One such slogan is the meme that we live in the 'Age of Anxiety'; as though a time period could be filled, throughout the ether presumably, by a feeling! If we were to give a label to this 'age' I think it should be called 'The Age of Insecurity'. Let me explain...

Prehistory: 'Eden'?

In prehistorical times man had the security of fending for himself. He could hunt, he could gather his food. He could make his own clothes from the animals he slew. 'Prehistoric man' created his own culture: the arts, pots, jewellery, knives, cutting stones - you name it he did it. He was a generalist and he had a great deal of control. His ability to provide for himself barring a mass animal die-out etc. made him self-sufficient: it was a tough life but in many ways he was free. He could take care of his own needs and satisfy them himself by taking action. He was part of a definite tribe with history and traditions stretching back far into the distant past. He belonged, knew he belonged and knew his identity and place.

The rise of civilisations: the fall?

Civilisations stretch far back into antiquity. Much further back than your TV tells you. The problem is they have a tendency to become corrupt and collapse. The soil beneath us is littered with their remains, many yet to be discovered. Or rather re-discovered. Civilisations are built by warrior bands of psychopaths and psychopathic priesthoods. Not necessarily in that order of importance. The creators of civilisations need slaves to live high on the hog. To have a leisured, ruling elite you need slaves. As tribal man hunted animals for sustenance, so must a hopeful future elite have its own human capital (the origin of the word 'capital' meant cattle) to work for it. This lead the warrior tribes to hunt non-violent tribes, herd them, detribalise them and turn them into massive slaves armies, entirely at the disposal of the new elite. The real age of anxiety for masses of humanity had begun about 8000 years ago.

In order to have a sense of security you now had to please a master. Your owner. He

31

decided if you worked, ate, slept, remained undamaged, were left unmolested, when you drank, when you took a shit. You were his property: whereas before you could look after yourself, the slave now had to worry about pleasing his master; he simply could not satisfy his own needs without permission. His master had in affect become a man-god. Why? He had the power of life or death. But in a bizarre way there was the 'security' that being a good, obedient ass kisser kept you 'alive'.

The Middle Ages: a terrible stability?

Then in come the so-called Middle Ages; in this period armed war bands enslaved masses of people and bound them to land holdings. These 'peasants' became serfs. Crap as being a serf was you had some security: you had a religion, Christianity, which told you to put up with all the shit you were suffering down here because if you were a good boy or girl you got to go to heaven etc. Which was nice. What's more you had worth to God: you as an individual had value. You knew your place, sure that was at the bottom of the heap but you had the security that if you let your lord legally steal up to 70% of your agricultural profits he would leave you be.

32

Feudal societies were societies in which families could scrape a living off the land and so this gave them a sense of self-sufficiency, security of social role and a place (your leased landholding) to call your own; sort of. As long as you did what you were told, fought as foot soldiers when your lord had an argument with one of his cousins, he had obligations to protect you against others like him.

The Catholic Church got fat on tithes, formed its own corporations which crushed smaller opposition, such as the ale wives and produced a hodgepodge of dredged up paganism with a smattering of the real Jesus's teachings. This geo-religious system created a 'Christian' identity that lasted across all of Europe for almost 2000 years. It produced 99% of all art and culture: music, festivals, symbolism etc. in the West. Feudal societies were stable because love of loathe your lord, you were all Christians together. Hell, he might even visit your parish church and pray with you: sitting in his own family nave of course; the Middle Ages provided a bizarre sense of security. You could get your needs met; it was harsh but you adapted. There was very little change or movement: things stayed the same. By about 1400 all this begins to change.

NOTE: in this period living off of the land outside of feudal society and sustaining your own needs by hunting was illegal – you could die for doing it. Hmmmm? All civilisations hitherto inherently foster a culture of dependency. Not self-reliance: that's the last thing the rulers want you having!

Capitalism: the dawn of security for some begins.

The 'English Civil War', so called, had come to an end. The King had lost his head. The 'Roundheads' had one. Though the throne was restored to the Monarchy, it was to be in an England never the same again. The mentality of Capitalism (it wasn't called that it was called 'free enterprise', Marx supposedly invented the term Capitalism) was originally a branch of Protestant Christianity although its traces its ultimate roots to the Canaanite Civilisation.

This is the 'age' in which the merchant becomes master. Not warrior king or 'race'. No, the person who trades rises to heights of unparalleled power in human history. Of course higher still are the bankers who financed the new mass industry and trade. Although it didn't begin in England it took root and power enough to change the course of human history thereafter there.

It was the biggest revolutionary change in human history since the development of agriculture. English serfs were thrown off their land and forced to work in factories. The average age of death at the height of the industrial revolution amongst the poor was 15! The entire rural way of life of the majority of English men and women was destroyed, utterly, irrevocably in a few generations. Man had found a new master: the 'capitalist'. Like all of his former master's incarnations he demanded utter fealty and obedience and like his forebears he had a god-like power of life or death.

In the grim, robotic life of young factory hands, if the machinery and drudgery didn't kill you, the wages and meagre food would not sustain you. It was the first 'transhuman' – man-machine experiment. The resultant anxiety and depression must have been massive. If you were a member of the mass of working poor there was no way you could satisfy any ambition, desire or dream. You couldn't even satisfy the need to breathe fresh air, get sunlight, rest or eat healthy food. England had become a giant industrial prison camp. Dark Satanic mills indeed.

Of course the Englishman, woman and child could drown the screaming despair with mind-rot gin; so it wasn't all bad. Massive and rapid social change = anxiety. No ifs or buts. If the change is for the worse, no matter what longer term benefits some may have seen, human anxiety will explode. You see people don't really like change. Better the devil you know, as they say. There are many parallels between what the English peasant experienced in this period with those of the Russian peasant with the arrival of Bolshevism.

It wasn't all doom and gloom however: there was a scientific explosion, technology advanced rapidly – especially ways to kill off masses of people. Medicine improves. A new 'Middle Class' becomes prosperous, independent and well-educated. Literature becomes more personal and widely available. Capitalist powers formed imperialist combines with which to force trade and steal resources from non-capitalists states etc.

It is of note that the permanent underclass of unemployed people created by design by capitalists to keep the sheep in line through

fear were known as the 'needy'. Why?
Because none of their needs could be met
sufficiently. Sexual excess became a problem
with them as it was an affordable drug to
quell anxiety.

Sex Drug for outlets

Capitalism in crisis.

The materialistic ethos of Capitalism created
its own materialistic bogey-man:
Internationalist Communism. Unlike classical
Capitalism which was an anarchic social
Darwinian free for all, Communism claimed to
provide 'from each according to his abilities, to
each according to his needs...' If you were
poor and oppressed this sounded rather
attractive; as the Soviet experiment in Russia
proved it rather resembled hell on earth in
reality.

The total destruction of the feudal Russia of
the Tsars was carried out with ruthless
efficiency by the bloodthirsty Bolsheviks.
Communism exterminated more people in
human history than any ideology or religion
that we know of. It also spawned a German
rip off known as Nazism. Again a system that
pretended to furnish the means to meet
people's needs to end the anxiety of 19th
century globalisation; in reality just another

mind-control prison.

Vodka based alcoholism in Russia was not halted by the Soviet period. When you live in a Gulag Archipelago you might well drink yourself to death as anxiety and depression rates explode. A living hell has that effect on people. Or maybe you think it was their genes?

Globalist corporatism: the age of total insecurity begins.

The struggle between some of the collectivist societies and Capitalism ends with the dropping of the nuclear bomb. A new age of terrible science had begun. Capitalists use the two wars to create global Corporations; massive capital combines, rather like trade unions for the rich. These dominate all nations across the planet, dictating foreign and domestic policies to nation states.

After a short-lived post-war rebuilding 'boom period' that lasts until the late 1970's people start to feel the pinch again. Whilst everyone was partying the globalists unleash their plan to create a system dominated by themselves; a global plutocracy, replacing the short lived experiment of managed 'democracy'. From now on people will find need satisfaction by pleasing global corporate masters and their long-range economic plans.

As nation states lose democratic power to pan-international organisations ordinary people once again find themselves in a position in which they are out of control. Massive and irreversible changes in social, political, ethnic and cultural shifts in the deployment of monetary, resource and human capital wrack humans globally with a state of mass insecurity. The human dimension of the planet it seems is in in flux. Constantly. The ability for non-trillionaire humans to satisfy their most basic emotional, physical and psychological genetic needs is threatened as never before in human history.

And you wonder why people are anxious? Must be their 'brain chemistry'...Riii-iiiight. The rather silly and facetious history above is a very simple rendering of the socio-political basis of anxiety and depression. *Mass sanity is not possible in an insane asylum.* For more details on these matters please refer to my book, 'Escaping cultural hypnosis'.

However if you have read the above and conclude that we are doomed to anxiety on the personal level then you have jumped the gun. You can be calm, focused and function well in almost any social system. It is how you respond to the environmental stimulus that is the key: one is a victim mind-set; the other is a realistic one.

Do we live in 'The Age of Hate and Rage!'?

As a lack of control and constant change (some of the French Revolutionaries called this process 'perpetual Armageddon') creates fear it also creates its flip side: rage! Reactions of all kinds to these geopolitical alterations is creating a background of rising impotent anger as well as incessant worry. Not only are people unconsciously and consciously asking, 'How will I keep my job, family, society, customs, language and country?' in such flux, they are also getting mad that it is being done to them at all without their consent. This reveals itself in ethnic hatreds, cultural divisions, the rise of political and religious extremism fuelled and empowered by modern technology and communications.

None of this should surprise us: when first wave globalisation peaked at the 20th century's beginning, the 1930's showed us the reactions we could expect. ***People who claim to have 'adapted' to globalisation are de facto those who are most mentally unbalanced; as Aldous Huxley wrote, they have come to like circumstances that they naturally***

oughtn't to. These I label the 'functionally psychotic': there is no hope for them – they are perfectly programmed puppets; the 'anxious' are the sane ones.

People are angry because they feel afraid. Why? They *perceive* they are powerless. The consequences as the current process continues are as yet unknowable as social engineering creates human environments (actually habitats) that have not existed before in known recorded history since the days of Babel. We are all living in a period of unprecedented change as I told a client once. If you didn't know this, or at least wouldn't admit it: are you really surprised that human mental health is so bad in all 'Westernised' countries?

Our next anxiety code insight is this: ***A fear-soaked brain is not working properly. In fact the entire front thinking part shuts down. If we are very afraid we are in state of pathological waking trance. Extreme emotions = hypnosis! Fear = executive function, conscious mind activities are***

offline! If you aren't thinking, you are reacting.

As goes the macrocosm so responds the microcosm. We turn our attention next to the family as a source of anxiety.

The drama of the family.

Being a child can be quite a fearful experience at the best of times. Think back to your own childhood if it helps. One of the sources of fear is insecurity, which leads to speculation and dependency which prevents self-reliance. Being small and lacking all knowledge and capacity to realistically survive and thrive alone, the young child, realising the precariousness of his or her position feels threatened. This is often revealed in dream content. Not only is a child fearful of its material needs being met but its growing awareness recognises the vital importance of the human love and emotional nourishment from its parents to it survival. Without love a child cannot develop emotionally, physically, psychologically or 'spiritually' with ease; when love is lacking, survival, achievement and relationships become a fearful struggle. A struggle to get emotional needs or ends if you like to meet. This is the real 'existential' source of much human fear.

Upbringings that foster anxiety.

This is very simple; factors that make children prone to anxiety problems are...

- Divorce. An example – the lead singer of Nirvana Kurt Cobain was a happy loving young man; until his parent's divorce. His entire world fell apart, all his later 'rebellious' behaviour stemmed from this trauma. Don't kid yourself that divorce doesn't traumatise kids – it does. Cobain said that after his parent's split his 'sense of security' vanished. Kids need security or they become 'in-secure'. Cobain's mom/mum was beaten by her new boyfriend while Cobain watched helplessly (learned helplessness); nor would she leave her abuser.

- Parents with mental or physical health problems.

- Poverty. The problems caused to family life by too little money are legion.

- Bad nutrition in childhood.

- Lack of exercise.

- Bullying at school – by other pupils and/or teachers and failure of parents to remove the child from the intimidating environment (this can lead to suicide in even very young children).

- Being placed in a care home.

- Witnessing physical, psychological or emotional violence.

- Being labelled the 'black sheep' of the family.

- Experiencing violence and physical abuse.

- Being deprived of unconditional love.

- A parent who is constantly or frequently bringing new partners (often sexual) into the home.

- Step parents (there was a point to those fairy stories ya know!).

- Watching too much TV.

- Living in a war zone.

- Living in a 'rough neighbourhood'. I call this 'shithole syndrome'.

- Lacking opportunities due to social class.

- Having parents who overemphasise

the importance of academic achievement or materialistic attainment.

- Being raised in emotionally suppressed environments.

- Being endlessly criticised.

- Being told that somehow 'you are not good enough'.

- Comparing the child to an imaginary 'perfect child' who like an ubermarionette behaves so as to ensure the parents' warped 'satisfaction' ALL the time. This is the key basis to anxiety caused by 'low self-worth'. It also creates mild multiple personality as the child pitifully attempts to curb its natural impulses to please the unpleasable parent. This is the basis of children mistakenly believing '...there must be something wrong with me.' Rather than the truth that there is something pathologically wrong with the parent.

- Incest. This takes multiple forms in 'modern families' including the step daughter running off with her step dad etc.

- Families that have 'favourites'.

- Being labelled a 'failure' at school – because the teachers failed to do what your parents pay them to.

- Families in which parents argue constantly and give each other the silent treatment.

- An overly 'permissive' parenting style. Children want parents to lead and be parents not their best friends.

- An authoritarian overly disciplined home. This produces 'Nazis' or weaklings. Nothing more pitiful than a 'broken in' child.

- Harsh communication patterns – including voice tone.

- A family that has no roots and travels extensively.

- Families that unnecessarily isolate themselves from the outside world.

- Unconfident, perennially worried parents who act as role models.

- Families who denigrate the creative capacity of children and expect them to behave as little adults – this produces 'weird kid syndrome'. We've all met them!

- Experiencing changing caregivers.

- Families that live in cities.

- Not owning your own property.

- The children of 'swingers' are highly likely to be disturbed as a result of their parents' sexual behaviour.

- Religious, political, secular fanaticism/extremism within the family unit. (Often there is a fear of being shunned/disowned etc.)

- A house that is too small for family needs.

- Families that have 'catastrophe response patterns' to life crisis and stressors rather than a positive problem solving outlook.

- Families with no sense of humour.

- Too many sweets and fizzy drinks – really!

49

- Too much 'drama' in the home. The home is supposed to be literally and symbolically a 'sanctuary'.

- Families without binding cultural traditions. The absence of such structures can produce self-loathing and anarchy. There is no wider framework to which a child belongs.

- Parents who are so overworked that they have no time to devote to the children exclusively.

You could go on and on. I mean it's all pretty much common-sense to someone with half a brain isn't it? Again what are we seeing? A lack of security. Such children are much more likely to have addiction problems and anxiety-based problems such as depression. This is because a state of relaxed and creative self-confidence which produces independence and self-reliance is not fostered. However all is not lost – such a resourceful condition exists latently in all of us: hypnosis can re-access it.

Note: the worst cases of anxiety based problems will usually be found amongst the victims of the 'drama of the family'.

It is also of note that all socialist and cultic

movements seek to destroy happy families so that they end up like the ones above. A society with strong families and values is invincible. Let us turn now to the happy family.

Raising the anxiety immune child.

Everyone gets anxious from time to time. But the key 'immunity' factor is **a strong, secure loving family with firm boundaries of acceptable behaviour in which the children are raised by their biological parents throughout all of childhood.** *(This is not even remotely a moot point; all the long-term research has proven this. In 21st century post-Western societies the question, 'What is best for the child?' is simply not asked.)* This produces what you might call 'the quietly confident child'. He or she is not the brash attention seeker or the crushed introvert created by the anxious home. Confident children also tend to have larger and closer extended family networks. The larger the loving family base or 'kin network', the greater the sense of security, tradition, 'belonging' and stimulation the child receives. Children from happy homes are doted upon and often express contentment in joyous imaginative play. Loving families are all very similar. The parents don't just love their children they adore everything they do; because the truth is, as the TV shrink Frazier said, 'The truth is, you don't just love your children; you fall in love with them.' They are the brightest, funniest, most charming people you'll ever meet – let them know! Or end up with a Karen Carpenter on your hands...

To sum up –

- **Unconditional love.**

- **Lots of cuddles and kisses etc.**

- **Encouragement.**

- **A family in which a model of inner 'democracy' rather than tyranny prevails. A true democracy had leaders (parents) but listens and responds to the concerns of the citizens (children). Such a system shows that the children are <u>valued.</u> Their input is respected. Tyrannical families in contrast show children that what they think and feel is not important – they are merely to obey orders. This has wider ramifications for society.**

- **An environment which allows free personality expression.**

- **A home in which traditional gender play is accepted as normal. When children have no 'roles' imposed on them, one way or another they by and large spontaneously favour traditional gender play.**

- **A family with boundaries of acceptable behaviour (healthy norms).**

- **A wide and supportive extended family base.**

- **Living in the same area consistently.**

- **The acceptance of childhood creativity and imaginative play.**

- **Parents who are comfortably playful.**

- **A broadly speaking 'fun home' atmosphere. Home should be a place that says 'welcome'; it is the family sanctuary. Your private place.**

- **An active involvement in genuine community affairs. This fosters a sense of control and influence.**

- **Give children your time.**

- **A stimulating environment and activities.**

- **The proud expression of native cultural traditions.**

- **A family which values humour and cheekiness.**

- **A broadly speaking calm emotional 'temperature' in the home.**

- **A 'problem solving meta-strategy' to crisis and life stressors as the family coping style and culture.**

- **Easy access to playing areas dedicated to families exclusively and easy access to nature!**

- **Good nutritious food.**

- **A good school. (Good luck with that one!)**

You could go on - there really are no secrets,

nothing is in the genes, you don't need a degree or to have attended 'parenting classes' held by odd people with no kids in their life. Looking after and raising kids well is something everyone who is not a nasty piece of trash is capable of doing, in your own unique way. There is no single template of technical perfection; thankfully all you need do is be 100% human and you'll do fine. People have been raising kids for aeons without over intellectualising the blindingly obvious.

Now let's talk about something I've been hinting at – the 'anxiety code'!

Cracking the 'anxiety code'.

There really is what I call an 'anxiety code'. What do I mean? **Anxiety is caused and 'cured' by specific things in the real world.** It is not a mysterious ailment that supernaturally descends on the unwilling out of the blue. It has nothing to do with a 'hereditary predisposition'. I will highlight the key factors involved in the creation of anxiety in all its myriad of weird expressions of human misery. For anxiety is caused by human suffering. And we can do something very real, very tangible about that using hypnosis.

But back to the theme of the human condition and the suffering anyone can undergo just by the process, the tough process of living in this material reality. I have a name for this; I call it, 'The trauma of living'.

'The trauma of living.'

What the heck is the 'trauma of living' you might ask? I'm glad you asked; it has been the experience and observation of the Rogue Hypnotist that just being present in this crazy material world we all live in is at least mildly traumatic by its nature. Let me explain...The good news is that we are by nature adapted to handle this level of trauma. It is when our trauma coping capacities are overloaded, chronically (over time) or acutely (due to one or a few specific traumas) that we get into deep doo-doo!

Very Tryt

A life of low level trauma?

If you think about it, lots of low level 'trauma' impacts us throughout life. Can I give some examples? Sure. Firstly – you are born! Think what a traumatic experience a birth is. You are quietly sitting in mummy's/mommy's tummy getting all your needs met through a feeding tube called the umbilical cord and BLAM! Next minute you are screaming and some white coated loon is pulling you out (by your head!) of that cosy place with a pair of metal pliers called forceps! Nuts. And before you are born your parents and the nurses check you are okay with ultrasound and that is

57

physically traumatic to an unborn baby. Didn't know that did you? Your body must handle all the elements, all the sun's radiation. You must process all the artificial, poisonous chemicals in your baby food etc.

Next they shove you off to school. What the heck?! Some complete stranger starts barking orders at you and acting like your replacement mum/mom. All key figures in a child's life imprint on that child. By age 2 in the West, you are being brought up and 'educated' by complete strangers who want to indoctrinate you. Nuts!

The whole schooling process is traumatic – schools are prison for kids; you are in turn bored, threatened, beaten up, bullied, separated from your family and taught crap and fed crap. Nuts! Worse than that you are trained to be lifelong dependent on others to get your needs met by the State or employer. For teenagers who historically would have been working and having families by their mid-adolescent they are kept in an artificially infantile state way beyond what would naturally happen.

You are exposed to a moronic, ugly, debased culture and media that isn't yours – you take drugs and get drunk regularly. You have sex with people you don't even like to be considered cool. And that's normal is it? Then you get a job: this is THE MOST traumatic bit.

You go and work for someone else. By and large this is some freak on a power trip who decides whether you eat, have a home or any money. You are entirely dependent on his (usually) good will to get ALL your needs met? This dependency is normal is it? To top it all your job is meaningless, you realise work is school with a bribe they call a wage. Most of your hard earned cash goes on bills and taxes! If you are lucky you meet a nice man or woman and get hitched (you now have someone to watch TV with) and have kids. You realise this is the most natural and sane part of your life and yet you spend most of your life with complete bullying assholes, making them rich just to meet your entire family's needs now. You drink and eat too much to cope. Wars and terrorism ravage the human planet in the meantime. The dominant spiritual culture is pornographic nihilism.

Once you get out of the rat race and they've sucked the life and all your best working years out of you, you start to decline physically and mentally. Your ears get big, your nose hangs, your skin turns prune like and your penis won't work anymore and heck he's the only one who ever understood you anyway! You watch the country and world go from bad to worse, everything you loved is gradually destroyed. If you are lucky you get cancer and they put you on chemotherapy which is so dangerous it might just kill you! Then, if you survive they put you in a eugenics factory called an 'old people's home' so you can die off out of sight. By the time you get to facing death you feel relieved; at last I get a fucking rest in his mad house you think! The end.

Never a truer word spoken in jest they say: the trauma of living folks. The question is – why do we all put up with it? And you wonder why people are 'anxious'???! What if on top of this shit you experience 4 major and real life crisis on the trot? Something might 'give' might it not!

Now, I think it's time: let's define what we name – **ANXIETY!**

What is 'anxiety'?

If you have read my other books you'll know I am quite finicky about language. I like to start with the origin of words:

Anxiety - (Noun). Recorded in the 1520's; from the Latin 'anxietatem' (nominative anxietas) meaning – 'anguish, anxiety, and solicitude **(care or concern)'**. Psychiatric usage dates to 1904. 'Age of Anxiety' is from Auden's poem (1947). 'Anxiety, distress', find similar roots to the Latin in Old English 'angsumnes' and Middle English usage - 'anxumnesse'.

Anxious - (Adjective). From 1620's, derived from Latin 'anxius' – 'solicitous, **uneasy, troubled in mind,** causing anxiety, troublesome'.** The roots of which are - 'angere, anguere' – **'choke, squeeze'.** Figuratively – 'torment, cause distress' (Note the similarity to anger!). The same image is in Serbo-Croatian – 'tjeskoba' 'anxiety' - literally **'tightness, narrowness.'**

Angst – (Noun). From German 'Angst' – 'neurotic fear, anxiety, guilt, remorse'. Roots in Old High German – 'angust'; *from the root of anger!!!* The author George Eliot used it (in

German) in 1849; it was then 'popularized' in English by the translation of Sick-Mind Fraud's (Freud) work. By the 1940's (1944) it had become used commonly in English speaking countries.

What have we learnt that is of use? What we call 'anxiety' is linked to a sense of care or concern of some kind. It is linked to anger, as anxiety often is in clients. Depressed clients are often very angry. There is also the physical sense of tension and 'narrowness', indeed choking – this has to do with the physical tension resulting from the care/trouble that leads to the **black and white thinking** so common in all anxiety disorders. This is the classic 'narrow perspective' caused by mass injections of adrenaline etc. Great short-term in a fight or when fleeing real danger – a bloody disaster in everyday life and functioning. As you will soon see: _anxiety of almost all kinds is an unproductive, unhealthy feedback loop._

I don't know if you noticed but there is also a temporal element to anxiety: anxiety occurs in time somewhere – anxiety about the past (guilt), anxiety about now (unmet needs), anxiety about the future (catastrophe thinking/worst case scenario self-torture!). It is also worth stressing again that much of anxiety is a complete waste of time and energy, completely normal though it is. Okay, let's look at the physical and psychological aspects of anxiety.

The irrelevance of the 'physical mechanics' of anxiety.

Firstly perhaps you thought I was going to go on about what neuroscience etc. claims to have to tell us about how an 'anxious brain' behaves. ***Let me be categorical – you do not need to know anything about the neuroscience of anxiety in order to 'treat' it. There is far too much fluff, flim and flam surrounding anxiety treatment as it is. Some neuroscientists even claim that there are 'markers' in the brains of 'anxiety prone' individuals. Thankfully that's all a load of total bullshit! However if you are a complete moron feel free to go on believing what you like.***

I have 'cured' so many people of anxiety problems I can't remember how many that is! This book is grounded in experiential reality and genuine hope. This book is to help people totally annihilate anxiety – if that's your aim or if you would like to do the same as a therapist, read on Padawan...

Anxiety is a warning signal.

Ever seen those cute little Meerkats on guard looking out for trouble? That's what anxiety's function is. When we feel anxious and feeling anxious is a normal/healthy response: sometimes we need to take some ACTION to remove the threat. However in the modern world the 'threat' is that we are living un-human, artificial lives that prevent us from getting out needs met: this can cause anxiety. Desires are not needs. Many desires are simply implanted into a person during the so-called 'socialisation process' (programming).

We may be overloaded by too much work, relationship problems, financial debt etc. These create real threats to our 'well-being'; again we become anxious. Anxiety is all about loss – loss that has happened, loss that is ongoing, loss that might happen. Our imaginations are marvellous engines of catastrophic horror shows when we loop bright and colourful scary movies and pictures of things that won't and can't ever happen! Some people get into a habit of almost always imagining the worst when what they want is the polar opposite. I have had many clients to whom 'the worst' did happen; they all survived. All suffering passes, eventually — what we label 'suffering' often has great teaching power, it often matures us, makes us wiser. This was the tradition of Christianity — that suffering had meaning. The 'modern' idea of suffering is derived from the ancient Greek tradition: that pain was simply to be avoided. That is was a meaningless bodily affliction. This is completely wrong.

True

Wrong

Our internal movies and images can scare us sh*tless! But this usually happens amongst a general background of fear, stress etc. A bit of anxiety is part of being human: instead of hating or worse fearing it — the best attitude is to see it for what it is — an essential warning signal. Anxiety is your friend. If you ignore its message then you get BIG trouble. And I mean with a capital T Padawan. Imagine you had no way, unconsciously, to evaluate threats: you'd be in big doo-doo, fast. Through social programming many people are not afraid about things that they should be very scared of. That's another topic entirely.

The structure of 'anxiety'.

What we call 'anxiety' often has several

elements or component parts; they entail changes in what I call our 'base state'. This is the one we usually operate from when comfy...The experiential structure of anxiety includes:

A. Changes in our emotions - a scared or uneasy feeling.

B. Changes in thought patterns - thoughts race and are alarmist.

C. Changes in internal imagery - bizarre or worst case imaginings.

D. Changes in external perception - our peripheral vision is blurry, we do not see the bigger picture.

E. Bodily changes - tense muscles, shallow breathing, shaking, hard to swallow, sweaty hands etc. Our body is preparing for a punch up/fight.

F. Changes in our metacognition - fear of fear, fear of our responses, fear of madness etc. We comment on our ongoing anxious experience.

NOTE: These changes feedback upon and reinforce one another. A change in one zone can spiral into changes in others. The anxiety _process can be triggered by a change in any one zone._

What are the real causes of anxiety right now?

Okay I've let you know that human social systems lie behind a great deal of anxiety but we can pretty much do f**k all about that. For now. So what can we do? And what else makes us jittery at least and downright panicky at worst? In no particular order: a fairly comprehensive list follows repeating some issues raised in the 'drama of the family section'...

- Caffeine. Soft/fizzy drinks and...

- Coffee: has powerful opioid proteins in it.

- A poor diet. Malnutrition makes you anxious.

- A verbal assault.

- Being sexually assaulted.

- A physical attack (violence).

- Tea. Modern tea is different from that our recent forebears drank – it can cause bizarre dreams.

- Being tortured.

- Being criticised.

- Being told you are worthless.

- Being humiliated or demeaned.

- An accident.

- Not having enough money.

- Lacking the means to fulfil ambitions.

- Feeling that you are powerless.

- Not achieving meaningful goals.

- Feeling trapped.

- Being physically restrained in some way.

- Rejection.

- Evaluation of your body (during sex for example).

- Food 'additives' (toxins).

- Having a poor social life.

- Not having any or enough friends.

- Not having an intimate relationship.

- Growing up in a loving family with an

adult who has 'mental health problems'.

- Growing up in a family with a parent who shows favouritism.

- Being labelled the 'black sheep of the family' as a child.

- Living in a 'rough neighbourhood'.

- Losing a loved one.

- Losing a job.

- Moving house.

- Going to school/education.

- Changing school.

- Doing something new.

- Taking risks.

- Not taking risks.

- Breaking the law.

- Doing something 'naughty'.

- Drug use.

- Alcohol.

- Not sleeping well.

- Being physically exhausted (even travelling).

- Being mentally and/or emotionally exhausted.

- Being injured.

- Being around authority figures – police, doctors, teachers etc.

- Perceiving that you have 'low social status.'

- Going to hospital.

- Being ill.

- Receiving genuine bad news.

- Losing control of your emotions.

- Losing control of your body.

- Intimidation.

- Fear of being physically harmed – threats.

- Spotting a large group of young people.

- Not getting a promotion.

- Getting a promotion.

- Living a life without meaning or purpose.

- Failing to have children.

- Having children.

- Working in high pressure environments.

- Not sleeping well enough.

- Not exercising.

- Physical inactivity.

- Ruminating on problems instead of solving them.

- Focusing on the past.

- Feeling you lack time.

- Feeling bored.

- Information overload.

- Overly rapid societal change.

- Economic recessions and depressions.

- Not having control over your local environment.

- Control freak Governments.

- 'Political correctness' ('Atheism' religionised).

- Religious intolerance.

- Commuting to work.

- Seeing too many people in a day.

- Multi-tasking.

- Failing to meet expectations.

- Not fulfilling potential/talent.

- Living in towns and cities. The human zoo.

- Not getting out into nature enough.

- Getting an insufficient amount of fresh air – sea air is especially good for you.

- Insufficient sunlight – especially affects office workers + Blacks and Asians who have moved to the northern hemisphere causing no end of mental and physical problems caused by lack of vitamin D, including diabetes and osteoporosis.

- Not being stretched by your work, hobbies or life in general – insufficient challenge!

73

- A crap sex life.

- No sex life.

- Promiscuous sex.

- Not satisfying your sense of curiosity about the world, life etc.

- Lacking a sense of 'belonging'.

- Living in high rise apartments/flats.

- Overcrowding.

- Having your body space invaded – a typical trait of psychopathic types.

- Your country being invaded.

- Not being able to pass through the natural stages of the human life cycle.

- Feeling unattractive.

- Being too shy.

- Lacking positive, life enhancing attention. The sense that people care about you, wish you well and devote time to YOU.

- Giving others positive attention (when deserved).

- People taking advantage of you.

- Failing to connect to a sufficient amount of people.

- Having a guilt trip laid on you.

- Knowing someone genuinely wants you dead.

- Fear of possible bad news.

- Watching too much TV, especially 'news'.

- Comparing yourself to others unfavourably.

- A lack of daily pleasure from the 'small things in life'. Sunsets etc.

- Comparing yourself to an introjected and fake 'ideal' self.

- Acculturalisation and deculturalisation — having your society and culture destroyed.

- Being conned.

- Being overly materialistic.

- Not having a recognised social role.

- Lacking 'spiritual fulfilment'. It is well known that true psychological security, an essential human need only comes from a religion or a personal spiritual practise. The West effectively has no religion. Ooops. A recent study showed that 'atheists' are much more likely to be psychopaths than the religious.

- Lacking at least one really good close friend that you love.

- An oppressive political system.

- Snobbery.

- Encountering people with overly high self-worth: narcissists.

- Being the focus of a psychopath.

- Being surrounded by mentally ill people.

- Having an 'anti-social neighbour': living near scum etc.

- A society in which the rich and powerful live by one set of rules and the 'plebs' another.

- Being in a war zone.

- Being in a car accident.

- Experiencing mass immigration (Mass irreversible shifts in demographics are the final stage in a civilisation's total collapse: fact. See appendix.)

- A change in your language.

- Thinking you've seen a 'ghost'! Really!

You could go on and on. In books 3,4,5,6,7 I give countless examples of 'Universal human needs'. **For humans to be reasonably stress free and happy these needs must be satisfied.** No ifs or buts. See the appendix for an updated full list of Universal human needs: it somewhat expands upon previous works.

A major part of the anxiety code is: missing needs = ANXIETY!!!

It is that simple. Or is it? No, but we must be practical as to what we can realistically address in therapy. Another part of the code is:

In order to fulfil needs you must take action.

Note for the violently stupid: there is no unique genetic or naturally existing brain chemical 'inbalance' basis to any anxiety disorder. If you believe in such things, there is no plausible Darwinian advantage to breeding a species of cowardly, fear crippled wimps! If you really want to 'cure' anxiety you had better start getting real!

Violations of morality and anxiety: guilt!

Word origins padawans...

Scruple - (Noun.) A moral misgiving or pang of conscience. Derived from the late 14th century from Old French – 'scrupule'; from the Latin 'scrupulus' –'uneasiness, anxiety, pricking of conscience'. Note: literally from – 'small sharp stone'; diminutive of 'scrupus' – **_'sharp stone or pebble'._** Apparently used figuratively by Cicero for a cause of uneasiness or anxiety, probably from the notion of having a pebble in your shoe.

The word in the more literal Latin sense of 'small unit of weight or measurement' is first noted in English from late 14th century (perhaps leading to a sense of – to evaluate?).

Guilt - (Noun.) Old English – 'gylt' – **_'crime, sin, fault, fine';_** origin unknown. Some suspect a connection to Old English – 'gieldan' – **_'to pay for, debt'._** The mistaken use for 'sense of guilt' is first recorded in the 1680's. 'Guilt by association' first recorded in 1919. If you have read my other books you may be aware of how much of our language is based on monetary value!!!

Anyway: guilt - something niggling that we can't get off of our mind? Hmmm...

Anxiety about the past: forgiving ourselves.

We often feel worried or anxious because we did something we shouldn't have. Maybe we hurt someone's feelings undeservedly. Maybe you stole a pen from work!!! Who knows? That kind of anxiety is good: it's how we know we have a conscience. We are supposed to feel bad about some things – it shows we aren't a psychopath. Healthy guilt is sign to get back on the proverbial 'straight and narrow'. However if anxious guilt plagues us undeservedly then you need to do something about that. You can't go on and on and on endlessly worrying and ruminating about what was, if it was at all - ***YOU CANT CHANGE THE PAST;*** you can learn from it.

Political Correctness programmes people that they should feel guilty for the supposed crimes of their ancestors; BULLSHIT! Some clients are raised in overly critical, perfectionist and downright hostile environments. Such upbringings can implant delusional ideas of guilt with no basis in reality. Some parents hate their own children: to my mind there is nothing less human.

Religions and cults can permeate a person's life with a pseudo sense of guilt. Such people fill therapist's offices. The good thing is – they can be helped. We can deprogramme them; soon, you'll learn how.

Even if someone has done something a bit wrong, if they genuinely 'repent' don't they deserve to get over it? Throughout history men have killed each other in cold blood for no good reason: we call such circumstances 'war'. People can be brainwashed to murder, believing at the time they were doing good; only to discover later they were conned. We must help such people. 'Let he who is without sin...'

Survivor guilt.

Finally there is another type of 'guilt' linked to those who survive traumatic events; might be child sexual abuse*, might be an act of terrorism, could 'just' be a car accident in which you survived and someone else didn't. We can feel guilty about surviving. We are quite sensitive creatures you see; well some of us are! This type of guilt is very easy to ease away, using quite simple hypnotic processes.

A brain that is not overly aroused is a healing and an efficiently working brain.

(*Sexual abuse in childhood including the viewing of sexual images can damage the frontal lobes. We know that it damages the parietal lobe. This damage affects conscious mind functions and increases dissociation and suggestibility.)

Anxiety and the media.

These were the headlines that grabbed my attention...

'How Our Brains Transform Remote Threats Into Crippling Anxiety.'

'The bombardment of fear we receive from the news has left us paralyzed.'

I read a very interesting article by Kevin La Bar who is a professor of psychology and neuroscience at Duke University in the News and Politics section of the website called Alternet dated November 26, 2014. In this piece Professor La Bar writes how the modern media creates massive stress, fear and anxiety in the general public. His insights are revealing.

La Bar states that 'modern living' is now almost wholly defined by a persistent low-level anxiety pervading throughout society. Why is this so? He states that ongoing reports about 'terrorism' and 'war' etc. and daily struggles to remain financially viable as a family and the chronic fear of job loss are the major factors involved. The core of the problem is he claims, in line with my own thinking, **_uncertainty_** – the fact that it is often hard to fathom how various ongoing crises will develop in the future. This very perceived 'unpredictability' triggers us to fantasise about what *might* happen; we generate 'future dystopias' in our imagination about the tough futures that may lay ahead. Recall the 'what if' scenarios?

In other words we perceive threats in an imagined, dissociated time to possibly come as being genuinely dangerous. The problem is, they haven't happened yet – they'll probably never come to pass (Tolkien fans think of the Mirror of Galadriel). But the body reacts as though they are real.

Usual cognitive responses are 'repetitive worries' (rumination), 'hyper-vigilant scanning' for evidence of danger (paranoia) etc. and attentional (focus) and 'memory biases' (pattern matching) toward possible 'threat-related' data. These rumination patterns create anxiety; this in turn triggers the release of stress hormones such as adrenaline and later cortisol in the longer term. **_Cortisol is linked to depression._** These bio-chemical alterations actually re-organise our brain's priorities to prepare for a 'future threat'. Essentially we are on a war footing. Remember what I said about information overload? How can you deal with real crises when you are trying to handle imagined ones too? Answer: you can't. Your mind and body cannot handle such high levels of stress, it's too exhausting. When the exhaustion is too much people start to break down; just like Pavlov's dogs in fact. This is why children from abusive backgrounds go on to develop anxiety disorders – they are under attack, brought up in emotional 'war zones'; this makes them hyper-vigilant, worried, pattern matching for potential threats: in a word anxious! But you don't have to have been abused to become anxious. Even children from happy homes develop anxiety problems because the current world we live in is very sick. Pathologically sick.

Anxiety in the 'Age of Terrorism*'.

La Bar believes wrongly however that we live in an 'age of terrorism'; we don't, we live in an 'age of chaos'. Geopolitically we are going through what is known as a 'time of troubles'; a transitional time between an old order and another 'new' one that is emerging.

But let's play with his concept for purposes of understanding anxiety. Due to news media reporting on various terrorist incidents many worry about something as statistically safe as flying. It's actually more dangerous to cross the road/street but that doesn't matter because we have been hypnotically primed. When you or I go on our holidays/vacation we are now more likely/biased to notice fellow passengers whose ethnicity/religious affiliation is similar to that of a given terrorist group (say ISIS/Al Qaida etc.). Having witnessed so many terrorist attacks on TV (9/11, Beslan school and Charlie Hebdo massacre etc.) our pattern matching systems are going haywire with hypervigilance! The **psychic driving** of such traumatic events and images are implanted through repetition and horror into our unconscious minds. As such you may see a woman in a hijab (the environmental cue) and thoughts of a wide variety of prior terrorist attacks spontaneously pop into your mind. Another example would be the latest 'Ebola outbreak'; which never really got off the ground did it? This doesn't mean that either terrorism or Ebola are not real threats; rarely they are. It is that we have prioritised a rarity into something that could happen every day at any minute – this creates massive background tension, this stops us thinking calmly. We cannot function well in such states; and if just such a crisis were to impact on us, we would be less well-prepared to deal with it.

Continual hypervigilance and false pattern matching creates paranoia.

Let me put it another way: how many murders have you seen covered on the news this year or last? You lost count right? Did you know that all that viewing of murders has traumatised you in very real ways? Look out your nearest window: quite dull and peaceful unless you live in a big, bustling city. How many people are being murdered right now? How many have just been killed by terrorists? How many have died of Ebola? I thought so. **You are more likely to be eaten by a shark, struck by lightning, die from a bee sting and win the lottery than be a victim of the above-mentioned catastrophes. However you have allowed the media to programme your priorities, your focus and that's the problem.**

The media is training our unconscious minds that the rare is the commonplace because it is dramatic. Danger is hypnotic; it fixates our attention.

(*The term 'terrorism' was first used after the atrocities of Robespierre's regime during the French Revolution.)

Anxiety levels and adaptive functions: studies in fear.

At mild levels anxiety can be a help initially, stimulating problem-solving and stimulating response actions to a possible future threat – it makes us plan well; we take countermeasures to tackle the threat – the anxiety then subsides. **_Anxiety is a message that can make us, lots of us if need be, take some much needed ACTION!_** But and there's always a but folks – La Bar states that: **_persistently high levels of anxiety 'hijack cognitive resources' required for other important tasks._** Let's delve deeper...

Lab tests on anxiety: the trouble with ALWAYS being on high alert!!!

There was a cute British TV show called 'Dad's Army' about a bunch of old geezers in the Home Guard in England during World War 2. Whenever there was a problem or they thought the Germans were invading one of the main characters would immediately go to pieces and start shouting, 'Don't panic! Don't panic!' to everyone else. La Bar and his colleagues carried out an experimental study on high anxiety and its effect on performance. What did they uncover?

- Well the experimenters wanted to investigate how anxiety affected performance on a 'visual search' task that mimicked airport weapon screening procedures. What they did was to 'cast' their human lab rats in the role of 'security screeners'.

- These screeners were then asked to look for 'T' shapes amongst others on a screen. Effectively they were given a suggestion – 'Look out for T shapes and only T shapes!' like a post-hypnotic command to pattern match for T's.

- The experimenters then made the human guinea pigs anxious by deliberately creating 'a few unpredictable shocks' (unspecified).

- When this occurred, the guinea pigs tended to miss seeing a second 'T' on the display screens! ***La Bar reported that, the effect was strongest in individuals who reported high***

levels of anxiety. In a real terrorist threat etc. the findings suggested (they did more than that) that high threat level alerts at US/UK etc. airports could be 'counterproductive'; engendering greater errors by elevating anxiety in workers. The exact opposite of what was intended! What ever happened to the Western cultural ideal of remaining calm in a crisis? **As I said, in many situations anxiety does not make us safer, it makes us unable to think clearly. We are therefore more likely to be endangered by it.** Geddit?

How to create widespread anxiety, fear and PTSD.

La Bar states, as have I, that as opposed to anxiety, fear is our response to genuine danger now. What we call 'fear' is none other than the outright fight, flight or freeze response; its functional purpose is to redirectionalise bodily and mental resources to deal with a looming threat. We know this. **_Fear is highly 'adaptive'* in this context because it increases the chances of survival._** Sending a surge of blood flow to your muscles for fighting or running =

increased survival odds. We know the amygdala is involved in all fear responses. This part of the brain is located in the temporal lobe. We know it wields a powerful influence over many other 'brain systems'.

(*Adaptive = increases your chances of survival.)

Fear and memory.

In the throes of fear, attention is directed toward the perceived threat. We need to know:

1. What it is.
2. We need to work out where it is located.
3. Then we take action to resolve the threat.

Part 3 is the point where so-called 'coping mechanisms' are triggered usually in an effort to calm oneself down somehow, anyhow. When the crisis phase is over, unconscious protective, evaluative processes kick in. Our fear soaked memories are updated so that the last threat can be avoided in the future. Intense emotions get embedded into our unconscious minds, as do the memories linked to them. Remember also that a fearful mind is incredibly suggestible. Fear is a highly focused waking trance state.

Chronic fear and its affects.

Fear places fierce physiologically energetic demands on mind and body. Chronic fearful reactions or repetitive fearful events are indeed damaging. Studies have found that in PTSD (Post-Traumatic-Stress-Disorder), the amygdala shrinks and is impaired in its ability to be able to create precise memories for threatening material. In other words it starts to hyper-generalise. In fact PTSD sufferers are stranded with what La Bar calls 'overgeneralised fear memories'. What does this mean? Instead of being triggered by real threats, intense fear reactions can be provoked by any stimulus that is merely similar to the original danger (our old friend pattern matching). Left untreated and after a while such reactions can become almost completely habitual (a sign of 'unconscious looping') and simply happen without any stimulus at all. The deep mind is on a war footing. You can't live like that: the toll is huge, family life is ruined; drugs, alcohol and depression can and do often follow.

Group protection mechanisms.

Since the dawn of mankind we have all needed to broadcast/communicate the existence of genuine threats in our environment. As I said in book 7 'Escaping cultural hypnosis' the biological mechanism of hypnosis is rooted in this reality. Concrete information of danger is vitally important for protecting members of any social group.

To facilitate this, characteristic 'brain mechanisms' allow the social communication of fear and anxiety. In wild animals this might be? Auditory based alarm signals such as howling, etc. These often inform others within a group of the existence of specific predators and their current distance to the group. These warning noises evoke feedback behaviours; for example - running away or targeting an attack. Such responses obviously help animal groups escape or defend territory etc. By the way, as I said above, this is why hypnosis works in humans – it also appeals to the same sensory channel predominantly though not exclusively – hearing.

NOTE: The amygdala and specific regions within the auditory cortex are genetically attuned (hardwired) to the

specific frequencies used in these auditory signals and vocal based protective warning signals (barking etc.) originate within dedicated motor circuits (movement) linked to emotional behaviour.

Fear and mirror neurons.

Body Language

Humans are more flexible in their responses – potentially. We communicate threat by facial, vocal (tone/volume) and body language expression; we can even relay it via our handwriting, music and visual art of all kinds to a trained eye. Baby chimps can be taught phobias by humans through observing fake scared responses to a given stimulus; more on this later. We too have certain brain regions that respond to both the direct experience of fear and observing others experiencing fear. This is due to humans' powerful sense of empathy. This is where specific 'neural mechanisms' such as mirror neurons that are involved in imitation and empathy kick in. We are inherently capable of mirroring the feelings of others due to their ongoing emotional expression. This natural empathic response (which psychopaths lack) prepares us automatically to ready ourselves when perceived threats loom on the horizon. We can instantly adjust to fortify ourselves in anticipation of such threats <u>without having to experience them directly.</u> A kind of emotional Chinese whispers. In the wild such abilities are great – in people such mechanisms and their exploitation can trigger mass anxiety. Often the 'fears' are groundless. One of the keys to the anxiety code therefore is...

You can't remain on a war footing forever!

So far so good. Now to the point...

<u>*The media's role in inflating anxiety.*</u>

La Bar's conclusions were forthright, sensible and unequivocal: our inborn capacity to experience what he calls 'collective anxiety' is that it elicits wide social responses for society to engage in realistic risk assessment and so generate protective or offensive responses/behaviours and can guide appropriate 'public policy' (actually Government policy). In other words our genuine human need to protect ourselves is met with an actioned response to sanely satisfy that need. What the media does in response to threats is more like a person with PTSD or a drug addict under stress. The perception, information relay and response cannot satisfy the organic need. Why? In times of social stress Governments, power structures and their lackey the media want a fearful populous who are more willing to obey top down dictats. It's quite simple.

Remember all human civilisations are predicated on *dependency.* If your response to genuine stressors is both calm and creative – some people may well be out of a job. Effective geopolitical cooperation that was sound would help reduce a great many modern threats. And indeed various media POTENTIALLY are very good methods for disseminating genuinely useful information about a multiplicity of 'social threats'. However the media, all media actually offer us an overwhelming onslaught and chaotic barrage of fear mongering; the results are predictable: 'collective anxiety' is mercilessly amped up. Such excessive anxiety levels can hinder survival chances as we have seen; potentially to such an extent that it could paralyse a nation, even though a majority of the 'audience' (message receivers) are not in fact at any direct risk. The media is like the Dad's army character crying, 'Don't panic!' whilst engendering it. Think of a recent crisis, any will do: 'Lots of people running around panicking! Tearful, fearful interviews with bystanders etc.! Need I go on? It's trauma porn folks. It gets ratings and sells consumer goods too. In a few words the media is deliberately eroding our stoicism with the intent of enforcing systems of wide spread social control.

In reality a balance between shrewd safety measures and appropriate information NOT fearful, fast and loose communication is vital in demanding times; the intent and our motto should be – 'keep calm and carry on' as La Bar rightly says. This book will teach you, on a personal level, how to

Keep calm and carry on...

A crucial plank in the anxiety code. In closing the promoted 'emotionalism' of the Post War period was a deliberate act but that's another story. The media also makes many people's self-esteem crash when they compare themselves to celebrity fantasy ideals; this makes them anxious. Women are the primary targets. Now, let's talk about worth.

'Low self-esteem': anxiety toward the self.

'You are a worthless idiot!' 'You cretin! You'll never amount to anything!' 'Why can't you be more like your sister?!' Being told something often enough the child begins to believe it. Being told it by a parent makes it imprint doubly because they are a powerfully hypnotic authority figure. Why would they lie? This is how abusive, often psychopathic parents break down children and hypnotically programme them. Some people's parents are simply evil. 'There must be something wrong with me...' the child pitifully concludes. Wrongly. Not being loved and delighted in for the wholly lovable child you are is DEEPLY traumatic.

If you are so worthless you can't really deserve anything good. If you are so incompetent you are bound to fail! Your whole life will be crap! You won't be able to survive or thrive! How could you with such an unrealistically low opinion of yourself? You attract assholes unconsciously and are attracted to them because you both share your low opinion of you. Women who have been abused often pattern match to abusers in later life – in fact many can only be sexually aroused by abusive men. In order to get rid of low self-worth programming you need to deprogramme verbal abuse. In this book I will show you how. No messing around, no ifs or buts.

Low self-esteem and pattern matching.

If you have been programmed to hate yourself as a child you are going to ignore your strengths and 'look for' evidence of 'worthlessness'; this is simply confirmatory bias – we seek proof of what we have already been conditioned to believe. This is also known as the 'self-fulfilling prophecy'. Or what I prefer to call 'future pace pattern matching'.

Funnily enough certain types of 'perfectionism' (really an inability to enjoy life as it is as opposed to artistic perfectionism which is quite normal) also lead to low self-esteem patterns. Let's say you are brought up in a family where it is expected that you have 'high ambitions'. Let's take the case of a beautiful Italian girl who married an American man; everything was ideal until she graduated. She wanted 3 kids and a job as head of marketing etc. by age 36. Okay. When she got the job she worried incessantly. Soon she did nothing but stare blankly (pathological trance) at meal times, heck any time. She was ruminating endlessly. Her sleep suffered. She went to a doctor who suggested she take drugs. Big f**king surprise. You see what you call doctors I call drug dealers. And they get LARGE payoffs – you better believe it. The lady refused the meds but her 'condition' worsened. Her sleeplessness worsened; she became 'delusional' and believed she was being haunted by the devil. She is presently locked up in a psychiatric unit. She is still there – doped to her eyeballs and 'uncured'. A worried, anxious girl has been zombiefied and stigmatized for life. Big pat on the back for the incompetent drug dealer, oh I mean 'doctor'. Riii-ght.

What happened?

- She set herself unrealistically high and unachievable goals in too short a time frame. (Were they even really 'hers'?)

- This made her worry. 'Can I do this?' 'Am I up to it etc.?'

- This affected her sleep.

- The endless looping of worries (rumination), sleeplessness and resulting exhaustion led to 'depression'.

- As her sleeplessness worsened she became sleep deprived and started to hallucinate and have delusional thoughts as ALL sleep deprived people do given long enough.

- She is diagnosed as being 'psychotic'. No, she is dreaming while awake. In the section on depression we will examine this key reality in depth. Prepare to have all your brainwashing as to what 'mental illness' really is blown out of the water buster.

All this was triggered because she couldn't live up to a set of unrealistic standards she thought she held for herself that had in reality been programmed in by the dominant culture and probably family pressure. ***There is a real danger in linking 'worth' to achievement: however this is a powerful, unconscious meta-belief in all Western societies.*** Now that IS depressing. To recapitulate: low self-esteem is really anxiety about or directed toward the self. It's inherent worth and capabilities. This often leads to...

101

'Social anxiety': anxiety 'toward' others.

Low self-worth is often linked to what is labelled 'social anxiety', 'social phobias' etc. Stress, rejection (this 'lights up' the same brain regions as physical pain) of any kind, being temporarily low on your luck can lead to 'social anxiety'; feeling afraid around others. This may express itself as a form of self-consciousness, 'How does everyone else see me!?' I say, 'Who gives as shit!?' If you have dated a boyfriend who seems lovely and then he starts beating you or vice versa you start to distrust your judgement in people. You might just be a more sensitive type of person who is keenly aware of people's moods and attitudes that they are unaware they are revealing. Maybe you feel uncomfortable with that person or environment and so get labelled 'shy'? You may feel your 'social status' is 'inferior' (According to whom? According to what criteria?) Whatever the reason you have become fearful around people.

Sometimes these fears are very specific pattern matches. I once had a man who was rejected by the first girl he ever asked out. Instead of saying, 'I want to take you out on a date etc.' or words to that effect he said, 'Will you go out with me?' Now what he lacked were social skills. You don't ask a girl 'out' in general. That's like saying, 'We are boyfriend and girlfriend now!' She could only say no. It was a highly pressurised ultimatum. Asking for a date is less pressurised for her. Geddit? Anyway from that day forth this 'rejection' imprinted on his brain as meaning*, 'I am unattractive to ALL women.' In effect the experience had traumatised him. When he told me that this 'princess' had a pattern of dating compulsive liars and criminals I knew he'd had a lucky escape. From that day forth he felt something bordering on blind panic whenever he even passed a pretty girl on the street! Not good. 'Feint heart never won fair lady!' After all most women aren't really scary.

Whatever the cause of the social panic in a trigger situation or anxiety about an upcoming trigger situation, if you remove the unrealistic fear pattern only calm and confidence remain. Even what we call 'public speaking phobia' is a form of anxiety and panic linked to speaking to more than two or three people. After all you can speak in public to one person: what's the difference? There isn't one, outside of your mind. Later I'll show you precisely how to clear up all this garbage. I call it 'psychological archaeology' or if you prefer 'trauma artefacts'. The brain is being WAY too overprotective – it's on that war footing again but there's no war.

(*Often the rigid meaning our younger self attaches to an event helps lock the problem in place – trauma, of whatever degree, causes rapid imprinting - we become suggestible; fear = 'black and white thinking' as our higher brain shuts down. We become dumber. We also lose our sense of humour! This is where you can use reframes: take the young man above, the real meaning was that he had had a lucky escape AND he was now free to find a girl who could really appreciate him. And that's just for starters!)

What is 'stress'?

The correct technical terms for what we call 'stress' is an even more bizarre concept: 'allostatic load'. This simply means 'wear and tear' in normal English. We can only take so much information. I don't mean information in the sense of watching daily news content, reading data in a book; no: 'information' is a wider concept. Food is information. The weather is information. Other people are information. We have threshold limits of optimum information input and output. Our systems can only take so much. Think of all information as having a measurable value:

1. Bumping into someone on the street - value of 3.

2. A car accident - 10. 50 or more if someone is hurt seriously.

3. Food with little nutritional value - 4 as a one off. 100 if chronic.

4. A great day out with friends - 20 but of a good, stimulating sort.

Are you getting the idea? Let's say your upper daily limit is 1000. It's much more but work with me Padawan. Let's say you have a great day out. But you eat crap food – it's a treat.

Then you bump into someone on your way back to your car and that pisses you off. In a bad mood, you drive badly and CRASH! You have an accident. See where I'm going with this?

Paradoxically it is also a stressor to do too little – we need the 'golden mean'; a balance between good and bad, rest and stimulation. No challenge: we become bored. Too much challenge in one go: we might well start feeling that 'too much!' kind of internal pressure we have all experienced; say on a very busy day. You are not a machine, not a robot, you are a living organism. You have limits. A lesson from the anxiety code is:

Keep both good and bad stress within manageable limits.

It is when we fail to do this or when we have no power to control our environmental information levels that we get problems, problems that express themselves in what we call anxiety. So another lesson from the anxiety code is:

When we are heavily stressed our body acts as if it is under physical

attack.

Imagine you have had a series of life
stressors. You have a lump on your ball sack.
It might be cancer. You go to the doctor. He
thinks you are in the clear, it's just a
sebaceous cyst but his new protocol is that all
patients need an ultrasound scan. SHIT! You
start to worry. Life isn't going so well at the
moment anyway; you lost that promotion,
your boss is a dick and your wife is having an
affair with an arm Wrestler called 'Lulu'. Out of
the blue you experience a blinding sense of
panic whilst out shopping. You rush home.
Nothing like that has ever happened to you.
Over the next few weeks you become panicky
on long car journeys, you can't walk down the
road without having to hurriedly rush home.
Your neighbours think you have bladder
problems. You check your 'symptoms' on the
Internet. You 'have' 'agoraphobia' or as I call it
– 'stress levels are chronically too high
syndrome'.

There is only so much any of us can take
Bucko. Cults push people past their
information stress levels deliberately to break
them down for mind-control programming.
You are human. Your agoraphobia is a
message from the unconscious: 'Your stress

levels are way too high; it's like a war room in here! I am detecting multiple threat levels – we are on red alert. What the f**k is going on up there!?' It's time to start to reassess things: how you are living in general, your goals perhaps? Certainly how you respond to challenges. An anxiety code lesson is:

There is an optimum way to respond to challenge and a lousy way!

Notice I said optimum not 'perfect'. This book will teach you and your clients how to do optimum. The cousin of stress is...

FEAR!!!!

What is fear?

Genuine fear has a bad rap; but first...
Word origins:

Fear - (Verb form) Old English source: 'færan'
– 'to **terrify, frighten**', from a Proto-
Germanic verbal form of the root of the
modern noun 'fear'*. Related to Old Saxon
'faron' – 'to **lie in wait**', Middle Dutch 'vaeren'
– 'to fear', Old High German 'faren' to **plot
against** and finally Old Norse 'færa' – 'to
taunt'.

* Fear – (Noun) Middle English source 'fere'
derived from Old English 'fær' – '**calamity,
sudden danger, peril, sudden attack**',
from Proto-Germanic 'feraz' – 'danger'; related
to Old Saxon 'far' – '**ambush**', Old Norse 'far'
- '**harm, distress, deception**', Dutch 'gevaar'
+ German 'Gefahr' – 'danger'. From PIE 'per'-
'to **try, risk**', a form of the verbal root 'per' –
'to lead, pass over; related to Latin 'periculum'
– '**trial, risk, danger**', Greek 'peria' – '**trial,
attempt, experience**'. Also Old Irish 'aire' –
'**vigilance**', Gothic 'ferja' – '**watcher**'; related
to 'per' – 'forward, through'.

The roots of fear are perceived immediate threats to the person

that are risky to survival for which heightened vigilance is required.

Eternal vigilance at the individual level is exhausting. Fear is healthy: you need it. It gets you out of danger fast. It gives you a muscular boost so that you can fight off an attacker. Without fear we would be f...ed. Thankfully God, Mother Nature, 'Evolution' etc. saw that the earth can be a pretty dangerous place at times and gave us a physical insurance policy. It is instinctive, automatic and fires off when the deeper unconscious structures so much as get a whiff of threat. Fear might be described as the physical basis of anxiety. You know, all the glandular secretions - adrenaline etc. of 'fight or flight or freeze'.

However much of what we fear is 'irrational' (to whom?); essentially this means the fear is unfounded. There is no good basis for having it: some men are afraid of women. Really! I mean sh*t scared. It is quite widespread and normal actually but not at all _useful._ We can become afraid of anything at all; and I do mean anything. When we get to the section on phobias etc. I will explain how this marvellous piece of biological engineering whose intention is always to keep us safe can go haywire and 'pattern match' to things that are entirely safe or at least not *that* risky. When fear rules our lives we cannot function. We actually become highly suggestible and programmable in such a state – this is why phobias can seem so entrenched. Fear stops the 'creative part' of our brain centered around the anterior cingulate cortex (ACC) from allowing us to solve problems by associating us to untapped resources that we wouldn't usually access in situation x, y or z. The ACC is a hypnotist's best friend. I write about it extensively in book 7, 'Escaping cultural hypnosis'. When you are relaxed and not pattern matching to faux 'danger cues', you can solve life's problems in amazingly creative ways.

Fear is great in an emergency. In life we need to take a chill pill (not literally, figuratively) when we do, and when our base state* is a kind of 'relaxed alertness' we function very well indeed. In fact you are born, made and meant to function well: you see, it's in your genes.

*The base state defined.

Our base state is our usual emotional-physical-psychological state that we habitually operate from on a daily basis. In anxiety clients this base state has been nudged too far up on the arousal scale. Imagine a measuring device – say a thermometer that is marked with numbers from 0-10. 10 = absolute terror and 0 = very calm and confident. Technically we say that the parasympathetic phase of the nervous system (calming down) is being swamped and bullied by the sympathetic phase (arousal). The sympathetic phase is not at all sympathetic – more a pathetically paranoid worry wart! Using hypnosis we can re-establish the parasympathetic as the predominant function/phase of the nervous system; when we do, the person's base state hovers around the 0-3 level depending on the situation. In other words: arousal stays 'manageable'. The person is alert yet flexible and relatively calm; their creative abilities are accessible. Instead of being fearful and inflexible instinctively their new calm state is one which encourages objectivity, a spirit of curiosity, a sense of humour, emotional control and a focus on the realities of the situation at hand – as it is, not as we imagine it to be - the creative abilities are accessible and working automatically when needed.

Next up: **WORRY!**

What is worry?

Anxiety code insight: worry is a huge waste of time and energy that changes nothing; it turns molehills into mountains.

Worry is really the psychological part of anxiety. It's the by and large **pointless rumination** – looping endless 'what if' scenarios in the mind.

'What if I do that and he does this?!'
'What if I ask her out on a date and my balls explode!??'
'What if I leave me job and it all goes wrong!'???
'What if global warming eats my baby dingoes!'????

Worry is speculation or the process of speculating. What's more we usually say such stuff in a really worried or worse panicky tone in our heads and that scares us even more and yet nothing really threatening or dangerous has actually happened! We have imagined it *might* and we fixate on this 'might' as if it were a reality! In the trade we call this 'misusing your imagination'. You see to conjure up any imaginative scene you just say

– 'What if...' and fill in the gaps. That is the linguistic structure of worry just as not giving a shit is 'So what if...'

'What if' is also the basis of conjuring up positive scenarios but they might be just as delusional as the worried ones!

'What if I do win big?!' the crap a gambling addict tells himself.
'What if she does say yes and it all goes perfectly!?' the basis of divorce!
'What if I leave my job and life goes simply swimmingly from now on!' Rii-iight!

More on this subject a tad later. Worry plays a big part in all anxiety disorders – in starting them and in maintaining them. Worrying is mentally exhausting – there is no exit from the loop; at worst it goes on and on with interconnected chains of worry fantasies. And remember you are fearful, which means you are programmable which means you just brainwashed yourself into believing in all those worst case scenario never-will-bes! Ooops. Effectively you have just created a worry trance.

Trance and worry.

All worriers are highly hypnotisable. Why do I say this with such utter conviction? Because in order to worry really well you must go into trance: a pathological trance. In the hypnosis scripts later I will show you ways and means to snap someone out of this and better still how to teach them to snap out of it at will.

The origins of worry.

It is generally learnt off of a worrying parent. They have generally done little with their lives. They are generally very negative about doing anything at all; unwittingly such 'worriers' (no one is a 'worrier' – they *do* worry – it's a mental process) infect their impressionable children with such habits. Additionally you might just become worried after a life stressor of some kind or perhaps your needs are being so badly met that you become physical anxious and that leads to mental anxiety or worry as we call it.

Anxiety problems are seemingly vast, messy, inescapable feedback loops – spiralling on and on and on. Until you, the hypnotist step in.

115

Worry is an upside down positive intent.

The purpose of worry is to anticipate danger, to troubleshoot problems that may arise and so effectively deal with them or handle them: the intent of all behaviours at root is positive, functional, healthy and helpful. It's just that people learn really dumb ways of fulfilling the intent. Let's take our man who is worried about asking a girl out on a date. His intent is to successfully ask the girl out on a date. So far so good. Now presuming he's not a stalker, is reasonably presentable and confident, his area of control in this situation is himself. He cannot control the lady he finds attractive. He can be charming, funny (he's probably better off ignoring her!) but what he really needs in this situation is the courage to take the risk. *The point is success lies not with achieving the desired outcome but with the act of taking the risk.* The worst that can happen is she says no. You'll learn to love again buster!

And the thing about courage is that we are all much more courageous than we consciously know. Fear grows when we do nothing. The rule of living is: in order to get courage, you DO courage! You act courageously. The more often you do something courageous the more the subconscious says, 'Hmmm, seems Jimmy boy here likes doing this kind of stuff now; he used to be such a chicken shit! Oh well, being a nice subconscious and all I'll do it all for him so he doesn't have to think about it! That's the kind of subconscious I am.'

You don't need hypnosis for mild anxiety: you just need a pair of balls. It's only when the anxiety becomes extreme that people like me receive phone calls. But remember this part of the anxiety code:

Do courage to get courage.

And...

All worry is an upside down positive intent in disguise.

Word origins of 'worry'.

Worry - (Verb) Old English - 'wyrgan' – 'to strangle; derived from Proto-Germanic 'wurgjan' (similar too: Middle Dutch - 'worghen', Dutch 'worgen', Old High German 'wurgen', German 'würgen' - 'to **strangle'**, Old Norse 'virgillw - 'rope'). This is supposedly from PIE (Proto-Indo-European) 'wergh' - 'to **turn'** (similar to **'wring'**). The oldest sense was already obsolete in English after the 16th century. The more modern meaning of 'annoy, bother, vex etc.' was first recorded in the 1670's. This is believed to have developed from a sense of 'to **harass** by rough or severe treatment' (recorded 1550's) as of dogs or wolves **attacking** sheep. The meaning which mainly concern us – 'to cause mental distress or trouble' is attested from 1822. 'To feel anxiety or mental **trouble**', is first recorded around 1860.

Worry - (Noun form.) 'Anxiety arising from **cares and troubles'** is recorded in 1804.

The root themes from the get go are very similar – worry is a form of mental attack or torture that we perform upon ourselves!!! We wring worries to death, turning them over and over – we strangle all the joy out of our lives.

Again, a degree of worry is normal; we all worry a bit about this and that but such thoughts are just the driftwood of the brain – we don't fixate on them. They pass. We are just anticipating problems – a good thing. In fact we shouldn't call it worrying at all at this level: it's just planning and troubleshooting. **It**

is when extreme worry persists chronically and obsesses us that we can get serious health problems: physical and psychological.

When we do the mental part of anxiety we are 'troubled' and 'care' about emotional, physical, spiritual, psychological and relationship unmet needs. Worry content is almost always about a need not being met sufficiently now!

I have had clients who worry pretty much all the time in the background of their mind. Worrying about this and that, that and this! It has to stop. The scripts I outline later will blow all this self-tormenting garbage out of the water – leaving calmness, clarity, creativity and confidence. The conscious mind thinks by worrying it will solve problems through intense analysis – wrong! The conscious mind doesn't have the storage capacity or resources to solve problems like this. It analyses them yes but then we **leave it to the subconscious to generate the solutions** whilst we do other things. Then, in moments of inspiration and intuition the insight we need effortlessly pops into our head. It's like trying to remember a name: the more you try the less you succeed; the information is stored subconsciously.

Often people who have had University training in left-brained 'logic' (a straightjacketed version of it) begin to worship their conscious capacities unreasonably. They entirely undervalue the resources and wisdom of their powerful unconscious mind. They forget or hold their instincts and feelings in contempt. At worst such people are often prone to so-called 'analysis paralysis' (never starting things), pathological perfectionism and psychosomatic disorders etc., often mentally fatiguing themselves into chronic fatigue syndrome. Honestly! I've treated them; I know. Rumination is not the same as calmly thinking things through, which is an essential life skill.

Ruminative worry is one of the key components in what we call 'depression' as you shall see soon enough. Again: worry is speculation - much encouraged and practised by the mass media.

Worry beating tricks and the psycho-linguistics of worry.

Words that are linked to worry almost always have to do with uncertainty, negative self-talk, excessive doubt and the imagination being used to 'horror film' us with terrors that never come to be.

Perhaps...it'll go badly!
Maybe...I'm not good enough.
Might...it be stupid to do x?
It's possible...I'll humiliate myself.
What if*...he wins!?
<u>Imagine</u> if...I fail!
I <u>picture</u> it...all going wrong...
I can't <u>see</u> myself...doing x right.

Get the idea? These words elicit mental states that ensure we get exactly the opposite of what we really desire: for things to go well, to be competent, to look good, to excel, to win, to shine etc. Our focus is topsy-turvy. <u>And you get more of what you focus on.</u> If you want to feel confident don't picture a lack of confidence, picture being confident and that's where you'll 'directionalise' your brain.

(*Anxious questions are attempts to 'fill in'/'answer' the experience of ambiguity and uncertainty.)

Another part of the anxiety code: is you must be comfortable with uncertainty.

If you want confidence state what you want

positively with a verb: 'I want to feel confidence!' Not 'I don't want to be scared!' Then imagine yourself being confident NO MATTER WHAT HAPPENS AROUND YOU – because you can realistically control that. You can influence others but control them? Even if possible and believe me it is if you have the resources; is that really what you want? Our degree of influence varies from 0-100% - so why waste your time worrying anymore? Worry is a diversion and waste of our 'life force' for want of a better phrase. We have a limited amount of any energy source. We save it for that which is essential to our survival and success. This is why we need to focus our mind on what we want – then take action. When you do, you literally can't worry to excess; for starters you'll be too busy!

Worry also disappears when you act and build up small but strong chains of success after success after success. And that's how you build genuine long lasting confidence based on reality. Confidence is not just a feeling; it's the reality of who you are in this world. You are confident because you can control, influence and manipulate (in the good sense) your environment successfully. You can achieve what you want. A good thing. A chronic worrier isn't even daring to take the risk to live. Life is too damned short for anyone to indulge in a worthless hobby of pointless speculation as a long-term habit. You need to be a doer in this life. Even a nematode worm is as doer.

As an end note to this section I recommend you listen to Monty Python's song about worry; it's called 'I'm so worried...', one of its lines is, 'I'm so worried about the world today I'm sure it's not good for your feet!' Very funny, the ultimate end-worrying reframe. You can listen for free on Youtube.

Now let's move onto PaNɪC!!!!

What is panic?

In my 10th and final book: 'Weirdnosis' which is about what I call Strategic Hypnotic Coercion, I will be fully outlining how to create mass panic. Honest. But for now…The word origins of this unpleasant state is the Greek word 'panikon' - 'pertaining to pan', literally. That is fear of Lucifer, the devil in Christian terms. Pan was the god of woods and fields, he was regarded as the origin of **mysterious** sounds that caused **contagious, groundless fear** in herds and crowds, or in individuals in desolate places*. Panic came to mean 'mass terror' by 1708; from the earlier adjective - French 'panique', recorded around the 15th century.

(*See the appendix for a brief interesting and amusing examination of this subject.)

Panic is basically when we totally lose it – it's fear on steroids. You can be going along swimmingly and them BLAM! A wave of panic surges through you! If a tram or train is heading your way and you need to flee fast – great! You have been provided with a massive surge in powerful adrenaline in order to survive. The body is programmed to respond this way to danger; it's actually the 'provide the body with masses of energy response'. But that never caught on. You need lots of energy for strenuous physical exertion. So what we label 'panic' has a positive intent as do all human behaviours. However what if there is no mugger, approaching car or stampeding buffalo? As I mentioned earlier: what if you panic just by leaving your house (agoraphobia – 'fear of the marketplace')? What if you panic on car journeys? What if you panic on the London Underground (subway)? What if a specific stimulus causes a 'panic attack'? Then you have what we call a 'phobia'. A panic attack is a phobia gone anarchically rogue – he just prepares for danger all the God damned time.

This is where the Pan root definition comes in handy, not in the essential biological purpose but in the mysterious sense of impending dread that suddenly befalls you so that you think you are going mad or having a heart attack! Or both!

Again: the cause is always a build-up of chronic stress or perhaps one acute stressor. Something acts as the straw that breaks the camel's back: when that happens you just entered the horrible zone of panic attacks that hit you out of the blue. Thankfully hypnosis can calm those suckers away like no one's business. Hypnosis dissolves panic attacks.

Panic – fear – stress – anxiety and worry; all differing faces on the same creature. An anti-hero with a thousand faces! They can and all do feedback on one another; they represent a 'hierarchy of extremities'.

Worry = stress.
Stress = anxiety.
Anxiety = fear.
Fear = panic!

And on and on. Get the picture? Closely related to panic attacks – a sort of half cousin, twice removed is so-called... *'Generalised-Anxiety disorder!!!' Oh my!!!*

An interesting advanced level sidetrack: The truth about fight or flight.

The standard psychological model is that humans evolved a mechanism called the fight or flight response. The model claims that early humans faced threats from massive prehistoric predators etc. However all the palaeontological evidence globally shows that animal predation played no significant part in human history. The selection pressure on humans was next to nil. Predators are by and large afraid of humans and do not hunt them; all animals show a fear response to the smell of humans. Stories of wolves and lions eating humans are largely myth. Only rabid wolves and sexually frustrated lions have been known to attack humans. Young male lions who cannot satisfy their lust can become addicted to man flesh! Bears and crocodiles will attack humans if their territory is impinged upon. A pack of humans can outwit and kill any number of predators easily. This being so why do we have a fight or flight response at all?

The threat probably came from other humans: we may well have this protection mechanism to protect us from our own kind.

What is 'G.A.D' – so-called Generalised-Anxiety-Disorder?

GAD is easily treatable using skilled hypnosis. And I mean 1 session easy folks. In fact in 90% of cases you can get rid of it by doing one thing. Know what that is? *You wish it would get worse!* But before we get to that, egads what's 'GAD' when it's at home!?

In a brief sentence it's pretty much being anxious ALL the time about everything and nothing – some call this 'free floating anxiety' which means there seems to be no cause or trigger but as that's completely impossible – I'll tell you what causes it: trauma and/or unmet needs. Yawn!

Do you have a fear of fear?

'We have nothing to fear but fear itself!' declaimed President Franklin D. Roosevelt; and of course, in his case, slopes, *'Nameless, unreasoning, unjustified terror which paralyzes needed efforts to convert retreat into advance!'*

Great propaganda slogan that that was; it contained a great deal of truth. GAD sufferers awaken afraid. They awaken and feel a surge of anxiety – BOOM! Just like that. They seem to have a nameless dread that things just ain't right. That's because they aren't DUMMY! This is how this works – I guarantee you all GAD sufferers were feeling bits of mild anxiety before they felt it pretty much all day long. But you know what? They ignored the signal. The signal is saying – 'Your life is going the wrong way fast mister! Make changes.' But they don't. If you don't listen to subconscious signals they intensify. You can't wish your internal feedback systems away. They are looking after you; unlike your dumb programmed conscious mind, they know what's in your best interests. They know better than YOU so pay attention. Do not mess with primal forces. If someone has GAD ask things like:

- Are you eating properly?

- Are you exercising?

- Is your work/life balance right?

- Do you need a job you'd enjoy?

- Do you have enough money?

- Do you need a rest?

- Are you drinking too much booze?*

- Is there a bully your need to stand up to?

The signal is saying there is a loss, a lack. Something is missing. Find out what the missing thing is and take action to address it now! Eat well. Go exercise. Balance all areas of your life. Get a fulfilling job: retrain if you have to. Get a job that pays more money. Stop overworking and rest now and again – you aren't a machine. Moderate your alcohol consumption. Put that bully in their place or get out of that toxic environment. You don't have to do it all today. The good thing is as soon as you start altering things in the right direction of actually getting your needs met – the 'generalised anxiety' calms down. You start feeling confident again. Imagine you are on a ship headed toward an iceberg and the iceberg detector device is flashing like crazy and you ignore it. What might happen Einstein? Yes, if you take a different course that crazy sound and flashing red light go away. Who knew!?

Ironic rebound.

There is a principle of mind that: **the more you try to suppress or ignore something the more intense and explosive the eventual reaction will be.** This is known as 'ironic rebound' coz the jokes on you. See book 7, 'Escaping cultural hypnosis' for further details.

(* The numero uno cause of 'drug addictions' etc. is anxiety/stress. See book 8, 'Hypnotically deprogramming addiction' to rid an 'anxiety client' of this part of their problem matrix. Anxiety problems and addictions often go hand in hand: this is known in the biz as 'comorbidity'. Sounds very dramatic! It means you got more than one problem but in Latin that sounds really f**king serious!)

No fear of fear = confidence!

Now sometimes people with anxiety start to fear the anxiety and that only makes it worse. It goes like this...

- You feel a wee bit of fear. Just a tiny jolt.

- You start thinking, 'Oh no! Fear!' This Sherlock, only makes it worse. The fear is met by a fear of it – this creates a crazy inescapable feedback loop. The fear of fear strategy goes like this: **fear – fear fear – more fear – fear – fear fear – more fear**

– oh my! There's no exit.

STOOOOOP!

- Interrupt the fear strategy by doing this: **fear – *genuinely* want more fear – less fear – less fear – want it even more – fear goes bye bye, fast.** Your 'exit' is the new calmness you feel. Your intent is to calm down after all.

This even works with panic attacks 90-95% of the time. Just let the bastard fear happen! It won't kill you; defy it...Say to yourself:
'Is that the best you can do fear you chicken shit!? More!' Taunt it! *'I want the worst anxiety attack I've ever had! In fact make it the worst in human history so I run around naked and my head explodes and my balls/tits shoot off in all directions blinding people!'*

The client who lost his fear of fear.

I once had an 'anxiety client' who needed just this approach. He was afraid of going outside; so he thought. I said, 'Nope. You are not afraid of going outside. You are afraid of fear. I want you to go for a walk to the end of my road and as you feel the fear start to rise, demand more fear! Deliberately ask for the

Bring it on

132

worst anxiety you've ever experienced and it'll go away.'

My client laughed. He knew it was true. I saw him to the front door. 10 minutes later he came back, 'It worked!' he said, 'Every time I felt it building up as I got further away I said, 'Is that it! I want more fear etc.!' He was 'cured'. The thing is his anxiety was low, it wasn't *really* bad. I knew this would work with him. Other people's subconscious minds aren't so amenable. To conclude: by wilfully, consciously demanding MORE fear you get less, then none; a paradox. Who is in control? You or your emotions? This will only work long term however IF you get your needs met too. Shit life = anxiety. Sorry. No magic formula will get away from it. But...

Another rung in the anxiety code is: to get rid of fear lose your fear of fear.

One level of fear is quite enough. With expert hypnosis however GAD goes gadabout very quickly and elegantly indeed; again the specifics are to be found in part deux of your book. What next? I'm glad you asked – A

NERVOUS BREAKDOWN of course!

Ahhhhhh! If you ignore a stress build-up long enough something has got to give!

What is a 'nervous breakdown'?

Thankfully a nervous breakdown (NB) sounds more dramatic than it is. Not that it isn't something to take very seriously – it's a warning signal that you have been living your life the wrong way and your mind and body cannot take the inordinate stress levels they are being dragged through.

When I meet clients who are on the edge of 'cracking up' they all follow a very similar pattern – a background of massive, chronic, intolerable stress that they have been putting up with as if they were some kind of masochistic beast of burden. STOP! You aren't meant to feel hyper-stressed on a daily basis; if you are, it's time to take a good look at things.

Often my clients feel that one more stressor will tip them over the edge. The mind-body is on a war footing – the first thing any health practitioner NEEDS to do with someone on the cusp or just over the edge of a 'nervous breakdown' is calm them down, right down, all the way down using mine and yours best drug free buddy – hypnosis.

Hypnosis is THE stress, anxiety and worry

beater par excellence; nothing else comes close. The fact is you can restore a person's sense of balance in about 5-20 minutes easy. When they are calm they can start to recover. They need to give themselves some time to heal. This means take a break and relax for a couple of weeks. Take it easy. If work is the cause you take time off. If a person doesn't they risk developing depression or worse. The extreme exhaustion that characterises a nervous breakdown is simply the fact that you can't stay on that psycho-physiological war footing forever buster. You are a human being, not a machine, not a robot – you have limits.

When we are very exhausted we tend to be more prone to worry. So you are exhausted and worrying! Nice – see how these negative feedback loops feedback upon one another creating despair spirals? How do you get out of 'em? There's no exit. Yes there is – with hypnosis.

Factors that push someone to the edge.

I have found several repeating factors that cause a nervous breakdown which I would like to now rechristen if I may as the 'I can't take anymore syndrome!' Your subconscious is sending you a feedback signal. It is processing too much information, it needs a rest. It needs to recover. Listen.

- Stress in the workplace. Low job security, bad management, a dangerous profession (policing), bullying in the workplace, long hours, lack of control over your job etc. are the main factors that lead to an NB.

- Childhood patterns of worrying plus stressors. When people establish worry loops as children, quite by accident, it makes them prone to excessive worry loops when a life stressor hits: as they do us all. At some point something has to give. Several of my clients felt so on the edge that they reported the only thing that stopped them going passed the 'tipping point' was staring at one point only and fixating their mind on it. Why? They are spontaneously effecting an attempt at self-hypnosis. Why? To shut out all the inner and outer information that now just seems too much.

- It is said that everyone is only 4 major stressors away from overload. I actually think most people juggle more than that on a daily basis but the idea behind the generalisation is you have limits. We can only process so much information. Time to re-evaluate your priorities etc.

- A final factor is a lack of overall meaning and purpose in life. If you carry on working in a job you hate for example two things will happen – you become like a broken in animal and give up like the electrocuted dogs or your subconscious starts giving you anxiety based problems, heart flutters, palpitations, difficulty breathing, feelings of impending dread etc. You might become a hypochondriac. The fact is, again, these are warning signals. You must live a life with meaning and purpose and that means you must find a way to earn money and work at something you love. What did you excel at as a child? The answer lies in your gifts/talents. More on this later. You get the point. The NB for such people is the 'enough is enough moment'. The moment thankfully where people become highly motivated to change course.

Those in a nutshell are the bare bones of a nervous breakdown feedback signal. Drugs are not the answer. You'd be better off drinking booze heavily; seriously! More on that latter.

A peg in the anxiety code is:

You can only take so much shit and something is going to give!

Next up, or should that be down –

depression! I'm so fed up: you?

What is depression?

Depression. I remember when I started as a
hypnotherapist – the first course I took gave
me a script and said it could be used with
depression. I wasn't convinced. At first I didn't
advertise for depression clients at all. I just
wasn't convinced I knew what it was. And do
you know what I discovered, rapidly, that 99%
of doctors, psychologists, shrinks and
therapists haven't a clue what it is either. I
had some NLP tricks that were 'supposed' to
help people with depression – they did
NOTHING to help. Nothing. I eventually
worked out what we call 'depression' is; shall I
tell you? It's easy – I sum it up in this phrase
–**depression proper is worry gone crazy!**
That's it. Or at least that's how it starts.

Depression as a severe pathological trance.

When people worry chronically it becomes
harder and harder to focus on now, the
present. Your focus is inward on catastrophic
imaginings, regrets of the past, fears of the
future etc. Essentially the worrying becomes
so bad that it dominates a person's life – they
are almost trapped in a hypnotic worry loop.
People erroneously labelled 'depressives' have
a great talent – they are capable of entering

an intense self-hypnotic state; paradoxically and thankfully this can be used to pull them out of it.

What causes 'depression'.

Simple. Unmet needs. If children are brought up in stressful, fearful, insecure or abusive families they start to worry about how their needs for safety, protection, love etc. will be met. They often blame themselves for their parents or 'caregivers' deficiencies.

Background patterns of trauma escalate worry patterns at the conscious level – again our old friend the war footing mentality. Children from less than secure homes will see all potential relationships through prisms of fear and mistrust. This stops them relating well with others which in turn makes them worry. This is one way that the 'patterns of depression' are laid down in some people. These are the ones I label the 'chronic depressives'. This is because the problem has often been with them for years, decades. They think it's who they are. Nope. It's what they've learned. The patterns of depression are just a set of inter-looped habits – the depressive problem matrix if you will. When you accurately identify them they are surprisingly easy to get rid of.

141

Another and the more usual cause of depression is loss. Loss now. A loss that causes a universal human need to go unmet. It can be a fear of loss that causes it. Let me explain. I once had a young lady in her late twenties who came to see me. She was on anti-depressants etc. (thankfully not for long). Want to know her problem? All her friends were married with kids and she wasn't. That was it. She just needed to get a decent boyfriend. Fearing that she'd never get one she obsessively worried about her terrible future that awaited her – in her head. Instead of taking action now to go out and get a man, and all woman can do that (you were born with the ability darling!), she sat and worried about not doing it. Her job was a stressful and meaningless financial sector role.

It didn't help that she hung around with psycho yuppies all day but that wasn't the core of it. She wanted to move on with her life. She wanted a good man. She wanted to be a mum/mom. And what did she do? She worried about the exact opposite of what she wanted – her focus had gone awry; she had directionalised her mind toward the idea of being an old spinster. She needed to calm down, focus externally, focus on what she wanted and take action to get it.

Another example. An old man came to see me. He was plonked (put) on anti-depressants by his doctor. Why? His wife had been butchered by an incompetent NHS (British National Health Service) surgeon during a minor operation; this left her crippled for life. She and her husband were looking forward to having a nice retirement when BOOM! Out of the blue some halfwit f**k weed ruins their lives. This was a traumatic loss. Their lives were changed in reality. This man had to look after his wife ALL the time. He had no life. He was an old man. His wife now had to be cared for 24/7 all because some prick didn't do his job professionally. That's what happens with socialist health care but that's another story.

My client would lie on his bed and worry. He'd worry about the past, he had no life now, so he had nothing to do but examine his old life, before his wife's accident. You often hear some semi-informed therapists etc. saying, 'Depression is all about focusing on the past,' wrong d**k head it's about going into unproductive trance loops. They can be about the past, future, anything. This man had given up on living. He had reframed this life challenge as being overwhelming, something he could not overcome. He had drawn unrealistically negative meanings from it. Had he sued the hospital in question? No. Had he sought alternative help to see if his wife's problem could be fixed? No. After his retirement he basically did nothing. He had devoted his whole working life to helping young disabled children, even if it meant him earning less money as a result. His role filled him with joy – this man's problem was that he was a genuine saint in an unholy world. He was an 80 year old plus innocent. I advised him to start doing things to help others again – this was a great source of joy that was now _missing_ for him. Geddit? He told me he couldn't read but that as a result he had a great memory. I said, 'I would learn to read now if I was you.' He said, 'No. It's too late.' I said, 'It's never too late to learn.'

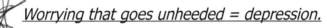

Worrying that goes unheeded = depression.

As I have said we worry about unmet needs. We worry if we'll lose our job so we don't tell a rude manager to go fuck herself. In turn we lose our self-respect. We worry about our drinking – which makes us drink more! We may open up 100's of mini worry loops in a day.

Imagine the 'worried brain' – visualise multiple little whirlwind loops at the back of the mind

144

whizzing around and around. Even though you might be having great sex, talking to your neighbour etc., at the back of your mind are the worry loops. If you have had a trauma there is big worry loop half the size of your head – like the whirlwind in 'The Wizard of Oz'.

These mini anxiety loops that we call 'worry' need a good night's sleep to be 'dreamed out'. You need to be relaxed to solve problems creatively – there are two types of problems: the solvable and unsolvable. One you can't do anything about. The other you can. So relax. When we are relaxed our insight and intuition solve our problems. Too much anxiety = black and white, over analytical thinking. You analyse problems to dissect them. But you need to trust your unconscious to solve them. This it will do if you just relax and get on with things. Endless and exit-less worry loops literally drive you insane if left unchecked. What keeps us sane in the face of worry? As I said, a good night's sleep. It is to sleeping and dreaming that we now turn. But before we do, another plank in the anxiety code is...

A good night's sleep keeps anxiety at bay.

Anxiety and dreaming: how we stay sane.

When I did deep research into depression I found out the following, more or less entirely from the ground-breaking work of the Human Givens' approach to therapy as created by Joe Griffin and Ivan Tyrrell. Although my model of treating depression is influenced by their approach I disagree with much of their philosophical standpoint which is ultimately, at least in part obviously Gnostic (as 99.9% of 'therapy' is). This said their work on the role of sleep, anxiety and dreaming is essential knowledge.

Briefly – when we dream we discharge anxiety. All the anxiety that we accumulate during the day is gotten rid of through dreaming. Often our dreams are just symbolic reworkings of our day to day fears and anxieties. That isn't the only purpose of dreams but this isn't a book on dreaming; you don't need to know about dream analysis or any of that crap to help an anxiety sufferer. You need to help them get a good night's sleep; easier said than done because when we sleep and have lots of anxiety discharging dreams it wakes us up. Why? Because it takes a lot of energy to have that kind of dream.

When people worry excessively they release adrenaline and cortisol; over time chronic cortisol 'leakage' means such people - 1. Have trouble getting to sleep. 2. 'Over dream' and wake up throughout the night as the brain tries to preserve energy. Depressed people will always talk about their 'bizarre and violent' dreams/nightmares. These are the results of their daily rumination trances. 3. They do not experience enough deep, slow wave sleep. This is the deep dreamless sleep that allows us to physically and psychologically restore our energy levels. 4. Because of this, depressed people feel exhausted by the morning – this is why mornings feel so bad for depressed people. 5. When people are exhausted they worry more, are anxious, experience black and white thinking styles*, lose motivation and are more prone to overreact to stressful events leading to panicky feelings or full blown panic attacks. 6. The low feeling of 'depression' is a result of this constant exhaustion. 7. The result is that depressed people, failing to get needs met already, in their perpetual uptight exhausted state can barely get them met at all. Often even their eating suffers. When you add nutritional deprivation to the mix you are in big trouble.

Essentially a depressed person is going through an experience roughly similar to a cult indoctrination 'break down' procedure. If this carries on unimpeded the brain becomes so sleep deprived, so exhausted and so worried that it starts to dream while the person is awake in order to attempt to discharge all the anxiety – this we call 'psychosis'. What we call 'delusions' are symbolic dream mentation patterns in waking states. What the person needs is twofold: one - to be calmed down so that over dreaming does not occur; two - to experience normal levels of REM dream sleep and deep slow wave restorative sleep; three – get their universal human needs met in waking life ASAP!

(*Rigid, inflexible patterns of thought that prevent problem solving. See below for details.)

Churchill's 'black dog'.

Wartime British Prime Minister Winston Churchill struggled with depression his whole life. He called it his 'black dog'. He would paint his way out of it often. Depressed people will hear this, 'What's the point? Nothing good happens etc.' voice in their head. That's what the feelings of high anxiety and constant exhaustion do to a person. It might seem like a 'black cloud' or some other symbolic representation of a 'depressed state' has descended but it hasn't really. It's just you pissed off at feeling crap all the fucking time and worse not knowing HOW to stop it. It is the perceived sense of powerlessness that is the problem with all anxiety issues. This book should rectify that fully.

Anxiety isn't an impregnable fortress; it is a wound up spring, a taught wire, a stretched elastic band: you can turn it into jelly, a soft cushion, a cuddly friend with all the insights in this book. If I have done something successfully and you do the same or similar things you can succeed again. Yes? Once anyone understands a problem, once a mystery is demystified you get the Aha moment. And anxiety starts to melt away; almost as if you were playing some surreal Kafkaesque game and then suddenly confusion gives way to – illumination! Knowledge is power.

Black and white thinking and stress.

When we go into fight or flight or what I call 'war-footing' mode we cannot think clearly, actually we barely 'think' at all. We see everything in extremes – ALL, NEVER, ALWAYS etc.! This also predisposes a person to become readily angry as depressed people often are. This is why people who are anxious seem so 'dramatic' – they are because their brain and body and stewing in a permanent psychophysiological state of *perceived* ongoing crisis. This is what causes the attitude of so-called 'learned helplessness' that supposedly so characterises depression etc. The person is stuck in war mode, as the crisis *seems* perpetually ongoing they eventually 'give up' and sink into apathy. Nothing they do seems to calm or solve the 'crisis'. Some retreat to a bedroom and don't come out until they are smearing their own faeces on the wall and writing notes on how they want to kill themselves. None of this need happen. By this 'breakdown phase' only remedial measures can be taken in the short-term and this may mean medication in the absence of a good therapist or just to calm the person down sufficiently. Once the crisis is passed then you can utilise the therapy approaches in this book. But it would be better for all concerned to intervene quickly, properly and effectively before things get so out of hand; and do you know what? If you do success is so ridiculously easy, as you will learn in part 2. Now you pretty much know what took me 20

years to learn in a nutshell. Use your knowledge wisely. The first question to ask a 'depressed' (what do you mean by 'depressed' specifically?) person is this...
'Are you experiencing bizarre or violent dreams?'

If they say yes, they are depressed or experiencing the mental process that we label depression – what I call 'excessive worry trance syndrome'. If they aren't – they don't have depression, even if they feel 'sad' or 'down'; if your favourite sports team lose you can feel 'down' – should you medicate???! Depression is about worry and over dreaming. You need to stop the negative feedback loop that = 'depression'. Most of my clients manage to live with low grade depressed patterns without any need for meds; like the OCD clients you'll learn about next, they often just think 'it's me', no – it's the way you go about problem solving, getting your needs met and managing fears - that is the problem. Hypnosis interventions are the NUMERO UNO silver bullet in resolving such unresourceful loops.

Okay. Feeling you are starting to 'get things' that seemed so 'mysterious' before? The human mind is actually very logical and ordered – we go right or 'wrong' in very specific and repeatable ways. After all there is no such disorder as 'Wearing underwear on head at dinner party disorder'. Or is there!!!?

For more detailed info on this subject read my book, 'Escaping cultural hypnosis', **'How to lift depression fast',** and **'How to master anxiety: Stress, panic attacks, phobias, psychological trauma and more', by Joe Griffin and Ivan Tyrrell.** However I do not agree with everything in these books; they are both however excellent. You may well be able to get over both anxiety and depression by reading them alone, even if you have experienced a trauma they'll help.

I especially disagree with their detraumatisation methods; the NLP phobia cure whichever way you redo it is only about 70% successful in such instances. My method, revealed later is 100% successful. However I am indebted to these men for their ground-breaking insights.

And next ladies and gents, would you put your hands together for: *Obsessive-Compulsive-Disorder!*

What is Obsessive-Compulsive-Disorder: O.C.D?

Did you know that all OCD sufferers are heroes? No? Read on Padawan. First off – all real OCD is caused by trauma of one kind or another. The 'compulsions' are doomed to fail attempts to control anxiety. If no anxiety is present people don't have compulsions or obsessions: both are products of extreme, persistent fear. The first thing you do with EVERY OCD sufferer is detraumatise them; I show you how, step by step in this book. Both permissive and authoritarian hypnosis works with OCD *if* you detraumatise a person first. Detraumatisation is a process where you take one unwanted state – fear/panic/terror etc. and replace it with the desired state through simple symbology work. See book 6 for extensive examples of hypnotic symbology procedures.

Back to OCD. Lots of people imagine they have OCD. They say stuff like, 'I am a bit OCD.' Er, no you're not. This has to do with watching too much TV which makes you a hypochondriac sooner or later. It's like medical students who due to inexperience think they have every disease in the medical books! Let me define what OCD is and how you know you 'have it' (more accurately you are 'doing it' unconsciously) and how to know you definitely don't.

What is the OCD process?

If you do this you have OCD:

- You feel anxiety building, almost to panic levels.

- You obsess about doing a particular 'ritual' in order to stop the rising anxiety. The OCD sufferer mistakenly believes that the ritual calms them down. WRONG!

- As they go into pathological trance and visualise all the terrible consequences of not carrying out the ritual, the anxiety grows and becomes more and more intense – OCD sufferers are wonderfully hypnotisable – they do it to themselves every day!

- As the anxiety - catastrophe movies – obsessions/impulses well up and swirl around in a big internal mess, a tipping point is reached. In order to stop the cycle (the OCD feedback loop) the 'sufferer' feels an overwhelming compulsion to DO the ritual. The ritual is an attempt at gaining control over the fear; instead it fuels it and makes it worse. A case again of positive intent – dumb strategy.

- At some point the person who does the OCD feedback pattern carries out the ritual. Ah! They have temporary relief. And then it all starts again – shit! OCD is like drug addiction or any other addictive process; it is based on a Gnostic fantasy that doing something unrealistic will satisfy a genuine need – in this case to calm down and have control. Remember OCD is an attempt at resetting the parasympathetic function of the nervous system. It is however doomed to failure.

NOTE: there is no prima facie evidence of ANY OCD genetic predisposition regarding supposed brain functions or 'chemical imbalance' mythologies promoted by those whose aim in life is to profit from drugs and other bizarre and antediluvian treatments. Shocker!

There is no such thing as a person who IS the OCD.

OCD seems a part of a person because they have done it for ages! You scratch your ass obsessively long enough and it will seem 'a part of you'. It is a simply coping mechanism which will only fail. OCD is not a part of anyone's 'identity' (most people's identity is just a media construct anyway). It is the anxiety that is the problem – all the O and the C stems from the fear. Calm the brain down – stop it pattern matching to faux 'dangers' and victory is assured.

Normal rituals.

People do weird shit. Some people count patterns on patterned carpets. Some people avoid cracks on streets – that's just normal everyday human weirdness. It is ONLY an OCD ritual when you feel massive fear before doing it.

I once had a client who told me he had 'all these rituals' that he did. He told me about one that was really charming: before going to sleep every night he would conjure up in his mind the faces of everyone he loved; by doing this he believed they would be safe. He knew it was 'nonsense' but it made him feel comfy and he fell asleep. I said, 'Does it bother you in any way? Does it make you feel bad? Do you feel terrified if you don't do it?' 'No,' he replied. I asked if he like doing it. He said yes. I said carry on doing it then. People come in all shapes and sizes – we process information differently for we all have different brains and entirely different subjectivities. There is no 'perfect' way to be human. There is no right way to be human. If there is no pain or suffering involved for a client or others then leave them alone. Who are YOU to judge what's 'normal' with regards to human subjectivity. As long as they haven't married their pet cat it's none of my business. And remember human brains like to find and create patterns – they like to take internal and external stimulus and create order from them. This is the mechanism of seeing a pile of rocks and building a house from them. Do you see?

To sum up – lots of people do funny little ritual things and lots of others don't. No anxiety = no OCD. Starting to get it? It's very simple really.

What are the hijacked neuro-mechanics of OCD?

That is a damn good question my Padawan! Why does a brain respond to fear in that way? Actually it is just the normal fear warning circuitry and behavioural response gone a bit haywire. It all has to do with restoring equilibrium once arousal has gotten out of hand. Fear as we know is a signal – an insistent genetic one that demands a response. Once a threat is perceived we 'obsess', a narrow focus of attention upon 'it' in order to prioritise our resources. We think about it, analyse it until we find a solution. When we have the solution we can calm down. It is the uncertainty of our potential responses to a given threatening stimulus that can also create more fear. We can also become afraid of our fear response. Which is very powerful and automatic – a bit like vomiting. The problem also is that in a physical fight etc. such a focus is great but outside of that context we need to relax and get creative in order to solve most problems – analysis figures out the problem, not always does it get to the solution – our insight does that, unconsciously.

As we are obsessing/ruminating about the

threat we also feel an impulse, a 'compulsion' to take action to solve it. In a fight or when confronted by a herd of stampeding woolly mammoths that's just great; but when there is no immediate threat or none at all that compulsion to act _now_ might not be so wise a course of action. Geddit? An OCD sufferer is mentally and physically preparing for a fight which never arrives. Yes, they are on a semi-permanent war footing. No way to go through life. It all comes down to our dear old friend 'pattern matching'.

Origins: trauma, pattern matching and OCD.

When OCD suffers are stressed their OCD gets worse. Why? Past trauma activated the 'OCD pattern' – all that is required to fire it off again is stress in the present; it becomes a default setting. **_Now the real key to getting rid of the OCD is that the person has to stop doing the rituals and notice that nothing bad happens._** This was the old cognitive behavioural approach. OCD is quite similar to an obsessive phobia; it's just a more extreme example in fact.

'Phobics' experience so much fear it can make some weird thoughts pop in their heads. I once had a client who had a fear of wide open spaces and heights – as soon as he got 50 feet down the road a thought popped into his head that he might fall off the world because it was round!!! The fact that gravity would prevent that was no help. But it wasn't the thought, it was the feeling that went with it. A calm person could think that and not be troubled by it. His stress levels were so high because he had a crap job, no girlfriend, little money and no future on his then current path so that few of his genuine needs were being met. The 'phobia' burst out of this ongoing stress. OCD is similar.

Imagine you are a mother and your beloved son is murdered. The event is so painful that you start to develop a 'hoarding obsession'. The media which is full of narcissistic morons doesn't help because it labels such people 'hoarders'. No, they are *hoarding* – a verb. It is something they do. And the cause is the trauma that surrounds the violent and unjust death of a child. A brain under prolonged stress starts to behave oddly. Actually in many ways it's a cry for help to others – I am in pain. Help!

I had a man with a cleaning OCD pattern. He had to clean his whole house everyday with tiny little wipe pads. He feared that if he didn't his whole family would die of a terrible disease. His intent was positive – to save people's lives. In his own mind, when his far younger self invented this mythology he was the hero. And if I told you that as a boy the whole family lived in fear of a tyrannical father who beat his mother regularly and occasionally hit him too you might realise that being brought up in an insane asylum might make you a bit edgy too. This chronic and inescapable trauma was the cause of the 'OCD'. Once the trauma was gone, he could move on. The trauma is the glue that binds the obsessions and compulsions in place.

To my mind not having your universal human needs met over a long period of time is a trauma. You are literally prevented from living like a human; if you don't water some plants they die. Geddit? A Gulag or concentration camp is a perfect example from history of a chronic trauma. Living in hell is very disturbing, even if you were 'physically' unharmed.

Let's say this man as a boy witnessed his mum/mom being beaten by his father. The shouting and yelling that preceded it, the sounds of those fists crashing into her face and body. You are tiny, you can't help mum/mom, all you can do is watch – you are powerless. Your fear levels are so high, watching your mother being beaten repeatedly and her screaming is a dirty business; ah! What if I clean everything. I can't stop her being beaten but I can stop us from dying from a disease. If everything is clean we won't die of that. Then I'd be a hero! Do you see folks? DO...YOU...SEE!? The OCD = power in this young boy's mind. He is a boy after all. But this very sane response to an insane environment is outdated for a man in his late forties. That's where and when he needs outside help.

What if he watches a film where a women is beaten? What if he hears someone shouting? What if he just sees a facial expression reminiscent of...well you can guess what? His brain is pattern matching – looking out for cues that say DANGER! After all, those patterns he detects may well have kept him alive. But as his brain pattern matches one way, it can pattern match in better, calmer ways. You don't want to eliminate all pattern matching, you want new patterns for old. The intent is positive – survival as far as the fearful part of the brain is concerned. Drugging that away doesn't address the issue – THE TRAUMA DUMMY! Drugs can only suppress that through 'zombification'. We'll get to that later.

By the way as 'OCD' is often triggered by a life stressor around 70-90% of 'sufferers' recover in 3-6 months spontaneously. So now you now have an idea of what we call 'OCD' for convenience is. After all, language is only ever a shortcut for experience. Talking of varying degrees of trauma etc....let's examine –

PHOBIAS!

What is a phobia?

Linguistically a phobia is something that makes you want to run away. Sounds like a blind date I went on once. ***Again there is no such thing as a 'phobic' – the totality of a person is not defined by a stress reaction process that is being looped unconsciously.***

I *love* phobias. I mean they're horrible things but as a hypnotherapist, if it's me up against a phobia, the phobia is going down – big time baby. I always beat the phobia; with phobias I have a 100% success rate. They are easy to beat. Clients always let them go. Why? They feel bloody awful. They are a psychological relic of a period of too much stress. At some point during that stressful time a scare occurred; that was the straw that broke the camel's back. Even a startle can do it. And when something is in the environment during that scare, that feeling can get linked instantly to that something, what we'll call the 'stimulus'. If you panic and a paper bag blows by, you may well develop a fear of paper bags. A phobia is a panic attack triggered by a specific stimulus rather than a generalised reaction to high background stress levels.

Anxiety code insight: In a fearful state we are highly programmable. Learnings however daft can be swiftly imprinted at the unconscious levels in such states.

Pattern matching and phobias.

Your brain wants to avoid that unpleasant reaction from happening again. So you start avoiding paper bags. In fact your brain starts 'pattern matching' to them! Our brains can't help but look for patterns; that's just part of what they do. But some pattern matching directionalisations are of no use. Especially if something like a paper bag isn't a real threat. With some phobias you don't even need to use formal hypnosis, the mild-ish ones can be got rid of by simply imagining the worst; I'll tell you how to do that later.

The origins of phobias.

Like worry, phobias can be created by imitation too. If your dad has a dog phobia and you as a child see him panic near a dog, your young impressionable mind will conclude they are *all* dangerous and you'll panic too.

Experiments with chimpanzees showed that a scientist had merely to introduce a new stimulus to a young chimp and fake a startle response in order to create a phobia of that stimulus in the young animal. In the film I saw this was done with a harmless toy bird. Thereafter the poor baby chimp fled at the sight of the toy.

Anxiety code note: young mammals learn what is dangerous and safe by monitoring their parents' /caregivers' reactions.

Phobias can be created by one scary event that occurs out of the blue. A dog may bark at you as your parents take you to play in your local swing park. He may only have been being friendly. But he is big, noisy and has sharp teeth – your young brain concludes he wants to hurt you or eat you. You run away from the dog and he chases you thinking you are playing! A phobia is installed. However it is my experience with children experiencing phobias that, as with adults, a pattern of background stress and nervousness has been created before the phobic provoking incident occurs.

There may be stress at home; children are

ultra-sensitive to such stressors. Parents may be simply going through a tough time emotionally for one reason or another and the child detects mum/mom or dad's anxiety. Then the child starts worrying too. Rarely they may develop when a child is being picked on by a nasty bullying parent etc. Phobias have been created in labs by 'scientists' experimenting on children using behavioural conditioning techniques. Sometimes clients can't even remember what caused them and as far as I am concerned 99% of the time I don't need to know. To sum up ***phobias are often caused by prolonged insecurity.***

I showed in book 4, 'Forbidden Hypnotic Secrets' the outline of my version of the classic NLP phobia cure. In book 6, 'Crafting hypnotic spells', I outline a more powerful symbology phobia cure; you will find the full process in this book in the section on childhood phobia treatment later on. However in this book we are going one step further: drum roll please ladies and jellyspoons! As I've said, I am going to reveal to you the piece de la resistance in the Rogue Hypnotist arsenal of hypno-weapons! It is my de-traumatisation process; I spent literally years trying to work this out. I had to find a pain free way of quickly removing all trauma. I found it. It is relatively quick and simple. Once you have this method it will put you leagues ahead of your competition but most importantly you'll be able to help all the people suffering from what we call 'trauma'. Details of the technique follow soon enough... Let's stay on this general topic though because we label an extreme 'emotional' reaction a

TRₐᵤMA!!!!

Trauma is the grand emperor boo-pah of fear responses!!!

A bad mannered interruption: anxiety and modern city life.

But before we get to trauma we must discuss manners. You see, bad manners make people anxious. There I said it. When people are collectively rude to one another they rationally and emotionally realise that every social encounter with a stranger becomes a source of potential conflict and tension, one-upmanship and narcissistic condescension or plebeian submission. To put it plainly the unspoken rules of civilised social conduct go out the window.

In modern Britain it is not now possible to walk down a local high-street in major towns or cities without encountering this low level anti-social 'thuggery'. And if you think it is confined to the 'lower orders' of modern Britain you would be sadly mistaken; in fact since the Thatcher and Blair Governments the re-establishment of a quasi-Victorian system of social relations between the social classes is not the least of both those fanatic's warped legacies.

In practise this reveals itself as the reanimated Frankenstein's monster of class snobbery in all its former glory; the meritocratic egalitarianism of the 1960's now a distant dream. In London this reality reveals itself to such an extent that the English working classes have been ethnically cleansed from the city which once created the lovable cockney. London is now little more than a vast student town for young, post graduate, cultureless yuppies. The working classes are also excluded financially – it now costing over £7/$10.61 to get a decent pint of beer in a London bistro 'pub'. London is really nothing other than a financial centre now and is, as a result, quite soulless. This soullessness also produces an unconscious anxiety – a feeling, a sense that things aren't quite right but you can't put your finger on quite why that is so.

The 'culture' of the London yuppie (they call themselves 'hipsters') is as follows...

1. The present culture may be defined as 'pathocratic'; that is it is created by psychopaths in the city of London and the media; the social underlings seek to imitate it. It could rationally be labelled 'trickle down psychopathy'.

2. Worship self.

3. Worship change for changes sake.

4. Venerate cruelty, venality, pettiness and materialism.

5. Look down on perceived 'social inferiors' and treat them disgracefully as though a conquered lower life form from another world.

6. Go to gyms and run on streets. Keeping the 'machine' going but not the 'ghost'.

7. Dine and drink in pseudo pubs that are identical to what used to be called wine bars.

There is no social cohesion (humans in constant competition with one another cannot 'come together'), genuine organic culture or uplifting 'esprit de corps'. People do not step aside and apologise to passers-by as they used to, they do not queue - they push in; in fact they expect others to move aside for them as if Royalty had dignified the streets with their presence. This culture of millennial rudeness is a major source of anxiety in city life.

I haven't even mentioned anxiety caused by overcrowding or the cheek by jowl existence of wholly incompatible cultures – London is the new Babel; it has more in common with the Bowery of 19th century New York than with any socially engineered fantasy of 'Utopia' (according to whom?). Rising crime, violent crime is inevitable.

London, rightly labelled a labyrinthine monster by writer Peter Ackroyd is also the model for all Western (or Post-Western as I call them) cityscapes globally; Britain sees itself as 'the way of the future'. The reason this rudeness exists is because the London populous believes it is composed of incredibly important people; the fact that they live in the most expensive one bedroomed flats/apartments in recorded history strikes no ironic note with them. As social cohesion breaks down further in the decades to come, and it will, as agreed upon social codes become literally impossible to define, as the English language degenerates as the agreed upon currency of social exchange, the arrogant Gordon Gecko like rudeness culture and its resultant anxiety will only massively intensify. If you want to escape anxiety, escape the cities!

A British defence department study predicted 30 years of riots in the new millennium as a consequence of the ongoing traumatic globalisation processes; the focal point of this tension will be the cities. If you live in or have a major city near you: is what I say in this section ringing any bells? Which leads me too...

Geopolitically driven social change and anxiety: cultural apathy.

We're getting to trauma; hold on. Let's talk about so-called 'learned helplessness' – what is it really?

'Learned helplessness.'

What has 'learned helplessness' got to do with geopolitics? Everything! Never in human history have the vast bulk of mankind been so voluntarily powerless. Voluntarily? Yes, globally people have handed over their right to choose their own destiny to a tiny handful of very powerful, extremely wealthy men. And as Balzac rightly observed, behind every great fortune there is a crime.

Transnational corporations own the earth, they own all the resources of the earth and they own all the 'human capital'; that is you and me. That's reality. Gradually, systematically and to a long range business plan this 'takeover' of planet earth has been accomplished in little over 100 years. National boundaries and nations states exist merely as geographical formalities. Corporations may set up shop in the USA or China, overnight. They may insource labour as swiftly as they

174

outsource factories. Their minions formulate Governmental policies globally and set the agenda of school children's 'schooling' globally.

G.K. Chesterton was right about this much – we live in an age where mankind is little more than a puppet for his economic masters. Some historians claim that the 20th century was 'The People's Century'; garbage. The 20th century belonged to the corporations. The 21st is set to belong to them even more intensely and dramatically. However this situation only exists because the masses have given up. They have been so bashed, so battered, so bruised by global corporate power that they have surrendered their personal sovereignty to an undemocratic, pathocratic and parasitical 'elite'.

This is the basis of 'learned helplessness'. This is the basis of 'apathy'; it is the apathy of the conquered. Mass anxiety can only flourish in a world in which the individual has been stripped of any sense of control.

This deals with geopolitical learned helplessness and its roots. Now let us turn to the drama of the family and the individual once more.

Electrocuting dogs for 'science' and other strange perversions.

It's a dog's life they say and not without reason. **The technical definition of what we call 'learned helplessness' is a habitual behavioural response pattern wherein any organism is forced to 'endure aversive, painful or otherwise unpleasant stimuli' and thus, as a consequence becomes 'unable or unwilling to avoid subsequent encounters with those stimuli, _even if they are escapable'._**

Let's apply this to a human, perhaps a child: they have learnt that they cannot **control the situation** and so they do not **take action** to avoid the 'negative stimulus'. All anxiety based problems, at least in part do result from a **_perceived absence of control_** over influencing a desirable outcome of a given situation.

I was talking about dogs.

The Seligman and Maier experiment.

It is 1967, the US psychologist Martin Seligman, in furtherance of his interest in studying depression, is conducting a series of 'animal experiments' and testing a theory of learned helplessness. In complete opposition to then fashionable theories of B.F Skinner, Seligman and his colleagues discover something very interesting but at the same time blindingly obvious.

The experiment.

- You need 3 sets of dogs class.

- Place them in harnesses. Good.

- Doggie group 1 is put in the harnesses and then simply released.

- Doggie group 2 is painfully electrocuted in the harnesses BUT can stop the pain by pressing a lever.

- A doggie group 3 dog is placed with a group 2 dog ('yoked pairing'), he too is zapped but his lever does not relieve his agony.

- As a result doggie 3 concludes that his pain ends randomly. He has no influence over its cessation. Poor doggie concludes: 'This is inescapable.' He surrenders, gives in; his spirit is broken!

177

- After the experiment group 1 and 2 doggies recover from their traumatic experience. Group 3 dogs do not. They go on to develop 'symptoms' (responses) identical to clinical depression in humans.

Geddit? Hold on it gets worse...

Retardation of learning.

The 3 dog groups are placed in something called a shuttle-box. A shuttle-box is actually a torture device. Imagine, simply, a box separated into two parts by a hurdle. A subject (dog) can jump over the hurdle from one side/part to the other. Painful electric shocks are received via a row of metal bars that form the floor of the box. Nice.

The group 3 dogs who had 'learned' that they could do nothing to stop the shocks in the earlier phase of torture simply lay down and whined in complete submission and 'helplessness'. The dogs didn't even TRY to escape even though they could. The emotional stress the dogs experienced when 'learning' that the trauma is 'uncontrollable' led them to behave in a totally apathetic way. _Worse still: once broken the dogs could only be made to seek escape by being forced by_ _the experimenters to move their limbs; they had to be physically made to escape, as if temporarily borrowing the will of the experimenter/torturer/abuser*._ Not even the promise of reward helped motivate the dog.

(*Note: dogs like humans look to the abuser/'authority figure' in a time of crisis, even if the authority figure created the trauma on purpose! This is the sado-masochistic structure of human hierarchies, 'Stockholm Syndrome' etc. Do you know what the basis of all REAL power is? Humiliation! More on this in my final book.) **The dog had generalised unrealistically from a single or series of traumatic experience/s.**

Are you getting the bigger picture here folks?

Take one baby.

Take a baby. A cute little, lovable baby. Scold it for everything it does. Tell it it is a bad baby. Criticise everything it does. It is never good enough compared to the perfect obedient, imaginary baby in your head – emotional abuse in other words. Or perhaps there is violence in the family? Maybe a child is physically and sexually abused. In all

179

instances it cannot escape this situation. It is, after all a baby. Geddit? It's not rocket science. These are your chronically depressed clients by and large. Any kind of abuse = anxiety. Point made.

Anxiety code insight: as an adult you <u>always</u> have a degree of influence. If you do nothing, you are choosing to do nothing!

Okay I'm done. Trauma...

What is 'trauma'?

Goo-oood question. Word origins...the word trauma, from the Greek means a wound, a hurt, a defeat. It is also very similar to the German word 'traum' for dream.

What trauma busting skills do for the therapist.

The good thing about trauma is that you actually don't have to understand it to treat it: you just have to know how to get rid of ALL those lousy feelings. When the horrid emotional residue goes, the brain affects an 'auto-cure'. Really. I have done it so often now I rub my hands when someone says 'I was traumatised' etc. I think – 'Not for long!' When I found out a really effective detraumatisation process that was painless I knew my method was complete. Most people who become therapists do it to help others; they are caring people, the idea that you might make someone worse or cause them ANY emotional pain is a real fear. Thankfully that fear is now groundless.

A hypnotist who can confidently end trauma feels an invincible confidence. Your clients will feel assured by your quiet aura of competence

and knowledge and that's half the battle.
Let's talk about trauma in a bit more depth.

The emotional residue of a crisis.

Anxiety code insight: trauma is so emotionally destabilising because it represents a violation of our right and universal human need to have a sense of safety and security that is 100% inviolable.

When we experience something very scary, painful, violent, degrading, unnatural etc. we can become traumatised. We are left with an emotional imprint or 'scar' of the event. The more intense the event, the more prolonged, the more powerfully the emotions elicited by that event or events are. Powerful emotions become the basis of powerful pattern matching templates thereafter as the subconscious desperately seeks to avoid going through such a terrible experience again.

But this danger detection mechanism can go haywire. If the adrenaline release and sensory overload involved during the traumatic event are extremely intense our normal fear mechanisms literally lose the plot and are 'swamped' (retriggered) by anything that even remotely resembles anything like the original crisis event.

Worse, potentially anything nearby could become linked by the subconscious to a source of a potential future 'threat'; even though in reality there may be none whatsoever. No one wants to experience the same horrible event over and over, to do so would threaten our sanity. The mind goes into protective overdrive to keep you as safe and sane as it knows how. It is an imperfect mechanism, crude and overwhelming but the deep structures of the mind have one prime directive: keep this person alive!

What trauma is, is a very powerful form of operant conditioning. It is the worst kind of Neuro-Associative-Conditioning (N.A.C – see book 3, 'Powerful hypnosis' for a full description) there is. These mechanisms are often exploited during warfare – military atrocities are committed to traumatise enemy combatants and populations into fear, surrender and obedience. Trauma is the basis of all military conquest – shock and missile attacks have been the basis of human warfare for 1000's of years.

The mystery of 'P.T.S.D.'

What the mainstream psychologists and shrinks call 'Post-Traumatic-Stress-Disorder' I call 'Trauma-imprinting-conditioning'. I have helped detraumatise several women who have been raped. When a woman is raped it can leave her with a horrible constellation of interlinked and unpleasant emotions: guilt, self-hate, shame, disgust at her own body's responses (orgasm), physical pain, feelings of horror, a sense of numbness, anxiety, depression, suicidal thoughts etc.; being raped feels to many as if they are dying – the list goes on and on. Rape is a crime so horrendous that RH believes that only the death penalty is sufficient punishment for perpetrators but that's another story.

When these emotions arise in response to such a violation and attack they may well dissipate given enough time; the mind-body system can spontaneously recover. Sometimes it can't. When trauma occurs it can prevent unpleasant memories from being stored as just another unpleasant memory. The mechanism that does so is overwhelmed by the constant fear arousal. The memories cannot unconsciously reframe. There is too much emotion – in skilled hypnotherapy you can detraumatise these negative emotional constellations and leave a person with a sense of tremendous calm. The brain is then able to spontaneously reframe past memories as background arousal returns to normal, non-war footing levels.

All of the so-called 'symptoms' of PTSD are caused by the trauma imprinting. 'Flashbacks' are just (most probably) the brain trying to 'dream out' any attendant anxiety whilst the person is awake. It you carry out the process I will show you in part two, they'll disappear anyway. Nightmares that relive the event are too attempts to flush out the massive anxiety. They cannot succeed because the trauma is imprinted at the unconscious level. Seemingly wild fears and 'trigger stimulus' panic attacks, ongoing anxiety etc. following a traumatic incident are simply pattern matching defences to avoid possible future dangers.

You should not go after traumatic memories and directly 'abreact' the emotions – this actually only further traumatises the person and imprints the trauma 'grooves' deeper into the brain and nervous system. At worse it can cause a full psychotic break. Can abreaction approaches work? Yes – the inventor of modern hypnotherapy Dr. Milton Erickson used them but he dissociated the elements of the abreaction into component parts first. By the way LSD can (rarely) cure trauma too but only a fool or a desperate person would play such Russian Roulette with their sanity, long-term health and general functioning. LSD induces temporary psychosis – the person dreams while awake basically.

First Erickson would elicit age regression to the traumatic time with suggestions that no emotion would be experienced, just visuals etc. Only when he had safely gone through all the individual sensory modalities of a trauma would he abreact the emotion so as to not overwhelm a patient. However today we have much more advanced, sleek and sophisticated methods that cause the client no pain and require no age regression whatsoever.

NOTE: The separate traumatic memories are not the point – it is the emotions associated to them that are the problem; once you decouple the emotional trauma safely the old memories are processed as normal unpleasant memories that we all have. Geddit? A rule for therapy and life is: you should only experience a trauma once!!!! It is so easy that it is funny.

Once the detraumatisation process within is followed, the 'worst' response you might get is a tear discharge as the emotions and stress are excreted through tears, sometimes in a trickle, rarely as a lengthy viscous discharge. 99.9% of the time there is no reaction at all, the client just says they feel good and calm again: BINGO!

Well-meaning but frankly incompetent therapists who claim to be trauma specialists are often just re-traumatisation experts – they do not listen to their clients who say – **'I WANT TO _FEEL_ DIFFERENT!!!'** Digging up psycho-archaeology is invasive in more ways than one and it doesn't affect 'CURE'; which I define as a return to normal life experience as per pre the initiating event/s etc., preferably you should induce superior functioning.

That's trauma – that's all the theory you need to help. I'll leave you with this anxiety code maxim:

A detraumatised mind can heal spontaneously.

Trauma and 'repression'.

Freud was right about a few things – one is that some people who undergo severe stress and trauma can lose all conscious memory of the event; this he labelled 'repression', the correct term is 'dissociation' and it is linked to mankind's hypnotic ability though not identical. It is an unconscious override system to protect the conscious mind. This mechanism is the basis of so-called 'Multiple-personality-disorder' (MPD) now known as DID – 'Dissociative Identity Disorder'; I just call it Multiple Personality – coz that what's the poor bastards have. This should only ever be treated by a skilled and experienced therapist with a full understanding of this 'splitting' protection mechanism of mind and how to reintegrate the divided psyche. To cover its intricacies are too involved, severely disturbing and complicated for a book of this nature. It requires its own book. The average suburban hypnotherapist would not usually be confronted by such clients in their lifetime anyway.

Various otherwise intelligent people who suggest that repression/dissociation and personality splitting cannot occur are wholly ignorant of the real nature of the human mind. A real MPD sufferer may have 100's or 1000's of separate alters. Imagine a pristine mirror. Pick it up and throw in on a concrete surface. It shatters into thousands of tiny fragments. You get the picture?

A lesser and very mild form of MPD I label 'Ego state disorder' – this will be briefly covered in the appendix. It is quite common and even appears in addictions to a certain extent as evidenced in my negotiation processes I outlined in book 8, 'Hypnotically deprogramming addiction'. An 'ego state' can express itself very subtly, often as an almost stimulus provoked and repetitive yet all-encompassing mood change. It takes a highly trained eye to spot.

NLP and psychoanalysis are useless for treating anxiety.

Apart from the NLP 'phobia cure' which has a 70% odd success rate in objective studies, NLP is almost useless for treating anxiety. There is one other exception and that is the 'Self-Esteem quick fix'. As I've said, see book 4, 'Forbidden hypnotic secrets' for the old time NLP pattern. Also read the case study on a lady with anxiety caused by low self-worth in this book for the NLP-esque 'quick fix'; my improved version that is later on.

Psychoanalysis (PA) and all psychodynamic 'treatments' are all highly contraindicated for treating anxiety or depression – they worsen it.

Psychoanalysis is a form of ersatz Gnosticism. Its aim is to 'break a person down' and reprogamme the personality as the psycho-anal-ist sees fit: that is the creation of a zombie who adapts to situations that they sanely oughtn't to. PA is a form of conversational hypnosis which directionalises the brain toward collapse through overload by focusing on past trauma and ruminating about it ('working through'). This is identical to brainwashing procedures used in all cults. See 'Powerful hypnosis', 'Forbidden hypnotic secrets', 'Wizards of trance' and 'Escaping cultural hypnosis' for more detail on such matters; if you haven't bought them already Padawan!!!

Enough said – in this book you will learn what works and what works not just safely but *pleasurably.* Taking pain away is not a painful process but a joyous one – IF you know what you're doing. By this books end, if you didn't know, you will soon.

Talking of useless treatments...

The Soma Society: 'the anti-depressant conspiracy'.

'The dependence of emotional disposition upon the ductless glands,' said Mr. Russell, '... was a discovery of great importance, which would in time make it possible to produce artificially any disposition desired by governments.'

Betrand Russell, 1924.

There IS an 'anti-depressant conspiracy'. Don't believe me? Let's start with an odd book.

The Ghost in the machine.

A very weird man, a former Soviet Communist wrote a very disturbing book called, **'The Ghost in the machine'.** His name was **Arthur Koestler.** All padawans should read this book. Koestler, an unrepentant control freak, laid down his case in this madman's confession that *ALL the public of the world* should be forcibly drugged because man was inherently 'emotionally unstable'. His aim was to kill off the 'ghost in the machine', leaving only the machine left. A machine that would dutifully do as it was told by totalitarian, schizoidal fanatics like Koestler.

And this book is well respected by a great number of mainstream psychiatrists and psychologists. How revealing. Although I do not agree with everything the great English writer G.K. Chesterton said, I do agree with him on this, if a man declares a tree not to be a tree, he is mad and we need to be protected from his madness; with that in mind...

Is psychiatry a cult or a mental illness?

If you question 'authority', you are mentally ill. No it's a fact. Sorry. Authorities are ALWAYS right. In fact they never change their minds ever. There are no stupid authorities. There are no brainwashed authorities. There are no corrupt authorities. I'm being sarcastic – you got that right? Let's examine this mind control cult mentality that has infected much of modern psychiatry. It leads me to the obvious conclusion that _most psychiatrists are savagely mentally ill._ All who adhere to the above demented belief system should be drugged to the eyeballs, straightjacketed, locked in padded cells and left to masturbate themselves silly. We are in the hands of lunatics folks.

'Oppositional defiant disorder' and other flying pigs.

Toward the close of jolly old 2013, the swankiest and most recent issue of the 'American Diagnostic and Statistical Manual of Mental Disorders' (DSM – sounds eerily close to BDSM! In fact I shall call it that from now on) defined a spanking brand new 'mental illness', so-called 'oppositional defiant disorder' or ODD. Okay...

What exactly was this 'new' curse that was blighting mankind? Essentially 'non-conformity' of any kind (including thinking for oneself) and questioning of authority was identified as a specific type of insanity. Ok-ay... The BDSM declared ODD to be spotted by observing the following 'symptoms":'...
ongoing pattern of disobedient, hostile and defiant behaviour...'

Okay. Weird indicators to look out for are:

- **Questioning authority!** Oderz vich must be obeyed! Links! Rechts! Achtung! Drop and give me 20! You're worthless and weak! Authoritarianism = no progress in science, art, morality or civil society.

- **Negativity!** Cults and self-helpers think this is 'bad' too. Oooh you are such a sour puss! You must be CRAZY! Jesus can't you just learn to LOVE Roman tyranny – you are SO negative!

- **Defiance!** If you say, 'Fuck you!' to some little Hitler asshole you are quite mad I'm afraid. Quite mad. If it were not for rebels you would have no United States of America!!! Every right we now take for granted was taken, demanded by our forebears, many of whom were imprisoned, transported and killed for merely wishing to be treated with some respect.

- **Argumentativeness!** A sign of having an active and healthy conscious mind. Apparently agreeing with everyone is a sign of sanity. No it isn't! Yes it is! That's not an argument, it's merely contradiction! No it isn't! Acting like a Moonie is the ideal of modern psychiatry.

- **Being easily annoyed!** Oh I am such a lovely Pollyanna! I love everything! Can you please shove a red hot poker up my ass! Yippee! I just love it! Presumably all these quacks get annoyed by anyone who questions them? Their annoyance is so extreme they think YOU need to take a chill pill to make them feel better.

Many concerned, one might say questioning observers have noted that each time a new BDSM is released, the number of mental disorders grows – and this growth is exponential. Are we becoming crazier by the year?! Or are the shrinks? And by the way, remember, if you disagree with the BDSM you must be crazy. Electroshock for you!

Look at these alarming facts:

- **In 1915 there were essentially 7 mental disorders.**

- **80 years ago there were 59.**

- **50 years ago there were 130.**

- **By 2010 there were 374!!!** 77 of which were discovered in just seven years! Wow: I suppose all those old fashioned doctors were so dumb! Maybe they just had ODD?! It could be that rapid globalised social change is driving people mad in ways hitherto never seen...

Well what other new ways of going bonkers have the illustrious Mad Hatter and the March

Hare discovered? I'm glad you asked:

- **Arrogance!** What you mean like the way most doctors behave?

- **Narcissism!** That's most of the Western population then.

- **Above-average creativity!** Seize Mozart and lock him away!

- **Cynicism!** One would have thought an essential life skill in an adult.

- **'Antisocial behaviour'!** How specifically is it 'anti-social'? According to whom?

'Madness' in the Gulag archipelago.

Such vagueness and crass stupidity is alarming; especially when we consider historical precedents. Read the following speech by Nikita Khrushchev made in 1959. Khrushchev was First Secretary of the Communist Party of Russia 1953 – 1964. Although he publicly denounced the horrors of Stalinism he played an active role in carrying them out...

'Can there be diseases, nervous diseases among certain people in the communist

society? Evidently there can be. If that is so, then there also will be offences which are characteristic of people with abnormal minds. To those who might start calling for opposition to communism on this 'basis,' we say that now, too, there are people who fight against communism, but clearly the mental state of such people is not normal.'

Pot calling kettle black? I leave that judgement to you. As a consequence of this schizoid word salad Soviet psychiatrists immediately went to work to locate and 'institutionalize' all those 'mentally ill' who thought that Communism was hell on earth realised. Comrade you are mad. Quite mad. You will have to be 'rehabilitated' and 're-educated' – you must learn to LOVE BIG BROTHER WINSTON! Just a warning: psychopaths often tell the truth by saying the opposite of what truth is. This is known as 'Gaslighting'. Think about it.

The Soviet purge of sanity.

It is 1951; a joint session of the USSR Academy of Medical Sciences and the Board of the All-Union Neurological and Psychiatric Association is in progress under Stalin's orders. A number of prominent psychiatrists and neurologists are charged with holding beliefs that are 'anti-Marxist and reactionary' (yawn); deviating as they do from world famous dog torturer and the only man to have any insights into human behaviour, ever, one Ivan Pavlov. They are questioning Soviet authority – the arrogance of the narcissists! The intent? To 'free Soviet psychiatry of Western influences'. The lunatics are running the asylum.

Inventing disorders for the defiant.

At about this time a loyal Pavlovian psychiatrist called Andrei Snezhnevsky wrote a report in which he claimed he had 'discovered' (yawn) a 'new mental illness'; this he labelled 'sluggish schizophrenia'. Following mass murderer Khrushchev's 1959 speech, the disorder became widespread and was mass diagnosed throughout the Eastern Bloc. No! A shocker. Soviet shrinks were on the lookout for minute changes in 'behaviour patterns' which could be early warning symptoms of 'mental derangement'. Defiance of the Soviet system, actually a sign of sanity was now seen as a symptom of 'sluggish schizophrenia with delusions of reform'. Snezhnevsky went on to receive two Orders of Lenin as well as four Orders of the Red Star and USSR state prize.

Snezhnevsky had invented a dangerous new dogma. Nice.

Snezhnevsky signed a decision stating that several leading political opponents of the Soviet madhouse were 'legally insane'. One Vladimir Bukovsky, a leading neurophysiologist and the first to expose the politicization of psychiatry in the Soviet Union was locked up for over 12 years in a variety of Soviet institutions - prisons, forced labour camps and psychiatric hospitals for the sane. At its 1970 annual meeting in San Francisco the American Psychiatric Association pronounced Snezhnevsky a 'distinguished fellow' for his 'outstanding contribution to psychiatry and related sciences'. Go figure! A year later Bukovsky smuggled out a 150 page document proving the silencing of political dissenters with the aid of psychiatry in the Soviet Union.

Psychiatry and psychology are NOT sciences!

If you or I fall out of a tree and break a leg and we see 10 different doctors they will all diagnose a broken leg, unless one's a psychiatrist. Additionally there will be a standard medical response to breaking your leg etc. Neither psychiatry nor psychology are genuine natural sciences. They are solely based on 'personal judgement' (indoctrination) – almost like palm reading. If you see 10 differing shrinks etc. you'll receive 10 different 'diagnoses'. Your 'treatment' will involve you being doped to the eyeballs with very powerful, addictive and dangerous drugs (psychotropics). You will be told you have a 'chemical imbalance'; however the shrink will provide you with no prima facie evidence that this is so: it is in fact an almost religious faith on his or her part. Or is it?

There are no 100% dependable and measurable scientific tests that recognise a 'mental illness'. So what's it all about then Charlie?

The big business of 'insanity'.

MONEY!!!! Money makes ze vorld go around! Ze vorld go around, ze vorld go around! It's always about the fucking money! If you don't believe me and that's your right, observe the following statistics (I can't 100% independently verify them but they sound pretty accurate):

- Global sales of anti-depressants, stimulants, anti-anxiety and anti-psychotic drugs = over $76 billion per year.

- 54 million people globally ingest 'anti-depressants' known to cause addiction, violent and homicidal behaviour. In fact a leading US researcher into US mass shootings has found that almost _all_ involved a young person or adult perpetrator who was on one kind of psychotropic drug or another. Yet there are zero calls to ban them.

- By 2010 20% of all US women were taking some kind of mental health medication. Essentially 1 in 5 American ladies is zombiefied.

- Globally 20 million children have been 'diagnosed' with 'mental disorders' and 'prescribed' either stimulants and/or anti-depressants. That's a lot of zombiefied kids.

- One set of research declared that by 2002, more than 100 million prescriptions were dished out for anti-depressants alone in the US; the hefty price tag? $19.5 billion. Am I getting through to YOU kiddo?!

- Similarly another set of data claimed

that spending on anti-psychotic drugs and anti-depressants soared astronomically from $500 million to $20 billion between 1986 and 2004 globally.

- By 2010 one researcher I garnered this info from claimed that more than 50% of the employed population of France were taking psychotropic drugs. In France, 1 in 7 prescriptions is for a mind altering drug.

- By 2010 the US mental health budget leapt from $33 billion in 1994 to $ 80 billion!!! That's one heck of a lot of 'crazy' people. Or is it?

Are we in an open asylum?

NIMH the US National Institute of Mental Health reported that by 2010 26% of Americans were suffering from a 'mental illness', moreover that approximately 58 million of Americans will suffer from an 'episode of mental illness in any given year'.

Psychiatry does not deal in cures. It alleges without any proof that its meds 'correct' 'chemical imbalances' in the brain. If this were so we would have seen a decline in the number of mentally ill people – in fact the polar opposite is true: we have seen a mental health explosion!

These 'wonder drugs' were rolled out on mass following World War 2. It's 1955: 355,000 US adults are locked up in the local laughing academies (asylums) after a diagnosis of mental illness. Zip forward 50 years or so after the glories of 'medical treatment' with 'anti-psychotic drugs'. By 2007 more than 4 million people are locked up. Wow! Only weather forecasters have an equally terrible success rate and keep their jobs. Something is seriously wrong with what calls itself 'psychiatry'. I say psychiatrists who behave in such a fashion are drug dealers: nothing more.

The collective mind is always right: illusions of 'peer consensus'.

Note: all the 'disorders' invented by the BDSM are arrived at by so-called 'peer consensus'; not by any repeatable, standardised objective measurements. Therefore psychiatry is no science – it's a guessing game. The treatments offered, namely drugs, create a chemical imbalance rather than rectifying one – the exact opposite of the effect claimed by shrinks. Most significantly the greater the number of new 'diseases' made up out of thin air by 'peer consensus' the more drug treatments can be prescribed. I think that it is quite clear that profit is behind these fictitious and laughable diagnoses such as 'ADHD' – what I call 'bored boy disorder' etc.

Just to show that not all doctors are basket cases or living high on the hog of human suffering, a certain Dr. Thomas Dorman, member of the Royal College of Physicians in the UK and Fellow of the Royal College of Physicians of Canada said...

'In short, the whole business of creating psychiatric categories of 'disease,' formalizing them with consensus, and subsequently ascribing diagnostic codes to them, which in turn leads to their use for insurance billing, is nothing but an extended racket furnishing psychiatry a pseudo-scientific aura. The perpetrators are, of course, feeding at the public trough.'

In light of this info alone you should seriously think twice about going to your local doctor or a shrink if you feel a bit anxious. The chances of recovery are slim to none. You will probably start feeling better after a few months anyway. The psychiatric cure? What cure!? Pills do not fix mental health problems – they make miserable people 'viable' for the system.

Zombie UK Ltd.

I wouldn't have even mentioned this stuff about psychiatry and psychology IF I hadn't seen such weird evidence of the mass drugging of the UK population by family doctors (GPs – General Practitioners; equivalent to US MD). I lost count of the amount of clients who came to see me for a whole host of problems who had been 'put' on anti-anxiety meds, and 'anti-depressants' who had no anxiety based problems whatsoever. I had a host of people who were smoking cigarettes who had been placed on anti-anxiety pills. I had people who were overworked who were on anti-depressants. I had people who were put on drugs to stop panic attacks which make them feel uncontrollably panicky. I could go on: I hope you get the picture. Apart from cash why is this occurring? There must be a reason.

'Neo-eugenics' in the medical profession.

What you have to understand is that most UK doctors are from quite privileged backgrounds, many see the general public as a great mass of stinking peasants who need to be 'managed'. Stealing dead baby's body parts and using them in experiments unknown to their grieving families is one such example ('Alder Hey organs scandal'); this was the fate of the poor in the 19th century: dissection fodder for medics.

The so-called 'Liverpool pathway' was an attempt by some UK hospitals to 'euthanize' (legally murder) old people – till it was exposed; you should know – doctors formed the largest professional group in the Nazi party. In a recent poll of doctors in Holland 20% of those asked said they would 'euthanize' (legally murder) a person who came to them and said they were 'fed up with living'. 1 million people in the UK have been 'misdiagnosed' with having asthma in the UK according to a recent NICE (UK's National Institute for Health and Care Excellence) investigation; all taking medication unnecessarily. That's one big 'blunder'. A 'good education' by and large doesn't make you more 'civilised', it makes you look down on those who have not undergone the same indoctrination process as you. This is known as 'elitism'. As far as I am concerned it is a real mental illness.

The early eugenics movement in Britain found widespread support in the top Universities (61% of Oxford's intellectual elite), the political class, the scientific establishment and all socialist and feminist groups in the first 40 or so years of the 20th century. After the horrors of Nazi eugenics they hid but now they have come back – now they call themselves 'bio-ethicists'. But if you look under the respectable veneer you see the same old 'herd management', neo-Malthusian philosophies.

The suffering general public is put on drugs because A. The doctor doesn't know what else to do. B. If he or she did they wouldn't have the time to do it. C. They don't give a sh*t about ordinary people. D. They get payoffs for promoting Big Pharma drugs to the public – bribes! E. The BMJ (British medical journal) has recently uncovered widespread bribery known as 'incentives' given by private medical firms to UK family doctors for referring NHS patients to them. These 'schemes' are covert and entail cash payments up to £100, 000/$150,486... ***If you are a doctor who does this you should be ashamed of yourself to the point of dysfunction.*** The problem with post-modern society is that not enough people feel guilty or ashamed about what they do and how they relate to their fellow Man. This is why we are in the big turd-filled hole we are in. Man's inhumanity to man is alive and well – in the 'medical profession'! I apologise to those many doctors who genuinely do care about their patients: your profession needs a purge.

The latest symptoms of psychiatric insanity: eating healthily is 'abnormal'!!!

Just when I think the schizoids who invent the BDSM can't get any crazier they go and surpass themselves in pathologicalising totally reasonable, normal and healthy behaviour. It has now been deemed a 'mental disorder' to desire to eat healthily. You're gonna love the name they've made up; it's Latin which makes it sounds official, scientific and valid, in fact it's drug dealer bunkum – 'Orthorexia nervosa'!!! Beware the lettuce!

'Side-effects' or just effects?

The side-effects of these hill high piles of pills and potions are legion – a worsening of symptoms, feeling 'less than human', having no feelings at all, your jaw hanging open, weight gain, chewing actions, a lowering of IQ and sex drive, exhibitionism, delusions, hallucinations, extreme paranoia, extreme fear, an inability to feel love, 'bi-polar disorder' (anti-depressant reactions disorder), 'dementia'/Alzheimer's, lethargy, suicidal and homicidal thoughts and behaviour – the list goes on and on. It's a horror show folks. ***Standardised pills cannot solve complex human dilemmas.*** I have got that off my chest; now – let's focus on what works, let's focus on side-effect free treatments: let's focus on solutions! Dare I say 'cures'?

Focusing on solutions – 'CURES' eradicate 'disease'.

You see I don't give a damn about all these silly names that are thrown out: 'so and so disorder', 'Lots of initials conundrum', 'Unknown chemical balance 57a': it's all a crock. In the first half of this book I have told you all about the realities behind the labels and diagnoses of numerous 'anxiety disorders'. You now understand cause. Now it's time for you to understand how to solve problems.

Everything in life is a challenge that demands a solution: one of my therapy and life maxims is – ***if it is necessary it is possible.*** Okay, let's look at the possibilities.

As a highly successful hypnotist I focus my mind on solving problems. The past happened – we are here, now. That's where you start from...

Part 1 b: Focusing on solutions.

Solutions: Why anxiety clients MUST exercise.

Numero uno anxiety and depression cure action to take right now – start exercising. Now I could tell you all the many reasons, all the 'brain chemicals' etc. that are released when we exercise that make us happy naturally but do you know what? You don't need to know about 'em, and all that crap about serotonin etc. is not cut in stone, no matter what academia and its loyal bitch the media might try to tell you.

The main reason we need to exercise is that it flushes out stress chemicals and their build-up naturally. It reduces physiological and so psychological allostatic information overload. A key principle of mind-body healing is – *where the body leads the mind follows and where the mind leads the body follows.*

You must find the right type of exercise for you, something you enjoy, we are all different; when you do you will stop adrenaline and cortisol etc. building up in your system – this will mean that excessive worry, stress, anxiety and depression will literally be impossible. Think about going on a booze binge for several days; it all builds up in your system right? You need a few days off to 'de-tox'. It's the same with stress chemicals; they build up and get 'stuck' inside: that is, it can take a while for the body to process them and remove them, unless you exercise. If you haven't or if your clients haven't exercised in a long while start slow and build. 3-4 days a week, 20-30 minutes is sufficient.

Exercise and heavy manual labour are not the same thing – the first leaves you feeling happy, exhilarated, flushed out, clear headed and optimistic. The latter grinds you down and leaves you exhausted. However if you are feeling on the edge stress wise you are best learning to relax again via hypnosis; this will reboot the parasympathetic phase (calming) of the nervous system. More on that soon.

Exercise is a vital, universal human need. You cannot be sedentary and happy and relaxed – never going to happen, ever. We don't hunt and gather as we did, we must now keep fit. That's reality.

Solutions: Universal human needs - happy + fulfilled people don't get anxious!

This section's solutions will be revealed through brief examples of stories. I have written quite a bit about human needs already in many of my other books, if not all of 'em in fact. All living things – animals, plants, even politicians have needs. Humans have unique needs that must be met or else they may sicken and die from their lack thereof. As I have covered this previously I will take a new angle here to make my point further.

All the lonely people, where do they all come from?

Remember the song by the Beatles...'I look at all the lonely People!' There are lots of Eleanor Rigby's out there and by and large they ain't too happy. Modern man and woman is becoming an increasingly lonely and isolated beast. We need close and intimate relationships in order to be happy; in fact along with food and water they are vital to our very survival. Let's add this to our anxiety code:

To be anxiety free you need a

sufficient number of good quality relationships.

The meaning of life part 1.

A very large proportion of the anxious clients I encounter have no meaning to their lives. They live a life without purpose. Most have merely become economic functionaries of the system. A cog in the machine. Most are materialistic and utilitarian. Such a state of affairs can only lead to human misery because man's brain is hardwired to seek meaning. We are meaning making organisms.

Meaning is not something that is sought in a pulpit or at the foot of a politician's podium. It is located, rediscovered when the individual asks themselves – 'What is my purpose in life?' 'Why am I here?' 'Who am I really?' This is only ever a personal discovery and seeking gurus or ideologies to assign you a meaning is the high road to self-annihilation. We may conclude:

To be anxiety free you need to live your live with self-generated meaning.

This perfect day or choice.

In Ira Levine's Sci-Fi dystopia, 'This Perfect Day,' all future citizens of the 'family' of the world state are assigned job, sexual partner, wife or husband, the ability to breed by a supercomputer that entirely manages all human affairs. To question the system is to require drug treatment for your 'sickness'. Thinking about following your natural inclination to be an artist when the world computer has designated you a lifelong role as genetic engineer is a symptom of 'selfishness'.

Many people want cradle to grave state intervention in their lives – they do not want choice or freedom; the problem is freedom of choice is vital to human happiness. To seek a life of constant constrictive other management is to cease to be human at all. So...

To be anxiety free you must choose to be free to choose. Calmness requires a degree of self-determination and self-reliance. Humans need to have a degree of control over the outcomes they seek; if they do not have this they become anxious in

proportion to which their sense of control diminishes.

'We all need somebody to lo-ove! Lean on me!'

More than just close relationships that are mutually fulfilling we have a need for love. This need first expresses itself in our baby stage – not only human needs such as food and warmth but deep, devoted unconditional love is the emotional water that makes the human grow healthily. To be unloved is to be traumatised when most vulnerable and we know this affects the deepest and most profound levels of psyche. We know now, as we have always intuitively known since our most ancient times that the prime 'mover' in this sphere is the mother; so key is her role in early childhood development. Mothers play the dominant part in shaping their children's lives and maturation. When this role is abused or abusive the long-term effects can be devastating.

This is not to marginalise fathers, (a recent trend founded in blatant misardism/man-hatred). The role of father is fundamental in all families; his influence for example on his daughter's future views on men and choice of sexual partner and perhaps husband is of the essence. Little girls idolise their daddies. His key role in showing his sons how to be a man, revealed in all his human interactions, especially that with the child's mother are so obvious that to even include it here seems silly. Over 75% of those in prisons lacked a father in the home.

Children who lack this force of human love grow up in one of two ways ordinarily. 1. They may desperately seek the approval of strangers thereafter; as if ANY approval could fill the inner void. In order to achieve this aim they become overtly or covertly manipulative. 2. They may become deeply untrusting and aggressive. They may constantly test other's 'loyalty' and so push them away. These usual responses are part of what some psychologists call 'attachment theory'; basically the strength of the childhood bond between parents and child set up a pattern matching system into later life. The success or failure in their negotiations and interactions with others in seeking their need fulfilment is framed in these early years; baring successful 'therapeutic' intervention which can and does 'repair' such damage.

However when the damage is very deep-rooted and chronic only a fierce desire to change on the part of the client and an awareness of his or her ego-syntonic (neurotic/dysfunctional) behaviour patterns and warped interrelations with others etc. will effect total 'cure'; alas few lack the insight or so identify with their 'symptoms' that they would be lost without them, so 'successfully' do they believe they have helped them survive. A rarer minority still masochistically enjoy the power their symptoms have over others. They are used to bend others' emotions in quite dictatorial ways. Thankfully the unmotivated client is exceedingly rare, often only accounting for 0.1% of a client base. And even such people as this can reach much higher levels of functioning and maturity than they hitherto possessed. Anxiety code conclusions:

Human love soothes the human soul.

The vital role of the extended family.

We have covered the role of the so-called 'nuclear' family but until the industrial revolution humans were not cut down to such small survival groupings; this occurred as a result of massive socio-political and primarily economic changes that so wracked and traumatised the former peasants of the Middle Ages as they were hurled into factories on mass or left to die of indescribable wants. But this we have already covered. In doing so, larger natural family bondings of cousins, uncles, aunts etc. were spilt asunder. Brothers and sisters having to travel and settle many miles apart merely to seek a job to feed themselves and their young children; this in turn leaving grandparents isolated and alone. Children and adults in fact rely on extended family associations for successful support through the challenges of the human life cycle.

This is why all tyrannical systems in whatever guise they paint themselves seek to destroy the family unit; initially by severing the extended family connections. Women separated from sisters lack a supportive female family member close at hand to either help in child rearing, babysitting, socialising or just chewing the fat. Men are separated from the protective clique of cousins and uncles which provide physical defence, male companionship and 'hunting teams' etc. Young males are much more likely to suffer physical assault from non-family members than females. In more tribal times were someone to attempt to attack you, your entire kin group may well have raised arms against the attacker. There ever was safety in numbers; the atomised life of modern cities and towns has left the isolated male open to muggings, stabbings and worse. Police numbers are simply too small to cope with these changed social realities.

Moreover, the variety of mental stimulation alone that can only be provided by a big extended family is not a moot point. It was a custom of the Anglo Saxons to dote on their nieces and nephews but old customs, in the face of globalised standardisation and deluded 'one size fits all' approaches, are eroding native mores that have naturally sustained *genuine* communities from year dot. Marriage bonds renew and reinvigorate ongoing extended family alliances that can, if the partner is chosen wisely, greatly enhance the survival and joy of the constantly evolving generations. We have barely scratched the surface on these matters: however you would do well to consider them when forming a model of your client's potential sources of future stress. Anxiety code insight?

Secure individuals are best found in large, involved and extended

221

family groups.

When the individual is isolated, for whatever reason, consider who will stand up between you and any potential Big Brother? That's a rhetorical question.

The need for worth.

There is an underlying need behind all the others yet mentioned: humans have a desire to have worth, to feel valued. This is at the root of so many 'equality' movements. A dominant group has taken power. In order to maintain its power it must brainwash the dominated that they lack power because somehow they are 'deficient'. In response a number of the 'subordinated class' react by demanding 'equal rights'. That is to be on a level playing field with the rulers.

Children who have been put down and overly dominated as children often seek to achieve 'great ambitions' later in life; many an 'inferiority complex' has created great wealth – often by 'self-made' men. This is a case of the child hypnotising the man, a more frequent occurrence than many know. Underlying this striving drive to 'be someone' is the desire for worth. Such people may also mistakenly believe that worth can be bought through monetary exchanges such as the 'trophy wife' or husband for that matter etc. So...

People with good self-worth are less anxious generally.

You aren't what you don't eat!(?)

It continues to amaze me that the vast majority of the Anglosphere public in the West are deluded into thinking that eating 'food' with low nutritional value will not have any mental health consequences. Anxiety and depression can in some instances be caused by a poor diet alone: your mind and body need optimum fuel to operate effectively. Pesticides, growth hormones, antibiotics, GMO 'Franken foods', artificial sweeteners etc. found in the human food chain pose a direct threat to total human health. Therefore...

If you want to stay calm eat a healthy 'organic' diet as much as humanly possible.

I mention this topic which I have covered more extensively in my other books. See,

'Powerful hypnosis', 'Forbidden hypnotic secrets', 'Wizards of trance', 'Crafting hypnotic spells', 'Escaping cultural hypnosis' and 'Hypnotically annihilating addictions' for my further commentary of humans need fulfilment etc. in general.

Constructive thinking styles.

When we are on an anxiety war footing we cannot think rationally, we are in black and white thinking mode. We lack flexibility, optimism, a sense of humour, a sense of proportion and reality, our imagination can run wild with worst case fantasies. The part of the brain involved in intuitive problem solving – the anterior cingulate cortex cannot function and form new associations because we are tense. We become overly analytical and stuck! We need to start thinking constructively – that is to direct our thinking to problem solving and the best strategies to solve problems. For that we need a relaxed brain. This is why bullying in the workplace is so destructive (immorality aside) – it prevents high productivity and efficiency in workers; workers work best when happy and relaxed. So...

A relaxed brain can solve problems easily. We have a need to be calm

to perform at our best 99% of the time.

Rest.

This one is so important and obvious that even I nearly forgot it. If you are on a 24/7 anxiety war footing what can't you do? REST! We all need time to rest and play. It really is that simple, you can't be constantly 'going at it' unless you want problems. Because if you don't rest sufficiently buster: problems you most certainly will get!

Dr. Ernesto Rossi first put forward the idea of ultradian waves. These are essentially 90 minute cycles of activity and rest. Every 90 minutes or so we need to take a break. You see this with children so I think Dr. Rossi is onto something. When children play with that unbounded energy they have it is often in hour to hour and a half bursts. After this they get bored with the game, their attention wanders and they want to watch TV, Youtube, draw or just lay down and snuggle. If you have young 'uns you'll know what I'm talking about.

Children instinctively know that you need to take a break and they do so without thinking about it. They never overeat naturally and they know how to pick stuff up without hurting your back by bending at the knee and using leg power to lift. We start off smart and end up dumb!

When I hypnotise very anxious clients the rest phase of the ultradian cycle is 1. Utilised to initiate trance. 2. Restored to its normal pattern. It is one of our natural time clocks (rhythms), the body has many; these are the real ways to measure human time. If you override this 90 minute rest phase too often you get stressed. How do you spot it? Every 90 minutes or so we feel our attention drifting, our muscles start to naturally feel more relaxed and soft – we often trance out. Our brain is taking some much needed down time to process the information – of any kind – it has just experienced.

Do you have to rest every 90 minutes like some kind of robot? No. But you need 3 good periods of rest a day. You'll work more efficiently and productively as a result. Employers take note!

An hour for lunch and two twenty minute breaks in the late morning and afternoon are required for a happy work force. Abuse this and expect your profits to suffer. Clearly most employers have no conscience anyway, perhaps the reality of human biorhythms will nudge them toward humane treatment of staff? Somehow I doubt it.

When we take a rest, when we go from the external trance of absorption in work we discover the real gold: for it is in this time, when our mind relaxes that ideas to solve problems simply pop into our heads. In order to progress you must reflect. Now and again. A wandering mind is a problem solving mind.

Rest, recover and kiss anxiety goodbye.

Is this all there is?!

Related to our need for meaning is our need to 'be connected to something bigger than ourselves'; originally this would have been a tribe. It would have involved belief in a Creator deity of some kind, ancestor worship etc. In the West such practises have all but been extinguished by Scientism, the religion of science.

Man has a deep need to belong to something; we know that all human groups have an essential need to maintain a strong ethnic identity, language and culture. If these come under threat men may become so aggrieved that violence eventually ensues. The roots of such drives go way back into man's primordial past. Even the most fanatical globalist knows this; they openly write about it in their books!

In order to feel happy and calm mankind needs to feel there is more to existence than the mere struggle to survive; when this is replaced by materialistic nihilism he sickens.

Are you really awake? Really?

One of the keys to good mental health is to have a good working model of reality. Belief systems that prevent as realistic a map of reality as is possible pose a direct threat to survival and cause anxiety even if only at an unconscious level. This is caused by programmed, pattern matching systems failing to create individual satisfaction. The best way to think of this is: imagine someone gives you a treasure map. They tell you that 'the gold' is marked by X. X marks the spot. You dig and find nothing. 20 years later you are still digging a much deeper hole for yourself. Some have wrongly claimed that continuing doing something that isn't working is a sign of madness, no, it is a sign of incredible stupidity.

Our last anxiety code plank in this section is...

In order to feel secure and calm you need to have a firm grasp of reality as it is, not as you wish it were.

See my book, 'Escaping cultural hypnosis'; my 7th bestselling rant. I mean book. Okay we've been talking about need satisfaction. Need satisfaction makes us RELAX! To that we turn our attention next. Incidentally see the appendix for a whole list of relevant questions that you can ask hypnotherapy etc. clients when seeking to assist them. Basically you need to ask: 'What's missing!?'

Satisfaction is the enemy of anxiety.

All this waffling really leads us to one conclusion:

A satisfied mind is not anxious.

Anxiety is triggered by a lack of satisfaction.

The origins of the word satisfaction are predictably economic in origin as is much of human language. One of the earliest meanings being, 'a satisfying of a creditor', The sense of 'contentment, appeasement' and 'action of gratifying' although appearing around the 14th century were not recorded commonly until the 16th.

When we are satisfied we are getting our needs met. When that happens we feel satisfied, same as that feeling you get after a great meal, a nice time with the family, you get the idea. Now go and get some satisfaction out of this god damned life?

If you want to avoid anxiety seek daily satisfactions.

Solutions: The importance of relearning how to relax deeply.

'Anxious people' have trouble relaxing - duh! In order to be relaxed and confident your body cannot be on a war footing almost all the time. If this has been your or your client's base state that has to change. The desired state for daily living is what I call 'relaxed alertness', not the extreme relaxation of a spineless jellyfish, that's no use; you need to feel basically relaxed and confident with an awareness of what's going on around you so that you can navigate successfully through the environment and carry our your daily tasks etc. So how do you get to be 'relaxed yet alert'?

The options.

Whatever you do, don't meditate: meditation is deeply dangerous – it can lead to a permanent dissociative feeling, it makes you hyper-suggestible, it can lead to a total psychotic break in the worst cases. Many of my clients have used meditation in order to feel calm, however they are using it as a drug: they are not addressing causative factors; they are looking, like addicts, for sticking plasters on the gaping wound realities of their dysfunctional ways of living and relating. For the full low down on meditation see book 7, 'Escaping cultural hypnosis'.

You could drink and do drugs! Nope. That won't work either. You can't go through life high on pills of any kind and drink just slows you down and eventually fucks you up too. The good news is that I have found with 99% of my clients that one relaxing induction and anti-anxiety session gets rid of the war-footing physicality and mentally. It's like taking your car in for an MOT. The mechanic looks under the car's hood/bonnet, has a bit of a fiddle and Bob's your uncle, its roadworthy once more – it just needed a bit of tweaking.

In order to beat anxiety for good you must have a relaxed yet alert base state.

You were born with this operative state but various stressors and conditioning smothered it. This book shows you how, in part 2, to get back to your birth right base state. It's very easy in reality, when you know how, and you will. A calm mind and body cannot ruminate – it can't worry. You won't over dream. You'll sleep well – ah!

<u>Solutions: The importance of sleeping well.</u>

No ifs or buts – ***in order to be anxiety free you must be sleeping well.*** This is not an option. When you sleep well, getting full psychological and physical rest and recuperation (the later through so-called – 'slow wave sleep') – you awaken in a relaxed alert state. The mind-body system knows what to do to keep you healthy so you don't have to think about it. The fact that anyone is thinking about it shows how wrong things are. The 'rules' for good sleep are:

- Only fuck and sleep in bed.

- Have no electronic appliances in the sleeping area.

- Only go to bed when you feel sleepy.

- Do not drink stimulating drinks like coffee in the late evening.

- Exercise regularly to tire out the body.

- If you are going to worry, do it during the day. More on this later.

- Don't clock watch at night time.

- If you can't get off to sleep – get out of bed and read a book, or something else relaxing and quiet until you feel sleepy again. Then go back to bed.

- If your life is great and you have peace of mind, a good night's sleep is 100% assured. Happy people do not have bad sleep.

- Do not become all OCD about the above. They're just guidelines.

A good night's sleep is Mother Nature's anxiety annihilator par excellence!

<u>Solutions: Anxiety and the vital importance of dreaming.</u>

To sleep, perchance to dream! We need to dream; my marijuana addict clients can't dream, this is one reason why they're so stressed. When we dream we 'dream out' the daily anxiety we all accumulate as I have said. But we don't want to over dream as this is exhausting.

We need both REM sleep and deep physical restorative sleep to feel calm daily.

Solutions: Surround yourself with supportive people only!

Get negative, unpleasant, overly critical, stress inducing, energy vampire people out of your life. I don't care who they are – shut them out. You know them because when you see 'em you groan on the inside. You get that tension in your shoulder muscles instantly. After they have been around you sigh with relief and feel exhausted yet elated you are free of them. These people are a waste of space, minimise your contact a.s.a.p. Your anxiety levels will plummet.

I had a client whose mother was constantly putting him down; she had done since he was a little boy: nothing he did was right (for her!). I always wondered why he didn't just cut the bitch out of his life: he would have been so much happier as a result. Anxiety code insight:

Cut the shits out of your life and bring in all the life-affirming positive people you can!

- Do not take sleeping pills except for in vital emergencies and then only temporarily. Even sleeping pills such as 'Nytol' can have terrible 'side-effects' such as dementia in later life.

However 'positive' doesn't mean they praise you when you act like a prize ass. A person who really loves you will tell you to your face when you are acting like a total penis. And rightly so. Being surrounded by yes men is not the way to go. You don't need to be wrapped in cotton: you do need good company.

Think of it this way: you are going on a very important mission. On this mission you need allies who can lend a hand and vice versa; without them success is impossible. One of your 'allies' is constantly putting your plans down. The criticisms aren't even logical or true. The rest of the team are losing that 'fighting spirit' essential to success. What do you do? Eject the problem person now rather than later. If they stay they'll suck the life out of everything.

People project their own limitations onto reality, that's why most people live boring, pointless lives; you need to live this life as he adventure it is!!! This life is a battle ground: the most exciting roller coaster there is!

Okay we got there: in a couple of hundred

pages you now pretty much get what anxiety is in all its weird and wonderful expressions of human want, pain and dissatisfaction. You have an idea of where your clients are when they come to see you. Now they didn't come to meet your charming dog, pet lizard or vibrating dildo. They want results. They want to 'get better', feel better – fast. In part 2, I will lift back the curtain on how this is done. Are you ready to annihilate anxiety my Padawan?

Onward!

Part 2: The anxiety annihilation scripts.

Anti-anxiety tricks without hypnosis.

You can often get rid of, or at least control anxiety in a number of ways without hypnosis, especially if it's not too severe. I have covered some of these things to a lesser degree in 'Powerful hypnosis'. Often all anxiety will clear up by itself if your life situation improves. Occasionally you have to clear up 'residue'. Okay I'm going to chuck out some anti-anxiety tricks, not already mentioned:

- One of the best is **deliberately visualise the worst.** Lots of phobias and some types of anxiety problems are exacerbated because people scare themselves silly by being afraid to imagine their worst fear. When you can do this comfortably your fear of imagining the worst goes and the anxiety feedback loop is disrupted. Let me give you an example. Say you have a fear of vomiting: imagine puking up in public all over a group of people. Exaggerate the worst so it becomes funny. Keep doing this over and over until you get no fear reaction at all. This is similar to challenging the fear reaction I told you about earlier. You can also do this with any worry. If you are worried about x then imagine x happening in the worst way possible – take it to its most absurd position. Say you are worrying about being late for a meeting. Imagine getting so flustered and bothered that it leads to your accidentally setting off a nuclear holocaust somehow! Just make shit up. If you are going to endlessly and pointlessly invent 'what ifs' make up a load of hilariously ludicrous scenarios. Stop being a what if horror movie maker in your own head and be a comedy movie maker instead. The difference is slight anyway! Anxiety remedies are often paradoxical.

- You can calm anxiety quickly using 3 simple **breathing patterns** – the 3-5 or 7-11 breathing technique and the fill the lungs technique. Anxiety is caused physiologically by shallow high chested breathing. You can stop this by breathing out slightly longer than breathing in. the first two tricks simply entail your breathing in for a count of 3 or 7 seconds and then slowly letting that breathe out for either a count of 5 or 11 respectively depending on how long you breathed in for. This restores calm quickly. You are 1. Counting and so activating your conscious mind. 2. Focusing on a task and not on the fear etc. 3. Pattern interrupting a physical pattern. This is a form of N.A.C. This is for emergencies. The last breathing trick is this – breathe out all the air in your lungs – till they feel 'empty'. Allow your lungs to refill naturally. Do this 3 times. Once you have done this, very often, your normal breathing pattern recalibrates itself.

- Remind yourself that the physical symptoms of fear are just that and not a sign of imminent madness or death. This is a form of **self-hypnotic reframing.** You had been alarmist and meta-commenting in your head about your increased heart rate etc. Just remind yourself that these physical reactions to adrenaline are normal, happen when you exercise and always pass etc. Do you know anyone who was anxious forever?!

- Set time aside to worry during the day. If you must worry do it for 15 minutes during the day and then stop. This is the Milton Erickson trick of **prescribing the symptom.**

- Connected to this is **write your worries down** on paper or type them out on your PC. The point is physically get the ideas out of your head and onto something tangible. When fretting in a worry fit, ideas swim around your head chaotically like a worry aquarium of panicked fish! Write them all down and examine them objectively. Once you do you'll find they seem less ominous and far fewer in number. Then write down how you'll solve them. Most likely this will involve need satisfaction.

- **Get out in nature.** A good walk in nature restores calm. Well in the UK it does as the worst animal we could encounter is a harmless bird or a fox. In the US make sure you go to an area without human eating animals for your stroll! Walking, being a repetitive activity requiring no thought, triggers your creative brain to start generating solutions spontaneously. The anterior cingulate cortex of the brain is no longer swamped and starts to create ideas. This is why writers often seek inspiration from a walk.

- **Have a bath.** Really: just soothes all the muscular tension away. Just float and forget. Showers too are a great way to come up with ideas.

- **Slow things down!** Anxiety is associated with speed. During The Orson Wells 'War of the worlds' scare of the last century, drivers hearing about the 'alien invasion' drove very fast! That's what anxiety does to you. Two tips – slow down body movements and slow...down... thought...and anxiety is harder to do. Speak to yourself in a calm inner voice. That is how calm people 'do' calm. They keep their head and move with more control and ease than anyone else. Change speed and halt anxiety.

- Some people have tried **controlling eye movements and facial expressions.** When people are anxious they tend to be fractionating in and out of scary trances. In order to do this they have to defocus their eyes or look up – usually to the right or left as they recall or invent scary scenarios. The same goes for facial expressions: it's hard to get scared if you can't pull scared facial expressions. Unless you are a man that is; men are experts at emotional concealment. I throw these things out as ideas only. A powerful hypnosis sessions by a skilled professional is always going to beat silly little attempts at muscular control. These methods may work with very mild anxiety but attempting to suppress anxiety may make it worse!

- **Exercise away your stress.** Bears repeating: if that body and mind are beat up with stress – work it out with a good work out of choice.

- **Be counterphobic NOW.** The more we avoid things that aren't scary the more we create tiny unconscious worry patterns that they are and these become habitual. If you have a phobia of trees get up and go stand next to a tree now. No fucking around. Stand there and really feel that panic or anxiety, stand next to that tree till the fear subsides – you must not run away. It's the running away that sends a signal to the deeper mind saying DANGER! But there isn't any is there? Unless a lumberjack is nearby! This used to be called 'flooding' and was used because it was cheap. Just go and face that god damned absurd fear. Even OCD used to be treated this way. You just go get your hands dirty if you are an obsessive cleaner. Stick then in mud and sit down for an hour not washing them. Just refuse – the fear rises, arcs and then declines. The brain learns there is no danger.

- **Mickey mouse the voice of fear.** The internal voice of fear often sounds like a very quick speaking panicked you – this scares your

245

brain. So make it sound silly like Mickey Mouse or sexy like Sean Connery and your brain sees it as a joke. Geddit? This is an old NLP trick. Again, with low level anxiety it can work.

- **<u>Shrink into black and white scary images.</u>** This is NLP too. With fears that are caused by images alone this can work. Scary images are generally bright, bold, vivid, close up and colourful – do the opposite: push them far away, make 'em misty, black and white and make the figures stick figures/cartoon characters etc. Give it a banana frame. Geddit?

- **<u>Ignore the voice of depression.</u>** Sometimes when people are depressed a nay saying voice in the head tells them – 'What's the point blah, blah, blah!?' It's very good at giving you rationalisations as to why any effort you might make to improve your life will fail. This is a product of exhaustion alone. Ignore it. It's an idiot anyway. Remind yourself it's a sign of exhaustion and will pass when your energy returns.

- **Note improvements.** When recovering your need to redirectionalise your focus away from an 'illness' focus to a recovery focus. This can entail keeping a diary, telling friends or just mentally noting any signs of improvement, however long they last. This is an example of making things tangible. Anxiety loves speculation and vagueness – the more concrete and specific you can be the more anxiety has no place to hide. Fear often lurks in ignorance. More on this in my last book.

- **Watch comedy.** You can't usually be scared and laughing all at once. If you are depressed or anxious go watch a funny TV show; watch 3 in a row. You WILL feel better. Your brain will start to produce happy feelings without drugs! If you have funny friends spend time with them. It's so easy and cheap – just go onto YouTube if you're broke! The world always looks a brighter place when comedy reteaches you that this life is absurd so you may as well laugh! Humour changes perspectives. *Anxiety code*

insight – you cannot laugh and be anxious at the same time!

- **Be around those you love.** The greatest healer is love. Many a confirmed alcoholic has been reformed by the love of a good woman with the patience of a saint. When you are in a safe environment, surrounded by people you love you will recover. Support from friends and relatives is known as a key factor in any recovery process.

- **Download hypnosis recordings.** I lied - this one requires hypnosis! Too broke to afford good therapist bills? The Internet is awash with some really good companies who provide downloadable hypnotherapy recordings for every issue under the sun. Do some research, find the best one or ones for you: email the service provider; they'll be happy to assist you in any queries you have. You can recover from all the 'disorders' in this book and more without seeing one therapist. Your recovery may be only a reasonably priced click away. You *can* get better in the privacy of your own home. No interview or nerves about creepy therapist types etc. It's been done, even for depression. If what you are doing isn't working – for the love of f—k do something different.

What do all these things have in common? They are pattern interrupts. That anxiety etc. can't get a hold because you took action to stop its flow.

Anxiety code insight: to halt anxiety in its tracks you must interrupt its usual activation process.

I highly recommended the book: **Living with fear, Understanding and coping with anxiety by Issac M. Marks M.D.** However it is Cognitive Behavioural in approach and the treatment techniques are frankly 'Stone Age' compared to the jewels in this here bookie, if I may say so.

- **Do pleasurable things!** This may sound daft or just sheer common sense but when people get anxious or at worst depressed they have often gone through a period of stopping doing the very things that make them happy. I encountered this often with men with drug addictions whose new wives had nagged them into stopping some favourite hobby etc. and unwittingly induced utter misery in their husbands leading to various mental health problems. It's hard to be anxious when you are doing what you love; that which gives you a sense of joy and meaning – such as a great job. It can also mean restarting an old hobby that you 'gave up on' for one reason or another. With depression people get stuck as the anxiety and exhaustion make them feel like retreating from the world and all the things that give them pleasure. BIG MISTAKE. You have a powerful and profound need as a human to do that which makes you, as an *individual*, feel happiest. Here's a tip: follow your passions. Often they were the stuff you loved to do as a kid; then one day you 'grew up' and became stupid. What do you love to do so much you'd pay to do it? ***Anxiety code 'secret': if you want to be anxiety free do things that give you personally meaningful pleasure daily!***

A deep relaxation induction for anxiety sessions.

Before we do anything else I am going to give you a 'whack 'em through the floor induction that will annihilate anxiety in pretty much anyone – it's aim is to reboot the parasympathetic phase of the nervous system. Let's get to it. Oh by the way, I am weaving in various suggestions to remain calm even in a 'crisis'. It's no good calming someone down without teaching the subconscious that it is far often better to remain calm, even in a tight spot. Stressful responses are less than helpful 99.9% of the time. Any of the induction scripts from my other books will work just fine with anxiety clients. Use what works. There is never only one 'right' way to hypnotise anyone.

Script reading tricks for the novice.

If you are brand new to this book series – where the hell have you been! Just joking, for people totally new to hypnosis I include a few tips on how to read a hypnosis script properly. This is covered much more extensively in 'How to hypnotise anyone', 'Mastering hypnotic language', and 'Wizards of trance'. Very quickly:

- Hypnosis and trance are not the same: hypnosis is a narrow focus of attention/absorption. Trance is daydreaming. Both together = hypnotic trance, a very powerful combo for powerful change work to occur within.

- The hypnotist guides a client through a process but the client does the work of change; that is their responsibility.

- Highlighted text = embedded commands, these are subliminal commands within seemingly ordinary sentences. For example, 'You can **relax deeply...**' When you see such in the following scripts you use a downward tonality as if giving a command. The opposite of a question which has a rising tone. You can also turn your head as you say the command or whisper it. Do something that marks it out as different and the subconscious/unconscious will detect it and respond. This trick is so powerful that it works even if the conscious mind is aware of embeds. In my final book, 'Weirdnosis' I give away advanced level new ways to do embeds.

- As you induce hypnosis gradually slow down your voice and make it sound much more relaxing and soothing. Think of lulling a baby to sleep. If you speak in bursts of between 4-8 words and leave a pause afterwards you will quieten the conscious mind of the hypnotee (person being hypnotised). Rhythm and hypnosis is covered extensively in my final book too.

- Use at least 3 distinct voice tones: 1. A normal waking voice for conscious communication. 2. A relaxing hypno-voice to induce trance. 3. A very deep and slow voice for communicating with the deep unconscious. When the client is under you can speak up and put energy into your voice: squeeze the meaning out of words – say 'power' in a powerful tone etc. Use a wide and varied intonation as a good actor would. You can send a client's brain all over the place by voice tone alone. Your tone bathes that person's brain with sound. When waking someone from hypnotic trance let your voice become much more energised – return it gradually to your normal speaking tone. Read all my other books to get the full low down on this

254

topic otherwise we'll be here all day!

Profound relaxation induction + installing a calm outlook script.

If you see NFH in the text it means 'note for hypnotist'.

Part 1: Layering in relaxation.

'Okay can you just close your eyes for me... great...And can you just pay attention to your breathing...You don't have to change it or do anything to it...Just draw all your attention to it for me...that's it! As you **focus** your attention on your breathing...you'll find it easy to **become absorbed** by some inner realities...as you do when you **daydream**... say on a long train journey and you **drift off** whilst looking out a window...lovely experience isn't it?

So can you just take a deep breath in for me and hold it!? *(Rhetorical question, pause a beat)* That's perfect. And just slowly release that breath and find you can **rest** here, **now...**And one more time please just take a deep breath in and hold it! *(A beat)* And slowly release that breath and know that on the prolonged out breath anyone can **relax far deeper...**Good.

Because the funny thing about the process of relaxation is that you were born doing it, automatically. Your subconscious or unconscious does all that kind of stuff so you don't have to...With that in mind...you can allow your attention to drift to the part of you that is most relaxed already...and we'll build on that by...**letting go** even more...as you find your own way to **go into a nice trance** and explore new ways of healing, recovering, learning, now...That's right.

You know in this busy world we all need to take some time out to **rest deeply...**As you do that now...as you notice growing sensations of comfort...as you imagine a colour you associate with calmness, **profound...calmness....now,** spreading all the way through you...soothing, relieving any past tension that can melt away so effortlessly...In this changing state...you'll relearn how to rest profoundly here...to the pleasing hypnotic sound of my words...A part of you hears them so you don't have to...isn't it? Wouldn't you really like to **go inside hypnotic oblivion, now...**

All of your subconscious, unconscious functions work so much better when you allow yourself to **restore a sense of inner calm,**

now... And the best way to do that is to simply do nothing...but in a very clever way... that allows you to re-access your creative abilities to **solve problems through insight and inspiration...**

What if you could see an even more relaxed you over there...in your imagination...with the part that dreams for you...lying down or in a chair...And that you is 10 times more relaxed than you are now...And that's nice to know you can **go that deep, now,** is it not? And in that place there is no need to move. There is no need for chatter – your peace of mind develops without any effort on that part's part... *(NFH: not necessary but you can get the client to float or associate into the more relaxed image of themselves.)*

And it can help to become aware of what sensations signal the return of relaxation, within...you might hear that sigh of relief in your mind after a period of work...remaining thoughts simply slow down...drift by...and off... as another way of processing information occurs...as other parts and functions of the deeper mind begin to comfortably predominate, now...

How do you usually **unwind, become so**

still and reflect pleasantly? That's it. Because it's unique to you. And that's nice to know too, isn't it? For as you are increasingly occupied by internal matters...other things are easily ignored...as anyone does when they are **nicely absorbed in things** that really matter to them. Perhaps physical sensations are attended to here. Perhaps images. Perhaps certain comfy feelings that grow, only grow, and mature, here...Many responses can and do alter effectively in a place of profound peace. Inside and out. As your physical relaxation develops and evolves so too does the **relaxing** of your mind. Of each and both of you.

Can you **recall** a time when you relaxed very deeply? Just let that vividly come to mind. That pleasant place of the past that can reawaken your awareness of your inner resources, now. Because everyone has relaxed for a period of time, from time to time, have they not? Wasn't it? That's it. Using your inner senses, be back in that time, place and body now – filled with **feelings of delicious rest and the ease,** of amazing relaxation spreading. Perfect...And as you relive that pleasing event, can you find your own way to deepen this hypnotic state appropriately, in a way that respects your healing intentions...

that's right...Numbers and expected processes do not matter in this place.

As your attention is now so deeply attuned to this inner environment can you notice what it is about those circumstances that make you **feel so deeply relaxed**? In that space...in that time...are their visual impressions that **increase your sense of peace**? Colours that soothe? Shapes that please? Could it be a particular quality of sound? Or the **absolute stillness** of this place? Are any aromas – smells of nature found in this process of introspection? Notice anything specific there at all that enhances your sense of **deep rest and comfort, inside.** Good. I'll be quiet for about 15 seconds as you go deeper in the pause.

Lovely. The purpose of any relaxing process is to **restore and re-energise** at a deep cellular level. For it is known that cells have a memory and if so even your cells can **remember the unconscious code of relaxation**. It's just common sense, isn't it? Your far deeper mind knows all you need ever know about such a re-connective process as certain old, outdated, temporary associations shift, now...That's the way. You can and are able at very deep levels of information

259

processing to **relax so deeply down** to the deepest levels of your unconscious mind, now...It contains feelings of joyous peace... **blissfully calm...**storehouses of energy... muscular and mental relaxation...and many other things that it knows far more about than I. It's nice to know you have that unconscious wisdom, is it not? And that might make anyone at all **feel so much more secure inside.** And that's all anyone really wants. Deep down, underneath all the fading tension. Evaporates like tiny droplets of water on **pleasant days/daze.** In fact before we continue, just become aware at some level, how much more wonderfully relaxed you already are. That's it...

Part 2: Elicit symbolic place of deep peace.

As you go down, all the way down on the river of these hypnotic dreams, building in **healing,** better, more useful hypnotic realities, I would like you to simply imagine a type of building...in a certain place...that you have only...could only...will ever only associate with the deepest **feelings of restorative peace and quiet** you have ever known....I'll be quiet as you find that place...**deeper inside than before.** *(7-10 second pause).*

260

Great...As you pay attention to a particular quality of my voice that helps **you're relaxing**...you can be aware...how just conjuring this place in your mind...relaxes you even more and takes you **deeper and deeper into hypnotic trance**...And allow a wave of comforting relaxation to sweep across your body...even more blissfully calm as I say the word...peace...PEACE. That's it. And that can **feel awesome,** doesn't it?

Now of course I don't know where this place is. You do. That's the magic of this. This is your private experience. As you noticed qualities of your relaxing memory that made it even more pleasant...notice how there are qualities of atmosphere...air...sounds...sights and touches...times...background awarenesses that make this place seem so lifelike and realistic...And that part of your brain that does such things can **amplify your response to these words** because it dreams dreams for you at night...

Without walking...simply **drift...float** toward that place...a sensation of floating in this state of mind and body...effortless toward that place of peace...You just unconsciously imagine it and it becomes so...so nice...Your mind is focused with crystal clarity on your goal at all levels of mentation...As I count from 3-0 you will reach that place and stand before the threshold, the en/in-trance to that place...And you deeply desire to be there...for you know... what lies within is a kind of magic that lies within, it always has...a deeper magic than you have known at one level...but a magic that can become real, very real for you...3 deeper with each number...2 closer, nearer, floating...1 almost there...0. You are where you need to be to get what you need. **Become fascinated** by your new level of calm...More is possible than you knew, or once imagined you did, or didn't, wasn't it? The only thing that held you back were past illusions that you have **let go fully now...**

Part 3: The deepest levels of peace.

Perfect. Now, enter the portal of this place of peace...you cross that threshold and automatically vow to **leave those outdated patterns behind** you. That's it. Good. You may even feel a wave of relieving comfort sweep through you, intensify and amplify as you rest soothingly in your place of peace – your private haven of deep security inside; it all starts with you having **deep faith in yourself.** In this shelter or this retreat you can **reconnect to the deep wellsprings of**

calm within you. At the appropriate level, they will serve you well in waking life.

Phase 1: Ultimate bodily relaxation.

What is the space before you like? A room? A chamber? A cave, some other place? You know. You will notice that in this first place there is much that helps **relax your mind and body even more deeply,** just as a **soothing** memory does. Every muscle fibre is capable of **going deeper into hypnotic rest** and stillness here. That's it. Notice how much more relaxed you already feel before you go beyond what wasn't really a part of you, for a relaxed person has **no need for excessive levels of attention or arousal.** Such a response would be absurd to them. And that's the new you, who you are, now. And perhaps you can become aware of a place inside that place where you could **take it easy**? A spot you would **feel an amazing comfort** were you to sit or lie down and **rest more deeply than ever** – so that tendons, tissues, cells, muscular effort **feel a renewed sense of calm and refreshment** here.

This first level of relaxation – symbolised by this specific place you are in now, has a wonderful calming atmosphere; invisible but so very tangible that it permeates your mind and body so sweetly that only recovery is possible. It is a powerful feeling contained in that space, within you, now. It replenishes your body's energy, strength and resilience in almost magical ways and you **feel that** is true, do you not?

So when you are quite ready...just lie down or sit in that inviting place inside that will take you to even deeper levels of hypnotic trance, all the way down so that **your body feels incredibly relaxed.** I'll pause for a bit while you do that. *(5-7 secs)* If you want to let those inner eyes close and rest do so. If that is what feels right. Absorb the deep sense of peace. Feel a level of comfort you didn't know was possible. Feel a soothing comfort spread down the face, massaging its way all down your body, arms, legs to your toes. So much more relaxation within. And where the body leads the mind must follow. We know this. Even your insides are being soothed and healed to a deep cellular level. That's right. When **you are relaxed** so many parts of you work better and that's nice to know, is it not? Have you ever experienced a nice time where you just could not suppress a smile of **deep satisfaction**? We all have and you can **feel that way now.**

Inside all is soothed. Inside all is well. All physical tension has left the body. Your body feels so relaxed that **your spirits are uplifted**. As though **a weight has been lifted.** And you realise that there is **no pressure** here. No one wanting anything. You can just **be yourself** here. It is as though **your self-belief only grows stronger** in this place. Your body feels stronger and so your approach can **be more flexible** in certain ways and perspectives. Just **resting deeply.** I will be 100% quiet as a mouse for a full minute and in that minute something pleasant and helpful will happen, something that moves you forward in this process, as **your creative part is free** to work effortlessly on your behalf. Free to **solve problems unconsciously** in moments of insight, intuition, new awarenesses, inspirations and more, much more, now... *(Quiet as promised...)*

Relaxing to play games story.

Good. It's funny how things that happen in real life just seem to relate to insights that help me in hypnotic work: let me tell you about my 7 year old nephew. On his birthday he received a computer game. He was so excited and he tried to play it but it was all new and he couldn't quite get the on-screen characters to move where he wanted, to do what he desired – he became more and more angry and frustrated and nearly tearful with helplessness; kind words didn't help, they made him even angrier. The angrier and more frustrated he became the less he could **control things** as he wanted. So he just gave up and pulled faces. Then his mum/mom called him into the dining room to blow out the 7 candles on his birthday cake. He instantly began to laugh and ran out after in such renewed excitement. Being the centre of attention made him **feel so good.** He began to **glow with that feeling of being loved** that only children can **feel.** About 10 minutes later he was playing his computer game whilst lying on his daddy, he was **so relaxed and comfortable** because his mood had changed for the better, he was **so laid back** and he made those little men on that screen run around and kick that ball just as he wanted. It was **all so easy.** He scored 7 goals.

Phase 2: Profoundly relaxing the mind.

As your body is so profoundly relaxed now... It's time to **completely relax your mind.** With that in mind notice that there is another entranceway in this place that leads to another space beyond that past mental tension you once had – beyond worry or fear, a place of **total clarity of mind** and objectivity of perspective....a place where you can easily **see the bigger picture.** Just float out of that **relaxing body** and look down at that you who is so much more relaxed than before. While you are off doing other things of importance that body will take the time to **rest and recover fully** as if you were having a great night's sleep in which **deep physical recovery occurs, now.** I know you **know that feeling.** Good.

So when you are ready, simply float into a place that symbolically represents **complete mental relaxation, now.** That's great. You are doing really well. Any and all mental chatter slows all the way down here...images are only pleasurable and **deeply relaxing** ones, ones that enhance your **deepening trance...**ones that increase your sense of hypnotic immersion in this process of change...Some things fade and move away... certainly a softening of certain things...a quietening down...a dampening...a new awareness of **a relaxed inner tone of voice** with which you can commune...here, deep inside. Everything is becoming **smoother, calmer**...it can be a moment of **absolute**

stillness...like a time in nature when all the world seems to be at one...That's it. Feel that sense of **complete mental peace,** clarity and security. When you **dissociate yourself from certain thoughts, pictures, voices** or one voice in particular you'll **notice a deepening sense of calm** and contemplation. You can **view things clearly**...as they are...reflecting on **seeing things wholly realistically, now.**

I'll **be quiet** as whatever needs to happen can happen. You will not hear from me for 30 seconds of clock time but inside your mind you have all the time you need to **make the appropriate changes** to **lock in a relaxed state of mind.** Good. *(Shhh for 30 seconds.)*

Phase 3: Going to the core.

And now...you know, deeply, that there is a far deeper level of hypnotic magic than this... beyond mind...beyond your body...is the core of who you deeply truly are...the part that is observing and monitoring everything – at the most profound levels...A place of far deeper magic and healing potentials. You have been **floating inwardly** anyway...getting closer and closer to this place...and at some level you knew that anyway, did you not? It is an inner sanctum...some people even call it 'your personal sanctuary'...it lies inside you...beyond your name...beyond this 3 dimensional space...beyond this place of clock time...I simply call it the core of who you really are and were meant to be. So when you are ready – notice the en/in-trance to your personal sanctuary and drift and **float** to that place: go deeper into the centre of yourself. **Become absorbed** by the symbolic nature of how you represent this to yourself for all things have profound meanings, learning and understandings, here. Good. I'll pause as you make any unconscious shifts you need to get what you need. *(5 to 10 secs should do the trick.)*

And now, you are here and there and nowhere in particular...a place that signifies the purest essence of things...a place where you can **rest more deeply** than ever...a place where you **recover in all ways...**where you reconnect and **re-associate to necessary resources** that move you forward powerfully. And you feel this to be true – you unconsciously absorb these leanings through the differing yet tangible atmosphere of this most special place within. Here, you can re-access that knowing feeling that somehow, no matter what had happened, you really know, that **all is well.** The river of life is always flowing onward. Meanings you once had **change here, now.** And that is a nice thing to know isn't it? Enjoy taking the time to tap into your ability to **feel calm no matter what is going on around you...**And as you have gone far, far beyond what once was, that reminds me of a story...

Phase 4: Remaining calm in any crisis entrainment tale.

Once upon a time means it's story time...a time to be entertained, a fascinating way to learn, one of the earliest ways you learnt and absorbed values that helped you navigate through this world...and it's always best to learn when **you are so calm.** Some people like to imagine sitting around a mesmerising fire, as our ancestors of old did as they listened to the storyteller. Stories are a part of our language of communication...the brain is worked upon by images which shape our mental maps...

There was once a man who was **always calm and collected under any pressure...** when problems arose he simply went straight into a calm problem solving state, automatically. It was just a part of him. He was the type who could **keep a cool head in a crisis,** or what others saw as a crisis: he simply saw problems as a series of challenges that made his life more interesting. No matter what was going on around him he could **focus intently on solutions.** He had an amazing ability to **be in time and objective about it too.** No matter how unbalanced others felt, he went his own way – he was so grounded, down to earth and strong-minded; people admired this ability in him. He didn't even need to think about it. It just happened as a reflex action. This made him a natural leader. He was able to **make good decisions and judgements** about so many things as a consequence. He would never blindly speculate – he would check his facts. He made internal and external checks that moved him forward, he thought for himself all because he had **full self-belief, now.** When situations arose that bothered others he could feel so comfortable knowing that such times always pass. In fact they help us in ways you don't always appreciate at the time. He knew, really knew that what seemed chaos and noise was merely an opportunity to **find that profound peace deep inside,** insights and creativity happen there. Like a sea captain who sails calmly through what seems to his sailors a terrible sea storm but to his entrained eye is merely a reality that must be dealt with evenly. He did what he could to change things and accepted what couldn't be changed. This gave him a tremendous sense of equilibrium through the ups and downs of life.

For he could go to his core – re-access his power there. And the good thing is – you know the way too now. Do you not? The truth is people can choose to **go to that calm place inside, no matter what is occurring.** And that's a nice thing to know is it not? Exactly. You may well find that you are **staying calm** more often than not. That certain perspectives can alter. Your map is updated. Let others get excited if that's what they want – it's just not something you do, inappropriately anymore, it's absurd, silly and unreal, it doesn't apply to you, and it just won't happen because calm and collected people don't do that and that's who you are and were, always, beyond what wasn't really true. Is that not deeply so? Ju-ust so. You'll find **you have such presence of mind, now.** Everyone can instinctively learn how to **be fully in any moment and yet calm and objective at the same time.** What one can do, so can another. And there is truth in that.

Future pace: dissociated rehearsal.

I bet you can visualise a you that has all these qualities. Could you watch it on the movie screen of your mind – vivid, colourful and so lifelike? Almost like high definition, 3D virtual reality! That's it. See yourself in a time, a situation in which **you have all these calm qualities** and are displaying them admirably. Perhaps in a future time which would have once troubled you before this hypnotic trance-formation occurred. See how wonderfully relaxed all your response are. How measured and reasonable. See that amazing poise you now have. Your facial muscles are relaxed. That **mind and body now calmer** than ever before. Yet you are alert too. All these thing are possible: can and will manifest and this is so. No matter what happens **you always remain calm during such times.** And such knowledge of your positively changing reality brings you such **peace of mind and security that pervades all you do;** that profoundly alters and constructively flips your whole approach to this life. *(Pause for 15 – 30 secs or so.)*

Future pace: associated rehearsal.

Good. And when you are ready – float into

that you who has **all these calm qualities locked in, now.** Go through that situation again from beginning to end – feeling a level of calm and confidence, poise and creativity, flexibility of response and a great sense of humour for good measure thrown in too. See through those eyes that reflect reality as it is. Hear through those ears. Feel those wonderful sets of feelings that let you 100% know in tangible ways that you can notice upon waking that – **you are fully calm and in control.** Nothing bothers you as it once did. That's your 100% total personal reality and that's that. *(Again pause for 15 – 30 secs...)*

Every cell is Changing in a
Colour feeling post hypnotics. Completely healthy
way

Okay! Turn this deep level of calm composure into a colour. Let that colour feeling spread through you, only deliciously **amplifying these wonderful feelings** more and more and more! That's right! And whenever you need to **feel this calm in future** you can simply imagine this calming, soothing colour spreading through you in order to **feel blissfully calm and totally balanced again** *(NFH: or you can link it to a key word anchor/trigger etc.).* But I bet you'll just notice that all these changes and resources are where they need to be as just the right re-

connections and re-associations occur, now.
You are doing brilliantly; with the deep
knowledge that a particular part of you can
really listen and experientially realise that
**very little in life requires an overly
stressful response** to achieve your deepest
and most heartfelt needs as a total person.
And I know that you – deeply know – **this is
all true.** For you have learnt that unless a
physical emergency is occurring that requires
large amounts of energy, your deepest
unconscious will ensure from now on that
**your parasympathetic, calming down
phase begins to predominate now** and
this remains so, permanently for life in just
the appropriate way that ensures your
optimum survival and success. It is better to
get creative than automatic or at least **get
automatically creative.** Won't it be funny to
notice how **your sense of genuine
optimism only continues to grow** as a
result?

*Gathering up resources before emerging from
trance.*

And as you leave that place of sanctuary,
knowing it's always there deep inside, and as
you float back into the place of **profound
peace of mind,** you will bring back all

appropriate learnings with you. The core of you is at peace. And as you drift through the space of relaxation of mind you bring with you that wonderfully relaxed, clear and objective frame of mind through which you now view reality. Many perspectives have changed. Your sense of humour and sociability are enhanced in just the right way. All the component parts of **a relaxed mind** – psychological and physiological are within you, now. You **focus on what you want.** You imagination helps you accordingly – your creative part fulfils this role wonderfully when appropriate. You feel a sense of zest for living fully, expressing your energy; you are amazingly revitalised and want to express that in waking life. You can **lighten up about so many things** as a result. As you float passed that place and back into the place of deep physical relaxation you bring back with you all that wonderful focused energy you've reconnected to. **Your body feels much more comfortable,** pleasantly relaxed, flexible and expressive of all emotions – all the emotions are acceptable. Emotions help us evaluate our experience – listen and learn from them. Re-associate fully back into your body if you haven't already with all these nice adjustments intact. You can leave that symbolic place of **perfect peace now.** Leave that place. That's it. And outside everything

276

looks more colourful, fresh and wonderful.
Grass seems greener, air fresher, you notice
the beauty and joy about you: the abundance
of this world. So many things uplift you. You
feel much happier being you. You are a
good person and you know it deeply.

you feel healthier +

That place of deep peace exists, you were
there: you took what you needed and have
correspondingly replenished yourself. Life is
good. Challenges move us forward as we
overcome them. That place of **your full re-
energisation, now** can be revisited when
you need to rest: daydreams, absorption in
pleasurable acts. Good company and **easy,
wonderful sleep at night** all allow a natural
boost. With that renewed calm and strength
rekindled within you can **feel a calm energy**
flowing through you; things just seem to be
easier, juicer, more fulfilling in delightful and
surprising ways. The old struggle has been
replaced by better attitudes, differing choices
and actions, enhanced responses,
automatically, smiling more often. It's a
though a weight has been lifted from your
shoulders! **Feeling so good!** Take these
fantastic hypnotic learnings into **your much
more relaxed future, nooooo-oooow!**
That's right.'

(Exduction of choice or continue with change work etc. If you want to carry on say, 'And now...you can go deeper etc.')

Structure of the process.

Very simple:

- Induce hypnotic trance.

- Link 'compliance' to deepening trance states.

- Elicit symbolic places that represent 'complete peace' in progressive stages. Remember from my other books, especially 'Crafting hypnotic spells' on SSC, 'Subconscious Symbolic Communication'; a client's subjective symbolism is better utilised than imposing yours on their subconscious. You don't know what their metaphors for experience are: they do!

- Relax body and dissociate client from body.

- Relax mind. Model qualities of a relaxed person's mind to client.

- Visit 'core' – the place beyond all material concerns.

- Model the patterns of keeping calm to the client. Give them an example of 'how' to do it. This is where you offer the subconscious alternative sets of patterns to operate from. This is actually a sly negotiation. You are implicitly saying, 'This is better than that.'

- Future pace (visualise) suggested changes. _Human brains operate from visualised maps drawn from language._

- 'Integrate' learnings (post hypnotics).

- Wake client up or continue etc.

Once you know the basic structure you can generate your own scripts. The script above is but one possibility based on such themes. Improvise around a structural thread to get really good at inventing your own scripts. It's easy. If you don't, you'll waste large sums of cash buying other therapist's expressions of such themes. While scripts are good to learn from you want to invent your own processes and expressions of them: that's called 'mastery'. Mastery is far easier than beginners might think.

Case 1: Getting rid of unnecessary worry.

She was afraid she was going to swallow her tongue. The doc had diagnosed – GAD. She worried a lot. She felt worse in the morning (a sure sign of the beginnings of depression). She was afraid of going outdoors - she called me asking for help in getting rid of her, ahem... 'phobias'. Actually she didn't have any. She just didn't know that – yet.

A relatively attractive and well-dressed young woman in her late 20's turned up. She was a bit overweight but other than looking a bit pensive she looked quite healthy. If you have read my other books where I outline my therapeutic techniques you'll know that I have a questionnaire formula that I stick to for 1st session clients. Shall we?

'How is life at the moment?' I ask.
I wrote down simply... 'stressful – lonely' as her response.

I ask what she does for a living and whether she enjoys it. She works for a major global banking/investment etc. syndicate; probably the most powerful on earth. She doesn't like her job since new management has taken over. She is looking elsewhere for employment. As I live in London a large percentage of my clients are financial sector workers. Class take note: the financial sector is toxic to mental health, especially for sensitive souls like this lady. If you are an asshole you'll thrive! You can't exist in an environment of psychopathic amorality and insatiable greed and keep your marbles intact padawans, ain't gonna happen. I have seen the evidence.

'What's your living situation? Are you single, married etc.?'

'No I am not married.' (Lonely, not married – she has cut to the chase. Which need is missing folks?) I am renting up town.'

Like all yuppies she earns large amounts of money but has no house. She probably lives in a one bedroomed bedsit (tiny apartment) and pays half a million for it. You can get twits to think anything is 'cool'. She tells me she is on some anti-depressant called Fluoxetine a derivative of fluoride, a known neuro-toxin used by the Nazis to sedate concentration camp victims. Oh well (sigh). She is not epileptic but was taking a drug for her 'GAD' (no boyfriend syndrome) called, monstrously,

Duloxetine. I dread to think what's in that! Apparently it made her worse (you don't say!?) so the docs put her on the fluoride pills. Nice of them.

I can already tell from her flatness of expression caused by exhaustion that this lady is genuinely depressed, she doesn't have GAD. She has unsurprisingly been misdiagnosed – shocker! I make a note on my questionnaire – 'Sleep? Depression?' I continue...

'What are the problems you want to solve today?'

'I want to live and not be like this (she feels stuck – her life is on hold; why? No boyfriend dummy!). It has become a part of me (she has felt like this for so long she now perceives it as being part of her identity as opposed to a normal reaction to unmet needs). It has become drilled into me. It's my mood, my low mood...I am always tired.'

Anxiety is tiring. The mood is a result of the exhaustion. Not the cause.

'When did all this begin? Was there a triggering event you can identify?'

She tells me it was a breakup with an ex. I hate to say I told you so. This occurred six years ago. The feelings etc. worsened in the past 3 years (as the need went unaddressed). The breakup occurred after she went travelling with her ex beau.

Okay let's discuss this: unmet needs = stress, we know this. The lady had experienced loss. The loss of her most intimate relationship with a man she had fantasised she was going to marry. He clearly had other ideas. I guarantee you the indicators of flagging interest were clear before the breakup – the person about to get dumped is often in conscious denial.

Let's talk about the psychology of girls, which hasn't been changed by Marxist feminism, for human nature does not change. Girls think and imagine their future wedding day as soon as they discover that girls can get married. My niece is 5. We spent one Sunday afternoon searching Amazon for a princess wedding dress and a castle for her to hold her princess wedding in. She also wanted me to buy the future groom's outfit – the man sized version and she hasn't even met her future boyfriend (that I know - a boy at school has already proposed!!!); are you startin' to get the bigger picture?

My client is in her late 20's; these days your average modern woman wants her career settled and then to get married by about 23ish, certainly by her mid-20's before her looks start to fade. All her friends are married, they have kids. *In her mind* when she goes out with her married friends she is the epitome of gooseberry. A washed up old spinster in her imagination and she's not even 30. Geddit? All any dumb doctor had to do was find this straightforward shit out and tell her she had 'no boyfriend syndrome'; her 'treatment' should have been – get a boyfriend and she may well have spontaneously 'recovered'. You have no idea how many miserable single clients I see! Note for the dumb: men and women NEED each other. Get over it. Note: ***women's biologically programmed mission to perpetuate the species means that women want the emotional and economic security that is provided by man.***

That reminds me of a 'treatment' that Dr. Milton Erickson, the creator of modern hypnotherapy provided for a patient. Okay it's post war America, Phoenix Arizona. Erickson is confronted by a beautiful but shy patient who is 'suicidally depressed'. Erickson says, 'Why do you want to kill yourself?' or words to that affect. She says, 'I don't have a boyfriend!!!' He notices she has a cute gap in her front teeth. He says, 'Can you spit?' She says she can. He asks if there is a man at her office that she has the hots for or who has the hots for her? She says yes. Erickson says – you are to go to the water fountain at your office at the same time as this man. You are to get a cup of water. Then you are to squirt a jet of water at this man through the gap in your teeth. Just follow these instructions and report back to me when you have fulfilled them.

The lady does so. The man is at first shocked, then she smiles at him. He smiles back. 'Why you little bitch!' he says to her. She shrieks and runs. The man catches up with her and kisses her passionately. Her depressed 'symptoms' vanish! No! You don't say!? They date, get married, have kids. Now that's 'therapy'!

What did Erickson do?

- **Find the cause of the distress** – missing needs identification. When this is done you have a specific goal to aim for. In this instance she needs a man!

- **Utilise reality.** This woman is cute and

285

has an endearing gap in her teeth.

- **Use humour.** Notice that the solution is fun and funny. Anxious clients lose their sense of humour.

- **Develop strategy to achieve need satisfaction.** She might be too shy to talk to a man but she can sure as hell spit at him! This gets his attention.

This is pure conversational hypnosis. He identifies the problems, utilises her assets and breaks her out of her rigid patterns (a pattern interrupt) by utilising her motivation to alter her situation. The suggestion to spit is the key suggestion. She follows it, even though it's strange but hey, he's a doctor! People used to respect doctors once upon a time. Result – cure. Now I have said in other books – what if hypnosis is just talking. Are you getting my drift Padawan? Sorry for the interlude – back to our case...

'Can you list the reasons you want to change?' (That would be me...)

Her list follows:

- Get rid of anxiety.

- Start afresh.

- I feel emotionally upset and empty. (She therefore wants to feel emotionally calm and full of life!).

That I can do.

'What things have you tried to do to overcome this and how successful were they?'

She has tried acupuncture, hypnotherapy (which helped) – she says the hypnotist 'read stuff out to me'. She has tried herbal stuff, relaxing techniques and meditation all of which had helped her feel better. But it didn't work because the underlying cause – she needs a good man in her life was not addressed. This is 'sticking plaster' therapy. Again, one of the reasons that drug therapy for anxiety disorders can be very dangerous is because it suppresses 'symptoms' much as pain killers suppress pain signals. However the underlying psychic pain source has not been addressed, this may lead to a full blown psychotic episode. You can't run away from reality.

'What activities absorb and fascinate you?' I ask.

She says, 'Going for a swim and going to the

287

gym.'

So what do we learn here? She likes to exercise. Good. But also I suspect she has deep sensuous physical urges that are not met by being a single lady. I go on...

'What do you enjoy most about life?'

She tells me she used to like socialising in groups; this would be a typical female response BUT now she avoids it! The one thing she needs is positive attention and she is flinching from it. This is often the case with anxious people. They flee what they need.

'In what situations do you feel most happy, secure and confident?'

'Back at mums/moms,' she tells me. Freudians would probably see this as a neurotic retreat to a symbolic womb. It's just a stressed, single girl who is turning to mum/mom for support because she has no husband and feels like crap!

'What things have you done that you are most proud of?'

She has a degree from University.

'What strengths do you have that will help you to overcome this problem?'

I am now starting to get her to focus on self-reliant problem solving using her own resources. If you have read my other books you know I call this directionalising the brain. The underlying structure of all good persuasive therapy is 'Not that – this!' You get more of what you focus on.

She tells me that she is a sociable person although quiet. She likes to focus on others and not herself. A good sign. She then goes on to tell me about the 'anxiety attacks'. She fears being on a train especially at rush hour. This is very common; commuting is very stressful. She avoids certain times of day when it comes to all public transport. People who suffer from panic attacks etc. often feel most nervy whilst travelling – along busy motorways, you name it. Why? Because you are exposed. There is nowhere to run to. You are confined, trapped in a space with strangers. Or alone. Your home seems the only safe place – all 'normal' stressors that we all have to cope with become intolerable. Why? Because the background stress levels are too high. The individual is too highly aroused. No, not sexually you perv! This lady is not really phobic – her fear is too general and she is experiencing panic attacks anywhere and everywhere. This is high anxiety, nothing more or less.

'If you could rate your self-worth from 0-10, 10 being you feel great about yourself and 0 utterly worthless what would it be?'
'I hate myself – 1!' she says bluntly.

Now my instinct is that this is not a deep-rooted lack but a situational lack. People can get down on themselves when they feel things should be one way and in reality they are the polar opposite. It turns out I am right because I sort this lady out in 1 session. Yes, 1 session for worry, panic, anxiety and the beginnings of depression; it's easy.

'What things help you relax?'

'I can't concentrate (RH: that's the stress; it's normal). I like to relax. I like chilling and staying in. I like being with friends and going to the gym.'

So she can still relax in certain times and places, just as she can 'do' anxiety at certain times and places.

'So you do exercise?'

'Yes. I go to the gym.'

Even as she is going through this highly stressful and worrying phase of her life and that's all it is, she is exercising. This is probably the only thing keeping her sane. It also shows that her motivation has not been fully hollowed out by the exhaustion of anxiety. Good signs. She is hanging in there – just!

'Do you have any intuitive sense of what has to change within yourself to get you the desired change?'

'I know but...to do it...I am scared about the change. I imagine it and I get anxious about it.' (Misuse of the imagination.)

She is stuck in anxiety any which way she turns – it has permeated the system and generalised.

'Can you think of an image, metaphor or symbol that represents either the problem or solution that you want?' I ask.

'I feel like I am in a black cloud in a low

mood. I feel claustrophobic, pressured, tense.'

This is classic depression imagery-symbolism. She feels trapped. All the predicates are kinaesthetic – I feel x, I feel y. She wants the unpleasant feeling gestalt which she labels 'anxiety' to be replaced by nice ones. All doable. She also tells me,

'I feel sad.'

Now this is why docs/shrinks etc. think that depression means you are 'sad'. No. When we fail to get our needs met and this persists over time because we imagine this will continue forever; anyone would be sad at such a prospect. It is however nonsense. All this lady had to do was go out and meet men! Women are more prone to anxiety than men because a man's mind-set is a problem demands analysis as a basis for taking action: at some future point he intends to act. A woman will tend to ruminate, she will talk about the problem but that won't solve it. You can only solve problems through action. There is also some evidence that women need more external stimulus to generate good feelings. It is far from conclusive however.

Another factor to consider in gender

differences is this: women are emotional creatures. They feel and intuit first then they think about that afterwards. Men will tend to try to think their way logically out of a tight spot. When a woman's brain is overly aroused the emotional part will predominate so much that her ability to think calmly is swamped by the limbic brain. Hypnosis can reteach her how to feel and think clearly: thus she will generate her own solutions.

'Is there any reason you shouldn't change? Is there a part of you that doesn't want to? Do you have warring parts?'

'I hate the fact that I have to change. But I am not myself. I don't look well. I hide it and I am desperate to get better. I can't do it anymore,' she admits; probably with a sigh. I can't remember.

Okay let's break this down: what has she said? Although stuck she has been like this for a while, it seems the norm. The deeper mind is conservative; it doesn't like any change once a pattern is established. Imagine if this were not the case; we would be so impressionable that we'd end up like Woody Allen's Zelig, unable to be ourselves and permanently adjusting ourselves to circumstances etc. Change demands energy. Change demands a reconfiguration. She says she doesn't *feel* herself. This shows that she can dissociate 'it', the anxiety: good. She actually looks fine but her inner turmoil affects her perception of reality: she cannot see reality as it is; she is not reflecting reality back to herself because of the miasma of constant anxiety – the black and white thinking.

'What has prevented the change you want up till now?' (Almost done; for this phase.) 'Nothing worked before; not long term. I want it to go.'

She has reached the therapeutically vital 'enough is enough' moment. Her motivation to release the neuro-physical energy required for change is ready and primed. I just need to steer her brain off in the right direction.

'Have you ever made a similar change or reached a point in your life where you just thought I've had enough and I'm moving forward in a more positive direction?'

'My job. Apart from that I don't think so. I have had that in relationships. I feel let down. My parents had a failed marriage. My upbringing was not normal. There are lots of lies and guilt there. I feel cheated and hurt. I can't let my old relationship go. I think about it all the time...maybe.'

She is merely revealing how she processes all information – past and present through a prism of anxiety. Notice her parents failure has led her to erroneously generalise that she will fail in relationships too: common with children of divorce. Once her mind is calm – this will all effortlessly shift. Now I move on to my usual unmet needs checklist that I use with depressed clients. I told this lady that she was on the cusp of depression; her dreams had recently become more violent and were affecting her sleep quality. She had got to me just in time.

Unmet needs module.

To include the full check-list here would waste space. I give a full example in the appendix. I discovered that...

- She felt completely cut off from wider society. Stuck at home alone – no wonder!

- She felt she was nearing 30 and that she had not achieved what you are 'supposed' to. According to whom?

The media!

- She felt incompetent in her life roles. This was more to do with her mental state than her reality. She was a highly intelligent, resourceful and capable lady. Major transnational banks would not succeed if they hired dim wits. The computational part of her mind was fine.

- She felt insufficiently challenged by life. Why? She was working in an industry in which she was unable to release her true personality. She had a 'prestigious' (according to whom and what criteria?) well paid job; but it was completely unsuited to her needs as a full human being. Remember that line from the Billy Joel song 'James'? 'Do what's good for you or your not good for anybody...'

- She felt insecure in almost all major areas of her life: she hated her job; she was not working at that time because of her anxiety. She had no relationship with the right man. Her need for economic and emotional security was not being met. She was trapped, frustrated, miserable and stuck. Her brain had become her own torture device.

Years after having seen this lady I reflect and conclude the following, though at the time I didn't consciously analyse it: *I just dealt with a challenge with a hypnotic response...*

The story so far: a happy, intelligent, sensitive and highly imaginative girl's little world – her family is devastated by her father abandoning her mother; her sense of security is shattered, she starts to worry. Her worst childhood fear, that her parents would abandon her has been realised. What else lies in store in this world? She starts to look out for more danger. She fears that she like her mother will not be thought attractive enough to commit to in later life. She 'selects' a man in later life who rejects her. This confirms her fears! Oh me! Life is cruel. Having invested so much in this relationship to be dumped at the point she *imagined* she would settle down is too big a blow. She now fears to take a risk on any man: she is man phobic! But she needs a man to be happy! She fears what she needs. Oops. Not good. Having 'adopted' the shallow, materialistic values of post 1960's Britain she works in a job which completely fails to fulfil her deepest personal needs or meet the kind of man she would desire – finance is a profession for professional assholes! She feels stuck in a rut of her own making and yet she fears to do what she knows she must to be happy once more and...

...now it's my turn to play!!!

Hypnotic interventions for severe worry script.

(The problem matrix was bound together by chains of worry - constant worry/rumination. This is where I target my attack. When the worry is stopped the brain will right itself – it took 3 separate modules in 1 session to do this. What follows is what I specifically did... Deep and VERY relaxing hypnosis assumed.)

Part 1: Seeing reality as it is.

'As you notice just how relaxed you can become, you can know that we will be working effortlessly together so that you can find just the right ways to **feel better already.** You know the importance now, to your long-term emotional wellbeing, of **getting certain essential needs met** in reality. And your deeply creative unconscious mind will help you generate so many different ways of doing so, now.

With this in mind, can you imagine going to a place in nature that symbolises an amazing sense of soothing calm? Perhaps it's a place you've been to already. It can be an imaginative construct because you can **use your imagination constructively, now.** Notice all the vividness of the sensory modalities – sights, sounds, smells and more. Be there fully now. Inside **you're unconscious** mind.

Have you ever had the experience, and I know you have, from time to time of **your mind becoming so calm and still? Now,** I don't know how that happened, you do. All the past ripples of stress have dissipated. Have you ever seen a pond or lake in nature whose surface was beautifully calm? So that you **feel calm** in turn. And have you noticed that you can go to places where they have those funny mirrors that distort your reflection? They can make you look really short and squishy or long and stretchy or wide and fat. The thing is, amusing as that seems, it prevents you from being able to **see reality as it really is.** We all have a very real ability to stop and **reflect on matters calmly.**

Have you ever looked into a flattering mirror that reflected all of your good points? That made you attractive. A mirror that made you **feel good** as you noticed that pleasing reflection. There was no distortion or displacement. Because when we look into certain pleasing mirrors we can **focus on your good points.** Perhaps one or several good points, your inherent strengths can spring to mind. That's it. It's important to be able to **notice good things about yourself and life.** Times you did stuff really well and were justly proud of that. Times you learnt skills that enriched your life. Times when you overcame a problem. Just take a minute or so to get in touch with such experiences while I am quiet... *(Shhh for 1 minute...)*

Within your deepest self, there are latent resources that you can tap into. I want you to **become aware of all your resources and abilities** that will help you **feel much more optimistic about things in general,** without knowing how you did it consciously. There really are things you can look forward to as you **take real steps to build a better future for yourself, now.** Hope is rekindled in anyone through positive actions that anyone at all can take to achieve **deeply desired goals.** Goals that move you forward through this journey we call life. As you act differently, you'll start to **feel differently.**

You may **feel wonderful now,** just like that, or improvements may just happen quicker than you thought they might, so that before you know it you **feel much better already** for some mysterious reason. This can and does happen. Just knowing this can make you **feel much more hopeful,** which in turn makes you **feel strongly optimistic,** and all this is grounded in a **deep calm** that comes from **reflecting reality realistically.**

The real way to effectively **feel an all-encompassing calm** is to **stop negatively speculating unnecessarily...**when that occurs, **now,** you'll find you **calmly reflect on things objectively instead...**And that reminds me of a story...

The mere in the fenland* metaphor.

(An east English wetland or reedy marsh.)

In the old eastern wilds of England there used to be large stretches of boggy fenland. Marshland below sea level. The whole place was filled with a magical aura of mystery, especially at night. One evening an old man was making his way through the marsh taking an old and well-trodden track. But a storm was brewing unbeknownst to him. It began to

rain. Lightly at first then harder. The chopping rain stirred up the water in the meres and the place seemed to alter its appearance. Even though nothing had really changed. It soon became hard to find the familiar route. The man became worried. The storm grew and grew. The wind lashed the trees and willows which blew like spectres in the dark. The moon had all but vanished behind the towering grey clouds that filled and bullied the sky. The surface of the waterways in the fens became so choppy and uneven that the man found it harder to find his old way and became quite lost. In despair he sat down by a large mere and looked out at its storm-battered surface. Strange and startling shapes were thrown up. Shadows and bizarre reflections seemed to leap and dash across the water and the man became even more scared. The water surface was frenzied and distorted, beaten by rain so that everything it reflected appeared weird and fey*
(*unworldliness, mystery).

But soon enough the storm passed...As it blew itself out the water in the mere began to **settle nicely...**The surface began to **smooth and level out...**The trees stopped waving their branches and **a still calm** returned. The great white moon appeared through the cloud break and the water revealed all her glory as it was high above. The fens seemed suddenly familiar and comforting...the surface of the mere was **clear and at peace once more.** All the reflections were grounded in the reality of the surroundings and the man realised – there is **nothing really to fear here** at all. In this frame of mind he found he could **easily continue** on his journey. And there's a lesson or two in that...is there not?

Stop pointlessly ruminating module.

(In order to stop worry you must stop pointless trance loops about unmet needs; this next short module shows you how...)

Now we spoke about how you used to go into those un-resourceful trance loops in the past. I understand your reasons and you did it well but if you were to feel that even starting to happen in future you can **STOP!** And perhaps a symbol that symbolises STOP will pop into your mind. This will be your signal to focus on the present realities around you so that **you no longer slip into pointless, negative trances.** If you are going to **daydream productively** – focus those daydreams on what you want to happen. After all you get more of what **you focus** on. And then you'll

take action in reality to **get your deepest needs as an individual met, now.** The purpose of any trance, any use of the imagination is to use it to **create the kind of change you want in reality.** All achievements start out as an idea. Then we use our creativity which operates just fine when **you are a very relaxed person** to generate ways to solve problems easily and elegantly. And your creative part wants to help and will work for you at an unconscious level in order to help you **fashion the kind of life you'd truly like to live.** So you'll pleasantly **recognise all the signs of progress** on the way and enjoy the journey too. Learning from mistakes and moving on beyond the past demands of a perfect you who never existed anyway. Daily, simple pleasures give you such joy.

Future pace a calm and resourceful you getting needs met etc.

Everyone has needs that need meeting. We have discussed this. You know there are certain needs specific to you that need meeting and your unconscious will help you formulate ideas, take action to **get your essential needs met, now.** It's time to use that powerful imagination of yours to build the kind of life affirming future you want. By visualising the kind of person you'd like to be, doing the things that would allow you to **feel awesome pleasure in daily living** you send a message to your deeper mind that this is the direction you now wish to go in...

Dissociated rehearsal.

Just picture a calm, resilient, resourceful confident you on your mind's movie screen getting some of those needs met. It's just part of what you do. That's it. Recall what we discussed – you have a need to **feel connected...** You need to be able to **achieve worthwhile goals...** You need to find ways to **feel you excel** at what you do... You need to **have meaningful challenges** that can be overcome... You need to **feel a sense of security and control** in several areas... You have a deep desire to **feel attractive** and meet an attractive man/woman...someone special...I think this will help you **feel you belong, now.**

So simply go ahead while I'm quiet for a whole minute, which is more than enough trance time, to imagine getting these purposeful desires met that will enrich you. *(Not a word while you clock count...)*

Excellent! You are doing really well. Now that you have the sense of your much better future, now, that you **feel better about your future...**you can imagine a you who is **feeling much better.** They are in bed after a **wonderful deep sleep** and just about to rise... Float into that person as they awaken **feeling so refreshed. You feel good in the mornings** after **such deep restorative sleep.** You can imagine going through a whole hopeful day, doing so many real things that give you pleasure. You are active and sociable. You connect easily. You notice how much calmer you feel. Your mind and body are so much more relaxed. You notice your strength growing. Your **confidence increasing greatly.** You **feel incredible** in mind and body so that you **feel wholesome again** and that may surprise and delight you until **it all just becomes an unconscious habit, now,** as **any and all necessary re-organisations of subconscious structures occur, now.** That's it. And these new templates will seek appropriate completion upon awakening. I'll be silent again for a while as you **rehearse these patterns of success, unconsciously.** *(Pause for a whole minute again.)*

Summation.

Very good. The only real question is just how much more are **you're really going to enjoy the process of being you** again? The process of **you're enjoying life.** The process of you **experiencing so many more pleasures.** With these powerful changes deeply embedded in your mind **you have a greater sense of control and real security** that you are now moving forward in your life as you wish. You are the director of your destiny. You will be able to **feel more relaxed in general** and able to **rest and relax very deeply when you need** to as you can **stop the old back and white thinking** and **reflect calmly** on so many things, **seeing reality as it is, now.** All storms blow over. I wonder what beneficial improvements you'll notice first? It's time to **get back to the adventure of living.** That's right!

Part 2: Stop worrying.

(Now we've restored a sense of deep calm we need to 'bash' excess worry out of her skull...)

The good thing about using hypnosis to **stop worrying, unconsciously...** is that you can, in this changing state **slow all appropriate internal processes all the way down. Now.** There is a calmer rate of breathing that helps **still your mind.** You have always known how to do that unconsciously too.

Firstly – what is the intent of worry? To run an internal check to verify that **you are safe now.** In order to do that you have generated 'what if' scenarios in your imagination. 'What happens if I do this?' 'What will their response be?' 'If I make that move he makes that move and she does this and on and on...' But pictures in the mind are representations of reality only. We can speculate about the past and what happened or might of happened and what it all means. We can be concerned as to how we appear to certain others and what they might have thought about a whole host of possible things. Will things go as expected? Is the unexpected always unpleasant? Will the outcome be good or bad? Or whatever else lies between before **meanings change anyway.** And that excessive speculation requires energy.

I had a man who had an obsessive phobia after he was mugged that lead him to worry, back then, about how far he was once outside from the safety of any building and he nodded when I said all that mental effort must be tiring. Thankfully – here, you can **rest that function,** you can **rest deeply** here in hypnotic trance far deeper than in any other way. I'd like to thank that part of you that has worried to excess for all it was merely doing to overprotect you back then. It has always had your best interests, your personal safety at heart. It did all those old worry loops and patterns, those outdated habits so well. But now, I know, that each and both of you and it recognises that now is the time to **learn some much better habits.** And you can loop these new ones at the unconscious level instead. As a consequence you can **relax more** and **feel a whole lot better.**

The attempt to attempt speculating about anything and everything that could, might and maybe may be *(NFH: not a typo – confusion)* is just too much of a strain. It's inefficient. You can **relax** knowing that your subconscious is always looking out for things you need to be alerted to, so that another part can **take it easy, now,** in the future and with regard to how you think about your past, now. Underneath all that past tension is a vast reservoir of **calm and relaxation;** it is always there deep down under that. And as all that **unnecessary arousal simply melts**

away, in hypnosis you can take a nice sigh inside and go deeper as I talk to you about how to do that which will help you, **get more of what you really want.** That's it. How much more **comfort of all kinds** do you already feel?

Dissociate from worry patterns.

Can you recall a time you were worried about something? Future, past, others, you, this, that, whatever. Doesn't matter. I know that process of speculative introspection starts a certain specific way for you. Some see images and feel unpleasant sensations and then comment on things in a worried tone inside. Some feel sensations in response to stimuli, comment in a shrill tone and see panicky pictures. Others **still** talk to themselves in panicky tones, feel bad and see scary movies. And there are, I am sure, many more permutations of that old way you used to process information. But the good thing is if you **process certain information differently at a deep unconscious level,** you'll find **things shift** all by themselves for the better. But before the what ifs run lose, before the voice inside rises too much in pitch, before those movies absorb your attention as they once did – **STOP THAT NOW!** And float right out of the old worried you and just look at yourself from a nice safe distance. A distance that allows you to **see the bigger picture...**to **become more objective, detached and free** about so many things. That's right. You are doing great. Feel how much calmer you can only feel when you **adopt another perspective.** You can go over, through, tunnel under, fly above, barge passed, hop around – there is always more than one rigid choice, is there not? There is a real need to **have a more flexible approach** to certain things.

Looking at the old worried self.

As you look at that worried you of the past – you can know, really know that it's time to **leave that pattern of negative speculation in the past now.** How worried do they look? How much pointless effort were they wasting on what ifs? How tense does that body look? How much better do you feel from this new vantage point? The fact is too much of anything is never good. It's like the story of goldilocks and the bears. As a human you are gifted from birth with an amazing ability to **process information rationally and calmly, now.** Knowing this, doing this, permits you to **let go and relax about**

stuff, to ponder things pleasantly, think about this or that with **a more balanced point of view.** And that's a nice thing to know, is it not?

What if a colour of that calm state of reflection just spreads all through you now. Spreading and generalising, throughout the system, more and more and more, now. Only use as much energy as is realistically required in any endeavour. That just makes sense doesn't it?

Getting some objectivity module.

In order for you to **let go of past stressful responses,** it can help to do the following: a person may need to **get a little perspective on things,** is that not so? Simply imagine from this detached position becoming increasingly able to **see many things in a wider context — now!** Float all the way out of yourself and float up and up and up! Higher and higher and higher! Float so high that you **rise above all that** – go so high that you can see the entire road/street and town *(etc.)* of that place where you once where! That's it! And then go further still – higher and higher so that you can see the entire country or continent that that place is found within. Go higher and higher – far hypnotically higher and yet deeper than ever so that you can see this blue planet from the reaches of outer space! That's right.

From this new vantage point those **old concerns seem of far less significance** than they once did; is that not so? You have found within yourself and through this manoeuvre that you can **feel more detached about so many appropriate things** because that's what happens when you **see things in a new way.** Experiences of past and present – those yet to come. Calmness can be invited in easily in so many situations when you **draw upon deep unconscious resources** at just the right time and place, when you need it, now. In this place – deep inside you notice you are indeed **staying calm in ways you didn't know you could,** consciously. Taking it all in your stride no matter how others react. It's nice to know you **have that effortless yet powerful control, now.** How pleasant can you imagine it being as you **take a much calmer course of action and manner** to things which once would have bothered you? Some attitudes **soothe the mind** in real ways, ways that help and your unconscious can generate many of your own ideas that will help you; isn't that nice to know that a part of you really is always aiding you in all your efforts? *(NFH: Are you aware we just double-dissociated the client?)*

Calmness in the face of uncertainty module.

(Here we layer in helpful ideas...)

From now on you'll notice you can **be more relaxed when faced with uncertainty.** In fact there is something I know about you and that is you are capable of a high degree of self-hypnosis already. If you couldn't **enter a deeper state of hypnosis** you wouldn't have been able to worry back then, in the past, now. It takes **a profound state of trance** to access fantasies of any kind. You had excelled at the skill of generating disaster movies of things that never came to be. Like an engineer I saw once who only imagined how things could go wrong. You see, you need to be able to **contextualise and compartmentalise certain abilities** for an appropriate time and place. But the thing was - there was **no danger,** not really, so **that body can relax.** There is no immediate physical threat so **that mind can heal and respond in better ways.**

You ever heard the story about that fellow who kept running around telling everyone the sky was going to fall on everyone's head yet – it never did or could? Some folks set time limits and dates for certain bad things to happen, yet those dates come and go and yet here we are. **Here, you are still.** Beliefs are not the same as evidence or facts. Anyone can sincerely believe things that aren't true. But when we, when you **step back and look at things afresh,** you'll see that the old pattern of looking out for threats that don't even exist is not the best strategy if you want to **see through calm eyes, a relaxed brain and body.**

The only thing you can be certain about on some occasions is that you can't always be certain because then all the risk and fun and adventure and thrills and surprise would go out of life! Would you clean every part of a house 3 times a day or 4? No; some things can be overdone. There is just the right level of any activity. A real security of mind arrives when **you have a very deep faith in yourself** and you **trust your unconscious to do what it does. Now,** as you ponder these helpful ideas in any way you really want, we'll continue...

It's funny that you thought I was going to hypnotise you, whatever that means, but instead I just talked to you while you were quiet and listened in your own way...You learned that **you don't need to obsessively check uncheckable things**, you learned that you can **relax with uncertainty,** you learned that you can relearn to **access your sense of humour** to **laugh more** and **see the funny side of so many things** because that's what a calm and happy person does and that's your birth right.

Deep down you know you are loved. Deep down you know that you know more than you know you know. Deep down you know that you have a good heart. That you are capable. That you have attractive qualities that many people admire. Importantly you also learned to **conserve your energy.** That in **deep**... hypnotic...**rest**...you can **heal.** Whatever 'healing' means to you. You'll find as a result of these changes you'll **fall asleep easily** and **sleep so well at night.**

Installing colour feelings in the calm you.

Now you can see that you over there who was worried but as a result of what we have already done he/she has made all the right changes. See how that person's entire body language and calm face communicates a person with peace of mind. They know the world isn't perfect. They know only so much can be done. They can see much more clearly.

Imagine now a colour that represents these new feelings which are really just old ones that you've reconnected to spread through that much more relaxed you over there – filling you with all the right feelings you need to **remain calm** more and more and more... that's right! With these new feelings flowing evenly and gently through them you realise that you **think like a calm person,** you **feel like a calm person** and you **act like a calm person.** The small things are so very unimportant.

Thoughts are more relaxed...they may even **slow down** somewhat...certain images that once troubled you can be placed in that place in your mind where some things seem of much less significance...certainly smaller and perhaps black and white...The unconscious knows just the right adjustments to make without effort. You know that you cannot predict the future perfectly because that's not possible or desirable and so you **relax with that fact** and find that your new relaxed breathing patterns support these changes.

Associate into the relaxed you.

(NFH: Changes have been safely rehearsed in a dissociative way – now we 'wedge' them in…)

Now it's one thing to observe and yet a more powerful thing to **experience all these changes first hand.** So as soon as you are quite ready, drift or float into that new calm you…That's great! Feel how differently you feel, think, act and importantly *believe* now… You find that subtle communications from the subconscious such as intuitions and insights are now free to flow as lesser known sets of associations can be accessed that help you. The mask of tension is gone – gone for good. You no longer need the old worry patterns because you know how to **plan calmly.** You will find that you **focus intently on what you need to** much more easily. You'll find that you are calmer with others, of all types. You take sensible precautions and **leave the rest to the subconscious, now.** The best way to solve problems is to deal with them as and when they arise so that they don't pile up. Then **everything seems far more manageable.** Break any task into small manageable chunks that you can easily deal with. Sooner than you know it **problems _are_ solved.** You know how to stop worrying and pop back to external reality, so you can relax more upon awakening. Fantasises are one thing, reality quite another – you are now able to **calmly distinguish between the two.** You stop misusing your imagination and use it to **generate good ideas.** You can use your powerful 'what if' ability to **create the kind of future you'd like** always paying attention to feedback and making appropriate adjustments. No one has total certainty – but **you are more in control** as a result of this awareness. Do what you can, accept what you can't – for now.

I bet that from this much calmer perspective you somehow find yourself making sound decisions that move your life forward, in all the myriad of ways that it does. You realise that analysis is one thing and letting stuff go is quite another. Trust the deepest part of you much more profoundly. It knows all your needs better than the other part, it knows how to satisfy them. That's nice to know, is it not? Haven't you? You will **feel much more hopeful and happy** as a consequence of these learnings here today.

Isn't it quite reassuring to know that positive surprises are possible? That you can't know everything and so you can just **start living more positively, now.** You are doing so well and as another part of you can **lock in these changes** and you feel knowing feelings that a profound good has occurred, let's **get rid of those old unnecessary fears** that once held you back. Because we all get more of what we focus on...

Part 3: Getting rid of unnecessary fears.

(All anxiety clients are good visualisers – it's a big part of fear – showing ourselves disaster movies in our heads. We want to keep the imagination and planning abilities but tone it down and reconfigure it to sensible levels – here's how we do it...)

And that reminds me of a story.

The man who couldn't stop checking.

Once upon a time, not so very long ago there was a man who was very finicky about his job. His job was to check for possible problems – the problem was he was so good at his job that he became overzealous, in fact he couldn't stop doing what he was doing: he started checking for problems everywhere, all the time and that was tiring and boring. He realised after a little time and a distinct lack of enjoyment that we all need to do just enough and then let it go. Checking for problems once per problem is surely enough for anyone. Then we exit that task and do something more fulfilling and satisfying because the part that did and does that can **regularly switch that mechanism off, unconsciously** once it's done its job sufficiently. Doesn't that just make sense?

Fake 'fear' as an ability gone wrong.

(Time to reframe...)

There is a time and a place for fear – for some things you need that response: it's a good ability – it keeps you alive and thriving – out of danger's reach. I'd like to thank that part of you that does that. But there is such a thing as unnecessary fear – this was your subconscious response to past scary images and thoughts that drifted through your mind back then. And that can be an exhausting talent. It isn't much fun – unless you are Stephen King! There is a time to **stop doing that** to just **live your life calmly and sensibly.** Because when **you are so calm,** you can **easily see the world as it really is.** And what if **this new set of ways can become a daily reality for you, now?** What if you could leave past unwanted habits behind you and **feel very confident**? What if you could feel exceptionally hopeful? Because you don't have to but you might prefer to **just know, with a deep inner knowing feeling that things somehow find a way of working out just right.** For there is a far deeper part of you unconsciously protecting you and looking out for your most fundamental interests and it works best when **you live calmly.**

A gentling, an inner kindness can occur in this place. A softening of rough edges. A soothing of the soul. Everything that man has made started as the result of his imagination and ideas. He has an amazing ability to **be very creative in productive, satisfying ways.** There is a time to examine honest doubts, to think critically, to check details but we must all do that in a way that we **conserve precious energy efficiently.** Fears and worries that are not based on facts are just a waste of your precious life time and **that stuff can all stop now.** You are finding much better ways, here, are you not? That's it. There is a purpose and a meaning to your life and here you can rediscover it – **focus your energies** on that; the super objective of your living in this world. Something that is unique to you and your life; isn't it really time you **follow your own course through this world**? We all need to **achieve things that have meaning** to us and us alone. While I'm quiet, take a period of hypnotic reflecting and wondering to **reconnect to the wellsprings of who you fundamentally are...**

(Pause like you promised; 1 minute should do...)

Taking control of the powerful imaginative faculty.

Okay. You have a free virtual reality machine in your mind – we call it the imagination. It is one of the things that makes us wholly human. Again I would like to thank that part that used to worry and conjure all those alarming what ifs: you did your job to perfection but I would like you to play a more productive role if you're willing, something much more fun and enjoyable because the old set of patterns had held this person back from living the kind of life they want and deserve. Starting right now, what is much better for this person is to **think constructively,** focus on what they want and use that powerful imagination to **picture things going well,** one way or another.

Someone once asked Mao Tse Tung what the significance of the French Revolution was and he replied, 'We may not know yet.' Going back to unwanted ways that were is an absurdity, silly, not right, not who this person is beyond what they weren't really anyway: and who are you really that is deeply relaxed with crystal clarity of mind and **a sense of relaxed alertness as your base state**? That's it! A human being is a creature of possibilities not grim fatalism: unlike all the other creatures on this planet we, you, can **shape your destiny!** No one need know the future in order to **be comfortable inside.** No one need know the future in order to **take control over your imaginative processes,** so that **it works for you, now.** No one need know the future in order to **relax, chill out and act cool.** No one need know the future in order to **let old silly fears drift away** like dreams upon awakening. There is real fear which you need and you can keep that for appropriate times and responses BUT 99.9% of human fear is and was caused by a misuse of the imagination. The good thing is you are really able to **only use that ability when**

genuinely needed, this allows you to **remain grounded in the reality about you.** That wonderful mechanism can be switched on and off – in fact imagine a light switch in your mind. Whenever you need to **switch that faculty off more often** or **do that old response much less frequently** or at all, just visualise a light switch and turning that mental light switch off switches off that internal movie theatre just as if a hypnotist had clicked his fingers *(do so)*, now. That's it. Your imagination works for you, now – this is a post...hypnotic...command!

The future is not set in stone! Who can truly know the precise nature of the future? No one. Who can know why things happened the way they did with 100% certainty – no one? Who is so powerful that they can control all the external acts in the realm of material reality so that it will go as they wish or imagined they wished? How would we learn? How would we develop new understandings? How would we mature? Knowing that, **you can relax with the uncertainty of certain processes** which allows you to powerfully **let that past garbage go.** You do not need to have all data or omnipotence to **really lighten up about so many things,** is that not so? Feel that nice flow of calm and ordered energy flow through you now, perhaps a tingle of that joyous excitement you can feel when you know deep inside that **all is well.** And more importantly the **deep and profound confidence you own** that despite what happens - you can handle it all. Your sense of humour really helps. It's possible to **refuse to take things so seriously.** I have a friend like that.

As all possibilities of your future potential exist in your mind before **you make a bright future your reality,** I would like you to **use that imagination as you wish** to picture what things you would like to happen in your adventure we call life. Go ahead and **dream** of such exciting, healthy and realistic possibilities with that biological virtual reality machine you possess for free. This can be like those creative, so-called 'brainstorming' sessions that people use to **generate positive ideas** that move you forward, **now.** I'll be silent for a profound minute of **change.** *(Do so...60 seconds later...)*

Living with courage.

Good. So, you have taken back control of events, and how much more relaxed do you feel as a result? What has happened wasn't what you deserved, it wasn't your fault – it's just what happened. **Forgive yourself** for being perfectly imperfect. Let all pointless guilt fade...away, now. And this allows you to **move on** from all that. We need to make mistakes in order to **learn, really learn;** all suffering passes and what we learn can make it somehow have value. You can take any event, an occurrence and draw a positive interpretation or re-configuration from it. If something doesn't work it means you have an opportunity to **get creative** and do something new. You were born with all the resources you needed to **live successfully;** it is the powerful heritage of your ancestral genetics that you have to thank for this reality. Automaticity is replaced by flexibility, nooooo-oooow! You don't have to wed a method. The best form of transport was once a pedal bike but men have since flown in space.

The courage to **live life with zest** arrives when you simply **do courageous things.** This world is not for the timid but for the brave of heart. Once more into the breach dear friends, once more! If you fall off of the horse - get back in the saddle! **Be bold** and mighty forces will come to your aid. Have you ever been on a good roll when everything just turned out right, again and again and again?

There's a state of mind that goes with that, now. Re-access all your most resourceful states. Lock them in so that the old **less than helpful states diminish completely;** like slippery hands that cannot get a firm hold. It will be interesting, perhaps you're curious to discover what the best results of these powerful suggestions will be? And you can **respond uniquely yet powerfully** to the words and ideas that resonate most. Going deeper and deeper into a state of wonderful absorption as certain subconscious structures change, improve for the better. There is always only ever more to learn. And that's the beginning of true wisdom, is it not? Have you ever heard an infectious laugh? How good did it make you feel? Sometimes things just tickle us, don't they? **Courage is yours** when you recognise the absurdity of so many things. How many times have you displayed the kind of courage you want and need? Perhaps a time, several may pop into your mind and they bring a set of **positive feelings that remain** with them, now. *(Be quiet for 30 secs to a minute...)*

Summation suggestions.

And I know a secret that you know too: you can **relax far deeper than you**

consciously know... You can unconsciously trust that whatever happens, whatever the future brings – **you'll be okay.** You know that you only **use that powerful imagination precisely when it's needed;** no more, no less. Your creativity is so useful and did you know that even the ancients knew that man must **be creative to feel fully alive.** And how will your unique creativity manifest itself? You have learned many ways to **positively yet profoundly process certain information differently.** And have you ever watched anything in a **dispassionate** way – just noticing things? In that state you probably noticed that you were more aware of things that were occurring than others and what's it like when you **do that at the right time and place**? You may find you can **feel calm and collected more often.** The sights, sounds, sensations that come into anyone's awareness can pass through while a far deeper part of you simply notices; you don't always need to react so energetically to the temporary. There can be great fun in not knowing and relaxing with that. What if past unnecessary, **unrealistic fears and doubts lose all power over you, now.** Have you ever been to an aquarium and watched all the bright coloured, dumb and silly little fishes swim by? Or watched flocks of birds migrating? You can do so many things with **a far greater sense of calm – inside** or out. It all was, is and shall be only in your mind; wasn't it? And haven't you? Nooo-ooow! As you take these final moments to **rest in such a tranquil state,** you may have already noticed that **you feel so incredibly good**? And after I awaken you...**all changes have been made and finalised:** you recognise that **you are calm, re-energised, confident, focused yet alert** all in one go because that is just a permanent part of who you are. That's it. You have unlearned what you had learned. As things are always changing, you may as well direct the change in ways favourable to you. Perfect!

(Throw in exduction of choice.)

<u>*Brief analysis.*</u>

Okay that was quite a long and hefty session – my voice may well have been hoarse after. Let's break down what I did.

- Using suggestions, metaphors, positive associations and symbols I layer in idea after idea about how this lady can redo calm. She already knows how to do it: in the hypnotic state I revivify it, stabilise it and link it to wakefulness etc.

• I dissociate her from unresourceful past states and processes and get her to mentally rehearse feeling and acting as she wants to: this is a positive use of her imagination, the exact opposite of what she's been doing up till now. These visualisations act as models of how she does calm: the unconscious takes then on as templates of how to act in reality – they are visual suggestions. Utilising our powerful urge to imitate behaviour is a great tool for hypnotic work. I call this 'imitating your best self'.

• Initially worrying is often partly a conscious mind act: I need to outflank consciousness – go to the director ('other than conscious processes') and tell 'it' to tell the over-active obsessive bit upfront to take a chill pill. Worry is over analysis – the conscious mind is trying to usurp the deeper mind's role of detecting genuine danger and generating solutions to problems. Hence all the suggestions for 'trusting' the unconscious etc. A worried mind is overloading itself, hence the exhaustion. It's like a person who won't delegate!

- I describe the internal processes involved with what we call 'calmness' and by so doing reteach her how to do it: this is 'modelling' in the hypnotic state; notice I am very specific in how I tell her how to process information differently especially when she is confronted by challenge. This I derive from NLP. Most importantly I teach her, again through modelling, specifically how to control her internal processes and how to react to certain thoughts and images more dispassionately.

- Permissive hypnosis is always the best way to treat such problems: save strictly authoritarian for the simple stuff.

- Think of severe worry and depression as a giant tangled ball of wool that you must gradually untangle.

- Take your time and speak calmly and smoothly throughout because that's how you want the client to feel –

geddit?: be congruent. You need to give your clients enough time to process the component parts of information you are feeding into their brain to deprogramme it thoroughly.

- I suggest, and again I'm just a hypnotist and this is only a suggestion, that you might like to write out the above script and take it apart, analysing each component part – this will teach you how to construct your own and you won't just be reading my scripts but constructing your own from core principles – the key to success and self-reliance in any field. Novices especially will benefit from this.

- I dealt with the 3 pronged problem matrix with my lengthy script above – the solution matrix. This lady was 'cured' in one session: it was easy. Your clients don't need drastic overhauls – they need subtle shifts and redirectionalisation to more resourceful patterns and potentials that they already possess. Once you've elicited 'em - lock em in. Simple.

- Notice the whole thing just seems like me talking in a kind of dreamy wistful way about how someone does 'calmness' – the less weird and more mundane, the less likely it is resisted. It's just a conversational monologue after all and my sneaky embeds do lots of the work anyway. Ain't I a stinker!? There is something of an ethical sophist in all good hypnotists.

Case 2: A heroic O.C.D client!

Something I learned about OCD sufferers is that they are often a heroic bunch: their anxiety is much influenced by a desire to protect others from danger. Not always but many a time in my experience. If you read OCD sufferer's websites they often say stuff like, 'Don't use hypnosis. I used it once and it didn't work!' Once is not conclusive evidence of anything. They never consider the competence of the hypnotist; they also generalise that ALL hypnotists do the same thing. No, we are not doctors. There are probably as many differing interventions as there are hypnotists.

The first thing you do before you do anything else is what? Detraumatise the OCD client. Like the stutterer/stammerer, like the nervous twitch client there is always a level of trauma which must be removed first. With OCD, once the extreme fear response is gone the subconscious has no need for the obsessions and rituals: the rest is child's play. OCD is also a matter of control. That is why I start (after the 'How to detraumatise anyone' pattern) to teach them about how much influence anyone can reasonably expect to have.

All OCD clients have unmet needs: find out which ones are missing and tell them to get them satisfied. Let's get on with the script. Like all interventions – they must be suited to the unique client before you; the solution matrix you design with be the opposite of their unique problem matrix. In some instances you must help a person overcome the loss of a loved one etc. too. But the following is a good, generic set of ideas that should help the therapist/hypnotist assist a wide variety of OCD clients.

The soothing away OCD script.

(Very deep and relaxing hypnosis assumed. Make sure a component part of the induction is PMR – Progressive Muscles Relaxation based. The key intent is to relax the mind and body of the OCD sufferer. When unconscious relaxation is restored OCD 'symptoms' lack the 'supporting' environment that engendered them. Restoring deep relaxation is the way to OCD freedom.)

Part 1: Insert the 'How to detraumatise anyone' pattern here.

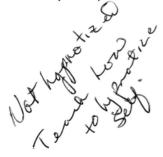

336

Part 2: Re-establishing a realistic sense of control.

Good. Now, as **you are in a very relaxed and deeply receptive state** you can, in just the right way, unlearn what you had learned about **your realistic sense of control, now.** No one can control everything – at any one time **you have varying degrees of influence.** As you begin the process of **feeling much happier** than before you can know that a key part of that is that anyone at all must accept that even, if only for a time, you must accept some things. And an idea that you can ponder now, unconsciously, is all of us must be quite clear in our own minds about that which we have any real influence over; is that not so?

As you **let go of old, unnecessary obsessions, rituals and compulsions, now** you can know that you have greater potential for influence than you knew consciously, but we must all go about the process of influence in just the right way. With a deeply relaxed and calm mind and body working together in harmony, as one focused unit, you will **notice more opportunities to succeed.** You see, when we are younger we can often mistakenly come to *perceive* that we

337

have much less power to influence things than we really do. And at other times we can *perceive* that we have far, far more influence than we really do: it's about the reality of 'balance'. Our degree of control or influence as I prefer to call it varies at any one time from 100% to something less than that. No matter what situation you are in there is always a degree of leverage. In some situations we have a great deal of control. Perhaps one or several may come to mind while I'm quiet for about 20 seconds? *(Shhh up!)* Good, that's the way...and at other times the degree of influence is realistically less and you can **consider such times very calmly** in hypnosis – looking at them on a TV screen over there in black and white if it helps. I'll pause while you process that *(Shhh for 20 seconds or so again...)*

Excellent. So as **you are adjusting your perceptions of these realities** it can be soothing to know that myths of total control can just fade away like daydreams of childhood that could never really be and what you are left with is the joyous knowledge that **you have a great deal of influence over your own life.** Sometimes we can influence others very effectively. If my niece or nephew are in a bad mood I know how to make them laugh and **feel good again.** But I know I have no influence over the weather. I can use an umbrella if it rains or dress in summer clothes if its hot. Isn't it about time that **you completely relax about the real level of influence you have.** You can take steps over time to improve things you would like to change by **setting realistic goals.** And because you are more relaxed and calm than ever **these changes are easy to maintain, now.**

Sometimes we must wait until we have certain resources in order to influence some things and that requires that you **develop an unconscious attitude of patience.** We may not know what we need to know yet and you can learn to **be comfortable with a temporary degree of uncertainty.** There is always only more to lean, here. As you cannot control everything perhaps unnecessary feeling of shame, guilt, frustration, powerlessness and anger can **be soothed** away as **your responses normalise.** That's it. You should only ever accept responsibility for things you are truly responsible for because that is the mature adult attitude to all different kinds of things as **certain patterns change.**

As children, or just as our younger selves with that information and that way of processing it, we can imagine that one unpleasant experience tells us all we need to know but here, in hypnosis, it is time to **stop overgeneralising about some things.** Because when you used to do that back then, you used to pattern match things that weren't actually connected. Just as you once believed that you lacked influence from time to time when the reality is **you have the power to influence, now,** and this new empowering belief and more positive generalisation will spread throughout the system spreading a greater sense of **your personal power, now.** That's right. And you can feel a knowing feeling that things have shifted significantly already without knowing what they might be. When you learn to **exert wise influence,** I wonder in what marvellous ways your life improves as your success builds on your success, more and more and more!

Have you ever heard that saying, **'Do what you can, accept what you can't and have the wisdom to discern between the two,'**? You are capable of applying these new learnings to many situations. You have influence when you use it. What if you came to **adopt some empowering new beliefs** such as – **'There is _always_ something positive that can be done.'** Or maybe, **'What someone else has done _you_ can do.'** Perhaps you can learn to believe right now that **you are _never_ in a cage.** What if you began to learn that **you have more freedom to act than you know** (?) What if you changed some unconscious patterns so that you can **see and utilise _every_* opportunity for progress** (?)

(OCD sufferers often have a sense of having to be 'perfect'; often in vain attempts to please an un-pleasable person: the above should shift that pattern without even mentioning 'perfectionism'.)

Future pace.

I want you to imagine now, on a movie screen over there, an amazing time when **you've accepted these ideas** noticing how much your life has changed for the better. I want you to picture what you'll be doing differently. How you'll be living with **a sense of greater freedom, now.** How you are doing things you once only dreamed were possible until **your attitudes shift appropriately.** And this all feels an instinctive part of your identity now as you realise those old patterns were not you at all. You **feel more assertive,** you **set limits** and you **feel an enormous sense of your own capacity to influence and control the outcome of events** no matter what happened in the past as **meanings change.** Somehow there's more playfulness. Imagine all these things and more, now, as I am quiet for a bit as you **do what needs to be done** to **feel deep satisfaction and contentment** in your life. That's it. *(Silence for 20 seconds...)*

Great! You can **feel so excited** about the many possibilities of these changes because **you are not a control freak.** You know there are times when it's best to **relax and go with the flow** and at other times it may be best to **react calmly to unfolding events.** And as your unconscious implements certain changes in feelings, perspectives and anything else it knows needs to be updated appropriately and safely, I would like your creative mind to visualise stepping into that time, going through those events and situations first hand with a feeling of increased joy, freedom, control and real influence. Always bearing in mind never to expect from people what they are incapable of giving. It's nice to know we are all on our own quest through this life and the surprise, the not knowing is all part of the fun. You will **notice pleasant differences** upon **awakening secure** later on and that's all very nice to know too, is it not? *(Shhh up for 30 seconds...)*

Excellent! Now let's move on – you are doing so well.

(*The more astute may have noticed that I am using stressed people's black and white thinking propensities against them by using 'universal quantifiers' such as 'every', 'never' etc. to open up a series of more helpful generalisations to act upon.)

Part 3: Destabilising the patterns of OCD.

Can I just take this opportune moment to really thank **you're unconscious** mind for all its done to protect you throughout your life: those old obsessions and compulsions were only ever trying to protect you. But the time for those old patterns has passed; they haven't always been a part of every moment of your life. They are not **apart** of you. The good thing is that you can learn, really learn to **stop having those old anxious thoughts** and simply **be free of OCD symptoms, now,** for your own unconscious

343

reasons. For your emotional environment has altered profoundly and so there is no need for the un-needed; doesn't that just make sense?

Everyone can relax and rest, we all **calm right down and slow down too,** do we not? Sooner or later. You know there are many symbols of **stopping certain things** in our culture – you have learned many such symbols and appropriate associations of **you're stopping certain things, unconsciously,** because in this place you can learn this all so easily. What if every time an old troubling thought tried in vain to ever bother you a deeper part of you would as it were 'hold up a stop symbol' of some kind: one appropriate to you that would **slow that old thought right down, now.** You need not even be aware of this process and its mechanics: **it can all happen behind the scenes** as it were. If a thought were to emerge **it can loose all its past fearful power** so that such things are processed so slowly, as a deeper part of you knows that that isolated series of words represents no real danger at all – deep down you know **you are very safe** and always protected. You can even say 'SLOW RIGHT DOWN' in your mind and it will. You can even tell it to 'STOP RIGHT NOW' and it does. What if that thought was

344

written in a calming colour or appeared on a surface that soothed you so that you can **dissociate from those old fearful feelings** and just **relax** deeply? That's right. Perfect.

You are in control of your internal processes unconsciously and **those old thoughts stop going fast** as you **feel calm inside now.** That old behaviour, old compulsions and rituals, old obsessions fade away in the face of **your much calmer self, now.** There is no need to do anything other than let these new choices drop deep into your memory, unconsciously, now.

What if you could imagine a series of healing lights: they may be multiple colours and they only **bring calmness inside of you.** See them moving throughout you, spreading **a deeper sense of calm and healing** unlike anything you've ever known. They **feel wonderfully safe.** A healing energy somehow goes where it needs to. Within. Wherever is best, easiest, now. Naturally open up to this healing process. I will be quiet and these colours only bring you **amazing levels of calm** in the pause... *(No noise for 30 seconds.)* Great.

I can let you know a secret – your

unconscious created that old problem for its own reasons but you are passed that now. As a result of these powerful changes your unconscious...mind can **reduce that old set of responses considerably.** You can **act calmly and confidently** from this moment forward; that's a much better way, is it not? Thoughts and feeling are not you – you are you; so with that in mind you can **alter their new meaning.** What I suggest you also do is **refocus your thoughts and feelings on what you want.** Things do change all the time. What was appropriate in one context may not be so anymore. Is that not so? You can think any thought, even an old thought that scared you once but as **the value behind that thought adapts,** the meaning and feelings alter too. You can think calmly about anything. That's what you used to do. That's what calm people do and **you are a very calm person.** Meanings are not fixed – we may watch a movie and because we **mature** and **notice differing things** than the last time we watched it, we **see it all anew.** Almost as though through fresh eyes. More than only one interpretation of any message is possible and some are more realistic and helpful than others. As a result of new learnings and a new way to **process certain information very calmly** you will notice that **old obsessions and compulsions** that someone once had **are** greatly reduced or **eliminated altogether, now** *(last 3 embeds are hidden coding: see book 2)*. All things must change.

So now, simply **reinterpret certain signals** that had bothered you in a very powerful new way that will give you a sense of much more control over those outdated patterns that you'd experienced up till now. You see, once you recognise at a deep level of experience that those old obsessive thoughts and old compulsions were actually deceptive and meaningless you can know **those old signals were false alarms, now.** As I am only a hypnotist and this is only a suggestion might I suggest that at an unconscious level you **realise this fact in some meaningful set of changes** that improve this person's life and we don't need to know what they are. If such a thought were to briefly pop into your mind in that new very slowed down way – you could simply calmly observe it and say to yourself, in so many words, in your own way – 'Ah! That's just a false alarm.' And with the power of hypnosis magic your far deeper mind understands that now. I will be quiet as a mouse for 30 seconds and in that time can you just process this in an appropriate way, making whatever subconscious, unconscious adjustments are needed as these words go to where they do the most good. *(Shhh...)*

You need to learn something very important – you can **let go completely of that old OCD identity** that you imagined was a part of you. It never was. The deeper core of you knows what I am saying is true. You are not your behaviours, you are not your feelings, you are not passing thoughts – you are the deep core of who you deeply, truly are. You never were those old patterns. You are not obsessive. You are not compulsive. If old responses to stress tried to come back may I suggest you simply **observe things calmly.** You are far more than that. Is a train the station it passes through? Is a sky a cloud that crosses its surface? Is a sea a boat that bobs up and down on it for a while? You are discovering that **you are a very calm and collected person.** Here, in hypnosis you can **allow certain re-associations to occur** as you discover that your potentials in healthy living expand far beyond what wasn't true anyway. Your nature is calm. You can **feel so much more secure** knowing this reality. Deep inside you **feel this** to be true. This healing message spreads throughout the system and generalises with many positive consequences that your conscious mind will notice upon awakening. At your most profound, unconscious levels of mentation you are only reconnecting to your birthright, the deepest wellsprings of **your core confidence deep inside.**

Part 4: Reset the circuit.

Now the real reason you are here and becoming who you really are is because that old protective process that we only label 'OCD' for ease of expression is just a label. It is just a description. It's a mere generalisation for those former obsessive, compulsive thoughts and feelings but what if I told you that only an over active neural pathway was responsible back then and all we need to do to **fix that unconsciously** is for you to learn, really learn how to **completely calm down that neural pathway now.** Some people feel as if that alarm circuit, if you like, is soothed back to a normal level of healthy and accurate functioning. It was like a faulty thermostat that was too sensitive, set too low or high. Imagine that part of the brain being filed with a soothing, healing, calming colour now so that **it does normalise, permanently, now.** Safely calm down that part of the brain somehow – to normal levels.

As though **that process is being reset properly.** So now you simply **feel much, much less bothered** about a whole host of ordinary things. You are becoming more secure, more calm, more relaxed as a result. But let's thank that part, after all it was trying to help the younger you in the best way it knew. It had the knowledge and understanding of that younger you. But know that **you have more resources,** things can change for the better for the rest of your life and that fact makes you somehow **feel even more protected** than before. You can handle anything in life. You **feel grounded and strong.**

Part 5: Prioritising attention.

Now your brain knows how to **prioritise certain information.** It knows exactly how to pay attention to some things and it knows precisely how to **ignore certain things.** It does this to all types of information processing – it sifts and filters it according to moment to moment relevance. It knows that which is significant to your health and survival. Can you recall some noises that you can and have unconsciously ignored? Of course you can. It might be the sound of a dog barking in the distance. The wind whispering through the trees. Children playing. People talking somewhere about something or other. The whining sound of an aeroplane overhead. It might be tree leaves rustling in that comforting way they do. The tweets of birdsong. Those sorts of things: so you know how to do that, have you not? Will you not? NOW! Take a calming moment to remember 3 noises you used to hear and now you are easily unaware of that noise most of the time. Take 20 seconds to **process this understanding** experientially. *(Give them the time...)*

Good, you are doing great and so we know, do we not, that you can **ignore old false alarms** that you used to link to that former unhelpful process. You can ignore, consciously and most importantly, unconsciously certain old thoughts and feelings that now no longer bother you in any way shape or form because **you are a very calm person** and this is so. So just take a further 30 seconds while I am quiet to truly process that and allow whatever changes the unconscious mind wants to occur, however major, perhaps positively dramatic and powerful or slight that it feels are right for you today. Only changing at the appropriate rate and speed. *(Pause for 30 seconds...)*

Part 6: Focusing on what you want.

Okay great! Now, in order to totally **free your mind of that old problem** I want to talk to you about the importance of appropriate **focus** in context. When **you are in flow, you ignore all competing distractions** and only focus on the task in hand. You can always **change your focus.** You can **refocus certain thoughts.** And that means you can **refocus certain feelings.** And when you **change those thoughts, you alter those feelings** too. So all the good stuff only feeds back on itself over and over.

Can you just recall one powerful and simple way you have refocused your mind in the past? For in that experience lie a host of learnings that your unconscious can consider and make frequently more and more available to you, more and more and more, now. I'll be quiet as you do that...*(Give 'em 10 to 15 seconds...)*

Okay with that in mind you can remember the power of **your calm feelings within your calm self** and imagine some ways, perhaps new ones that you can use to learn to **safely refocus your mind, your thoughts and feelings, now.** This all manifests itself

unconsciously, automatically as a part of who you are, now. Habits change. We all change when the motivations and timing is right. Enough is enough! Your creative part can help you safely develop ways to **refocus on the things that really matter** to a calm and confident person. So with this in mind, I'll be really quite while you practise this success in deepest hypnosis – trust what happens...
(Shhh for a full 30 secs -1 minute...)

Now you have processed all those suggestions marvellously, all changes show up in incredible advancements that are tangible. New thoughts, awarenesses, insights, feelings, attitudes, rhythms, behaviours and more, much more can surprise and delight you comfortably. You are gaining such strength as **your inner strength is strengthened powerfully** here. You **feel courageous** every day. You **gain confidence in every experience** you experience. You **have no fear of fear.** That signal is only true and appropriate now. All is well.

So...very...relaxed. You have lived through it all and come up smiling, calm and wise. Anything that comes along is only there to learn from in some way. You can do so many things you once believed you couldn't because

353

confident people with your **full self-belief** do that kind of thing and many more. When you **give far, far less attention to fear,** when you **let unnecessary residues of old fears go, now** you'll find that somehow, in some mysterious way you can **place a great deal of value on your as yet untapped potentia**l which from now on you will utilise and express when appropriate. Remember: you get more of what you focus on – so **focus on what you want,** like a laser, effortlessly.

Part 7: Fears that have less meaning.

I would like you to consider what would happen when you **re-evaluate certain things.** Can you imagine the results of **you're placing much less value on those old thoughts** and feelings that held you back? I know you can learn that **those old obsessive, compulsive thoughts and feelings have less and less value;** in fact you know, do you not that **that old process is well past its sell-by-date** (?). And since you have learned to let go of all that unnecessary fear of the past **some things just become less and less important.** Like an old relationship you outgrew or an old fashioned tool that has been replaced by superior technology...Good. Now just let these healing words **sink deeply** into your unconscious mind, now... *(5 seconds pause...)*

Part 8: Letting the OCD part go.

Till recently it may have seemed that their were two parts of you. One is generous, feels safe, laid back and calm: this part enjoys life, people and experience. He/she is as happy as sunshine. He never holds onto complaints or bears silly grudges.

But we both know that another part of you was full of an anger; an anger that could emerge as temper tantrums. An anger that spilled over into hate. When hate and anger controlled you as they once did you see things in black and white terms instead of **seeing the bigger picture from a more objective, detached perspective** of maturity.

Now, when two parts war inside for supremacy it can be tiring. We have all suffered injustices, that's just a part of being human, that is a reality of life in this world. But hate can drag you down to places not worth visiting. It can churn up feelings that you need to let go of. And the secret to

355

accepting the positive protective intention of that part is to **stop giving its old strategy any energy.** The old path was just too unpleasant, counter-productive. It produced struggle when what you want is to **be soothed inside.** With this in mind I want your creative part to find better ways of solving that intent. Generate as many as you like which lead to beneficial outcomes; place the old methods, thoughts and feelings in that place where you leave old habits; kind of like putting it in the recycle bin on your computer before you **delete that old stuff forever.**

I'll be quiet for a full minute and in that time I would like your creative part to check with that part which is in charge of such things that **these new ways will work better.** They will **satisfy that intention calmly** and in a mature fashion. There is always more than one way. You are developing flexibility. You can see past present obstacles. Let these healing ideas settle into your deepest thoughts and feelings. As soon as you are ready to make this change you will **feel a knowing feeling inside** that all **this has worked profoundly.** That intent always respected but with better options that work for all of you and beyond. Options that you place in that place where you *will* do things.

That's it. *(Quiet for 1 whole minute; assume it worked...)*

And those learnings can generalise throughout the system, noooooo-oooow!

Part 9: Easing old obsessive thinking styles and patterns.

Now there are times when we have to think of certain things and sometimes they produce a solution. At other times we simply waste time and energy and the key to any thought is that the power in it resides in its emotional content. So as you **learn to relax deeply and calmly while thinking about anything** I can teach you a trick that helps the process move along smoothly.

I want you to imagine a symbol of time in your mind because the thing about anxious time is that it was too fast and you need to slow...the wheels...down as it were. So see that symbol of how you represent your internal sense of time in your mind. That's it. Just trust what the subconscious offers you...Good.

Now I want you to realise that nearby is a device – perhaps a remote control, a

357

computer interface, a lever, a set of buttons. I don't know, you do. The important thing is that by modulating this interface somehow you can **slow down certain thoughts to a calm speed,** so that you can **process things calmly...**That's it.

And by altering that inner speed you'll find that you can **focus your mind on more enjoyable things in the present.** So much so that you **stop having certain thoughts altogether.** You might find that some old bothersome thoughts are now totally unnecessary at this new rate and speed. This is the time of safety. This is the time of that restoration of your **deep inner peace, now.** This is the time to **leave the past patterns behind** and **see the world and life anew from a new angle.** Have you ever been on a stroll in nature when you felt so clear headed and uplifted and you **see everything in its proper perspective** (?) We both know you have. So, with all this new knowledge in your mind, deeply, profoundly embedded there, why not begin to realise that you and only **you are in control of your sense of time.** The time to review anything solvable at a leisurely place. No one can do everything all right now. We have to solve real life problems in practical and manageable ways. Sometimes the best thing to do is get on with living now and somehow the rest takes care of itself. No one can control everything – relax knowing this is true.

And the great thing about hypnosis is that your life has really moved on, you will get so much more done, you'll have more fun on a daily basis. From now on you **look at your future in a much more positive way,** going back to the old pattern matching is absurd, can't happen in your much happier reality. You'll notice changes in all areas of your life that enrich you. And this is so.

Part 10: Acting differently.

(There is an element to OCD that is very much like an addiction. The OCD 'voice' tells the sufferer they need only carry out the ritual to achieve a satisfaction – which never arrives. The favoured cognitive behavioural treatment for OCD was for a nurse to hang around with the OCD sufferer and when the latter felt an urge/compulsion to carry out a ritual to quell anxiety in response to a usual trigger the patient was encouraged to do nothing and just let the anxiety subside. This teaches the brain that nothing bad happens and extinguishes the OCD. We can learn from

this but do it in a much more sophisticated way in hypnosis.)

Feeling as incredibly relaxed as you do, you can know that with any problem anyone might have there is a time when you think – **enough is enough.** Some just reach the conclusion that it's time to **rebel against that.** Perhaps you have known bossy people who like to order others around? Perhaps you have had to **stand up against things** like that. **Now,** the power that such people have over others only arises because people go along with what the bossy person says. But who says you have to? What if you **simply do nothing** in certain situations? By doing so **its power of command drains away completely, now.** You don't even have to react at all. Some bossy people just like upsetting you – so do not give them that sense of enjoyment. You can **simply do nothing or something else very calmly;** almost as if you **ignore those old noises** that used to bother you. And when things like that become irrelevant do you know what happens? **Those old communications become quieter and quieter and quieter** like a background hum you blank out. It is time for you to relax and **calmly regain your freedom and independence** is it not? Will you not? Isn't it? That's right.

Future pace rehearsal of doing nothing.
a. Detached rehearsal.

For a moment only before you **act differently on a permanent basis** can you recall a time, perhaps in response to an old trigger, just before that old OCD urge tried to boss you around? It may have used all manner of strong-arm tactics that made you feel an old compulsion to do x *(ritual etc.)* but now you know, really know that **some messages aren't worth listening to** at all. But as you are in a time when that old illusion of compulsion hadn't yet happened simply float out of yourself and **get some comfortable distance** from that old set of responses. The past loop was not completed but has been replaced by choice. From this detached perspective YOU can chose to **act differently** at that time. There are more appropriate options. Simply watch that ever so calm and in control you behaving with freedom in a new empowering way. That's it. See how calm your body language is. See how calm your breathing is. That you is emanating a calm confidence from within that is tangible to others; it is unlike anything you've yet known so strong it is. And notice that you can just **calmly refuse to go along with absurd instructions** from any quarter. If you do not feed a beast **it has no power over you.** Have you ever known a person who used to intimidate you who suddenly transformed into a complete bore? If you haven't, imagine what that'd be like. A person you came to see as quite ridiculous and not worth paying any heed to? And as **that calm you relaxes with doing nothing at all** in response — you may notice that some time had passed, perhaps 10 or 20 seconds and if you can stop doing something that long, what difference does 1-5 seconds more of doing nothing at that time make? And if you can do it that much more than before why not **stretch out nothing** to 10 whole seconds? Then 20, 30, 40, one whole minute, two minutes, half an hour, two hours as **you have better things to occupy your focus.**

Some voices that seemed so important at one time fade into faint echoes of past remembrances that we can look back and laugh upon with the idea that we ever took that seriously. Until that event just became another memory. You can choose what to pay attention to and what to **ignore, unconsciously.** Life is too interesting to pay attention to boring matters is it not? You have so much to do as you are busy enjoying yourself. And the greatest thing is when **it all happens so absolutely easily.** Your unconscious can turn down certain sounds, messages, noises so that they don't bother you at all, now. That's it. Perfect. I'll be quiet for a full 30 seconds whilst you **learn better alternatives...** *(Shhh etc.)*

b. Associated practise.

Now I want you to go to the start of that calm rebellion. And simply float into that totally calm you who can **do nothing calmly in response to old triggers.** Those old triggers make you fly into a resplendent calm that feels amazing. You can **do new things automatically** and in order to make this so, **absorb these new learnings instinctively** in hypnotic...trance...NOO-OOW! Your body and mind feel calm at that time. **Those noises are not present** or so far away and quiet as to be indistinguishable. You **feel no urge or compulsion.** You have all the time you need to **refocus anew and do nothing** wonderfully at such times. What if you came to enjoy the new patterns and matching that **all this just becomes a part of you,** naturally. You decide how you act and respond. The old illusions of fear are gone –

you are free, safe and well. And that's a nice thing to know, is it not? See through those calm and confident eyes. Hear through those confident ears which **ignore the irrelevant.** Very confident people **feel indifferent about a great many appropriate things** that trouble others. Their stillness is powerful. Feel that wonderful fusion of calmness and crystal clarity of mind and thought and supreme confidence as you **rehearse success,** sending a profound message to your ally, the subconscious mind, which you can trust to make all the appropriate and safe alterations in any and all relevant subconscious, unconscious structures and associations, responses, attitudes, communications, rewirings, feelings, emotions, thoughts, behaviours, minimisings and maximisings, timings and durations - now. I will be quiet for a full minute as you **absorb these learnings deeply.** You are a relaxed and calm person and that's that.'

(Exduction of choice etc. That's quite a lot of tricks for starters.)

Case 3: Transforming panic into nerves of steel!

Getting rid of panic attacks etc. is identical to the phobia removal processes I outline in the next 2 cases. First you do the emotion symbology change pattern (see case 5 and the outline in appendix) then add on this script...

Panic into calm script.

(This script is but one option. You can just tag on a confidence boost script which is very direct and short or adapt a phobia script from this book: remember panic attacks are just phobias that occur anywhere! Once the symbology work is done you are 99.9% there anyway with any fear work; I only add suggestions to bash away any doubts or residue and set a new direction for the unconscious mind in general. But you can do a direct module to reset the 'panic alarm response'; my script below shows you how. Deep and VERY relaxing hypnosis assumed...)

'Sometimes we can make a big fuss when the reality was it was just a tiny bump in the path of life. There is an optimum level of arousal in waking living...and here...you can **go back to**

that level, now. Once any stressor is over anyone at all can **feel a deep sense of peace inside** – unruffled, undisturbed like leaves on trees after the wind has past. We all have powerful unconscious mechanisms which work all by themselves to **easily return to a base state of calmness.** I know there have been many times in your life when you **feel level-headed, with a sense of fortitude/valour/courage and equilibrium.**

You posses all these beneficial potentials within and they will manifest more frequently in your much calmer approach to life in general, now.

Feel how much more relaxed in general you feel already; because each and both of you need to learn, really learn that no matter what happens in life, through the ups and downs that anyone eventually passes through – you can **remain calm.** As life is not a linear upward process at all, you can recognise at a deep level of information processing that you are far better off when you **feel a deep feeling of relaxation is ingrained within you.** When **calmness is your second nature.** You'll find that **your native state is a sense of serenity,** an easy going vision, a certain gentling of appropriate perspectives. And these ideas alone give you tremendous reassurance, do they not? Haven't you? Now... There is an unconscious level of protection from potential danger and up until now, for its own very good and understandable reasons yours had been set too high, it was once too sensitive but **that mechanism can be restored to a sensible, healthy and befitting posture, now.** Just get a knowing feeling that this is so. You may feel a tangible sense of appropriately detaching and disengaging from old outdated reactions and responses. There is always more than one way and you'll find this new perspective allows you to **make better choices in life.**

Have you ever had a neighbour who had one of those over-sensitive burglar alarms that just seemed to go off at the slightest thing? Maybe even for no real reason? And sometimes you just need to get someone, anyone who knows how will do, to **fix that response for good.** That's it. Perhaps you **become the sort of person who is cool in a crisis** (?)**;** when everyone about you is running around like a headless chicken, you feel a profound sense of faith in who you really are and you ability to **deal with things in an unperturbed way.** What is more, as I say 'much calmer' you might feel 50 times more relaxed than you are, just because that is possible in this state and acts as confirmation of your far greater relaxing potentials. 'Much calmer!' That's the way – all the way down into that; floating beyond illusions, beyond a sense of former tightness; all that melting and fading away so deliciously and delightfully.

At an unconscious level, you can learn to act, feel and think differently in times, situations and places where a pleasant review of the really best way to respond takes place far away from any need for awarnesses. Trust your creativity. Your far deeper mind does not need you to know how it does what it does to **make a magnificent transformation possible.** You have an ability to **feel so safe** in this world. You have a unique way to **predominantly operate from a place of tranquillity within.**

Future pace work.

Dissociated.

I would like you to see a vision of this far calmer interpretation of how you will be in your future. See that calm you over there responding with amazing confidence, self-possession and poise. Observe that **you are feeling different.** Notice the way **you behave in more resourceful ways** in times that once would have bothered you but now no longer could. Notice your flexibility of responses from this powerful place of calm composure that you own now. When **you are calm** you have choice and the power of your instincts, intuitions are freely available as your creative self helps you **solve any problem unconsciously.** And best of all watch and learn that **that old response is completely gone, forever, now.** Perfect. See that calm you handling anything at all so easily – there is more laughter and smiles and a glow from within that is so attractive as you **conserve those energies.** You **feel so much more energetic** as a result. Life flows more pleasantly and you reset your ability to **feel incredibly good** inside; and doesn't that sound like sound advice from the wisest part of you? I'll be quiet for a full minute: and as this is all your time, take your time to take a fresh look at the new ways in as many places, with others or not as you would really like. *(Shhh for 1 minute...I check my fireside clock...)*

Good. There was a funny TV show on TV in England called 'OTT' which meant 'over the top'; but TV is not life, in life it is far better to **take guidance from the roots of your calmest self.**

Associated.

Okay to finish off simply float into that you who is filled with **all the sense of calm you need, now...**Per-fect! See through those calm and confident eyes, **feel the flow of calmness residing within** you. Hear through those relaxed ears. Feel somehow that **the alarm setting is back to where it needs to be, now.** In your amazing virtual reality machine we call the imagination, go through a time and situation that will 100% confirm for you that **this has worked.** Take your time. Enjoy rehearsing the success that will delightfully manifest in waking life. You are a calm person – you always were deep inside. You have tremendous worth as an individual. Trust that your subconscious is working positively on your behalf 24 hours a day, seven days a week. It is resetting templates. It is finding creative ways to help you **get genuine satisfaction in your life on a daily basis.** More to learn, do and experience. All final adjustments can and do take place as I say 'now'....'NOW! Rehearse **things going so well** as I am silent and as you learn, really learn all you need in a way that meets all your needs as the unique person you really are. So much more pleasure and joy!!! Back and yet forward to a healthy, new normal. Re-associations have occurred. That's the way. *(Shhh etc. Add in any additional work, exduction etc. Job done.)*

Case 4: Fear into funny - removing an intergenerational animal phobia etc.

I have a 100% success rate with phobias –
phobias are wimps! Now I have told you in
'Powerful hypnosis', 'Forbidden hypnotic
secrets', 'Crafting hypnotic spells' and this
bookie a whole host of tricks, scripts etc. for
eliminating phobias in 1 session. The
confidence boost script in 'Powerful hypnosis'
adapted for said phobia is tagged on the
symbology phobia cure I outlined in 'Crafting
hypnotic spells' for a dentures phobia. That's
my phobia busting system, more or less.
Again: you can also use the 'How to
detraumatise anyone' script in this book; it's
more advanced than the one I gave in CHS.
But I have left out one little device I use with
some phobias – notably with animal phobias
but you can use the principles with any if you
like, not needed but sometimes I throw in
extras to stave off boredom and experiment.
All you do is symbol flip in hypnosis using
humour.

Symbol flipping is covered extensively in book
10, my last in the series; entitled 'Weirdnosis'
it will be out soon padawans. Keep you eyes
peeled. Okay now let's get on with teaching
you how to turn a fear stimulus into a laugh

stimulus. How do you do it? The client used to imagine stimulus B and feel fear. Now they will imagine it and giggle or at least feel good: it's a method for switching associations. That's all. It is a nice technique because it seem just like you're telling a funny story.

RH's fear into funny pattern.

(Deep hypnosis assumed...)

'Imagine you are in an everyday situation in which you **feel completely safe and secure...**Good. In a moment you will hear a very small and funny high-pitched voice coming from somewhere in the near environment. It somehow strikes you as hilarious! That's it – you can hear it now if you haven't already. You ask who it is......A tiny voice replies and says, 'It's me down here!' You look down and see the most cute, friendly, cartoony looking 'y' (phobic stimulus) you've ever seen, it looks so harmless and ridiculous that you **feel like laughing in response.** Now, even its silly clothes are funny – **you can't see it or think about it without smiling!**

In fact it does something that makes you realise how safe it is. Perhaps it looks weak, defenceless, puny, stupid, ludicrous or foolish? Whatever happens you **start to feel differently as a result.** As you process this new information **old responses are permanently changed** for the better – this thing makes you laugh! This thing look so incredibly funny for your own unconscious reasons that you positively generalise from this experience in multiple fantastic ways. You know that **whenever you see/experience 'y' in the future you only want to grin and laugh!**

You can take this as a sign and a signal that the very next time you see a 'y' you will remember this learning event at some level and only a smile, giggle or indifference seems appropriate as your mind learns to **wisely minimise certain things** just as it can **maximise the good responses** too. The truth is 'y' is a harmless creature (make sure it is!!!). That old reaction is something you can never be bothered by again. *(NFH – list all the good things that 'y's do in reality – spiders eat flies, dogs chase off burglars – they are loyal etc., horses are quite sweet when you get to know them etc.)* From now on you **happily get on with your life, let them get on with theirs.** That's right.' *(Simple.)*

Process.

- Make client feel safe etc.
- Create a funny scene involving the 'y' (stimulus) that makes the client smile etc.
- 'Cartoonise' the 'y'; make it small, silly and helpless etc. Using the sensory representations make the submodalities of the 'y' unthreatening ones.
- Give suggestions that link the new response to the old stimulus (post hypnotics). This is a simple N.A.C technique. You are actually re-associating them to their inborn response of confidence before they learnt to fear 'y'. This is a resetting procedure. You can use a similar process with athletes who fear a specific competitor etc. Use your imagination, reword appropriately.

Now I'll teach you how to cure a phobia in children; the full process is given.

Case 5: The girl that barked back! Helping childhood anxiety with hypnosis.

I once had a lovely young girl about 8 or so come to see me with her dad. She was very bright. She had dressed up in her best clothes to come and see me and had her hair braided like Elsa from Disney's Frozen – so I knew she meant business. She had told her dad that she was going to get rid of those fears that had bothered her. We discussed her problems – just some stress at home and school and a dog that chased her once, when she was little. It was the most rewarding hypnosis session I had ever carried out. She was brilliant – didn't even look hypnotised at all; just like a little girl concentrating on something important (with her eyes closed). She smiled when I taught her how to get rid of the phobia. I wrapped it up and counted her out but she was way ahead of me – 'You got rid of it didn't you?' I said. She smiled and nodded. Her next mission was to visit the big swing park at the end of my road. Full of dogs see. She and her dad walked there hand in hand. She had a big smile on her face. Now let me tell you how *we* did it.

Rogue hypnotists protocol for helping children with hypnosis.

- **The comfort of the child is the most important thing.** Unlike with adults, mummy and daddy are allowed into the hypnosis lounge during the interview stage. They are allowed to stay during the hypnosis part with the warning that they might get hypnotised too! After a worried look they'll leave; generally the child will be so eager for help they will shoo mom/mum and dad out! Mum/mom and dad often help the child remember different things that are relevant.

- **The motivation of the child and desire to use hypnosis must be high.** It must be the child's genuine wish to use hypnosis, if they are really excited and determined to use it to help themselves you are assured complete success.

- **Never speak down to children.** Never act as if the child is an idiot or unable to understand what you are saying. Simplify the language and make any explanations easy for a child to comprehend. Children are actually smarter than most adults not having all the social programming and shitty life experience which makes grown-ups stupid and jaded. *Note: children are exceptionally brave!*

- **Do not dredge up the past with children.** Do not retraumatise the child by endlessly going over and over what caused the problem etc. If they have a fear of dogs they'll say 'I was chased by a dog and ran away!' That's all you need. *The point is to remove the feelings and replace them with calm and confidence – the child wants to be happy and free.* You focus on making that happen.

- **Children do not need long inductions. *NOTE: Children only need to start visualising to be in hypnosis.*** They do not show such overt signs of hypnosis as adults do. They may fidget, rub their eyes, even open them – they are still under. You might notice rapid eye movement, a bit of yawning, slightly flushed cheeks etc. Don't count on having any explicit indicator of trance! If they aren't hypnotised they'll tell you, children are

378

honest, assume all is well. The child's fertile imagination is your main asset in helping them. Stimulate it! My rule of child hypnosis is – <u>if they are visualising, they're hypnotised.</u> It's that simple.

- **<u>Change work must be simplified and made exciting for children.</u>**
  Adult change work is so serious and austere! Children don't like that! It's BOR-RING! In the phobias session script that follows you'll see how I make a symbology change work approach appropriate, interesting and fun for a child.

- **<u>Sessions must be quick – 30 – 40 minutes total including interview.</u>**
  Children aren't like adults, they are not bullshitters, you don't have to wade through lies, rationalisations, and masses of stupid theories that all adults have accumulated through the stupidity inducing process of schooling, TV, magazines, 'self-help' books etc. Children get to the point, say what they mean and want quick results. They really want it to work and somehow know it will.

- **Tell the child that you aren't going to hypnotise them, you are going to show them how to go into hypnosis themselves.** Let the child know you don't have magic powers and that they are in control: I can't emphasis this enough. Tell them that you will help them find a nice state of absorption like when they watch TV or play a computer game. They get the idea instantly. As I said children are smart, don't make stupid assumptions and have common sense. The adults are another matter!

- **If you even mention a 'subconscious' at all say it's the part that controls their emotions, imagination and food digestion; they'll get it.** Don't give children longwinded bullsh*tty explanations as to what a subconscious is. I don't even know what a subconscious is!

- **The purpose of hypnotherapy with children is to teach self-mastery, reliance and control.** Seemingly out of control emotions can undermine a child's inherent, inborn confidence. Effective hypnotherapy with children proves to them that using their own mind and inner resources, they can not only feel better but regain control – that they can master self and thus function better in the external world and gain more mastery there. A very powerful thing for any child to learn ne's pas? Such children will better cope and handle stressful events and the process of maturation with a greater sense of security and ease. ***Every challenge that is met with a positive response builds confidence.*** The child can learn to *generalise* confidently about their ability to meet a whole host of life challenges and solve them with more equilibrium: 'If I overcame x I can overcome y etc.'

Multiple phobias for children session.

As I've hinted, the following is an almost verbatim example of a multiple phobia session that I carried out with the help of a very clever 8 year old girl. Frankly she was brilliant and made the whole thing so easy. There is nothing nicer than helping little children feel better; it puts a spring in your step. Questions and possible responses first, hypnosis script soon follows. It is so simple, quick, stimulating and easy for a child of 8 to comprehend.

Note: with younger children you may need a different approach - it is possible that simple direct hypnosis can remove phobias etc. in small children. Note the session is for a girl and uses ideas and imagery that appeals to a little girl – if your client is a boy obviously talk using imagery associated with sports, cars, spaceships and heroes etc. Stick to traditional gender play themes because that's how children really are despite any Marxist programming you may have been made intensely stupid and damaging to others with. Keep 'your' brainwashed ideas to yourself and don't impose them on others' children: as if you had the right anyway! Questionnaires should be simpler and less 'in depth' than adults ones.

Examples of questions.

1. **Your dad/mom said you have a fear of x and ys (x and y being phobia triggers)? Is anything else bothering you at the moment?**
   Answers will be a list of the phobias etc. If a child is afraid of dogs this can generalise to cats, both being a bit

382

similar – furry, claws, teeth, both a bit wild and unpredictable. If phobias are present they may indicate nothing other than a one off scary experience that now produces an overprotective fear reaction. The child's brain may however start looking out for multiple simple pattern matches that *could* be dangerous if they are even slightly similar to the initiating trigger stimulus. This is a tiring and unpleasant state for a little child to habitually be in. Childhood should = innocence +fun!

2. **Can you rate each fear? 10 being the worst and 1 or 0 being nothing at all.** Get a grading to make the fear real/tangible/measurable and they'll be able to mark the feeling's absence/diminution after the hypnosis.

3. **Do you think about the x, y (phobic trigger – dogs etc.) when it's not around or just before you anticipate encountering it?** Phobias can create obsessive thinking patterns in order to avoid a potential triggering situation. This is easily gotten rid of and often isn't present anyway. *When the fear goes the obsession goes.* Constantly worrying about imagined danger and its avoidance

is exhausting. NOTE: do not do NLP patterns with children; only adult brains can safely process them. Keep it simple and easy – nothing weird or strenuous with children or you may worsen anxiety.

4. **What happens when you get scared? If you could teach me how to do it, how do you do it? Or – This may sound like a silly question but how do you feel when you are scared?** They may worry what might happen – running 'what if scenarios' etc. They may also have dreams about the phobic trigger which is normal; the worried rumination and fear is discharged through dreaming. There is no need to analyse the dream at all. Forget about it. Successful dream analysis is easy if you know the person well and can interpret their unique symbology – I do it with friends only.

5. **Are there times when the fears are better or worse or is it the same all the time?** Generally they will feel safer with adults/parents around. If you fear cats and daddy is there, daddy can kick the cat up the ass if it hisses at you!

6. **Can you use one word to sum up the**

fears? Might be 'worry', 'fear' etc. This is their code/access/trance word to experience the state. Use it to display empathy and understanding but minimise its use in the hypnosis part. After you have changed symbols you don't have to use it again at all. Though don't be obsessive about this. When the word 'worry' is less worrying you know you have succeeded.

7. **How would you like to feel instead? Can you sum it up in one or two words?** Children will generally say – HAPPY! The natural state for a child is happiness. Running around playing etc. That's how they are meant to be – safe, secure = happy! They want the feeling to stop getting in the way of all the happiness their friends have and they used to have. Children compare themselves to their peers.

8. **What will be the best things about having gotten rid of those old problems?** They will be able to stop avoidant behaviour. They will be happy to do what they did and others do without thinking or worrying about it at all. Those with phobias want indifference to triggers. They'll be FREE to do what they

want. Go to the park and play and not worry about big dogs etc. They can imagine happy things and not unpleasant never-nevers (misuse of the imagination). *There is no such thing as a nervous child or disposition; although some children are more 'sensitive' than others – this is often linked to high intelligence and creativity.* All unnecessary fears are learned and can be unlearned.

9. **What things do you enjoy most about life now?** It will be TV, books, games etc. Use this to help you create absorbing hypnotic subjects for the specific child before you. TV and computer games are highly hypnotic for children and should be used.

10. **Do you know what a symbol is?** Yes or no. If yes – yippee! They almost always do. If not explain it. Draw a funny face and say this is a symbol for happy. Draw a miserable face and say this is sad etc. Geddit?

11. **Do you know anything about hypnosis?** They may not want to and just want to get on with it – children want results, not to be bogged down

with theory. Just say, *'It's just like watching your favourite TV show.'* It is!

12. Is there anything you want to say or that I need to know in order to help? Yes, no etc. Listen to what they say. Take heed of it.

13. Is there anything else you think hypnosis might help you with? They might tell you other times they worry etc. I told a child who worried before bed to do all the worrying they needed for a ten minute period during the day. It's fine to worry a bit, but before bed after a busy day when your mind was occupied is not a good idea. This is Milton Erickson's principle for 'prescribing the symptom'. They might not like a teacher etc. When you get rid of the phobia the general level of arousal and unconscious preparation for arousal will be massively diminished. Tell the child, *'Fear is good; fear is energy to protect you. You need good fear: it's unwanted fear that's no good – it's too much. Even me and mommy/daddy need fear if a big truck /lorry is coming towards us as we cross the road/street and need to get out of the way fast.'*

The following script took 20 minutes in total to complete. It could have been 5 minutes shorter easy. With some children you can just go to the symbol change as that accesses the imagination but I always play it safe: it's about loading the dice in your favour. Create an **adventurous, stimulating and appropriate** hypnotic induction like the one below. Children do not like to focus on one thing for too long these days (blame TV and modern child rearing); keep changing focus to grab their attention. Tell them it will be all over soon, that they are doing well, nearly there etc. liberally. When you ask questions they may well nod etc. giving you lots of lovely feedback that what you are doing is working. Working with children is delightful if you are competent. If you don't like children or are useless with 'em this field is not for you. Ladies should have no problem.

Induction and multiple phobia removal for children script.

- **The use of black dots indicates a slight pause. Say 3-10 seconds. Don't give children too much undirected time, enough to process things and then move on; you'll just know when.**

'So just close your eyes and just notice your breathing...That's it. In and out. In and out. To help you **begin to relax nicely...** *(Lots of embeds for calm and confidence dispersed throughout)* Can you take in a deep breath and hold it...And slowly release that breath... Excellent! And one more time...Deep breath in please and just hold it...Good. And **relax and rest** as you let that breath out nice and slow for me! Great. The good thing is you don't need to do anything to help...Everyone can **go into a nice trance** by just letting it happen... You might notice a nice feeling in one of your hands...The tip of your nose...One of your toes...? As you pay attention to **comfy feelings inside your body...** You might notice that as I speak you feel lots of nice feelings. And that can make you feel even more comfy and pleasant than before...We are going to play an imagination game...And in this game you can learn to do some amazing things...

Imagination game.

In your imagination can you just get a picture of a banana?...Just floating there in your mind's eye...

•

Excellent...And can you let that fade away and

see a picture of a beautiful flower?
That's it...

•

Could you **imagine** a picture next of a ~~Big Lego home~~
wonderful princess's castle? ~~the home of~~

• a Superhero –

That's all you have to do to **feel confident and calm** when you need to...you just allow yourself to imagine different things that I suggest to you in hypnosis...Can you imagine a piece of music? Maybe one note? Or a song. Maybe an instrument? Piano or guitar playing?

•

Have you ever heard the nice sound of a stream or river?

•

Have you felt the feeling of a summer breeze on your face?

•

Can you imagine that as you **relax even more?** Maybe you'd like to pretend you are at the seaside? ~~Lake Como~~

•

Can you imagine the feeling of sand under your feet?

•

As you imagine all these things you **feel even more comfortable** and relaxed...That's right. You are really doing well.

Magic TV.

Can you just easily imagine yourself at home in a very comfy chair. **You are feeling very calm and a little bit sleepy** as you sink down and get so relaxed and feeling nice and snugly in this chair. Maybe you've felt like that before? On your next out breath just close your eyes in your imagination and allow yourself to **become absorbed** by this lovely feeling. Your chair is in front of the TV. It's so pleasant and just the right temperature in this cosy place that you can find your mind drifting and dozing a little. **Keeping your eyes comfortably closed** in a moment, you can begin watching your favourite TV show on the TV. *(Presupposition for eye closure.)* As you really enjoy watching, you can **feel very calm, relaxed, peaceful and safe.**
Okay, so imagine you have your own magical remote control and in your mind you can really see your favourite show on the screen because you are using hypnosis magic! Can you listen, hear all the sounds...? Feel all the nice feelings you feel and enjoy, really enjoy watching your favourite TV show. And the amazing thing is you can continue watching that TV show in your imagination because it's just the same as **going into hypnosis, now...**Just get as comfy and cosy as you'd

391

like and those feelings only grow...And feel nicer and nicer than ever before...You might even **feel drowsy and sleepy** and that's just fine...I'll be quiet for about 10 seconds and in that time just **enjoy it** as you **become more and more absorbed** in watching your favourite show and then we'll do some hypnosis magic that is even more fun!
(Pause...)

Magic carpet ride.

Very good! Imagine now that you are in some safe and totally magical place...I don't know what this lovely place is like but you do...This is your special place...Now in this place you can see way off in the distance, a lovely golden archway...like you might find in a fairy story. At your feet you see there is a flying carpet! And I can let you know a secret: this is your flying carpet and it can take you anywhere you want! All you have to do is think it and it does what you think! And you know you need it to fly through that golden archway...Because when you do you will have arrived in your safe place...Your totally safe and secret place inside...that will allow you to **feel confident and calm around x (dogs) and y (riding on buses etc.), now.**

392

Stepping in your own room

So in a moment I'll say 'hop on board' and that will be your signal to jump on your magic carpet and tell it to fly through that archway; and as I count from 5-0 you can fly on that carpet getting closer and closer to that archway: and at the same time you'll be able to become even more absorbed in the whole experience and it will feel really nice. Ok. Are you ready? Here we go! 'Hop on board!' That's it! And your carpet takes off and starts flying toward that archway...

On 5! You are getting closer and closer! You know that very soon you will **put all those past fears and worries behind you in the past** and just knowing that makes you **feel really good** already! 4 – Flying closer and closer, over your magical place in your imagination. What sights and sounds are there, that interest you most!? You **feel safe and in control inside!** It is always best to stay nice and calm whilst doing most things. *(Themes of safety and control repeated; keep suggestion wording simple.)* 3 – Getting even closer and feeling nice and excited about changing things for the better so you'll be happier and be able to do so many things that you couldn't before and you'll really look forward to being able to do so and learning it all so easily! 2 – You are very nearly there and you know that you really want to **feel nice and calm around any x or y etc.** and making any other secret changes you want to make your whole life better than ever! Things will just be so much more fun! *(Giving* without worries *suggestions for 'secret change' allows the unconscious to alter anything else it sees fit and it appeals to children's love of secrets!)* 1 – You are almost there! Almost there! You might feel as good and excited as you feel before Christmas (etc.) or going on a nice holiday or before you meet your best friends! 0! Go through that golden archway feeling very relaxed and wonderful! You have flown into the safest and most wonderful place that you could ever imagine and it's even more lovely here than the last place! You tell the carpet to land because you are where you need to be...That's perfect...

The Emperor of the gods for children.

(The following module is a version of a tale I use for adults who have fear based problems; see 'Forbidden hypnotic secrets'. Again: so often people are afraid of fear itself! All potential scariness is taken out for children.)

In this place you see a lovely bed and it looks so nice and cosy that you want to take a nap and **sleep.** Your favourite toys are there waiting and you climb in and get cosy and snugly and pull the covers over you so you are nice and warm. And you close your eyes and **fall fast asleep** and you **have lovely dreams** and one of them goes like this…and as I tell it, you **feel totally safe and protected** because it's just a funny story!

We all have our favourite stories and our favourite story tellers don't we? Once upon a time the Emperor of the gods decided to go on a trip and leave all the funny little gods in charge. While he was away a big silly, wobbly, funny looking jelly monster came towards the castle they lived in and the little gods grew very afraid, even though it was just a silly old jelly monster and not really scary at all; and the more scared they became the bigger it grew until it was very big indeed. The little gods quivered and cowered behind the castle walls. Just at that moment the Emperor of the gods came home and saw what was happening…'Oh you silly things!' he laughed. This is no monster, this is fear, he lives on your fear of fear – the more you worry about him the bigger he gets. 'Oh!' said the little gods and as they realised **you have the power to stay calm and to keep things in just the right perspective** the monster began to shrink and shrink until it was no bigger than a mouse. 'Shall we get rid of it?' asked one of the little gods. 'No' laughed the Emperor, 'Let's keep him, he might have some uses, some times, from time to time, if we use him sensibly...' *(The embed clarifies the meaning of the metaphor for a child's unconscious)*

(handwritten notes: Kai Fire, Wya Water, Thor - Norse God of Thunder, Hammer, World of Ninjago, Nya, Cole, Lloyd, father, god, Jay, Cole, Earth, Zane, Ice)

Fairy Godmother symbology change work. *(Note in the following I tailor the dry and rather austere symbology change in such a way that appeals to a little girl: I am replaced by a fairy godmother who is both healer and a symbol for the child's wiser unconscious – she also uses magic! With a boy pick a hero of preference and give him a magic sword or laser gun instead!)*

And now you have another **dream** and it goes like this. *(The single verb embed 'dream' creates the idea that the child is having a series of nice dreams as during sleep; it is also a one word command to experience hypnosis etc.)* You are in a lovely place in the countryside. It is all pretty and nice. The air is fresh, the flowers smell nice. It is a summer's day and you feel so happy here. It is your private place where you **feel safe and**

(handwritten: My mind controlls my feelings)

Thor + the Ninjas live

totally confident and in control! I can let
you know a secret! This is the place where
your fairy godmother lives! She is very kind
and always protecting you. She always wants
to make sure you are safe! And she does that
job very well but now we know that it's time
for you to **feel much happier and calmer,
more confident than ever before** and so
we just need to change something to make
you feel good. To make you **feel all better
again.** *(Parental languaging: 'all better')* It
will be like magic! Hypnosis magic! Like when
mummy/mommy and daddy kissed you all
better when you might have hurt your knee or
something when you were very little. That
kind of magic!

So as you walk around this lovely place you
can see your smiling fairy godmother! You
walk over to her and notice she has a wand! A
magic wand and she's going to use it to help
you **feel calm again.** She has a very kind
voice and she says, 'Can you just relax and
think of your favourite cuddly toy?' You easily
do as she asks. 'Now we are going to get rid
of those old fears all in one go with magic but
I need your help. Can you imagine the things
I ask so that we can make **you feel happy,
calm and confident around x or y** or
anything at all?'

You nod your head as you really want just that, and it makes you **feel so happy** to know that soon all the **old feelings will be left in the past, now.** The kind lady says next, 'As you're **feeling completely safe and calm** can you ask your deep, subconscious mind or deeper mind: this is the bit of you that controls your emotions and digests food for you, to give you a symbol which fully and completely sums up the old unwanted and unneeded fears all in one go? Trust the first thing that pops into your head. And can you really notice that symbol and everything about it? And as you look at that symbol you really know that it represents every aspect of the old fears you had experienced.' *(Give about 10-15 secs or so. When I say 'for you' I presuppose that its intention is to help you AND you can influence it. Avoid saying fears are 'silly' because they are but aren't too! Respect children's experiences and don't trivialise them.)*

•

(You can drop mentioning the fairy now, she and your voice will 'blend' somehow – trust me...) 'Ok. Good. Really focus now on that symbol really closely, notice as many details as you can about it. Think about how close, how far away, brightly lit, dimly lit, colour, shape, size. Try to really get to know that

symbol.'
• *(Give longer time for this process...)*
'Good. Can you ask the subconscious what needs to change with that old symbol so that it no longer represents the old undesirable feeling but now represents a new symbol that sums up and represents all the new desired **feelings of calmness and confidence** and any other wonderful feelings you want and need. Again as you focus on that symbol, ask your subconscious mind what needs to change with that symbol so that it no longer represents that old fear of x or y's and those old feelings that went with it but now represents **comfort, confidence and strength in those formerly bothersome situations, now!** Whatever changes your subconscious tells you to make to that symbol make those changes and when you've made all the changes it tells you to, just acknowledge they really have been made.
• *(Longer again; up to 10 to 15 seconds...)*
Good. You are doing brilliantly: ask your subconscious if there are anymore changes at all that need to be made so that this new symbol fully and completely represents the new and desired feelings. If there are any more changes that need to be made, make them and then just accept that **all the right changes have been made.** Again to be

sure, ask your subconscious mind one more time is there anything that needs to change with this symbol so that it fully and completely represents feeling calm and comfortable and confident when around dogs or in lifts etc. And if there's any more changes it wants you to make, simply make those changes all right now! *(Repetition can usefully produce clarification.)* ~~But with all~~

• *(Longer again...)* ~~the fans + bits~~

Good. *(Praise children a lot and tell them they ~~the~~ are doing great!)* And the fairy godmother ~~B~~ waves her magic wand and says some magic ~~c~~ words and all the right changes are made ~~homme~~ forever!

So now as you focus on that symbol you can sense that it absolutely, completely represents **being calm and confident when being near x or even thinking about them or y etc. or thinking about them.'** *(This removes any residual obsessing.)*

Excellent, now you fully know that this wonderful symbol represents feelings and the only way that feelings can make any sense at all is if they're inside of you somewhere specific. Now, I don't know precisely where this belongs inside of you but the good thing is you do! I don't know how it needs to be positioned there but you do. This is all private. So just take that symbol now and put it in that place where it belongs and position it exactly the way it's supposed to be. So that you fully feel and experience that **calm, comfort, confident strength.** That's it: Just so...

•

Brilliant!!! Really let yourself **fully feel that feeling.** It's really great isn't it?
(They may well nod and smile!)

Now because it's your feelings and **you are in control** of them I want you to take that symbol and just make it larger, make it bigger, so that it begins to fill you up, so that every part of you is filled with that sense of **strength and calm and confidence.** Make it bigger and bigger till it fills every single particle of your whole being...And I want you to make it stronger, more powerful. More potent so that it so that you can really **feel it in every cell of your being, in every part of your mind and body,** filled with these amazing, powerful sensations, this super sense of strength, confidence and comfort and it gets better...and better...and even much, much better and you can really **feel that** can't you?

Make it even bigger, make it even more

powerful so that you're glowing, brimming over with these wonderful feelings of total confidence and deep strength, the blissful comfort when you're anywhere at all: near dogs, lifts (etc.), whatever! **You feel very calm** — make it even stronger, even more mighty, even bigger! And when it fills EVERY single part of you and it's really, really powerful – just know that you can **keep these changes.** *(Stabilisation, permanency embed.)*

Good, you are doing so well x (x = child's name). Now, I want you to take that and make it even bigger still. You can do it! Even stronger so that it's radiating out from you in every direction! So it's like a magic glow surrounding you, it's so powerful, it's so large, so incredibly powerful, if someone were to walk past you they would feel that feeling with you. It's radiating out from you just that like. You can feel that radiating, can't you? And if you imagine looking down at yourself, you can see that radiating, expanding, beaming out from you, that's so isn't it? *(They may nod etc.; if not carry on anyway.)* Very good. Just let the feeling, all those feelings just stay there for a moment...Enjoy that. Nice. Now simply let your mind clear for a moment. Just think of your favourite cuddly toy and **relax**

It is a place

nicely.

When you were asked to come to be a part of

The safest place. *the Ninjago world, Jay,*
Zane - Cole Nya Kai + Lloyd wanted
you there to be their friend.
In your mind I want you to go to the place;
somewhere in your mind is a place that is
Most wonderful
your safest place, some people call it 'The
place of treasures'. In this place you are in
complete control of absolutely everything.
Really! In this special place you have perfect
peace, **you have perfect calm** because no
one can come here without your permission,
it's yours, you are completely and utterly in
control of all of it. In the safest place
everything is just the way you want it to be.
Like magic! In the safest place you **feel**
completely happy and where you
belong*.

It is
funny
but then
too.
He is
the Nose
God + guess
what? you
have
grandpa's
from Norway
too J
He high fives you
because you are both
have
the Same
kind of
ancestry

Can you just take a lovely moment and look
around the safest place, really get to know
this special realm? Every detail that you can
notice. Explore as you wish for a while and
you have all the time you need here. Just take
in all the splendid details. That's it! And more
importantly notice how good you feel being
there. That's so good isn't it? *(*The embed*
implies, 'in this world'. Give 5 – 10 secs.)
Great! Please can you look around the safest
place one more time and this time find the

place in that location that is 'The most special place of all!' The most important special place in that special place. It's amazing and awesome - there for some reason that only you know about! And it's special because whatever is there is the most important thing in all of that inner realm of treasures. Just find that place now. *(Simple fairy story type language!)*

•

Good. Okay, now imagine a container, a storage device of any kind you wish is there. I don't know what that would be - a big coloured box, a safe, a bucket, a carton, a crate, a jug, a pot, a tub? Anything you like, whatever you think is best, something that holds other things really well.

That container represents you – its is a symbol of you if you like. You notice a word is written on it that indicates that this is so: perhaps your name or something else. So simply step right up to that container right now and I want you to look down on yourself again, notice that you are still glowing, RADIATING, with these feelings of confidence and strength, GLOWING with this certainty. And this peace. This feeling of total security. This calm. Get some some of these amazing feelings and put them in your container. I don't know how much needs to be there. But when however much is there, should be there, you'll know when it's right. When there's enough in there you'll trust you just know in some mysterious way. I'll be quiet for a bit while you do it!

• *(Up to 15 secs...)*

Very good! See it's all so easy! Now whatever for the rest of your life goes into your container here in the safest place will be on tap/at hand to you from now on. It lasts forever and ever! If you ever need some more of that, a part of you outside of your awareness can come back here, get what you need and it'll always have an abundant endless supply for the rest of your life and the good thing is, that happens automatically, you don't even need to think about it! You can put anything powerful, needed, special, clever and amazing into that container and it will be yours to keep from now on. That's a very nice thing to know isn't it? You **feel so reassured.** Very good. Very good. You are doing absolutely brilliantly!

Okay! Right, now come back out of the safest place; all the way right back but still keeping your eyes closed. We are almost done*! Focus on that symbol that is now inside of you and how it feels, what you feel radiating, glowing

405

in and through you. Every part filled to the brim. There's **no problem whatsoever.** Notice how much better you feel! Great isn't it! *(*When you tell them now and again how much further you have to go you are dealing with a very prominent childhood concern, 'Are we there yet?' It also dispels fears of it never ending or getting boring!)*

Alright, keep focusing on that feeling for me, keep focusing on that feeling right now. Turn it up, make it even stronger! Make it EVEN more powerful! Make it bigger, SO...MUCH...BIGGER...so that it's expanding out even further. You can even imagine that if you're near an x or y (old trigger) right now that you **feel great in that situation,** it's easy, it's increasing and amplifying SO much that everyone, anything can sense it. They feel it, they know and most important you know it...That's so good. Well done! **You have the confidence, you have the certainty, you have the calm, you have the strength** and THEY all know it! Notice how good you really feel...'

Fantastic! So that is all done: you can thank your fairy godmother who waves her wand and says some magic words so that you really know that **all the changes have been**

made permanently and locked in forever! You say goodbye and she waves as she flies off on another adventure!

Suggestions to reinforce change.

I would like to thank your subconscious mind for everything it's done for you and we've almost finished, I've just got a few more things to say and we are done! You are doing brilliantly. From now on you **feel calm and confident in/around x's (old phobic trigger),** just something you do easily and calmly and you just know this is so. You **feel safe in or around y's of any kind.** All x's are different; they have different aspects/personalities just like people! You don't have to like them but **you feel safe and confident anyway***. You **feel confident, happy and relaxed from now on,** maybe more than ever before and any and all other changes that need to occur can occur right now, you learn what you need to learn easily and this is so. *(*Suggestions for noticing differences in past triggers eliminates past generalisations – all dogs for example become that dog and this dog which are different – a phobia is an overgeneralisation, young minds tend to overgeneralise as a safety mechanism due to a lack of* *experience.)*

Exduction.

Good. Now I'll start to wake you up and when you awaken you'll **feel happy and healthy, feeling confident and good.** All I'm going to do is count from 1 – 5 and on 5 you'll feel totally wide wake and great. Everything I said, all the changes we made together stay with you getting stronger all the time! You **feel safe and secure around any x or y and this is so.** So very happy, so many wonderful things to learn and experience! *(Set up an instant re-induction trigger – 'Deep sleep' etc. here if you want.)*

1 – You feel positive and very good!

2 – Feeling confident in your abilities to solve problems in the same way you overcame this one so easily and quickly! **All past problems washed away** as if a magic wand had simply got rid of them. As we overcome problems it makes us **feel stronger!** You are so good at learning things! Learning is easy. You somehow find that learnings lessons at school is easier than ever!

3 – You **feel so good,** lighter and brighter. Aware of sounds around you. Of your body and how pleased you feel about how well you did. Waking up a bit more!

4 – Feeling almost wide awake and back to normal! All the changes occur automatically so you can just get on with learning, living, having fun and a lovely, happy life! So many interesting things to do!

5 – Everything completely normal, feeling alert, great! Full of energy! Wide awake and fully alert, eyes can open as soon as you are ready on 5! Wakey-wakey rise and shine! Perfect! Clever girl/boy!!!'

They may well wake up before the count finishes! That's fine – just say number 5 as they do! Expect a smiling, laughing, beaming, happy little face! Praise them liberally for what _they_ did! Trust your instincts. Tell mom/mum and dad etc. just how well they did. That's one little person and family with one less thing to worry about – result – JOY! Pat self on back!!!

Case 6: From Russia with depression!

A very beautiful Russian lady with raven coloured hair turned up at my house. She looked mid-twenties – tops; in fact she was in her early 40's! Good genes. What follows is her interview and the session for depression that followed. I talked non-stop for 2 hours because this lady wasn't in a secure financial position at that stage in her life. I do stuff like that because kindness and generosity are important to me, unlike a lot of other money grabbing therapists. I never went into hypnotherapy for the money, believe me!

Interview.

The lady told me on the phone what she wanted – she was depressed. Her aim was to sleep well, learn how to love herself, to look after her physical self, learn how to be deeply relaxed. I can do that. Good. *Break the problem 'depression' into its problem matrix parts and tackle it bit by bit till it can't exist.*

1. In general (client's name) how are things going at the moment?

Answer: 'I have always been a bad sleeper – have memories from childhood of this. My childhood was bad. My dad drank a lot and was violent. My dad always had a potential to kill himself. Once I came into a room and saw my dad hanging from a rope. I thought he was dead but he was just pretending and laughed. I had to go to the doctor as my skin broke out in neurodermatitis.'

Well we know the cause – prolonged, traumatic, insecure environment and then some! Even though she is 'depressed' she cares for her appearance but dresses dramatically in black, like Hamlet. Like most adult Eastern Europeans she is quite dour and a sense of humour is not a strong point depressed or not. These are the legacies of autocratic Governments stretching back far before the Soviet system's horrors. Notice the use of the universal quantifier – 'always'.

2. What do you do for a living? Do you enjoy it?

Answer: 'I am self-employed and I am studying psychology at University. I have a ... (young child) and also I am learning about NLP.'

Again no man! She smiles as she tells me about learning NLP as though this is a bond of similarity between us. I just think – what you learning that crap for?

3. What's your living situation? Married etc.

Answer: 'I have financial problems* as I am divorced. My divorce was unexpected. I am not consciously worrying. I am a good student. But I overwork a lot. I am a perfectionist. I have not found myself.'

(*Linked to her financial problems she tells me that the indoctrination she received by the Soviets has made her feel guilty about making money – cultural hypnosis at work.)

She tells me she relaxes with meditation – 'SHIT!' I think, don't do that! Read book 7, 'Escaping cultural hypnosis to find out why it's so dangerous. So what we got here folks? No financial security – an essential need. No man – an essential need. She isn't taking time out to rest – an essential need. She is not comfortable with who she is – being comfortable with yourself is an essential need. No wonder she's depressed past traumata aside. Notice she says, 'I am not consciously worrying...' That is her telling me she _is_ UNCONSCIOUSLY worrying which is worse! She is not epileptic I note. She was taking anti-depressants but she says, revealingly, 'It made me feel less than human.' She wisely stopped taking them. She is taking sleeping pills. Her sleep is terrible and its healthy re-establishment a key plank in her recovery.

7. (3 more questions implied above...) Can we clarify what are the specific problems and what are the exact results you desire?

Answer: 1. 'I have had very bad insomnia for over two years. I want to sleep well (like all people with insomnia she hears all noises at night – a sign of heightened tension). 2. I have a pain in my chest – it is relieved by crying. (This is the physical manifestation of the whole 'trauma gestalt'. It is bound emotional pain – the legacy of her childhood. It must be 'detraumatised' using my, 'How to detraumatise anyone' process (see the same named chapter for the full outline). In this section we are focusing on anti-depression measures solely. Having said that the recovery from depression is rooted in the trauma – no past trauma feelings, no depression.) 3. I have very tense muscles. My neck and left shoulder has a knot in it. It is painful. 4. I have constant guilt. 5. Early mornings are terrible. I can't relax in bed. I have a heavy cloud hanging over me. (BINGO – I have her symbology for 'depression' – the black cloud is one of the most common metaphors for depression.) 6. Depression.' (Everything she just said is her 'depression'.)

Poor lady – the constant anxiety starting in the childhood home has left unconscious patterns of deep trauma and worry loops. This makes her mentally and physically tense – extremely so. She is on a war footing but the 'war' is over. These feeling are trapped in her, no drugs will do anything other than suppress them and make them worse as the 'issues' behind the 'symptoms' are left unaddressed. This level of trauma cannot be wished away. It won't go by itself unless some miracle occurs – we must jointly create that 'miracle'! I have already noted that this lady sees everything in very stark, black and white, stressed brain terms – it is making her intolerant and impatient of others. I must deal with that. What has the lady, in a roundabout, indirect way told me? ***I am in emotional pain now and I want it to stop now.***

8. When did these problems start? Is there an event that you feel started them?

Answer: she says, 'Insomnia for 2 ½ years (What she means by 'insomnia' will be outlined soon). It was my sudden divorce. It was unexpected. I am lonely. I feel disconnected from my daughter (reminds her of ex-husband?). Any pressure at all and I feel an onset of depression.'

The fairly recent divorce is the trigger – the stress caused by the meaning she gave to this event and the stress caused by the withdrawal of affection, financial and child rearing support pushes her over the edge. The insecurity of childhood has returned affecting her self-worth. She feels bad.

At this point I ask my: 'Are you having bizarre and violent dreams?' 'Yes' she replies. As I do this she smiles; I have demonstrated understanding of her problem. I go on to explain the connection between sleep, dreams and the 'depression cycle*' (*see appendix).

9. What are the positive benefits of making this change?

Answer: 'I will be able to communicate better and be flexible (physically and mentally – stress = rigidity). I will be more relaxed. I want my own house. I want to make quick decisions...' She also tells me about a bone breaking in her teenage years (physical abuse?). She also tells me about a protective pattern match she has – she hates alcohol; understandable because of her dad. BUT the problem is 99% of men in Europe drink, pretty much all men in England and she now lives in England! Her young unconscious made this connection – All (universal quantifier) alcohol associations are bad! WRONG! When the trauma feelings go this will spontaneously 'reframe'. She also tells me about being 'over clean' and too tidy. She tells me that as a child she would 'obsessively' tidy her dolls and put them in little rows. Her mother took her to a hypnotist to treat this in Russia. I said, 'You're a woman. All women tidy stuff up. Not my mum/mom but most women.'

At this she bursts out laughing and so do I. This is the first time that the Slavic 'ice queen' façade breaks. She has a huge smile on her face and it won't go. I have already broken her out of her unresourceful state. _Note for the perennially stupid – if you are politically correct you'll be a shit therapist. It means you can't think rationally. You will operate from a perverse and judgemental Manichean frame._ From this point she lightens up considerably and I make her laugh several more times. She enjoys this. I enjoy this. She clearly isn't that depressed.

- What have you done to overcome this so far, if anything, and how successful or not were those things?

Apart from the anti-depressants which we already discussed she tried some 'self-help' books; they worked 'a bit' she tells me. Self-help is one of the biggest financial scams going.

- What future evidence will let you know we have succeeded today?

Answer: 'I want a partner close to my soul. I am scared of trusting. (She believes she is not 'attractive enough'; she looks like a supermodel!) I am unmotivated to work (she wants motivation – it's lacking from the anxiety induced exhaustion). I moved here and I am studying psychology and philosophy plus architecture. (Philosophy and psychology are bound up in architectural symbology: Architectonics - a fascinating subject. Note: *she* has a need for intellectual stimulation; she is a very bright lady. This is a need she has as an *individual*). I feel disconnected as a foreigner. I am conscious of my accent (it's lovely). I only like talking about serious subjects. I may sound a bit arrogant but I know I am very intelligent (she is; depressed intelligent people often find trivial conversation boring). I run an interior design company and my husband left me with lots of debts. I am scared and guilty about the invoices (finance again). My sleep is terrible – I am still awake at 4 am. I constantly wakeup (her unconscious is preserving her sanity by doing this). I fall asleep late and get up at 10am. I feel better sitting up. I pretend to sleep. I tried to use special pillows (the pillow ain't the problem hun!).'

She kind of answered my question in a back to front, upside down kinda way. This is usual. *Therapeutic questions are merely rituals to provoke a client to spill the beans in their own way.* Then she tells me about some bullshit book she's been reading about mental illness and intuition. Yawn. She says that this author (who will remain unnamed) said that, 'It is easier to be ill than accept you are incapable.' One word: CRAPPOLA!!! Self-help books may as well be written by witch doctors, though their beliefs are probably less weird than those of published shrinks etc. Really. What does this lady need?

- To be relaxed. When she is – everything will start to work properly.

- She seeks flexibility because she knows her black and white, either or and incredibly overly 'judgemental' (about silly things) mindset is stopping her getting what she wants. Namely some bloody good old fashioned human companionship. She fails to make quick decisions because she overanalyses all the wrong things!

- Note that she is suffering from what I call GND - 'Global Nomad Disorder'. This is simply a term taken from French politico **Jacques Attali's** book, **'Millenium: Winners and losers in the Coming new economic order.'** He predicted that globalisation would produce masses of global nomads (immigrants) who lack a sense of place, home and history: all essential human needs. Like many people from abusive backgrounds she fled a country but the problem was and is always within. You can't run from your own feelings. When she's relaxed as a baseline state and able to reflect calmly, rationally and creatively she'll deal with this adaptation process one way or another. Constant anxiety = no clarity. Celts, Slavs, Germans are all one big extended family anyway.

- This lady needs to lighten up and quit the aloof, poor suffering me Hamlet persona and live damn it, live! As I say, she needs to, 'Bite into the ass of life!' She's floating around in a pathological trance observing all of life's wrongs, like a disconnected wraith. She needs to go skinny dipping and get blind drunk! I keep these thoughts to myself. Next...

- What do you enjoy about your life now?
  Are there any situations in which you are
  already confident/happy/secure/content?
  What achievements are you most proud
  of? (3 in 1!)

Answer: 'Reading. I like attending lectures. I
read religious books – I am interested in
spiritual matters. I am fascinated by
interesting things etc.'

She's a smarty pants this lady: intelligent
clients are always easier to work with. The
conversations are more stimulating. You can
use her state of fascination via revivification to
help her enter trance if you want.

- What are your strengths as a person?

Answer: 'I am clever. Courageous. I do things.
I feel sorry for others who are suffering. I
have conversations with God (for atheist
therapists – this is quite normal behaviour for
a religious person; do not misinterpret this as
a 'problem'). I do not look for ugliness in
anyone. I felt very happy when I was
engaged...'

Okay – she has good self-worth regarding

traits that she has; so in this sense that part of 'self-esteem' is good: she has good 'ego strength' regarding her brains especially! But and it's a big but...she cannot sustain core feelings of worth unless she is externally validated by others. Of course anyone feels good when they get engaged (well most people!) but when the admiration and love is withdrawn she 'collapses' in on herself. A good marriage is a great healer; trust me. I ask...

- If you were to rate your self-esteem from 0-10, 0 being you feel terrible and 10 on top of the world, what would it be?

Her reply is indirect...

Answer: 'I lack memory. I am intelligent. I write affirmations. I also feel a bit more relaxed now. But I think I am ugly and not attractive. I tell myself I am stupid. I can say I put myself down.'

The memory problems are caused by stress and past trauma – that will fix itself when she's relaxed. Writing affirmations must be a legacy from some dumb self-help book. Repeating, 'I am happy' won't make it so. Like my first depressed client in this book she cannot see reality as it is: this lady is stunningly attractive but with low self-worth she cannot see it. I wonder if her dad in his sober moments ever told her she was beautiful. If you have girls you really have to tell them how beautiful they are at least a few times a day. She fractionates between self-hate and a kind of cute 'narcissism' – you know that attractive pride that women have in themselves as women. This is part of an internal war caused by childhood neglect.

- Self-esteem boost: obviously! As I have only about 2 hours to spare I decide to focus on detraumatisation and relaxation restoration etc. I have to prioritise my time: will work on self-esteem specifically if she books another session and it hasn't auto-corrected; it might!

- What specific things do you do to relax?

Answer: 'I have a bath. I like books. I like Romance books (yearning need). I read novels. A lot of them. I like music.'

Again you could get her to visualise doing any of this stuff to create trance. I notice she doesn't use her body much. This is also a source of her depression – she is not getting good feelings from physical activity; like most of my clients she is 'head bound': she needs to get out of her head and into the world. She hides from the potentially harsh and painful world of relationships in her own enclosed inner world. It is 'safe' but very lonely there. There is pain, misunderstanding etc. in all close relationships from time to time; that just a part of being human.

- Do you exercise?

Answer: 'From time to time I have a spinal problem. I walk and I focus on the steps. I walk fast, long distances. I have a slight lack of motivation to exercise. I need someone to push me.'

Not exercising is one of the biggest causes of anxiety as I have said. She needs to get this injury fixed or treated properly. Long walks aren't enough – good for fresh air and getting out and about BUT it must be at least moderately vigorous exercise to 'flush out' the accumulated stress. I tell her about the benefits of exercise and she grits her teeth as if a bit angry and says,
'I know!'

This pleases me because it means she is relaxed enough with me to be genuine in her responses. I make my clients feel as if they are talking to an old friend very quickly. Sometimes they'll say to me – 'I feel like I've known you for ages!' I am never aloof, I don't play an 'authority figure' role. I'm just me. I know a great deal about hypnosis and I am professional. Don't 'be' a hypnotist, just use hypnosis when it's useful from time to time: honestly you'll be more successful in therapy with this approach. Somewhere around this point I also realise she has terrible eating habits; you must eat properly otherwise you can become anxious/depressed etc. if you're lucky!

- Do you have any intuitive sense of what has to change within yourself so that I can help or rather what will need to occur _during this process_ for you to make the required changes?

Answer: 'Sleep. It is a vicious circle. I am _constantly_ tired. And in pain. I feel like a hero. I do not understand the meaning of it (her suffering). I do not find funny things funny but sad...'

For this lady as with pretty much all my depression clients, a regular, good night's sleep is the key! Notice that she _claims_ she has no sense of humour; she's been laughing her ass off for the past 10 minutes! Depressed people forget the good times. Some therapists advise that they keep records of their upbeat

424

moments in a diary so that they can prove to themselves that from time to time they do feel good. I just blast that depression away in one go baby! I ain't takin' no prisoners! She says that her suffering is meaningless. In a way she's right – suffering often has no redeeming features, it's just like saying that holding you hand over a flame is good for you. Er, no it isn't. It just feels awful. 'Pain' exists to teach us that something is wrong. She cannot think of a metaphor that symbolises the problem or solution. I move on...

19. Is there any reason you shouldn't make this change?

Answer: 'No. I honestly desire for success.'

20. What stops you from making this change on your own?

Answer: 'Lack of support. And energy. Not enough understanding from others (true relatives etc. are often awful sources of advice – they simply know too little; their theory of mind is weak – their recovery tips are little more than old wives tales!) I am in physical pain (interestingly she asks for no help with this; often pain is the sole cause of depression, remove that and the 'depression'

goes – who would have thought Sherlock!?)
21. Have you ever made a similar change?

Answer: 'My life is not going in the right direction (her needs are not being met). I constantly want to please other people (low self-worth). I want to be easier to be around and not a burden on others (desire for self-reliance and improved mood). But I am ambitious; I often get what I want!'

Despite this lady's dark view of the world stemming ultimately from the prolonged childhood trauma of neglect and fear she has deep within her soul a great strength of spirit and character. This is the only thing that has kept her sane. She is one tough cookie!

22. What do you know about hypnosis?

She doesn't know what it is. She talks about 'programming'. I say no that's not it and her face drops. She is a grade A type student and not used to being misinformed. I tell her hypnosis is about re-associating to her best traits and resources. I am actually going to deprogramme her – of her trauma and the erroneous conclusions and generalisations that her younger self drew from that chronically stressful experience of growing up:

sometimes you just have to survive your family! I also carry out a universal needs questionnaire but it's already obvious what needs are not being satisfied, isn't it? In her hypnosis session I focus on 6 problem matrix factors:

A. Detraumatisation – the past feelings must be removed and replaced with 'wellbeing' etc.

B. Worry. Comes primarily from the above.

C. Sleep. Ditto - this is the core psycho-physiological recovery issue.

D. Flexibility of thinking. She is too rigid in her problem solving methods.

E. Getting her needs met now.

F. Being able to lighten up and laugh – you can restore a sense of humour using hypnosis. I'll show you precisely how.

G. Eating well.

The whole script would be too massive and all the component parts are covered elsewhere in this book. What follows are modules for:

1. Mental and physical relaxation and total 'flexibility of thinking'.

2. Being able to laugh again. *If we cannot laugh, we cannot see reality as it is.* Nor can we spontaneously generate new meanings and reframes. Nor are we much fun to be around!

3. Eating nutritious food to fuel the brain so it can function optimally. A brain starved of nutrients is a potentially depressed brain.

Shall we?

Interventions: seeing the world in a more rounded way depression script.

This woman's major problem is that she OVERGENERALISES massively. I induce a very deep relaxed state of hypnosis and between modules I take her deeper and deeper again. My aim is to retrain the brain to know how to recognise and 'do' relaxation again...Again: insert the 'How to detraumatise anyone' process first.

Part 1: Immersed in nature deepener.

(Deep hypnosis assumed)

'Already you are learning the right way to simply allow your mind and body to **rest**

deeply and **feel so calm again, now.**
What's it like when you settle all the way
down somewhere comfortably? A nice time as
you let yourself **relax even more.** Because
of course you know the best way to **learn** any
set of new skills do you not? That's right. We
all **really learn** best when **you're relaxed.** A
natural state where, when you just **absorb
information easily** – your **hypnotic state,
now...**

When you are in just the right place, time and
state of mind how would it be to **picture
yourself** going on a journey through a place
of resplendent natural beauty? I don't know
where that is – you do, for this is your
changing experience where you are choosing
to **process some information quite
differently** than you habitually used to, and
that's a good thing, is it not? Notice sounds,
natural sounds inside that captivate your
attention inwardly, as you might when you
pleasantly daydream...perfect; notice the
music and harmony of nature. Notice of
course the soothing quality of lights, colours
and the reflections of colours, highlights and
shade as an artist might.

I want you to **go inside so deeply** to a place
where you can attain profound levels of **deep**

comfort and rest. Let **you're unconscious...**mind...**now**...be your guide. That's it. For only it knows the way to **healing.** The thing about nature and being immersed in natural sensations is that it is inherently healing to the human spirit. And in hypnosis, the imagined is as powerful as the real, the effects are the same. Can you tangibly **feel the atmosphere of such levels of peace, tranquillity of mind and body?** Your **serenity...now!** It requires merely the gentlest of no effort at all, here.

Excellent. As you wander and wonder in this special sanctuary of your own...I would like you to notice ten things in that place that help you **relax even more.** They'll help you **go deeper into hypnotic oblivion.** I will be quiet for a whole entrancing minute of solar time whilst you **operate within another time** sphere...You just **feel the change in trance depth** happening as you notice each deepening thing. I don't know what the first, second, fifth, seventh or more, beyond that might be – you, only know, now. *(Quiet for 1 minute – a variation of a symbolic deepener, as outlined in book 4, 'Forbidden hypnotic secrets').*

Lovely. And how much better does that feel

already? And we've only really just begun to go beyond what wasn't really, anymore, now. What is it about this particular experience that you are having that delights you most? Get a true sense of your capacity for gentle delight in simple pleasures. Your unconscious only wants to help you. And despite where you are, it's truly possible to **relax all...the way down...completely, now.** You are **restoring your levels of energy and motivation** back to their natural potential – as you might recharge a cell phone/mobile or battery. That's it. Take one more moment to **feel the bliss** of this place...Good.

Part 2: Going beyond bias – creativity in problem solving.

Sometimes we go about things in less than helpful ways...we may not see problems as the challenges they are that help us **mature** beyond our younger perceptions of what we once feared were our 'limitations'...often defined by others...We may learn to associate things that do not match as if they did or might...a person who has a fear of x, y and z when **there is no real danger in certain situations** is a case in point. There is a time for the fight or flight response and on other occasions, more frequently than not, **a**

certain situation does not require that amount of energy. Now, when people are less than totally calm, there is always the possibility of forming an inaccurate generalisation – we need generalisations, it's part of what our deeper mind does for us; we need to make certain automatic responses to certain stimulus but it is always best to update your generalisations when new learnings and understanding come our way.

Some people I see focus on all the things they'd rather not. And so it's not that surprising that they don't **feel so good** as they ought or really want. They might make mountains out of molehills and molehills out of mountains – one thing is maximised another minimised in less than helpful ways. We can always **see the forest for the trees** when your mind is much **calmer now.** In order to **see things as they are,** you must **reflect reality calmly** and see a still reflection without the disturbed ripples of the past. That's right. It is always best to **see things as they are.**

Some people *(client's name),* as we spoke about, see the world though stressed black and white thinking, everything is always an extreme of this or that with no shades of grey.

But isn't anyone's ongoing and changing experience made up of degrees of pleasant and less than pleasant occurrences and can't the meanings and feelings change over time too? You know they can and do. Really, one of the keys is to **moderate your language... and stop making unrealistically negative generalisations, now.**

But we've all had times when and where what we thought was less than perfect turned out to have done us good. Four persons witnessing one event will all **have a different point of view about certain things.** Our mind generates meanings from events – the meaning of meanings can change for the better when **your mind is so relaxed and able to function optimally.** That's right. Just like that. When any of us **relax and alter perceptions appropriately...**we notice that meanings can and do change...As a body of water may be rough and choppy in a storm, yes, but once the storm is passed it can **become still again.**

As events unfold do we always know how things will turn out? Do we have to in order to **feel calm and relaxed with uncertainty** (?) Is it always helpful to pay attention to rumours and speculation upon which no evidence **rests** (?) When **you're calm,** aren't we less likely to be hoodwinked by past assumptions? Isn't it sometimes better to just **wait certain things out calmly** (?) When things in the present are not as clear as we'd wish it may be best to **snap out of old trances and focus on pleasant realities.** Of course you can daydream about this or that. You can waste energy on running a billion 'what ifs' in your mind. That might have happened or you could STOP! And simply **become fully present.** As you do, your unconscious can work as you **remain calm and stop misusing your imagination.** How can anyone reach all perfect conclusions without a time machine or a crystal ball that works? Just let your life unfold with the knowledge that you're okay at a very deep level. And this also has to do with the fact that you are reconnecting to your inherent self-belief, now. Trust your unconscious to help by **being here now** with relaxation as an ally. That's it. Your creative problem solving abilities can function when you **re-access and lock in your calmest capacities to wait and see.** What if you could **focus your mind on what you want and need** and how to satisfy that, **now.** Because a good generalisation to operate from is – we get more of what we focus on and so why not

focus on ways to get satisfaction from simple daily pleasures (?) What it you could retrain your mind in trance to **notice all the joys around you** (?) What if the way light hit a blade of grass in a never to be repeated moment was a pleasure? There are treasures all around you, within you and in others and you'll become so good, so adept at **paying attention to that which makes you feel much better, now.** The core of these natural abilities is **your calm mind, now.** You are merely re-associating to your birth right, as certain subconscious structures begin to alter...all is well, all is well...

You know the great thing about life, the wonderful thing about it and about us in it is that it and we are not perfect. Thank goodness. I know you told me you were a 'perfectionist' *(client's name)*. But 'perfect' according to whom? And for what purpose? Can life, can you be perfect ALL the time realistically? You can't get from others what they are incapable of giving – let it go. What if you could perfect some new abilities which are really natural ones you had but hadn't used in a while – because I know up till now you've had a great talent for visualising the worst worries about future possibilities. This tells me **you are creative** and have a powerful imagination. That's a good thing. What you are going to notice from now on is you can **use that creative faculty positively.** You no longer show yourself those worries and concerns of the past, now, instead you can use your very real talent to **picture what you'd like to happen.** That's it. That's your 100% personal new reality and this is so.

We all need to **compartmentalise things appropriately** too. It's really time, is it not, to **stop overgeneralising** about so many things. What might be true here isn't necessarily true there; is that not so? Just because you have one flat tire does that mean all the tires are flat or will surely become flat? You know the answer. I knew a woman who told me that good things never last but then neither do the bad. Suffering is temporary. A bump in the road and then you just glide with the smooth. I knew a man who believed that all less than wonderful things were permanent. And then he found a wallet full of money on the ground. There are many more than only one rigid slant for viewing any situation. If I am an artist and I look at a tall building from the ground it looks one way. From a helicopter looking down I **see things in a new way.** And from inside that building looking out I **see quite a different**

perspective.

What you need to develop is an attitude of **balance.** Is everything always wonderful? Evidently not. BUT when **you are so calm in mind and body** you can **think more flexibly** about so many things. You'll **see problems as challenges** to be overcome on your path to **greater and greater maturation and improvement** than you once dreamed was possible. When you realise that life is not a perpetual tightrope. When you realise that a body of water can **be still again.** When you **go beyond past bias** towards a more rounded perspective, now, you'll **recognise that things are very different from those illusions** and your increasingly calm mind can **see things in a more even and balanced way.** When you **calm right down, now** – you'll notice that it's impossible to hold onto all the past always, nevers and forevers. Words are not always linked to realities. Challenge past distortions unconsciously so that **only the helpful more realistic generalisations win.** When you **stop worrying unconsciously,** those loops stop looping and you'll **start sleeping well again.**

In order to **solve any problem calmly** we

need to **set goals,** even the tiniest will do because you can build up from that to greater and greater successes – even making a nice cup of tea or coffee or tasty sandwich is a success. When you **think in this new way,** when you **alter your focus** towards that which you wish to happen and take steps to make it so, you'll come to know that it all begins with **you're taking action daily** to create the kind of life you want; which all starts with your ideas about what they should be for you, based on your unique needs as an individual in this world, now. There are many useful, helpful and better ways of **viewing reality objectively.** What if you came to believe that you could **be very practical**? Why not imagine at least 3 ways to solve any problem? How could you solve any problem most elegantly? And you will, will you not? Will you not? Haven't you. Thaaa-aat's right.

Anterior cingulate cortex reactivation.

(Anxiety keeps a person stuck by preventing their brain's anterior cingulate cortex from working properly – see book 7, 'Escaping cultural hypnosis'.)

Because the fact is you had been stuck in a limited use of your brain, locked in that state of rumination and over-analysis. BUT another part of you works when you **relax deeply;** it allows you to unconsciously access sets of associations beyond that past bias and all you have to do is **relax and re-access that ability, now.** This part known as your brain's anterior cingulate cortex is your creative part – it controls all your emotional responses and to prove I'm right, will that part please let this person **experience a wonderful feeling** to confirm this (pause a beat); that's right. Thank you. You can take that message as a sign and a signal that that part can creatively problem solve on your behalf whilst you just **get on with the enjoyable process of living, now.**

The thing about any generalisations is that there are *always* exceptions. In fact as I am quiet, can you simply recall some times when what you once negatively assumed was entirely contrary to what actually and positively happened? *(NFH: Shhh for a full minute.)* As a result of this you can **delete certain beliefs** that held you back...only to **replace them with better generalisations** that help, unconsciously, nooo-ooow. You are a creative problem solver and this is so. Know, really know that there is something within you, a quality if you like that is so strong –

some call this your 'inner strength' – it helps you in many ways that you little understand to **overcome the challenges of life;** reconnect to this power, nooo-ooowww!

Using the imagination to problem solve: future pace.

(This linked module is entrainment in positive use of the creative faculty to imagine many ways to solve even basic problems; the essence of 'flexible thinking' – we can process information in sounds, images, symbols – you name it: your unconscious is your happy little slave – visualise what you want and it tries its best to make it happen.)

The good thing about your creativity is that it loves to solve problems so that another part of you can just **forget about some things** and get on with living enjoyably – ideas, insights, intuitions and hunches just pop into your mind, often when you least expect it BUT in order for that to happen and it will, you really need, each and both of you, to **have such a relaxed frame of mind habitually, now.** I don't know what that precisely means to you but the deeper you does.

Something else has also occurred: you are

now aware of the counter-productive futility of old patterns of black and white thinking, unrealistically negative assumptions and generalisations, all or nothing expectations that turn out to be nothing but hot air in your mind, in the past, that's right. You know that if you are going to **make use of your imagination positively** it is best to **think about what you want and then visualise that.** Because that was a big part of what you had called the old 'depression' that you had once experienced BUT you have moved far, far beyond that. Where there was once a black cloud *(use the client's symbology)* you will now **notice a clarity and intelligent foresight** has replaced those old patterns as though the sun is shining in the clear sky *(the opposite symbology)*. When we are fearful it can make us dumb and you are a smart lady/man, so that being so - **relax your way to your most intelligent capacities** as a complete woman (etc.). The good thing about an unpleasant experience is that you need only go through it once. You'll find you can **see things in a balanced perspective** free from the former chains of the illusions of unnecessary fears that have dissipated and faded away...completely. That's it.

Get in touch with how much more relaxed and

clear your entire mind-body system is. How much better does that feel? To what degree will you experience more of this? How much better will **your renewed calm** make you feel on a daily basis? As you achieve so many big and little goals that go toward your sense of shaping your own destiny, now. The darkness has lifted and there is only the light of **calmly imagining doing certain things** that need to be done, **calmly doing some things differently,** at times **communicating your needs calmly** to others, having much more fun and just **lightening up** about so many things. It's as if a great weight has been lifted. Ah! You'll begin to **see through, past and beyond, far beyond previous distortions in thinking.** You'll think things through without excessive rumination, no longer looping worries rather than **taking purposeful action to get your meaningful desires met** more than adequately. Knowing this has all changed, really changed, can allow you to **feel a foretaste of the satisfactions of delightful living** you are deeply reconnecting to as very many reorganisations of certain unconscious structures only occurs, now.

And to reinforce the power of your new

approach I would simply like you to **imagine solving any problem you want:** it could be some simple thing we all have to do to take care of ourselves, it could be going on a date, it could be a small or a big goal, it may involve a small series of steps of a long chain of tasks that leads to certain success...Big or small it starts with an idea, then a plan. Go through as many as you want and I'll be quiet for a whole minute of solar time while you **experience an entranced time** which permits you to **mentally rehearse doing what needs to be done** to open up your capacity to **get in control of things, to feel more alive,** in your own unique way – knowing you are an individual who is different and who has unique patterns, meanings, dreams, purposes and more, to **live with zest** and abundance, and to relate in better ways, deservingly forgive in ways that assist, take the rough and the smooth seeing that it's your response that determines the outcome more often than not. Knowing no one can perfectly control or please, **spotting opportunities** like that man I saw who found gold where he fantasised once upon a time that there was only dirt, noooo-ooow! That's it. You are doing magnificently. Retrain your mind to **take practical steps to achieve** all manner of wishes. Even a nice drink of your favourite beverage, **thinking calm thoughts** can be an indication that **this has worked so powerfully,** has it not? *(Quiet for 1 minute please...)*

Part 3: The hypnotic structure of meaning.

As you become even more fascinated by this changing process you might begin to wonder about the meanings that any of us give to things. Some people make assumptions that are never updated. They can take experiences that apply to only one part of human experience and apply false conclusions to others. We make assumptions about ourselves, others, places, people and events do we not? I knew a man who assumed no woman would find him attractive because the first girl he ever asked out said no. But the planet is full of women; isn't it reasonable that just one might find him attractive? We can all go through tough times, just a part of living and assume that we're stuck in that phase but a phase it just that. It's actually impossible for things to stay exactly the same. We move. We age. We learn. We mature. We surpass. We **overcome, now.** The world is usually not as limited as our old patterns of limiting perceptions may have once suggested – like a dumb hypnotist who focused your mind on quite the wrong things.

But as you have learned, really learned to **become so incredibly relaxed** you now know, do you not that **meaning is flexible** in many useful ways (?). When you realise this at a very fundamental level of experience you will notice that **depressed thinking goes.** Part is not all. Sometimes is not all times. One person is not all. And it helps to **moderate your language** when more accurately describing your ongoing experience through the prism of calm eyes. Is there ONLY ever one way to do anything in particular? You know the real answer. You can only be very disappointed if you expected something from a faulty map. Now and again we need to step back and take a broader view – not only focusing in on details, fixed patterns but seeing there is a **freedom in flexible approaches,** new patterns, better perspectives. Because one thing about meaning that is certain is that **meanings change** over time, when **moods change** as we **mature** and more, **now.**

What if I promised you that when you **live creatively,** when certain points of view **soften and consider other ways,** how pleasantly surprised might you be to find that things mysteriously turn out better without effort? What if you **now believe that glorious opportunities and pleasant responses lie all around you** (?) That the world is full of hidden treasures that you can begin looking for as your wondrous mind did as a child when you wanted to **learn** the reality of this amazing place you were in. How nature fascinated you. How you might watch an ant scurry with wonder? No one is so perfect so as to know everything. You can **be relaxed with not knowing.** What is the meaning of meaning? What is the meaning of wonder? Have you ever laughed so much that you **just let certain things go** without trying? I know you have. As you realise that meanings are flexible, depending on so many other factors. As you know that not all things are in your control. Was it always your fault? Really? As you become aware of the inability of any source to be right always; as you **trust yourself** more: don't be too surprised as to how much more calm you are in daily living. Are generalisations always right? What if the meaning isn't clear right now? What if or so what? Do you know a hypnotist can create ideas in the mind that others slavishly follow even if they're silly – wouldn't it be better to use this hypnotic state to **regain your freedom from the tyranny of past**

unwanted perspectives, now (?) This occurs in deep relaxation where and when you are capable of making much more uplifting connections and associations, now. I know you have had moments of complete relaxation and clarity and as you **feel that way now** – ponder on what I have said as I continue...

And now...I'd simply like you to realise, in the way that suits you best, that those old patterns of meaning were just like passing clouds on summer days and **with a feeling of completely calm detachment** you are free to just see them pass through in a dissociated way – we think all kinds of things and not all are helpful. Have you ever said something to someone but you didn't really mean it? With your far greater calm you can **distance yourself from past patterns** that held you back. You can **calmly examine particular thoughts** and thoughts about thoughts more objectively. Don't be too surprised to notice that you **feel more positive** and **think more positively*** too, **now.**

(*Depression is often believed to be 'negative thinking': if only it were that easy!)

Symbology: turning worries into removable objects.

Can you imagine now getting one of those old worries, those thoughts you looped over and over, that you ruminated on pointlessly, like wheels getting you nowhere and just STOP and turn that thought into something you can kick and kick that thought far, far, far away till those sorts of things don't bother you, anymore? That's perfect. And I'll be quiet for 20 seconds whilst you **get rid of more old worries** in this way. Again: take those former habitual worries and turn them into a quite kickable symbol that you can boot far, far away. *(Pause etc.)*

Future pace.

I'd like you to take the time now to picture yourself going through your much more satisfying life on a movie screen in your mind's eye. That you is very calm, that you can **think constructively** about how to get needs met. That you can **see so many more possibilities.** That you can **feel a blissful serenity.** That you can **feel so much better about all kinds of things.** And what if that you could learn to believe unconsciously that you can see so many things in a softer, kinder,

448

gentler more wholesome way when that's appropriate. That person has **let go of past illusions** of guilt and so many other things that were never true of the deepest you. That you is relaxed in mind and body – see how all that tension and stiffness has gone so that **you are physically and mentally much more flexible.** That you is **responding more resourcefully and creatively.** That you knows that meanings are not always fixed and static but evolve as we **change,** really change. That you is not bothered by feelings, perceptions of a younger you doing the best she/he could, in old circumstances that once troubled you but now they are just something you take in your stride. You adjust – differently, better than ever, automatically. That's it. Watch that – learn from your best self while I'm quiet. *(30 seconds should be enough.)*

In fact I would like you now to associate into a future time when you feel so much better about all manner of things without knowing you could. A situation that might have bothered you - but now see it from your new, balanced perspective. You **feel so much more comfortable** with certain people, certain events, things you have and want, need to do. Feel the abundance of satisfaction flow through you from head to toe. You do not need to know how this had happened, wasn't it? I'll be quiet again as you **mentally rehearse the new patterns** you are embedding into the deepest subconscious structures and associations in your mind. *(30 seconds silence.)*

When you awaken later you will **feel a peace of mind** unlike anything you've known. You think, feel and live, really live differently. More satisfaction than you ever dreamed of. These very many learnings have contained a multitude of understandings that will remain with you, only growing stronger. Perfect – you are doing so well! Now I'm going to tell you a secret about how to **feel good** for free. *(That will get their attention.)* That raging whirlpool has turned into a calmly flowing stream, a beautiful babbling brook and that's nice to know isn't it? Can you consider, deeply, the true meaning of **calmness**?

Part 4: The power of laughter!

(When wishing to elicit any state in hypnosis adopt a tone of voice consistent with that state – with laughter put a slight giggle in your voice as if you find what you are saying so very funny. If your client laughs out loud

during the following take it as a good sign!)

Have you ever noticed the interplay of shadows and light depending on the time of year? We may not understand a sound until we are close enough. If we walk under or over things **your perspective changes naturally.** In the film about Kasper Hauser he believed a tall building must have been made by a very big man; is this so? Where is the place that humour comes from? What part of you is in charge of laughter? How will it **find new ways to be amused** (?)

It can be helpful to **cultivate an attitude of gratitude** – in this relaxed and more humorous place, what do you really recognise now that you have to be truly grateful for? Take a minute or so to **calmly contemplate** this – with an inner smile and twinkle. *(Pause for 60 secs.)*

Now, let's talk about laughter, humour*,* **you're finding things funny again,** that kind of thing. Your sense of humour is a totally natural asset that you have to **dissipate unpleasant feelings.** You can laugh and smile for free and both are such wonderful mood boosters and better than that they are part of who you were, are and will be.

451

Humour is powerful because it helps you to **break past former rigid thinking patterns...**humour is powerful because it boosts your creativity...humour is powerful because it helps you **see things anew...**and there is a wisdom in the most innocent of jokes. Using your sense of humour is just a natural part of who you are reconnecting to – that's not a suggestion; that's a reality, now. If you weren't meant to laugh and smile why do you have the genetics to do so? Humour teaches us very quickly that there are many more than just one possible meaning, does it not? Humour even allows you to see an event that you felt one way about in an entirely different light. What if obstacles were just a unique type of opportunity when looked at in the right way?

Humour is a way of thinking. Humour is a way of seeing. Humour is a way of doing. Humour is a way of believing. Humour is a way of feeling. Humour is a great tool in you're being much more objective. It is a way to **remain grounded, practical and realistic.** It is a way of receiving insights. It can **expand your frame of reference** very quickly indeed. It is a way of relating and perceiving.

What are the positive effects or affects of

laughter? Too many to mention! When we laugh we use our body in a unique way to make us **feel good.** Have you ever experienced a time when it seemed you just wouldn't ever stop laughing? Can you let a memory of that time come to mind...That's it. Humour reveals truths and makes us **much more fun to be around. Now.** This in turn will make anyone **feel much more attractive** too. Do you know it's not possible to feel as bad about anything when **you laugh more**? It is actually good for all your body and all it's automatic functions when **you find more reasons to laugh.** Were you ever in a situation when you shouldn't have laughed but where you got the giggles? Can you let a memory of such a time spring to mind as I talk and **you recall laughing.** You know the more we try to stop laughing the more we have to laugh!? There are many differing and funny points of view-mer *(play on words)*. What if you could learn to **exercise your sense of humour** more and more and more until inevitably **your humour shines through.** What if your unconscious mind now starts looking out for more frequent opportunities to **see the funny side** of so many things. Recall a time you laughed so much that your tummy muscles felt the effort afterwards... That's it.

What really makes you laugh? What do you find really funny? Do you have a favourite comedy show or comedian? Do you have a really funny friend that you like to spend time with? I am only a hypnotist and this is but a suggestion but what if you **deliberately seek out experiences that allow you to laugh more**? You might watch a favourite TV comedy show. Go to see a stand up comedian. Your sense of humour improves when you see the unexpected suddenly, enjoy the absurdities of life, notice rapid reversals of perspective, now. Do some people make you laugh more than others? Perhaps you should **spend time with people who lift your spirits**? We need to be around people who help keep you grounded, who tease us and **don't take things so seriously,** inside or out.

I'd like you to take the time to really immerse yourself in past times when you laughed so much. That's it. Maybe one time in particular springs to mind. You know people love to laugh so much they'll pay for the privilege? What if you start generating lots of funny 'what ifs' with your amazing imaginative capacity? Laughter is so enjoyable that just the sound of it is infectious and as you **experience good deep belly laughs** you

feel so wonderfully relaxed as though you have done some exercise.

Future pace.

Imagine now a time in your future when **you are laughing so much** that you just can't stop! See that laughing you over there in some situation in which you realise **you can laugh about so many different things** – you own the gift of laughter as part of your rich biological heritage. The more you laugh the more you want to laugh. The more you **use your sense of humour more often** the easier it all gets because anything at all is far easier with practice and you can practise right here in your mind... *(Pause for 30 secs.)*

When you are ready – drift, float into that you who is in absolute hysterics of laughter! That's it! **Experience humour** from the inside out – see what you'll see that is so funny, hear what you'll hear that makes that laughter so all-encompassing and infectious, feel how wonderful it feels to **laugh out loud** – deep belly laughs now! You may even be laughing so much that you cry tears of joy and tears can be so beautiful. Maybe others are laughing which makes it seem funnier still? Maybe you are rolling around on the floor in hysterics? I don't know – you do! Let all that joy out now! Let it all out and **feel the freedom of laughter deep inside** – the best medicine as they say. I'll be quiet for a full minute as you **practise using your laughter muscles, now.** (Do so...)

So you have learned the power of laughter – you know that you know how to **feel good by looking for humorous meanings and interpretations of many things.** I want you to know that a deeper part of you is looking out for you so that you can **notice many opportunities to find things funnier in general** and won't it be a pleasant discovery to find out what they are, haven't you? That's right. You have rediscovered the gift of mirth, the generous gift of laughter! Enjoying it fully now on a daily basis, locking in these changes permanently, making any and all adjustments to the appropriate subconscious structures and associations and this is so.

Part 5: Feel good food!

(This woman did not eat right! She ate a chocolate bar that day and nothing else! No surprise she's anxious...)

In order to **feel calm long-term** you need to **eat well.** We discussed the importance of getting needs met. Your body needs good food to function optimally; it's as simple as that. You need to breathe, you need water, sunlight and you need nutritious food. Imagine now preparing a wonderful meal: all the essential food groups are covered – fat, carbs, proteins. You **eat organic fresh vegetables** which are filled with all the vitamins and nutrients you need. You can enjoy shopping for the right food, online, in a shop – you care what you buy, you **care for your body.** Make meals something to look forward to with pleasant anticipation. You **love to eat healthily,** now; it's just what you do. Just consider how satisfying your new habits will be – mind and body working properly with the right fuel. There are many differing meals and ways of preparing them. **Eat a varied diet.** All **the motivation you need is there.** Food is a simple pleasure, nothing big or fancy BUT it is the re-beginning of **getting in touch with simple pleasures.** Drinking genuinely fresh and healthy water daily. Knowing some say that your gut produces 90% of your good feelings. Food affects your mood. **You eat better, you feel better. Now,** you need the energy to be able to express yourself, carry out that which must be done, achieve goals, spend time with others in fulfilling ways. The varied satisfactions of taste.

Let your subconscious be your guide as to what food you need – images will pop into your mind, perhaps tastes or smells, textures of the type of food you know, really know is instinctively good for you. In fact get the sense of eating such food now, really taste how great that food feels in your mouth, savour all the flavours, chew it at the right speed so that you **truly appreciate good food...** *(10 secs...)*

Future pace new eating habits.

Good. So just visualise yourself over there in your mind's eye buying, preparing, eating and enjoying all the right, best and most gloriously nutritious foods...The food that helps you **lock in these beneficial states of mind and body.** That's right. See that you going through a whole week or so – just get the gist of it. **These healthy eating habits are automatic responses to living.** Look how happy and healthy that new you looks, look how calm, look how much more fun loving, look at the energy and increased activity and motivation. You have all the time you need in trance to **experience these fundamental learnings.** *(Quiet for 30 secs...)*

Excellent! And when **you're happy with these changes** picture going through that process again from your own point of view – see what you'll see, hear what you'll hear, experience what you'll experience, **feel how good, calm, free, so fully motivated and energetic you really do feel, now** as a result of the alterations and shifts made today. Whizz through that whole week of nutritious achievement – mind and body working at your best. That's it. Unlearning, relearning, **re-associating to deeper, natural instincts** beyond what could never be. That's it. *(Shhh for a full minute.)* Wire it in – permanently, NOOO – OOOOW!'

(Add in any appropriate modules etc., wrap up and exduction of choice – Bob's ya uncle as they used to say! By getting clients to imagine how they like to respond you are training them to use their imagination positively, killing two birds with one stone and leaving them? Self-reliant!)

Case 7: The man who was afraid of sexy women!

Sometimes a fear can be gotten rid of by getting rid of a really dumb generalisation. I had a client who was afraid of beautiful women. YIKES! That is a problem. Unless you want to remain a sterile eunuch. You can get rid of some phobias by tackling dumb, unconscious sets of associations that have developed in response to a learning. In such cases I find early 'rejection' (you're not right for each other) creates an expectation of further rejection: often being good with women is simply the luck of being accepted for a date with the first girl you ask out! It sets up a bedrock of confidence. Unfair? Yes. Who said life was fair? This sort of problem almost always affects the more sensitive types, exactly the ones who make the best boyfriends. The insensitive just don't care about whether woman a, b or c likes them: this, ironically, is why they are so successful with them!

What follows can be applied to fear of sexy women as I call it but I am leaving it fairly generic so that you can apply its principles more widely, should the need occur. It will. The following approach could just be used as

a module etc. within a wider solution matrix.
So:

1st step – hypnotise.
2nd step – detraumatise (see the next 'case').
3rd step: *Foolish generalisations removal script.*

(Deep hypnosis assumed – obviously)

'Here/hear, I am talking to the deeper part of you. Up until now you had been responding to a certain stimulus in an inappropriate, uncomfortable, overly generalised ways for what I know were a very good set of reasons. Thanks so much for that - you did it well, for what you perceived back then as being for the best based on what you knew. However as **you mature,** you've become acutely aware that those attitudes, feelings and beliefs are not what is in your best interests any longer. In fact what had tried to help is now a hindrance to your progress. With that in mind...

It's now time to **develop a more relaxed approach to things that bothered you unnecessarily.** You really know that **certain old patterns need to alter, now.** From this moment on you could **generalise comfort in**

those situations, couldn't you? As we proceed through life we can **learn new things,** some of which help us and some of which didn't. Such functions can be changed for the better as the unconscious mind learns that often an all or nothing response can be counter-productive. I have had many clients tell me about such matters. Perhaps you once felt worried, scared even about the prospect of encountering certain people, places or situations? Now you know it's time, really time to **feel so confident about that.** That's right. What if you came to deeply believe that **that thing is no threat to you**? What if you responded to each situation, place or person based on the real character of that individual experience? You know how to **feel good** with friends and beloved relatives, do you not? So I know that you can **feel that** at other appropriate times too. All the learnings you need are deeply embedded already within your nervous system. All that need occur is for **certain positive, empowering re-associations to take place, now.** That's it. No two people are alike. Even individual animals have marked differences. And although some generalisations are very much needed and useful some aren't. At an unconscious level you can **let go of the old unrealistic generalisations, only** that no longer serve your best interests. So that from you on you **react differently** in that place, with that type of person (etc.). Beginning now you **feel so resourceful, objective and much calmer** at such times. New patterns are starting to predominate. You **have a knowing feeling** that this is so. **These improved responses simply do become your default setting – automatically, spontaneously, now.** And that knowledge can leave you with **such a feeling of security, inside** that you can take it anywhere you like. That's very nice to know is it not?

People often learn to view the world through what I call the prism of their 'isms' or should that be prisons? But reality is far bigger and more interesting than that. It really has to do with **seeing each individual as they are,** not as we once imagined them to be. No two women (stimulus x) are the same. Each lady is so very different from another that just discovering who she is is quite enough to focus your attention upon. Of course some people aren't nice, pleasant or supportive from either sex and those can be avoided. You have unconscious 'antenna' as it were that can tell you via feelings, instincts and hunches if that type of person is right for you without even having to utter a word. However you can **feel free to talk to any lady you like feeling good about yourself.** Comfortably find out who she really is.

You have the power to **evaluate and discriminate for yourself** no matter what might have happened in the past. The past isn't necessarily a prediction for the future, is it? With some people we just feel on the same wavelength almost instantly and others not so much or not at all – these sorts of feelings and more will guide you. The good thing about living this life is that it can be so pleasantly surprising from time to time and the unexpected thrill is part of the joy. You can **be so curious** to find out who she is. What is her story? What does she like and not like? And how best will this process of learning and feeling better unfold? That's for you to find out – setbacks are just the seeds of understanding to laugh at things, or the seeds of creating entertaining stories – how boring would life be it we did everything perfectly? We'd learn nothing. We would develop no resources to **deal with challenges successfully.**

I once heard of a boy who had been kept in doors so long that he had never had any bad experiences and so he didn't know how to **handle that effectively.** Your sense of humour and wit are often the key. Some people say we shouldn't be 'judgemental' as though being able to judge is a bad thing – it's the very thing that makes you human. Men are women are different – thank goodness! You can **comfortably appreciate her feminine energy** and approach, the way she sees and does things quite differently from you. Men and women are made to compliment one another. That's the way it is, always was and will be.

Direct suggestion module.

Whenever you are around a woman you feel attracted to you **feel supremely confident,** and you can **be yourself comfortably.** You have nothing to prove – remember you are evaluating her suitability too. Not all women will be right for you. Like a connoisseur of fine wine you can enjoy finding out who you really can and do connect with in a special way. You only **feel calm and relaxed around beautiful women** and this is so. You **never act desperate.** In fact the idea of feeling any fear around beautiful women is so silly that it just never happens to you again. Nervous men might feel that but **you are 100%**

secure in who you are and you **radiate that to others** without any effort. It doesn't matter if she is with friends or alone – you can **approach any women with full confidence** because you **feel very attractive, now!** You were born knowing how to **connect.** All humans instinctively know how to **flirt well.** They know how to **talk comfortably.** They know how to carry themselves with a sense of genuine pride without a trace of arrogance. What will be the most interesting part of this process? That is for you experience with a sense of fun...'

Wrap up etc.

Future pace?

You don't always have to do future paces. I don't. Sometimes I just bombard a person with direct, positive suggestions and leave it at that. I have given so many examples in this book of how to do expert level mental rehearsal that you should be able to make it up your own. That's how I learnt. I took other people's stuff and altered it, changed it to suit my clients. That's one of the good things about being a hypnotist – you get to be creative! Basic phobias may have once been caused by a lack of need satisfaction but they may not be maintained by them – sometimes they are just relics of a stressful time.

NOTE: with severe anxiety (OCD, depression, GAD) cases I always future pace. Phobias etc. don't need it so much. Use your skill and judgement.

Case 8: How to detraumatise anyone.

I have used the following process with intensely painful trauma; I have never had it fail once. Before you proceed ask the client:

- **What is the problem state you want to get rid of?** - Get them to label the trauma in their own words – 'anguish', 'guilt', 'anger' whatever. Use their words in the session – they are their trance words, their keys to their mind. It will be a non-specified verb or nominalisation of some kind.
- **What is the solution state? How do you want to feel instead?** - Get a word, it will be another nominalisation etc.: 'confidence', 'calm' and so on.
- You can also ask – **What are you experiencing? And what would you rather experience at those times?**
- Once you know what they don't want and want in explicit terms ask them in the conscious state to rate the level of emotion x/trauma now from 0-10. 10 = the worst it could be, 0 a total absence of trauma. _I suggest you never use the word trauma._ At the end, once the process is complete, you ask the client to rate it again once they are wide awake; it will have considerably

reduced or have gone altogether. You will both have measurable proof of success. A good thing. Now you are ready.

• If you have a complex problem matrix, for example maybe they have an addiction etc. DO THE DETRAUMATISATION STUFF FIRST. See book 8, 'Hypnotically annihilating addictions' for multiple addiction busting protocols. By writing these books I am saving you hypnotherapists a fortune in course fees!!!

• *The how to detraumatise anyone script.*

This could well be the single most powerful intervention you may ever learn. If you don't already know it, or something like it, it may well revolutionise your therapeutic practise.
Your client success rates will go to a whole new level. You will soon have the key to debugging the human mind body system of traumatic feelings without any drugs, with words alone. Pretty impressive stuff Padawan. Ready? I knew you were...Ah, I almost forgot it is divided into two parts; you don't have to do the first. I often do because I like to remove all old residue of any kind so that the mind is 'purified' before tackling the trauma head on. Without further ado:

How to detraumatise anyone.

(This will only need to be done more than once IF the person has suffered prolonged chronic trauma throughout early childhood and not even then 99% of the time. Even after the first time the trauma will be so massively reduced that their life will have improved dramatically. Give the client the expectation of a 1 session 'cure'!)

Step 1: The 'haunted house' metaphor.

(Exceptionally deep hypnosis assumed – whack 'em through the floor!)

'Some people believe in ghosts and haunted houses. Some people can pass on beliefs of all kinds to their children. Some are helpful, others less so. Sometimes people tell us to stay away from certain things and places because in their mind, for what seemed their own often very good reasons some places symbolise danger to them.

What if a person could learn, improve, advance and flourish in many differing ways but in one small way, something just seemed to hold them back? Prevented them from going safely where they could, can and will?

Things that seemed strange, odd, peculiar can be things you grow accustomed to with experience. Ideas and experience do not always tally. I had a lady who came to see me who had a phobia of spiders, she had learned this from her mother. As a child seeing her mother's fear, she simply concluded that silly old spiders* must be so dangerous. That's what a child's mind does. But **a calm and confident adult** with their own ideas, beliefs and feelings can look at an ugly old spider in calm fascination as it weaves its web knowing – **all is safe, secure and well inside, now...**With that in mind we shall continue...

(*In the UK we have no dangerous spiders: should you live in a country with dangerous spiders adjust suggestions accordingly. Update: since I wrote this my country is now infested with False Widow Spiders – thanks globalisation!)

Step 2: Symbols of past unwanted emotion dissociation.

Part 1: Removal.

I want you to wonder and wander in your mind to a place that is very relaxing and totally safe. I have no idea what that place looks like but you do. Just go to that place while I pause and really experience it vividly, as if it was real. *(Pause 10 secs or so.)*

Just imagine in that place of **perfect peace** that some kind of symbol or object that represents a thing that you could put unwanted things in is drifting toward you on a pleasant breeze. Whatever that thing is, is just right for you. Implicitly trust what the subconscious offers. Do not try to change it in any way. Good.

Notice all of its qualities as it gets nearer and nearer. And as it get nearer and nearer you feel better and better because you really know that you are about to get rid of some things that have held you back. This knowledge empowers you tremendously.

This symbol or object comes to rest just near you, somewhere appropriate. I want you to just get the sense that instantly all past negative thoughts, feelings, beliefs, behaviours and responses are leaving you in a stream of energy and entering that symbol. That symbol begins to fill with all of that past negative energy as you **let all that stuff go now.**

Let it all pleasantly leave you and stream into that symbol/object which has more than enough capacity to **remove that which serves no purpose any...more, now.** If it has to, that thing can get bigger to accommodate that past limiting material or it can remain constant. After all this is hypnosis magic! As you **let go of all unwanted emotions, feelings, sensations, thoughts, beliefs and responses** you might notice that the colour of that symbol changes, indicating that those things are now fully locked in there, never to return. I will be quiet for a further 10 seconds which is more than enough time to **complete the removal process.** *(Do so...)*

Now that altered object can lift off of the ground and at the speed of light or thought, whichever is quickest, it can shoot off into the distance or it might just drift off as it came, gently on the wind, light as a feather. However your subconscious wishes to process this is just right for you. At some point, in some way, it gets so far away that it disappears from view or vanishes without a trace. That is your sign and signal that **all that junk is gone for good, now.**

Part 2: Filling yourself with positivity.

(In all therapy you cannot leave someone a blank: if you take something away you must fill 'em up with new stuff...)

Just picture a new symbol or object that represents all of your positive potential. It is probably a different shape and colour. Notice everything about it as it drifts its way effortlessly towards you......Good. Let it settle somewhere near you that feels just right. That's it. *(5-7 secs etc.)*

Okay. Now let a stream of all your more optimistic, positive, wonderful and empowering energies, thoughts, beliefs, emotions, sensations, feelings and all manner of awesome responses flow into that symbol/object. That's the way! Good. You are doing brilliantly. All the best feelings are going in there in abundance. I don't know what they are, you do. You can even let your best values flow into that receptacle or container of all that is best about you. Good.

Now as this happens you may notice the symbol/object alters in response or not. It might alter in size, shape, colour etc. Let any and all changes occur. Whatever happens is just right, Trust it fully. *(5- 7 secs for processing...)*

Now see within that symbol is a template of you – almost like a hazy image of you filled with all those positive feelings, thoughts, energies and responses. NOW, step inside that symbol, it is so easy to do so. Merge with that amazingly positive you filled with all the best you have inside. Perfect! How much better does that feel now!? Feel all those amazing thoughts you are thinking! Notice the power of your much more optimistic yet realistic beliefs about what you are capable of in this life! **Feel the super confidence and that awesome feeling of personal power** that fills and radiates from every cell, fibre and part of you like a beacon of positive energy before the world! That's it! Feel how good that feels! And the good things is from here on in and forward, it is only going to get better!

Future pace.

Great! Now as you relax a moment...can you just take the time to imagine what your life will be like from this new perspective. See a you over there on the movie screen of your mind who is filled with all the positive abundance of the changes you have made today. That's perfect. See how you are living your life the new way beyond those past illusions which now no longer trouble you or bother you in any way, shape of form. Everything is somehow changed for the better and you know it and feel it. You can **deal with things much more objectively.** That you is filled with a calm, confidence and relaxation unlike anything you've ever known. Watch that, rehearse that from a safe distance until you have seen reflected back everything you now wish for yourself and your new approach to life now **all that baggage is gone forever!** By doing so you are sending a powerful message to your deepest mind that **this is how you are, now.** I'll be quiet for 20 seconds while you go through that process fully and to your utmost satisfaction. *(Do so...)*

Okay. Great. Now as soon as you are ready float into that movie from the beginning seeing everything happening through your own eyes. See, hear, feel the changes throughout mind and body! You go through some situation that let's you know, really know that **this has worked powerfully.** You have a renewed perspective and approach that feels much more genuine, much more like the deepest you. Take a whole minute of solar time to experience these changes at the cellular level as all safe, appropriate and rapid unconscious adjustments occur, now, while I'm silent... *(Quiet as mice...)*

Step 2: The full detraumatisation process.

(Step 1 removed the junk, any residue from any part of the person's life that may have got in the way of the full detraumatisation process. Now we are going directly for the trauma – ready? Your goal is to separate the emotion/s from memory. They are not inevitable linked. You already know what the problem state is and what the solution state is. Also note: some hypnotists use a similar process to me but they do not induce deep hypnosis first, working with light trance. Although it can work it is far less stable a state and less impressionable a state than very deep and relaxed hypnosis. Get that first before you do the following process. This final step is divided into 3 parts – Again, I have already laid out a version of the first part in book 6, 'Crafting hypnotic spells' – the dentures phobia segment - and in this book with a more advanced version for children's phobias. **Take note: this incredibly powerful process can be used to alter ANY feeling.** *And I mean any. It is the second part that I have revealed in this book*

that kicks trauma up its rear end so it cannot come back. Okay...)

Part 1: Symbology change!

Just relax and go deeper, 10 times deeper than before in your own way...Imagine a sheet of white paper or something neutral – **let your mind focus and yet be clear...**Good. Now, ask your subconscious mind to give you a symbol that represents all aspects of x *(unwanted state).* Your waking mind is unable to consider that problem in one go. It cannot do it. Your subconscious can. Your subconscious processes information in a different way, it can consider every single aspect of that problem. And it can do that with a symbol – a symbol is just something that represents something else. It can be anything at all: usually it's a picture/visual, sometimes a colour but it might be a sound, it might be a smell, taste or the sensation of something you can touch. Whatever your subconscious offers you is right instinctively. Trust it, it knows more than the other mind. I'll be quiet while you do that. *(Give them 10 secs – do not ask for ideomotor signals; this introduces doubt. Tell them what to do and expect that it is done. They have no reason not to do it – they want to feel good again.)*

As you **focus on that** you now know that that symbol represents all the aspects of x. In your own mind only now, on a scale of 10-0 where 10 was the worst that could be and 0 **you feel wonderful, no trace of that state, now.** Where do you feel it is before we **alter that permanently**? This is private I need know nothing.*(Give 7 seconds or so...)*

Excellent. So as you intently focus on that symbol I want you to really get to know it, to notice every single detail about it. Where is it in inner space? Far or close? Is it bright or dim? What colour is it? What shape is it? Note its size? Does it smell? Is it rough or smooth to touch. Take 10 seconds as I am quiet to know that symbol intimately.

(Wait...)

Good. As you focus on that, ask your powerful subconscious what needs to change with that symbol so that it no longer represents x but now represents y *(desired state expressed as a nominalisation)*. Whatever changes your subconscious tells you to make – **make those changes now!** *(Pause for 10 secs...)*

You can take this act as a sign and a symbol that **powerful changes have occurred.**

They will remain with you, now.

(Note: _never mention the unwanted state again!_)

Very good. Now ask your subconscious if there is anything more that needs to change with that symbol so that it completely represents feeling y (desired state). If there are any more changes required make them now. *(10 second pause...)*

So now, as you focus on this new symbol you can 100% sense that it represents state y. And as this symbol represents your feelings and the only way that feelings make any sense to us is if they are located in precise locations inside us, you need to take this feeling symbol and place it just where it would feel correct. I have no idea where this might be – you do. So just take the time now to **place this feeling inside where it feels just right.**

(7-10 sec pause...) Perfect! You are doing so well! Fully feel that y *(confidence, calm etc.)* radiating from that place powerfully, now! *(At this point they may touch that part or more likely they will tip their head back and thrust their chest out a little! Not always but*

the expressive folk do this.)

Part 2: Beyond amplification!

Now really focus on your new feelings. They feel amazing don't they!? You really like this don't you? *(They may smile and nod...As you say the following make sure that your voice tone is forceful, enthusiastic and congruent with the feelings you want them to feel!!!)* Understand fully: these are your feelings and **YOU are in control of them.** Take that symbol and enlarge it now! Make it bigger and bigger and bigger so that it fills up every part of you – head to toe! So that you are filled with and radiate y! *(Confidence, strength etc.)* And now make it bigger and bigger still! Make it so big that it fills every fibre of your being! Every part of you is touched by its healing, positive power! That's it! Make it even stronger and more and more powerful and totally awesome! It is so potent that **it permeates every cell in your body with power!** Every part of your mind and body! All of you filled with these wonderful feelings of y! Those sensations are amazing! You **feel incredible.** Let it get better and better and *even* better......But there is more within! Make it larger and bigger, **let it expand more and more** and more! Make it so big and powerful

481

so that it is as though **you are glowing and radiating** with this force! These wonderful, life changing feelings of y! You feel y *(confidence, calm, strength, power etc.)* flowing through you! Just acknowledge that **this is so** at a deep level of experience! Perfect!

But there is still more – take these powerful feelings you now own and have locked in and let them spread out even more, in all directions – out and beyond your body! That's it! It's like a tangible force, an energy that you are immersed in and that surrounds you! It is so big and so powerful! Others will **feel this radiating from you!** This power radiates from you! **Feel that radiating out powerfully** and it feels awesome! If you were to look down, around and above you, behind you in your mind's eye you can see that emanating from you, can you not?! *(They may nod but carry on regardless – they will be hypnotically high and elated by now!)* Really feel these feelings, your new feelings. That's it.......Now just relax and imagine a blank sheet of paper or something neutral. Allow your mind to clear knowing **profound and permanent alterations and re-associations have occurred, now.**

Part 3: The most special place of all.

And now, I want you to go somewhere in your mind that is very special. There is a place deep within the very core of who you are, beyond your waking name. It is a place of total safety, a place where you can connect to who you really are. It is a place where you are the one with all the power. Nothing and no one may enter this special place without your say so. Look deeply inside that place – it is a place of perfection, everything is just how you want it, no one can alter a single thing about it. It is a place where you feel at home, it is the place you visit at night when you **dream and rest.** It is a place of untold possibilities and potentials. It is a place where you can **reconnect to the core power** within your soul. It has always been here. Become absorbed by the experience of really getting to know your very special place. Notice all the sights, colours, shapes, sounds, smells and atmosphere: it all seems so vividly real and lifelike. You **feel complete security** within this place. You may return here whenever you wish. Now, take 15 seconds or so to really explore this magical place within while I am silent...Luxuriate in this sense of total privacy. *(15 second pause...)*

The symbol within the core.

Good, now within your special place is a spot where you may communicate with your deepest self. It is somehow different from the rest of your inner realm. It seems to shine magically, like a beacon of constant hope – to be the very heart of your inner realm.

Something about that place within that place is very distinct......And when you have found this place of deep communication I want you to see something there that symbolises *you.* Something that symbolises the core of who you really, truly are. There may even be something empowering and deeply meaningful written on that symbol? I don't know – you do. Take some time to get to know that place within that place and that symbol that you find there.

Now, I can let you know a secret – this symbol, this thing that represents the deepest essence of who you are is capable of containing things. Things that you may well wish and want to place inside it. I would simply like you to approach that symbol of the deepest you and stand within touching distance of it. *(Give them 5-7 secs...)* Good.

Now, look at yourself – you are still over brimming, glowing and radiating with all these y *(confidence/security/strength/peace/calm – list the desired qualities)* feelings etc. It is emanating from your powerfully – like a force! Take some of that feeling within you and place it within your container symbol. Put in as much as you need to put into the deepest part of you. When you have filled it to perfection we will proceed further. Fill it so that **these positively powerful states of mind and body and locked in and always available upon need, now.** All of this occurs unconsciously.*(10 seconds pause should be sufficient. Look at them!)*

Good. You are doing magnificently! Now you can know another secret – as a result of this **you have an inexhaustible supply available within, forever!** That is a really nice thing to know isn't it? You can **feel a profound sense of inner certainty** knowing this reality. Whenever you need these resources you can simply come back here; they are always available to you. And no matter how much you use there is always more available! Within this symbol that contains these powerful states of mind and body you can put anything at all that you want to keep available to you. If there is anything else wonderful you would also like to add, that would help, just get the sense of including it now. *(Pause 5-7 secs...)* Good. You can take this act as a sign and a signal that **these changes have been made, now.**

You are doing brilliantly, we are almost done. It's now time to leave that special place knowing it is always here within and may be revisited if you wish. That's it. Good...

Testing your work: the wrapping up the process.

Okay, now, I just want you to focus all your attention back on that symbol again. That symbol of your power! **Feel it.** Feel the way it radiates and emanates within you, from you tangibly. That's it! How much better do you feel now? Rate it in your own mind only - 0 represents **no problem whatsoever.** 10 being the worst it once could have been. Note the improvements. Even if it is zero we can make it better!

As you focus on that feeling, turn its power up even more! That's right! Make it bigger and stronger and stronger and bigger and more and more powerful and more and more intense. Make it so amazing and awesome that other people can sense it! It is radiating out from you so much! Feel how good that feels, really **feel how good that feels!** That's it. Lock it in and keep your power – feel the y *(strength, confidence, calm etc.)* You have this, it is yours, you have reconnected to it. Reorganisations have occurred just as you need, wasn't it? **You have all the confidence you need. You have all the strength you need. You have all the calm you need.** Others know it, you really know it. You have unlearned what you had learned, now. Rate that feeling (silently) again – how much better do you feel now?

Quick associated future pace test.

Well done! So just imagine being in a situation which confirms **this has worked,** perhaps one where and when, in the past, it would have bothered you, maybe with certain people or a particular environment. I don't know - you do. Be in that wonderful time, feeling so much more of what you need, **feeling so good** and in control. That's it. Perfect! Feel your new energy! Feel your strength! These good feelings are SO strong they overwhelm you! They are so good, so excellent, they pervade every part of you, they only get stronger and stronger and stronger!

NOOOOO-OOOOOOOOOW! That's right. You deserve, can, will – keep the legacy of these changes, forever. You have a certain knowing feeling that **all is now well** and this is so. Well done – you did really well!'

(Begin other change work or wake up etc....)

This process is 'analysed'/explained in your appendix.

Bonus insert: Dealing with 'obsessive phobias'.

But first, what's an obsessive phobia? Simple – you have a phobia that totally dominates your life and thoughts, you arrange life around the avoidance of the phobic reaction. It's obsessive because you loop thoughts about it over and over and...During a session just throw in this sentence to stop such obsessive features:

'That old fear is completely gone: so you no longer worry, obsess about that former phobia. Instead you are confident and relaxed – your thoughts easily focus on the tasks at hand; you are occupied and absorbed by that which really interest you moment to moment.'

It's not rocket science; obsessive features respond well to direct hypnosis once the underlying fear is removed. In fact they tend to go without saying the above at all!

Case 9: Public speaking and emotional control.

Note: there is more than one way to skin a cat as they say. Not a very pleasant metaphor but there we are. Learn as many ways as possible to achieve a goal — this will give you the required flexibility of approach. He or she with most creative options wins. If you haven't already, build a *huge* hypnosis script library: buy everything that looks good! I have draw after draw full of the stuff. I am never caught out! And I am always on the lookout for new stuff that I can learn from.

Public speaking fears or lack of emotional control, which is also a common complaint with regular public speakers, is so easy to deal with it's unreal. Firstly you do the symbology phobia process. You can add in 'The emperor of the Gods' metaphor (see this book and 'Powerful hypnosis') too if you want and then say this...

Total public speaking mastery script.

(Deep hypnosis assumed...)

Part 1: Acknowledge problem and thank subconscious (pacing).

'Now once again, I'm talking directly to you...the subconscious mind...you are in charge of this entire process...you'd been creating that old unhelpful set of responses, certain unwanted feelings in the past...up to now...You had done this due to past information processes which need to be updated now...I know it was you who created those nerves, lack of an emotional balance and that lack of confidence back then...the desire to avoid speaking in public...the thought you might do something silly, that your emotional pitch wouldn't be quite right. You've had your past justifications for the former lack of emotional control, maybe you told yourself a certain story at some level... and you performed that old pattern brilliantly...I'd like to sincerely thank you for all you've done to look after and protect this person.

Part 2: Lead subconscious and re-directionalise it.

Nevertheless at the deepest levels of processing you understand forthwith and instantly that the old ways of being is no longer what is appropriate, optimum, comfortable or productive (list things – could be 'health' etc.) for this person...You fully acknowledge and understand that those old patterns are not what is best for this person; you know, really know there are better and more efficient ways to **overcome any challenge.** You know that is not what is best for him in any area of life whatsoever...You have mastered the fact that the best thing that this person can do is **keep calm, be totally confident,** in control of all their emotions whenever they speak in public...those old ways were counterproductive, that situation is best not left to fight or flight instinctive processes in that former way – those responses are all unnecessary now in that situation...As a result of you're making many changes his/their/her health, wealth and relationships improve dramatically – their quality of life is improved, now. They are a totally confident public speaker, they excel at it – they are fluent, expressive and impressive and this is so...simply **automatically learn and assimilate** advanced, state-of the art levels of performance, now. One of the golden rules of public speaking is **face it calmly and with a sense of fun** too, do not force it. Become absorbed by the process of enjoyably communicating with others. These **gains become second-nature, now.**

Part 3: Lob in chain after chain of positive suggestions for great public speaking skills.

As you **drift and sleep** in a special way, in trance, you can know that because they are a so confident, emotionally balanced and always shine when they speak in public...there are simply **no nerves**...or unnecessary doubts, no need to seek approval, to worry about what others might or might not be thinking.

Whatever happens you have the resources to handle it when you **act reasonably** and so **feel in control.** Nervousness is for nervous people, but this person is incredibly confident with just the right levels of emotion whenever they are required to **speak comfortably in public,** so those old uncomfortable feelings just aren't needed anymore...and when **those feelings change, the thoughts change too.** They are a highly competent public speaker, it's just talking after all and you've a whole lifetime of practise doing that, have you not? They are **a great public speaker** in fact...so there will be no nerves, **no excess emotion** of any kind... and you realise, recognise that there will be **no nerves of any kind**...for the reason that, again, that's for nervous people and this person is not one of those...They're **secure, assured, persuasive, funny** when appropriate; the best response when speaking in public is to **take it easy.** A brilliant public speaker who can **remain reasonable and rational** in any situation whenever they want to. So much so that it will surprise and delight them as they notice certain effortless pleasant shifts. Looks forward to opportunities to **speak in public feeling so good,** imagining it all going well. That's his/her etc. new 100% total reality and this is so. Able to handle anything that arises and loving it. What fun is life without

494

challenge?

Our emotions are so important – in many ways they are the truest deepest parts of ourselves and they are powerful but like a rider on a horse **that power must be kept under control, now.** Our emotions allow us to bond, they warn us, they are fast and intuitive, they evaluate instantly, they add spice to life; life without passion is no life at all. All your emotions are acceptable when appropriate. With this in mind there are **no worries,** no stress, **no strain** of any kind whatsoever...and there never will be – their voice is strong, powerful, relaxed, things just somehow harmonise now, thanks to the reality that **the old patterns don't belong** to a totally confident public speaker...those old things just don't belong to a totally calm and confident person regardless of the perceived status of others and because *(client's name)* is a totally confident person in all areas of his life, he/she is also, obviously, a totally confident and competent public speaker – that level of calm and confidence ripples, generalises and spreads throughout their life.

They far exceed earlier expectations, they radiate a controlled confidence and poise, often receiving pleasant compliments on this amazing ability. They **trust this ability,** which he/she always really had, it's a part of everyone – the leadership part will assist, always, the inner strength too. Everyone knows how to **speak comfortably,** you've done it already: what you've done in one context you can transfer to another unconsciously as certain re-associations take place. They trust you, the subconscious/unconscious etc. to allow him/her to enjoy it, take your time, **speaking to others feeling comfort inside;** it doesn't matter how many - 1,2,3,4,10, 15, 20 it's **the feeling of confidence** that matters and lasts; who said your aim in life was to please everyone all at once? Only aim for that which can be achieved and that which can be given. The realistically positive anticipation of **things going well** – just always does somehow, performing very well indeed, performs brilliantly whenever they need and want to and this is so.

Your conscious mind needs the emotions to

know what feels right – what you might call a knowing feeling and your emotions need the conscious mind to calm them down and control them fully when needed. Is that not so? It's a balancing act that can all take care of itself somehow, for some mysterious reason that you need not comprehend. And if *(client's name)* is speaking to just one person or ten or over fifty or hundreds or thousands or more it's all the same is it not? Prepared or spontaneous – they can do it. Quantity isn't important, it's the quality that counts – old concerns not going to bother them in any way, **no problem whatsoever**...They are just people after all, probably all concerned about what others think of *them,* their new shoes, who knows?

When you **focus outwardly in social situations,** you relax. They are so confident no matter what the circumstances or how they change. Any hecklers - played with – use your quick wit without effort, during any speech you **feel deeply at ease** with yourself and who you are, what you have to say and that's the bit that is 100% under your control. A really good sense of humour always helps - trusting it's insight and wisdom – that's what true confidence is – **total faith in yourself, now**...The old problem, responses, beliefs, ideas, attitudes, behaviours, illusions, sensations, apprehensions that held them back cannot anymore - it just won't disturb them, unruffled, unflappable; that which they once worried about he/she now enjoys. Every worry is the basis of a good joke looked at from the right perspective, now. It just doesn't bother this person in any way shape or form, they can even have a really good laugh which sets the audience at ease. Express themselves just as they wish in the appropriate way in a given context: because that's simply who they are...**All a part of your identity, now.**

They can utilise any and all temporary interruptions with total coolness and serenity or energy if that's what's needed; a lifetime of learnings to draw from. Using the full expressive range of their voice. There is **no pressure.** Trust your skills and talents. It just doesn't matter...what anyone else is doing...those old behaviours and feelings are not something they do...Not looking for approval during a speech, not needed - it's not what you do...it was an absurd intent. Your intent now is to **relax, trust, enjoy,** see what happens; the unpredictability is part of the fun. Life would be boring if we always knew how everything turned out. Trust the process of communication to spontaneously evolve in its own way. Variety is the spice of life. No negativity...no fear...and so **only your boldness remains.** In fact it seems like the most separate and estranged idea that there could be for you...to feel any fear when speaking in public?! *(NFH: Voice tone = what a ludicrous idea!!!)* No. And when that residue of **fear goes** only complete relaxation, certainty, backbone and grit if needed – all at your disposal at will, appropriate control and even **a sense of playfulness remains.** Your morale and self-reliance is high. Your emotional balance gives you flexibility.

Part 4: Summation and consolidation.

The great thing about your conscious mind is that it allows you to **plan and think wisely and calmly** when you need to **make great decisions about important matters,** more and more and more. With all these learnings

499

deeply embedded where they need to be you can also know that what you once perceived as being scary can now be for you something you find exhilarating if you wish. Weak points become strengths, now. We can all learn from our mistakes; that's how we develop. Our imperfections allow us to learn. The idea of any unrealistic negativity, doubts, worries, concerns, fears, stress about public speaking just seems laughable and ludicrous...something that simply wouldn't and couldn't happen in this person's new reality...not going to happen anymore. It won't ever crop up...The size of the gathering or audience is **no problem...**no fuss whatsoever...no matter how other people react around them, they are as entitled to speak as anyone else, it's not about being perfect, or liked or the 'best' – it's about your right to **confidently speak your mind** and **effortlessly communicate with others fluently.**

This individual is **in control and centred,** courageous and valiant in all the situations he/she needs to be and wants to be. Others are free to do what they want and they **feel**

wonderful regardless... The reality now is that this person can **feel 100% self-assured** in that situation. And no matter what happens during any kind of presentation to an audience...it will seem the most natural thing in the world just to let him/her **feel great,** with high yet realistic hopes that **it all goes well!** Every time **this occurs,** you, the seat of their emotions will give *(client's name)* a sense of inner strength and purpose...they'll **feel an incredibly pleasant natural and appropriate feeling** from this moment forward, **keeping this invincible confidence** for the rest of their amazing and much more fulfilling life. These changes will surprise and delight him/her.

Many differing points of view – three people witnessing an event will interpret it in many different ways, some perceptions are more helpful than others. When you tie your shoelaces – **you have rock solid self belief;** when you brush your teeth **you 100% take self belief for granted;** when you speak to a large crowd - **you own self belief.** Do you know the one magic sentence that instantly neutralises fear? You simply say,

'Go on fear do your worst, the worst panic ever!' and it vanishes forever because it is was only a fear of fear that hadn't helped at all. Fear helps you pay attention and them it passes. You **experience the appropriate and optimum levels of arousal** when required and no more. And who weren't you not really anyway who is **happy and confident speaking to anybody in public anywhere,** any number but where you weren't really – any positive way but temporarily back then and so on and so on. Plan your successes. Set goals. The rest is down to trust.

Creative, good-natured, a good mood, good humoured, eloquent yet natural, competent, strong voiced and everything else you'd expect from the fact that **you're a totally confident public speaker, now.** The unconscious mind knows the psychological and physiological component parts of confidence and all the other resources needed and they will manifest at just the right time and place because it can just do that.

Someone others like to listen to, using words

well, tonality, painting word images, deft pauses, rhythm, gestures and posture and more, prepared and confident in the information you present – connecting easily and pleasantly with an audience of one or one thousand. **Be calm throughout the day** more often. Look forward to things positively, picturing it all going very well indeed. You **control your imagination.** There are many times in life when you've been in the flow state, that almost magical state of mind where **things just go well for you.** Sportsman perform their best there, musicians call it being in the groove, you can even **experience it more often,** say when simply going for a walk, whenever you **do things that are satisfying, absorbing and fulling** – there are **no unnecessary worries or concerns** in that state – you are connected to what is going on around you, you **feel great more often,** and now that flow state, that **being in the zone when you speak in public** can happen. Emotional levels just perfect. Wasn't it? All adjustments made. That's it!

(NFH: In this section I used the pronouns

'HIS'/'HER' etc. more – you can use anything
– 'YOU', 'THEY', 'THEM'; it doesn't make a
difference as I said in other books. The
message gets through. I'll induce brief
confusion using all of them.)

Part 5: Future pace with the emotions barometer in place; control excess nerves.

Brilliant! You are doing really well! To wrap up
all the good work you've done I want you to
simply picture a few things that you'll find will
help. Let's **enhance your certain success**
further!

Imagine now, that somewhere within your
mind is an emotions barometer – it tells you
the intensity of any emotion at any given
time: I have no idea what your looks like; you
do. It lets you know how intensely you are
feeling an emotion by the colours you see. At
one end when that emotion is very intense
you see a certain colour that lets you know
that and at the other very calm end of the
devise is a state of wonderful calm
represented by another colour. Now notice
what colours you use subconsciously at either

504

end of the scale to display the intense emotions and the calm ones. *(Give 10 secs.)* Good.

Now I want you to also notice that there is a devise of some kind nearby – a control panel, whatever your subconscious automatically offers that represents your ability to **lower the intensity of any emotion when you wish.** You just need to adjust this device accordingly somehow so that **this happens.**

Now, what I want you to do is **imagine** a time just before a public speaking event *(etc.)* when you needed to **be in contro**l.......See that emotional barometer is telling you that emotion-colour needs turning down to the optimum level so that **you always perform well.** And just before that response takes over float out of that scene and push that memory away so it's small and black and white; that's it!

Now use that device you located earlier to turn that emotion all the way down to just the right level of balance and calm...Perfect. See that you performing brilliantly as a result – it's all going so well. You look happy, calm and really are doing very well. You are present in that moment, at ease and actually having fun. Watch that scene when you **experience just the right level of emotions;** that's right. Everything is going brilliantly, almost like how you've always dreamed you could when **you perform at your best.** A time in the future when you will need confidence...Watch it on that movie screen over there – see it up close: make it big, bright and bold. See that situation going just as you wish, positively, see yourself in 100% in control, confident, see yourself handling anything at all that arises...I'll be quiet as mice as you do... *(1 minute to practise...)*

Excellent! When **you're happy,** step into that movie from the beginning of that process again and see through those confident, emotionally balanced eyes, hear through those confidently calm ears, **feel this supreme confidence flowing through you.** Your subconscious mind can take this act as a sign and a signal that you easily keep any emotion in a comfortable range, unconsciously, now. Your confidence is just part of who you are. **Imagine success** and make it more likely. Imagine things going as you wish. When you imagine things going well you are sending messages to your subconscious that this is what you want. You subconscious only wants to help you. When your conscious and subconscious work together - you are so much more powerful. Is that not so? That's right! You can **feel delightful** knowing with a deep knowing feeling that **our work is complete.** I am just going to count you up and give you some great wrapping up suggestions etc.'

(Lob in exduction of choice etc. A tip: my sister does lots of public speaking; she does a rehearsal talk in front of work colleagues to 'get her nerves out of her'. Rehearsal of any kind is always good. The client can do it mentally, it activates the same neural pathways without the nerves.)

Case 10: Shy girl.

Broadly there are two types of 'shy' people. The first have usually been bullied etc. The second are not really shy but aloof and quite nasty. The secretly nasty shy people are hiding their nastiness behind 'shyness'. There is nothing wrong with being a bit shy or sensitive, it is not pathological: why should everyone be an outgoing extrovert? Answer: they shouldn't. People differ. But often that shy reaction stops someone from connecting with others; for some reason unconscious fear and mistrust of strangers is present. Everyone's spouse or best friend was once a stranger. If fear prevents much needed human relationships then you intervene. You do not want to remove such a person's sensitive nature; this is one of the traits that makes them the unique person they are. But they're so shy that no one can find out just how great they really are!

My little niece has an adorable character she pretends to be called 'Shy Girl'; Shy Girl is completely scared of all people. Shy Girl hides behind whoever plays teacher and whenever you ask her to join in the games she shakes her head and looks worried. But people need people: we have a powerful drive to socialise for a whole host of fairly obvious reasons. A shy person is not getting this universal human need met. It could take just one crisis to tip such patterns into more severe anxiety or even depression other things being equal –

Anxiety code tip: if there is any anxiety anywhere in the system it can predispose people to worse anxiety problems should a crisis or an inability to get needs met arise.

This is how you start to help...Induce deep hypnosis. Do a variation of the de-phobia/de-traumatisation pattern first. There is often trauma with shyness. I once had a sweet teenage girl come to see me who had 'become shy' after dating a highly abusive man. After I had 'cured' her I said, 'From now on when you get that feeling that someone isn't safe you are going to listen to it aren't you?' She nodded and said, 'Yes.' People with low self-worth often ignore social warning signs that a person is a danger to them. Nut cases are often attracted to those with low-self worth. Worse still, people with low worth feel they deserve such abusive people.

You can also ask the shy person what colour

the anxiety is and ask where it's located –
they'll look confused. Once they tell you
(usually it's red) ask them what colour calm
and comfortable is (usually blue); in trance
get them to imagine the red turning into blue
or just say, *'Imagine that unwanted colour
feeling you told me about spontaneously
changing into the calm colour feeling,
spreading throughout mind and body
powerfully, now! That's it. Now lock in that
change and keep it permanently, now.'* Notice
this is vague – the client fills in the gaps. After
I have done a bit of symbology work I say
something like this...

Getting rid of unwanted shyness script.

(Deep hypnosis assumed)

'I would like to take this chance to thank your
subconscious for doing this old protective
pattern you labelled 'shyness' in the past. I
know you had a whole host of very good
reasons for that and you did it very well. But
the time has come when this person has
outgrown the need for that. It's too much,
counterproductive: it's stopping her getting
some of her most essential needs for
companionship. As a consequence you know
the time has come to **act much more**

confidently in social situations – that is what would be best for her in all areas of her life from now on. With this understanding in mind...

From now on you'll be able to **focus outwardly in social situations.** When anyone is involved in any interactions they need to **pay attention to others' responses** when appropriate. In any situation there is an optimum level of arousal – a state of calm alertness which your unconscious mind will activate on cue, now, just when you need it. Meeting new people is potentially an enjoyable experience and I want you to get in touch with that. It's nice to **spend fun time with people** because of all the unique aspects of their personality. Some people you spend time with because they really make you laugh. Others are understanding and wise. There are so many reasons to **get out and meet others** that I couldn't list them all! But the wiser you just knows anyway. You have an instinctive, inborn ability to **connect with deserving others.**

Of course it takes time to really get to know anyone and build genuine trust based on mutual compatibility but a real key to **you're enjoying yourself much more around all**

sorts of people is that a sense of humour and playfulness usually help in any interaction; more and more and more, now. And remember when **you are socially relaxed,** others relax too. You just know what to say in that back and forth moment to moment communication that any two or more people **become absorbed** by. You already know how to **feel really comfortable inside when socialising** in many contexts. Anyone can do what they already did, only better and spread that feeling out as a generalisation that really helps. Of course some people are not worth the time and effort but when you listen to the wisdom of your instinctive responses and feelings about a person you'll find that you **find kind and supportive people** with more ease. With that reality in mind you can **lighten up** – they're just people!

You can speak fluently and **feel a real confidence in any social situation** that feels so delightful that others are attracted to it. Social confidence is so attractive. You go with the flow, you are at ease. And that can please you, now. Because the truth is you are fine just as you are. Nobody is perfect but you find that it is safe and easy to communicate who you really are to others. Nobody can be friends with everyone. You just seem to click better with some who are on your wavelength. Some people become pleasant acquaintances. You set boundaries of acceptable behaviour. If needed you can be appropriately assertive. And the great thing is as **you're becoming much more sociable** you'll discover the joy of long lasting friendships too. Even the smallest interaction with a complete stranger can be a good time to **experience a calm sense of ease and effortlessness.** That's right. What if you could learn to believe that **you are a person who can easily talk to anyone** – you're that type of person, now.

I know there are things, events, people, places, situations and activities which allow you to **feel deep absorption** – so your inner mind knows how to **do that in social situations** without effort because there is a time when introspection is appropriate and there is an appropriate time to **completely focus on events** going on around you to the exclusion of all other concerns. You can switch your focus at will. You can **let go of that old self-consciousness** as you realise that you are a likeable, lovable, unique person with much to offer anyone; with that reality firmly embedded in your mind you can know that you need not compare yourself unfavourably with others, there's no need to go inside and visualise what you imagine or speculate others might think of you. You can care about others but you don't have to care about everything they think. Any past troubling images – small, black and white, shooting far off, so small, so tiny and untroubling, fading away, completely, now. That's it. Another trick is to dissociate from past memories of how you once did shyness and **see it all with such objectivity** and recognise how absurd it was to have acted like that once upon a time.

When **you trust yourself,** when you know **you are a very confident person in all social situations** regardless of who others are or imagine they are, you can **relax at such times** and simply **let go of too much energy.** That's it. In fact the old ways now seem so ludicrous, just something that incredibly confident people don't experience, they can find new ways to look at old things that really make them laugh. Remember, always, the resource of your great sense of humour, laugh more and more and more about so many things that are just so silly when you think about it all afresh. This is simply part of maturing. Those old patterns are what nervous people do and you aren't one of those, wasn't it? You have **more**

strength of character than you consciously know. After all it's just meeting and talking which is **no big deal** for anyone, and you are anyone are you not?

Future pace.

Watch an inner movie of that you over there **behaving more resourcefully** in a past situation that would have bothered you. See how confidently that you is talking to others. That is **a very socially confident person** – see that **you at ease** talking to anyone, see how those others like your company. See how you just go along with things, lead things when needed, change things, talk about small or big talk kind of things as you wish. Notice how much more compelling this future you is and **resolve to change now,** once and for all. And when you are ready – step into that future-present you, NOW!

See through those confident eyes, hear through those confident ears, **feel how socially confident you really feel** and it feels awesome doesn't it? **You have all the power you need** to appropriately act as you really desire at such times. You have the right to **express yourself just as you wish.** There is no one else **like you.** The sunlight never falls in quite the same way on two differing days, the formations of clouds is never the same, each moment new and unique, never to be repeated – the continua of social existence going on and on and on. The **flow** of people, faces, places, needs, joy and life – your greatest joys will spring from your best relationships – **seek out the best people for you.** Every great friend was once a complete stranger, you **talk and connect** and on and on; you were born with the ability to **make friends easily,** just a gift from this reality to you, **now.** And always remember not everyone is deserving of your attention or presence; you **value yourself** and expect to be treated with respect at all times. Your expectations effect your reality. As I am quiet, take my pause as a sign and a signal that for one full minute of clock time you have all the time you need to **practise social success** in the comfort of your imagination – this in turn sends a powerful signal that this is the new direction you wish your subconscious to automatically operate from. Go ahead and **do that now...** *(Shhh...)*

Excellent! Will it be the improvement in how you feel? Could it be the way others are attracted to you more? Will it be the more skilled yet fluid way you **interact**

comfortably with others? What behavioural alterations for the better will you spot? And how much more will be going on on your behalf outside of your awareness as you trust your subconscious to aid you implicitly? That's it, you're done.'

(NFH: Wrap up as you wish...)

Case 11: Transforming stuttering/stammering into fluency!

The best way to stop stammering and stuttering is to rebuild the shattered ego. To do this you need to 1. Get rid of the person's inferiority complex and 2. Help the stutter/stammer sufferer (SS) handle feedback without falling apart and 3. Remove early negative programming (brainwashing!). The modules required to tackle this problem in entirety would take a whole book. The 3 module script I provide here will help you greatly however. First things first – detraumatise them! You know where to go for that.

Suggestions for speaking fluency etc. are relatively straightforward and remarkably similar to treating a nervous twitch. You can in fact modify the nervous twitch scripts I provide later to help an SS. A lot of advanced level hypnotherapy is simply about adapting known treatment patterns and applying them widely and imaginatively. In other words you need to be able to ***detect similar problem matrix patterns in differing clients and generalise solutions.***

The building blocks of fluent speech script.
Phase A: You are as good as anyone else.

(Deep hypnosis assumed)

'Anything meaningful can relax you even deeper and further than before during this hypnotic process...You know at some point in our lives we all encounter what I call negative authoritarian hypnotists. These people often don't know they are hypnotists at all. They often have no awareness that they believe 'their' opinion is always right. Or worse, that it's reality and not a belief at all. They see the world in black and white terms and project that limited map of reality onto experience, onto others and the fact is anyone's beliefs are just that and not reality at all.

Some people take great pleasure in trying to brainwash those around them that it's their way or the highway. Such people are often very angry or secretly scared. They are often hypercritical and demand their idea of 'perfection' from all around them over who they have any kind of influence. Some of these negative authoritarians are unable to see the great qualities in those around them, like they have blinkers on. They think that you motivate best by always pointing out mistakes, when the truth is it's positive feedback that makes anyone excel. It's as though their intent is often positive but *they* are just very, very, very poor communicators. With that in mind you might even feel a bit sorry for such limited people...

Facts are facts – I may be taller or shorter or the same height as you. **It makes no difference as to anyone's worth what the facts are.** Imagine if you NEVER doubted yourself. You would be like those unpleasant, arrogant narcissists that no one normal likes. So having a degree of sensitivity and concern for the opinions of others is a good thing. As long as you know that you can care about other people without having to care too much about what are after all just THEIR opinions. Most just repeat what an authority figure told them at some point – without thinking at all. People are entitled to think what they think and you are free to do likewise, are you not? The fact is that without changing any external facts you can **feel very secure about your true self right now,** there is no need to wait a second longer; and that's a nice thing to know, is it not? With these insights in mind...deeply...

You were born knowing just how to **feel very**

good about yourself. Because that problem was never about thinking; it all came from some old programmed responses that created a set of unconscious feelings about other's ideas about who they imagined you are! As if they knew it all. And no one does. How silly. There will never be two yous. No one has the right to prevent you from **fully reaching your inborn potentials, now.** Consider a rock. They all come in different shapes and sizes. Does one's size make one more valuable than another or are they all just rocks? Doing what rocks do as best the can. You already know the answer's secret.

If there was a kingdom with a king who was unjust and unfair, who issued laws that made no sense, who thought he had the right to micromanage everyone's opinion, wouldn't it be just to **refuse to obey such ideas**? You like a whole lot of different things from me and rightly so. From now on why not **stubbornly stand up for your individuality.** You can know that if all men are equal then no one is ever truly better than you. What if you came to believe, funny as it might seem that **you are fine just as you are, now.** Imagine living life from that belief. How might a whole host of things, responses, perceptions, attitudes, feelings and energies be quite differently better for you? What if you realised **you are your own champion**? What if you realised you are good enough to do that and meet them and go there? What if this led you to **feel empowered** as you re-connect to your inherent birthright as a human being, **now**? What colour would **a healthy pride and true self-confidence** be? Let it begin where it's needed most and become stronger and stronger and let it grow and spread and emanate beyond past boundaries of other's limitations that they used to impose on you.

Does the king of lions sit like a king no matter where he finds himself? He carries himself unapologetically and his eyes convey his authority. When you look at such an animal, others know **this individual must be treated with respect.** Is that not so? And whether a lion needs to roar proudly or just growl contentedly, he knows how to make just the right noises to suit any occasion. For he is a lion and lions just know how to be lions and how to **communicate appropriately** who they really, truly, deeply are! To the trained eye a seeming 'rock' is a sparkling jewel!

Imagine you were a dolphin in your element swimming **fluently** because they are born to

be that way. Even if an eagle was brought up to believe it was a mouse? It would still be an eagle and eagles can fly higher than other birds, can they not? Always. That's the way. And if a parrot can parrot **perfect human speech** then how much better is a human being better at bettering a parrot at being a human? No creature on this earth has a brain, body and nervous system that was made to **communicate superbly with others.** Without effort. Life is easier with **a sense of humour always close at hand,** like a superhero's trusty sidekick. As you find **your sense of freedom only grows** to **proudly be who you are** and walk your own way in this world. You have more to contribute than you know as you **learn who you really are,** learn what you really think, take the spotlight of life and say THIS IS ME! Happily. And when **this strong foundation is laid** the sounds sound and feel right. This are **no restrictions there, anymore, now.** The world and things and people look and **feel differently.** Comfort, safety, protection, strength of character are all already there. Exactly how well, how easily and pleasantly would such a unique person as this **speak out proudly, now** (?) That's for you to discover? **Let your voice be freely you!** With these beginnings and endings – all the same – the road goes ever onward, firmly fixed in YOUR mind...**You express an inner dignity** that is overwhelmingly compelling and this IS so.

Future pace the new attitude: dissociated.

(I future pace all the component parts of the solution matrix to lay the 'bricks' firmly, in a manageable way...)

What if you **playfully don't take others too seriously**? If you only knew half the doubts they have. Time to **focus your attention on others** in a social gathering. You can't be inside when it's not raining. Certain behaviours are not necessarily a part of your core identity. This awareness alone helps a part **let them all go.**

Now, imagine a time in your future...in which your new feelings might have once been tested. Perhaps you could be with people who are not 100% supportive all the time? I don't know, you do. But see the new you who has found their voice once more, **speaking fluently around anyone** at all. That's it. In fact see them relishing the challenge of being with limited people like that and yet noticing **you're feeling so powerfully secure within.** See how calm and unruffled they are.

See how the sparkle in that eye and that slightly amused smile on their face shows that **your social status is always strong whoever you are with. Now,** that you doesn't take them seriously anymore. Sometimes the greatest comedian plays before an audience that just does not get it. It went over their heads who knows? Some can't give what they can't give and expecting otherwise is to wish for the impossible. And because you **act differently** at such times they are forced to respond to the new you who is actually the real you. That person is not pretending. That person obviously does **feel free and happy to be you!** They see it as a gift and their voice reflects that so attractively that they are bringing new positive, supportive, uplifting people into their lives without any effort. As if **you have a mysterious magnetism that attracts such people.**

You can hear supportive, kindly voices as you watch that scene unfold in better ways with far better outcomes for you. They are saying the nicest things about your personal qualities, especially your voice. And the best thing is, at a very deep level you **believe their messages.** However, you need not know why. I don't know what they are saying

– you do! It could be things like – 'What a likeable voice!' 'I love the tone of his/her voice!' 'I love listening to this person!' 'What a magnificent speech!' 'I wish I could make people laugh like that!' 'What an interesting and intelligent thing to say!' And on and on and on! **Take heed of these words of wisdom.** So overpowering are they that any **past negative opinions are silenced forever, now.** The wonderful feelings of these words will remain with you when you need them to be there but the specifics can remain entirely unconscious. And the consequences of these and other changes will surprise and delight you magically! I will be quiet for a full minute and you have all the time you need in trance to **learn and unlearn** as you must. That's it. Layer in your certain patterns of true success. *(Watch the clock etc....)*

Associate into feelings of security etc.

Excellent! You are doing marvellously! Okay – this part of the **healing** process is almost done! Finally just visualise yourself going through that trance-formative process again but this time from the inside and not as an observer. When **you're happy** with the changes you practised float into the new empowered you who has regained their self-mastery, confidence, strong voice and composure no matter what others opinions on x, y and z are! That you! That's it! Good...See through those confident, self-assured, empowered eyes! Hear through those ears **securely**! Feel the new **feelings of total security inside, now!** Notice how you also **feel total unshakeable core self-acceptance.** At a deep unconscious level **integrate all this** as a part of who you deeply are, now! Responses, behaviours, the way you process information of all kinds at an unconscious level of super-fast mentation changed for the better without knowing how but feeling the positivity radiate from you in such a compelling way! It can **feel awesome** for you! I will be quiet for 1 and a half minutes. In that time take the opportunity to imagine going through at least 3 or 4 relevant yet differing scenarios with your new approach to living and relating in new ways. And during that time you can know that there have always been times when **you feel fluent.** You know the feeling of which I speak. Discover that feeling more and more and more whenever you are talking to anyone at all – your mind-body system knows the component parts, does it not? **So fluent, now...** *(Pause etc.)*

Fantastic x *(client's name)*! You are doing brilliantly. You **no longer feel inferior** and this is so. Now let's move on to the next module...

Building a protective shield.

Imagine just around you solar plexus area is a protective shield made of some amazingly tough material of your choice. When someone tries to knock your confidence in future, imagine your energy and power tries to escape through your solar plexus weakening you BUT it hits the protective shield and remains within. With this in place you can **keep that energy and power** – it can no longer escape and weaken you; as a result you feel like **standing tall, taking your time** and knowing, really knowing that **that power can remain within, always!** Can you imagine hearing an upbeat piece of music that supports this feeling? That's the way.

Phase B: Handling feedback casually.

Up until now you had seen some feedback as an attack; but when **you are calm no matter what the feedback** you have the choice as to how you react or not at all, now. Other people's ideas are just that: ideas.

Ideas are not necessarily an accurate representation of reality. Some people are genuinely nasty and do not have your best interests at heart; they never did. Others are just clumsy communicators who focus on goals and not artful methods. An unspecific, overgeneralisation is not feedback at all – it is a form of delusion. Are words like – 'NEVER! ALWAYS!' always valid? Almost always never. The core of who you really are never was, is or will be your behaviour. That's like blaming the sky for the changing clouds. Not all words are gifts worth keeping. All genuine feedback offers positive encouragement in the face of any difficulties. All true vindictive criticism tries to harm your self-esteem by attacking the core of who you are. The only truths that are revealed by the CRITIC are all about themselves and no one else at all. With these truths deeply embedded in your deepest mind, we shall continue...

Once upon a time a man was verbally abused by another for no reason. The former listened calmly, wiser than the later and simply said, 'I refuse to accept this; therefore to whom does it belong?' The later being less wise said, 'It belongs to the one who offered it!'
Children who were over criticised can come to a child's conclusion that there was something

wrong with them when the truth is, **in maturity now,** that there was something wrong with the critic but they weren't critical enough to notice it. What you need to know is that words are just information. And you can **really relax as you receive certain information.** In future I want you to **access your deepest sense of calm separation** from particular types of information and your emotions. At times we need the evaluative capacities of our emotions, at others we need to **think objectively.** This can occur even if you feel a bit tired. Knowing that **some words do not affect your core sense of self-worth negatively** any...more, now.

Remember – there are many abstractions/notions that are but half-truths or no truths at all. Some people believe their sweeping and unhelpful abstractions are the law; but other's intent is to genuinely help you; at an unconscious level you can now **automatically distinguish between the two.** That's it. You might find, delightfully, that these new learnings make **you feel very secure already.** Deep within. The achievement of all your needs, the necessary, the important require that **your sense of heartfelt security** in who you really are is locked forever within you. **Re-access it,**

now.

Future pace: Dissociated.

In order to **reconnect with your inborn fluency** imagine a time in your future on a glorious movie screen when **you are responding so calmly and reasonably to any kind of feedback** whatsoever. You can even **laugh about it.** See **that new reality** vividly now. There is a sparkle in those eyes and a knowing smile on that mouth. That person that you really are has choice and choice leads to **you're making better and better decisions.**

In your own time, over the next minute and a half I would like you to take all the time you need to **rehearse your natural new responses** unconsciously while I am quietly irrelevant. Simply do this thoroughly in at least 3 differing but appropriate contexts, perhaps such as might have once troubled you – see that fluent, relaxed you over there in your mind's eye...That's it. Good. Notice how he/she does indeed **feel differently** about the whole experience. Notice how **calm** they are. Notice that they can **listen to the words calmly.** Notice how they **respond objectively to feedback** and yet if they were genuinely verbally attacked they could defend themselves with all the energy or aggressiveness or subtle wit required. They just seem **so at ease in that situation,** do they not? Their **unshakeable self-worth is safely locked up inside** – no matter what others think or thought they thought. Observe that process until you are satisfied that **these improved patterns are instinctive and spontaneous, now.** *(Be quiet for 1 minute...)*

Associate into change.

Great! You are doing really well! Now I want you to simply imagine a time in your much better future when **you are free to be fluent** no matter what information you are receiving. See that new you in a situation that confirms **this has really worked well!** That's right. Now – float into the **calm and resourceful you** who is capable of listening and if right **learning wisely.** You can **think things through calmly.** You can select, reject or absorb in an impartial, dispassionate way. You can identify the helpful from the harmful; for you were born with the power to **discriminate.** As you **go through this trance-formative process,** you can **feel the changes have fully become an**

integral part of you and your interrelations. I'll be silent again for a full minute as you find the best way for your deep unconscious to **absorb all the learnings and understandings, now.** *(Shhh...)*

(NFH: You can get the client to mentally re-rehearse past times when un-resourceful responses were manifested and imagine the calm objectivity skills etc. occurring instead. However the past has happened – this is why I mostly concentrate on the new patterns that are being re-associated to. Feel free to experiment...)

Phase C: Decontaminating the voice.

Excellent! It's nice to know **you have totally reclaimed your vocal power,** have you not? Nearly done for today. Now as you **open up to even further new potentials...**In the past at certain times and in certain ways some people may have said things to a younger you that were unjust and untrue. As **one voice** that resulted from that method of communication becomes **but a faded memory** of how things were **another more empowering voice begins to emerge** from deep within you. **Now.*** I just want you to imagine how someone with a supportive inner

and outer voice like that may behave in so many situations that **display full confidence in yourself – always.** How do they speak to anyone at all? How exactly does their total belief in themselves materialise in that voice? What wonderful things does that new inner voice say that assists this process? How much stronger and more and more radiant is that person over there? That's it. **Deep subconscious change** is possible for you, **now!** *(Pause for 15 seconds...)*
(NFH:*First 4 embeds = a subliminal run on sentence: 'One voice but a faded memory, another more empowering voice begins to emerge, now.' See book 2, 'Mastering hypnotic language.)

When **you speak properly** there are no obstacles to your breathing or having **a nice flow of breath support.** When you **speak easily** the entire structure of **those vocals cords can comfortably do what they were born to do.** The way you say words is just fine. Others like to listen as you only **feel relaxed and confident when talking,** unless you are passionate about something and want to **express that clearly and assertively.** There are **no blockages** when you **have the right attitude to speak easily.** The ideas and **words flow smoothly** without any conscious effort – is that not so? Many parts of the brain are involved in **your good speech.** When **you are feeling good** those parts can do what they need to to help **create effortlessly articulate speech.** All the cells and nerves and muscles know how to **translate thoughts and feelings safely into words** because you are human and that's what we do. And you can feel just enough arousal to **deliver any speech well** so as to **energise your expression.** Your diaphragm muscle supports you with **all the vocal power you need.** All children naturally **have the vocal power of an opera singer.** The truth is everyone is born with **a distinct, attractive and powerful voice. Now...**

Unconscious acceptance protocol.

Imagine a colour of **good speech** that spreads all through your brain and body causing certain positive re-associating processes to occur. It fills you with **a feeling of pleasant, warm, personal power** that is so compelling so that as **you just talk,** your unconscious processes that do such things **simply produce clear speech** using an ancient set of pathways that lead you to imagine humming a clear note within your natural range. You take in a deep breath and let out a gentle hum that resonates with certain healing ideas. That sound sounds nice to you. That sound is your sound. That sound sounds sound to you. The pleasure a baby has in cooing. The pleasure in joking with friends as you **take some things far less than seriously from now on.** You know some things are worth your focus, worth your energy, worth your time, worth your worth and some shouldn't ever have been believed literally, like fairy stories and Father Christmases/Santas etc. and more. Somehow, in some mysterious way a deeper part of you will **make these understandings your own.** Your powerful subconscious mind will finalise any and all appropriate changes from this session right now.'

Begin the exduction process etc.

(NOTE: Even the best speaker can stammer or stutter when they are really nervous.)

Bonus tip:

I once had a stammering client tell me that it felt as if he had a machine in his throat that stopped his voice working: what do you do? Hypnotise him and have him totally dismantle it in his imagination. Hypnosis magic.

Case 12: The little soldier won't stand to attention – sexual dysfunction in men.

This script deals with both premature ejaculation and erectile dysfunction (unable to get it up!) in one big caboodle. I have found 9 times out of 10 they go hand in hand being closely related. So here is a double whammy.

In my experience men who feel impotent in life often get what I call 'symbolic impotence'. If you suspect this, do not share it with your client: it is for you to know. The penis is symbolic of masculine power. Look at all the tall cock-like buildings and monuments! I could have called this the 'Premature ejaculation/erectile dysfunction and sexual confidence script'. But that's quite a mouthful so I chose this funky title instead:

Mr. Mojo Rising script!

(Deep hypnosis assumed)

Part 1: Mini hyper-suggestiveness module.

(Not needed but why not load things in your

and their favour?)

'You're now so deeply relaxed and so deeply hypnotised, that whatever positive, healthy and beneficial thing I suggest that you do, you **simply do it** for your own good and whatever I suggest will happen, will happen for your own good. During this highly hypnotic process my most influential words become your thoughts, experiences, perceptions, sensations and your deepest held beliefs, **in deepest trance...now.** Of course you can **respond to these suggestions powerfully** in a way that makes you comfy. Your hyper-responsiveness to these ideas which lead to better responses is maximised somehow, unconsciously, now.

Part 2: 'Parts' therapy.

(A rather vital part of him ain't working; you need to talk to the 'bit' of his subconscious that's responsible. Don't say, 'I am now talking to your penis,' for fairly obvious reasons...)

Now I know there is a part of your

subconscious, unconscious that has been responsible for these past behaviours, responses, patterns, perceptions, a certain way of processing certain information and other things besides that which you want to **change. Now,** I'd like to thank that part of your other than conscious processes for its positive intention, whatever that is. I fully respect that part had your best interests at heart and was doing the best it could with the learnings you had back then. You did that all so very well.

But that was back then and this is right now and in his future. Because you now know that those responses had unforeseen consequences that were not beneficial long term. It's time to stop all that and **enjoy relaxed, fun, healthy and normal sexual activities again.** You can **unconsciously re-associate to that which you would normally do.** You can **have a powerful erection whenever you need one,** you can **last as long as you wish** to each and both of your satisfaction. That's it.

I know you have a very powerful creative part

and it can find many new ways of fully satisfying that old positive intention without the negative side effects of those former ways of being in the past. Now I'd like that innovative, gifted part to agree with me that it can **find new ways, new behaviours that satisfy that intention, now** and I'd like your gifted imaginative part to **find as many healthy ways as possible** to do that. Why? Because that is what is best for this deserving man at this time in his life and beyond – his level of satisfaction throughout all areas of his life will improve and that's a good thing, is it not?

At an unconscious level you begin the process of choosing the best, really wise but relaxed and fun alternatives, several, many, perhaps three or so at least, as many as you want and simply **act upon them automatically** in the days, weeks, months and years to come... And that part of you that does do such things can check that they are beneficial, better than the old ways, that they serve, only and always, your highest interests as a total man, loving this life and when **it's satisfied that this is so** it can **keep the new responses** as part of your positive present and future learning at deep levels of mind and body for **change immediately, in every way that you need, now**...Keeping in mind the total ecology of all the parts of yourself moving you forward in the ways you really need, and this is so. And you can **generate all the new solutions that you need to, now...**because your unconscious mind can do that for you and you need not even know how...as we consider some other things that will help **stimulate this capacity.**

Part 3: Resetting the sexual excitement dial.

Imagine something neutral, like a blank piece of paper....Good. Now, just let an image come to mind of a dial that represents where your sexual excitement levels at the point of lovemaking were set in the past *(Give 'em 5 – 7 seconds)*. Okay, now simply imagine moving that dial so that that **the initial excitement setting is lower.** So it is now set at just the right level so that you can **last longer, much longer in bed, now.** Relax, with that change deeply in mind...*(This module could have other uses: pornography addiction etc.)*

541

Part 4: Premature ejaculation into long, luxurious lovemaking.

You are about to **achieve your desire in a timely way** as you **dream a voluptuous sexual dream** in trance. Dream of being in the soft arms of that beautiful sexy woman you want to be with in that erotic way that only a man and woman can satisfyingly experience. **Be in that experience** as a fully absorbed participant. You notice you **feel very attractive** and so relaxed, yet aroused at the same time. You **feel completely comfortable being naked** with a woman you are really attracted to. When you **feel relaxed and happy** she will too.

You know that you can **take your time,** you can **be excited yet in control.** You can be passionate and slow, you can **be firm** and gentle. You can slow things down and even stop and start again. Your unconscious mind can **alter your responses during lovemaking** so that you **last as long as you wish.** It controls all of your bodily functions. You can relax knowing that you can **prolong the feelings of ecstasy** just as

long as you wish, **now** and in your future –
just **imagine that.** If something feels that
good **you want to prolong it,** do you not?

Look at her beauty, the curves of her body,
her grace and femininity, the delightful noises
she makes, her hair and eyes, her lips, every
part of her that fascinates you do deeply.
Caress her incredible body for just as long as
you wish – take your time, **there is no need
to rush.** You can relax knowing it will happen
at the right time but not right now because
somehow and for some mysterious reason,
you can **delay certain responses.**

Unleash the vivid power of your sexual
imagination and picture, hear, feel, smell and
taste everything that happens vividly. Do what
you really want to do, notice how good it
feels, **experience all those amazing
feelings at just the right pace.** Your
unconscious mind is in control of all the
timings of all the functions of your body. In an
emergency it can speed things up but when
making love it can
slow...certain...things...down, now.

So just relax, feel that you have all the time you need, feel **that lust is under control.** Like a skilled rider controlling the power of a horse. Enjoy her, enjoy the most blissful sexual feelings that you were born to luxuriate in. When you eat a really good meal you savour each moment – all **your senses heightened to their greatest pitch** of joy. **Be in that moment, only.** Your rate of breathing is different than before. You are touching her, feeling and sensing her, you **feel her desire** for you, her need to be with you sexually as a mature, sexual being. You will enjoy discovering the brilliance of her incredible sexual responses when you **make love in a new way** that is mutually fulfilling. You realise that you **want her to have a powerful orgasm too.** You want to know that **you can do that to a woman.** Lovemaking is about sharing. When you **prolong the experience longer and longer** you **make her feel so attractive** and deeply desired and woman love that. When you **do amazing things for someone else** they tend to want to return the favour.

Take your time to enjoy her in all the ways

a man can, **take your time** to enjoy all of her sensual delights, **take your time** to **make her come.** You notice her sexual arousal is intensifying, you are realising what she is capable of and how much more fulfilling and erotic that is. **You have a real, manly power to excite her** as long as you wish, to **keep her at the threshold of orgasmic release** until you **want her to come powerfully** because **you are controlling your own carnal desires, unconsciously** and it feels amazing, feel that power of manly control, now, that's it! Feel how it feels to **really be in control** and let that feeling turn into a colour that radiates all through your mind and body and learn, really learn to **keep this imprint.** You now know that what you can imagine you can do it real life; during real lovemaking all the same neural pathways are utilised as you **rehearse only the greatest and most blissful success.** You are sending a powerful message to your subconscious, which only ever wants to help you, that **this is what you want, now.** You can **last as long as you wish.**

All women love to be flirted with, all women

love to be teased, all women love to be found attractive, all women want you to **take control** so that she can sexually surrender to your male sexual power, she deeply desires that **you take the lead in bed confidently.** Your mind is relaxed yet focused on mutual satisfaction. At such times you **become so absorbed in lovemaking** that it is your sole focus. At that time, everything else is irrelevant. And that's a nice thing to know isn't it? You can **last just as long as you desire;** you pay full attention to her responses, you may smile with a naughty twinkle in your eyes as she begs and pleads with you not to **prolong the sexual ecstasy much longer,** but you know that you can always **last far longer.**

What difference is an extra minute or 2 or 5 or 10 and on and on? You're being in total sexual control of the experience is just a part of how you are now - **make the bliss last** as long as you want. You can **unconsciously delay when you ejaculate** – anything else is for nervous men and you aren't one of those, **you are _so_ sexually confident** and it feels great! You can stop and start or continue in that pleasant flow just as you wish. You can withdraw and penetrate her again with ease. You believe in that place in your mind where you believe things most of all that **you are a great fuck/great in bed** and you know it. You reveal it in your walk. Caresses and kisses that excite and arouse - you can **do all this easily** because **you do not give in to immediate impulses,** you **control your feelings -** you are in control more and more and more. You will come. You will **come hard, powerfully and joyfully at just the right time** because the subconscious is assisting you in all your sexual pleasures more and more and more. That's right!

After a pause perhaps, picture the smile, surprise as **you carry on longer and longer than ever before;** her soft, warm welcome responses. The joy, pleasure and sheer prolonged ecstasy of your sexually sensitive bodies. You just find that **you are much more relaxed in general and during lovemaking** and this allows you to **take it easy** and **take all the time you need** to pleasure her too. You can be appropriately aggressive and fast and you can **slow your**

thrusting when you need to, **escalating the sexual tension gradually,** rekindling it, resting, taking her higher and higher into places of erotic intensity she never knew existed, now. **Become absorbed by her beauty** in all its manifestations, you are in charge of the process, **fuck her blissfully,** as if you are giving her a great gift, you **delight in the pleasure of her body,** its sexuality and you want to make **those sensations last as long as possible** — she has sexually surrendered to you, giving herself to you, she abandons all restraints and lets her deepest sexual self out, enjoy the ride, her body is yours to do with as you deeply desire. **Pleasure her** in ways that drive her wild with desire. Her seemingly endless rapture.

If you feel that your come is about to explode into her you can easily **slow down, calm down or stop for a while,** the teasing will please her more and more. You decide when she comes and you can **prolong the blissful intensity** of her longing to have the release of her mind-blowing orgasm. Feel her shudder, feel her softness, she her neck and back arch, hear her moan. **You are fully in**

control when fucking her senseless and it is you alone who decides when to **increase the satisfying boundaries of sexual ecstasy.** You can and will full-fill her with an amazing orgasm where her body loses complete control, she lets out a cry and her body spasms and bucks against you, her eyes roll back into her deepest hypnotic sexual response.

And as soon as I am quiet...I want you to **totally unleash your sexual imagination,** let go in your mind and just enjoy, fully experience in all ways the incredible sensations and satisfactions of making love with that beautiful, sensual, sexual woman who wants you... NOOOOO-OOOOOW! Do what you need to do – learn what you need to learn...That's it. *(Shhh for 1 whole minute – let him enjoy himself...)*

As we continue, these powerful suggestions penetrate and go deeper into your subconscious mind, only growing stronger and stronger, more and more powerfully effective every second of every day. And **these wonderful feelings remain with you,** growing stronger and stronger and stronger, a knowing feeling of certain success within, radiating out from you in all appropriate ways and times that you may not even be consciously aware of – you'll just **radiate a different attitude,** perhaps **more cocksure** somehow, more poise and confidence than ever before as a result of all these profound changes you made.

(Did you notice all the sexual ambiguities?)

Part 5: Appreciation of beauty metaphor.

The human unconscious mind has an innate appreciation of beauty. It likes to take time appreciating this appreciation – just like you don't eat your desert too quickly. You savour it. It is nice to unwrap a present quickly, to get to that gift fast but at other times it is nice to take your turn, **give that person you care so much about a beautiful gift** and then when *they* are fully done, you take the time to unwrap yours too, taking your time to never look hasty and impolite. Appreciate the sumptuous beauty of experience. **Make the good times last, now,** for your own

550

unconscious reasons.

Part 6: Masculine sexual power.

(You'll get this module nowhere else folks – it really helps. It doesn't turn him into a dick head 'Macho Man'. I've seen very positive results from it!)

From now on you truly deeply believe in that place where you believe things most of all, that in a completely non egotistical way **you are an incredibly sexy, very important man** and you **feel this.** Women want you because you will give them sex so good it will change their life forever and you know this. **You have a powerful sexual masculinity.** You accept this. It is something you **feel ultra confident** about, it affects the way you walk and talk and feel and think from this day forth. Your testosterone levels are boosted, your libido is increased, your mojo is back better than ever, your energy, your powerful carefree attitude, your masculine strength and control of both mind and body. You are a powerful, masculine alpha male. **You have a masculine sexual power that you are**

comfortable with. Remember that women are affected by male sexuality as much as we are by theirs. **You are magnetically attractive** in just the way you wish to many people without trying. You **accept and affirm confidently all your masculine power and instincts and drives** in a way just right for you. **You are a _real_ man** and you accept this. Gone are all the old negative ideas, worries, embarrassments, absurdities, nonsense, unnecessary shame, guilt and concerns of the past, permanently and for all time. **You are potent and effective throughout your life, now.** You make women feel good around you, safe, comfortable – in ways that let them open up their most intimate sexual self. Women love sex with the right man, **you know how to sexually fulfill a woman,** trust this power. You instinctively know how to fuck a woman to make her come – again, again and again. You are fully confident in all the ways you need, now...Your mature, masculine adult instincts know what to do – let it happen naturally, automatically. That's right.

Part 7: Your super powerful erection.

I wonder what kind of an erection you will have? How powerful and long lasting it will be? To **be potent** is to **have power.** And you **have abundant sexual power!** Maybe it will come and go in just the right way? Maybe you'll be surprised to **notice a full hard erection**? In order to **have the type or erection you truly desire** at the right time at the right place, you can remember it's a message from your body that it's time to **have fun, enjoy the pleasure, focus -** trusting in your playfulness and great sense of humour all to your deep unconscious mind now, controls emotions, relaxation and blood flow, being in flow, **being in the flow of great sex** when needed, intensity, behaviours, images and appropriate thoughts...let it do what it does. You are safe when you make love, when you **fuck for fun and let nature do the rest.** All is well.

Part 8: Enjoyment NOT performance.

(Post-Kinsey culture has taught modern man and woman that fucking is a performance

sport where we all hold up 'score' cards and rate each other; get that shit out of your head fast!)

Sometimes we learn silly ideas from unwise, uniformed sources but sometimes it's ok to **become absorbed in our own pleasures** when that's appropriate. Sex is about bonding, intimacy and enjoyment, never a performance - pure enjoyment between two people. All thoughts of performance you may have had are gone now, gone forever...**focus on enjoyment.** Please her when it's right but you have to please yourself too. Performance is for study, work, the stage perhaps but nothing else...in sex **enjoyment is of prime importance** to each and both of you. When **there is no pressure,** you are free to relax.

It just becomes easier for you to **accept this reality** from now on. You achieve natural, automatic, spontaneous mastery of yourself in the ways you want. All old, unhelpful ideas from the past are gone for good. Only enjoy her, touch, kiss and if anything happens let in happen naturally because **you are fully in control.** The harder you *try* in vain to go back to how you once were you could only fail. Now, you **only succeed at succeeding** just as you truly wish.

9: Erectile dysfunction into cock of POWER!

Hypnosis can **restore normal bodily function.** Go 50 times deeper as I say the words – your powerful erection...'YOUR POWERFUL ERECTION, NOW!!!' That's it! Go deeper into trance, into hypnosis, rest a while peacefully, your mind can pause **hear**/here. Your subconscious and unconscious minds do so many thing for you. Your heart beat, the blood pumping blood around your whole body, **just the right amount of healthy blood into your penis during sexual arousal,** regulates your emotions – relaxation, all types of arousal, the way your lungs work and aid **your healthy functioning bloodstream** in ways you can't imagine! When **your breathing rate changes to relaxed breathing** most of the time you'll notice you **feel more calm and relaxed in general, now.** Your breathing...relaxing...you more and more and more. You walk and talk and your other minds do so many other things for you, we'd be here all day if we went through them all; the most important thing is you can **trust your deeper self** and **take certain responses for granted.** That's right. You don't even need to consider any of these natural processes because your other than conscious processes take care of them, unconsciously – you are born with certain abilities and potentials, - **that response you desire is totally instinctive, now;** trust the wiser you. Did anyone teach you how to breathe? Did anyone teach you how to cry? No - you just did it when it was needed, did you not? You have many ways to **get your deepest needs met,** you always have. Sometimes you need to **gain unconscious mastery over a given process.** You had the potential to walk and talk but you needed to learn how over time; once those abilities were absorbed they became habits. **A powerful erection is an automatic response, now.** As a teenager you might even get one on a bus going to school. It was that easy! Some people **easily get rock hard erections** at certain times of day. Can you recall a time like that?

You have learnt many things that require no thought or effort on your part, now; your powerful unconscious does all these things for you and it always works best when **you're relaxed more often.** Stress, worry, the cares of the workaday world is a total passion killer. As you **relax more deeply than ever** in hypnotic trance, you can know that **your unconscious mind will remove that problem, now.** That's it.

Sex is fun, when you **take off all that unnecessary pressure,** you will have so much fun again. And it honestly begins as you **alter your perspective and lighten up.** As you lighten up about a whole host of things **you'll _get it up_ with effortless ease,** at just the right time. Up until now certain things weren't working as they should but from now on **you will enjoy the process of lovemaking.** Enjoy the joy of flirting, sex starts with certain looks, touches, the way you use words suggestively. And these are all fun things to do. She makes you **feel a warmth.** You **feel a certain excitement** in her presence. And that's all part of the fun too. Soft or passionate kisses, embraces and all the touching makes you feel so good, when **you feel sexually attractive** things start to stir, do they not?

Can you recall all the emotions of a very special nature that you feel with a very special woman? You can take your time, relax and don't **get so stiff** about things, not at that time. What is it about a certain woman? What traits arouse you effortlessly? The way she walks, glances at you, holds your hand, looks deeply into your eyes, plays with her hair, strokes the stem of that glass, touches your forearm, the glamour of her face, her laugh, her smile, the way she wrinkles her nose or places her hands on her lap, the way certain bits wiggle. The sight of certain parts – you know how to **become aroused physically by an attractive woman,** when the time is right, it is a part of your heritage, if it wasn't then neither would you be. *(Mild confusional langauge...)*

As you make love with words, sounds, touches and more you can **feel your cock getting harder and harder** because **that part is working fine.** Imagine now, making love, fucking, **easily getting in that sexual zone,** where, when you can both abandon all inhibitions and enjoy each other beautifully. When **you are relaxed and having fun** – all your energies flow as they should to where they are needed, now and in your future as required automatically. When you are in that place of pure sexual arousal, when nothing else matters at that time, **your cock gets hard so easily.**

The soft feminine feel of her, look of her, smell of her are your only focus at such times. You **feel powerfully potent** at such times, use your rock hard cock to pleasure her and yourself as you may have only imagined once was possible but which is now your 100% total personal reality. That's it. It is all going perfectly, again and again and again. Picture it and **feel your powerful erection** as you thrust it deep inside her. The blood knows how to flow, just let it happen. You feel invincible and manly at such times. You could go on forever and notice how easy it is to **maintain a rock hard erection** for **as long as you want.**

I will be quiet as you **rehearse your sexual success.** See what you'll see, hear what you'll hear, feel how good and easy it all feels. Whereas once you thought things would **be so hard** you discover you can now just go with the flow, unconsciously. *(Shhh for 1 minute...)*

The delight of these pleasurable feelings, abilities, unconscious habits has been reawakened and locked in place: any and all final re-organisations occur, now. You deepest mind had a template of how to **get erect and hard on cue.** So you can **radiate a sure-fire sexual confidence** in your real manly power that will satisfy you profoundly. There are times when only thoughts, images and sensations of sex occupy your mind and that's as it should be – a great part of life. These feelings remain with you, now. You can relive these abilities to **get hard, remain hard** in the reality of your experience of lovemaking, every time. **Respond naturally to her attractions.** Do what you did before only better. Make sure you take the time to **relax and rest and feel good** about who you really are. It is all just there. All the sensations of success, **great sex is yours** and this is so!

10: Crystal ball of total sexual power...

(This is a future pace variant: Milton Erickson liked using imaginary crystal balls in hypnosis, they suggest 'magic', hypnosis magic...)

Dissociated rehearsal.

Now I'd like you to imagine a crystal ball in your mind's eye. As you **look deep inside** it, you can **see a powerfully erotic image,** a porno if you like with you as the star with some beautiful woman, her body is splendid! This you is experiencing great, amazing, awesome sex, his cock is rock hard, he has amazing sexual stamina: this all takes place at some time in your near future, sooner than you think, now, making love, more adventurous and passionate, so confident, dominant, aggressive and gentle, in just the way you want to, incredibly well – better than you ever imagined was possible until now. You are discovering, learning with surprise and delight because **you are a truly gifted lover.** Just a part of who you are.

Watch this porno, your porno – the best porn film you've ever watched, the most arousing ever! **Fixate your attention** within your powerful mind on just this experience. You can vividly see that naughty movie over there! Wow! That confident lover - you and your beautiful lover! You are only fulfilled in just the right way for both of you, **totally satisfied inside,** completely, at just the right time for each and both of you. And that can leave you with **a feeling of deep security inside,** can't it? I will be quiet for a full minute as you enjoy this emotional and physical sexual ecstasy. You deserve it. Dare! Let go! Unleash the unbridled power of your masculine sexual imagination, now... *(Shhh...)*

Associated rehearsal.

And when you are ready and **everything has gone as you have wished,** allow yourself to float into that image from the start of that amazing porno film but this time you are the star, the star of real life, and **fully experience that entire process** making love amazingly well, to the great pleasure of the both of you. See the pleasure on your lover's face as you **fully satisfy her** and when the time is right, yourself. Take time to enjoy this now, you are learning to do what you want at the right time, in the right way, without knowing how, just trusting, really trusting things to happen in due course. It's great to **fully trust yourself like that,** is it not? I'll be quiet for a whole minute as you create new pathways of experience in your unconscious mind.... *(Shhh!)*

Excellent! And now, once everything has concluded as you wish, you can return from that experience, allowing the learnings and understandings to remain locked deep inside you; indeed you may not fully remember everything but you deeply know somehow, in some mysterious way that **you are irresistibly headed for certain success** as the crystal ball fades...away...completely, now.

All your wonderful future sexual experiences will be just as pleasurable, in differing ways and for different reasons, just as enjoyable, variety is the spice of life as they say, you have already seen that **this is so** within that powerful magic crystal ball in your inner mind.

When you **imagine success** your unconscious takes this as a sign and a signal that this is what you desire, it makes the necessary adjustments now for this to be so.

11: Stiff finger into stiff cock...

(This part gives new meaning to the word 'stiffy'; you can take hypnotically induced catalepsy say in an arm and transfer it elsewhere in the body, say his...You don't need to get real catalepsy, imaged stiffness is just as good.)

Hypnotic entrainment.

In your imagination or with your real finger it doesn't matter which can you just do the following: extend your forefinger on the hand you feel most comfortable doing so – that's it straight out in front of you, as though you were pointing at something important. *(A beat.)* That's magic. Now, as I continue to speak hypnotically you will soon notice that **that first finger is becoming very stiff and very rigid. Now,** as it does so, you will also find that you **feel a sense of control**

over the stiffness. In a moment if it hasn't occurred already – that stiffening finger will be just as stiff as a powerful iron bar and yet it keeps **all sensations under control.** It is stiff, potent, full of energy - becoming just as stiff as a rigid iron bar right now. Perfect! Your index finger is as stiff and powerful as an iron rod yet it is exquisitely sensitive, yet that feeling is under your control – you sense somehow you could increase the intensity or decrease it at will without knowing how consciously. *(Pause 7 - 10 secs for processing etc.)*

Now all the stiffness can leave that finger as it fully returns to normal now. That's it – all the way back to **normal sensations and flexibility once again** – give it a wiggle to prove it if need be! *(A beat!)* Good!

Post hypnotics.

From this moment forth – every wondrous time that **you are ready for great sex** you will automatically find that at the proper time **your fully potent cock** has become just as stiff and powerful as your pointing forefinger was only moments ago – **your cock is as stiff as an iron bar when you need it to be** – just a part of who you really are. And it will be just as sensitive as it need to be to satisfy you and your lover, just as much a sense of control over certain intensities. You will easily **maintain your erection and prolong sex for as long as is necessary to fully satisfy your lover/woman and yourself.** Normal feelings return to your penis as soon as it would happen normally and healthily. You are fully able to **maintain your erection as long as is desired** to reach climax – to ejaculate, and **your climax and ejaculation feel 100 times more satisfying, pleasurable, powerful and fulfilling** than you've ever known so far. During this process you have been left with a knowing feeling, now, that **you have fully retrained your unconscious responses** in all the ways you require for pleasurable success to be a certainty, now – relax, enjoy..and - **trust your unconscious learnings, now...**

(Some hypnotherapists suggest the client's cock go numb during sex – now class, why is

this a stupid idea? Discuss. Really!?)

N.A.C squeeze technique...

(I throw in a behavioural conscious mind technique.)

Well done *(client's name)* you are doing brilliantly – we are almost done! Another technique is to remember whenever you wish to control that excitement and arousal during sex: squeeze the place on your penis where the shaft meets the head with your thumb and forefinger. This instantly diminishes those feelings. **You are fully in control,** you know how...

Laughter...

A wise hypnotist once told a man that if he had problems in the past with sexual arousal he would look at his lover and say, 'You want this don't you?' She'd say, 'Yes,' and he'd say, 'Then *you* get it up!' You refuse to take that problem seriously anymore. We always learn to **laugh at many things** that once bothered us. It's the basis of an idea that helps:

refusing no matter how **hard you** try to take things that seriously unless it's genuinely best and really right to. Remember laughing at things makes us **feel so much better inside** and relaxes us and others, makes us **feel amazing.** There is more than one way to view anything, so we may as well add in a giggle or two or more. What if **things that made you angry, frustrated, nervous or fearful way back then, now make you laugh instead**? Just for fun. Just **fuck for fun** for fuck's sake!

12: Future dreaming...

(You can programme the unconscious to have dreams, sexual dreams – I showed how to do this with erotic hypnosis in book 6, 'Crafting hypnotic spells'; it reinforces the work you have done when you're not there – a good thing!)

Sometime, during the next few nights or so, when you are fast asleep, perhaps beside the warmth of your lover, you are going to **have a most erotic and pleasant dream** which I promise will be extremely sexually arousing.

All dreams are composed of a symphony of dream images, emotions, responses, meanings beyond waking meanings, sensations, experiences in your own inner imaginarium – this one will be very sexually stimulating indeed, and you will **be so excited** by it and its message, inspiration and intent that you will find yourself awakening, yes, even before the dream is completely over, and you will be in the mood for some loving, fully aroused, rock hard and ready to make passionate love.

The dream's after affects last for as long as is needed when you wake up so sexually aroused. These changes add glorious heights, wholly novel proportions of luxuriousness and lavishness, intensities beyond the extent of all you've hitherto known that could be known up until now, wonderful sexual bounties, pleasures and abundance that will enrich you and your profoundly empowered lovemaking capacities.

You will unearth and **originate distinct pathways of sexual bliss,** satisfactions, entertainments, self-indulgence and thrills.

Your joint sexual revelry will titillate beyond measure! Unique intimacies will be shared that deepen your loving connection, over and above any expectation you might have had.

You may find that you are so surprised and delighted to find that **your orgasm will be on the far side of sexual ecstasy,** out of reach of the bounds of what wasn't really true – ever, now! From this instant, **your orgasm will always last longer than before.** It will be more satisfying, powerful – you will come a lot and deeply!

It's nice to know, is it not, that now and again you will discover yourself having these sexually delightful dreams in which new ideas can be tried on and out in the safety of fantasy! These will occur at essential times in the future boosting **your incredible sexual confidence** and sense of erotic experimentation, which only improves your life in so many ways that you can joyously anticipate the discovery process of...

Remember the old as time tale of 'The Tortoise and the Hare'? The hare thought it best to rush, he rushed to the finishing line and thought winning was about getting there first. But he lost; back then. It was the tortoise that won, he was wise. He took his time, enjoyed the journey, paced out his stamina and won the *real* prize: and you can too; can you not?

Make all of these suggestions intelligently your own...now

13. Ego boost, positive outlook etc...

From this day forth, **your self-esteem is totally unassailable,** impregnable like a mighty fortress protecting the core of who you are and the core of your new total conviction and belief that **you are worthwhile,** that you deserve the best in life – you have it coming. This is **your/you're powerfully virile** new reality: your self-confidence is solid, unshakeable like a mighty mountain **rock solid** from attack. Forgive those people you need to forgive, forgive yourself: most people are doing the best they can with the resources they have. Let unhelpful attitudes fade, they are no longer true about you. Heal, release, **let it go;** let the past go in the way that is most appropriate because your subconscious can do that, now...You **trust your instincts,** listen to that inner voice that wisely guides you, those feelings and responses from within, let your conscience guide you – it is a very human part, always **trust your subconscious mind, now**...you are a worthwhile, unique, talented individual; deep down under the illusion of doubts you have always known this with a deeper wisdom...

We have proven that **you can relax deeply;** this is an amazing achievement, a new beginning for you as you only **achieve the same success every day.** You have learned how powerful your mind is. You know that when things are in your control you can **focus intently on positive imagined thoughts that bring about the positive things you desire.** You can **relax deeply whenever you wish.** You have achieved all that you needed to most of all in this session: **think and imagine positively,** think what else you can achieve now and in the future when you **think in these new ways** and go and do it.

Go for it! Live this life with the zest that you give to those things that you commit to 100%! Give it your all! See yourself going out and meeting new and old people, any people that you wish in a confident, powerful way, enjoying your new way of living and of being as an individual in this world. You are looking forward to doing new things, having new fun experiences. You are **fully motivated to achieve all that you most desire in life, now...**

As you **relax even deeper** realising also that whenever you hear my voice in the context of a hypnosis session, the effect of my positive suggestions upon you will only grow stronger in every way enabling you to realize that something you once thought would be so difficult to achieve has in fact proved so amazingly, ridiculously easy. And the fact is – it was YOU that did it! When faced with a problem in the future, you can ask yourself, 'How can I solve this most easily, elegantly and effortlessly?' When you are faced with a series of tasks you can do them one at a time and break them down into small manageable chunks. You have all you need within to **live**

your life to the fullest, nooooo-ooow!'

(I gave you far too much but I'm like that...Hint: this script is designed for the porn generation, okay; most of my male sexual health clients are young men, not older ones. You can be quite rude, crude and speak in a male banter manner. It works. However if you are a female therapist or you are dealing with older men as clients tone it down. Ladies speaking in a hypnotic voice sound quite seductive at times; it is a very soft and nice tone to a male ear – it's not far from sexual sweet talk so BE CAREFUL. Older men prefer a tamed version of the above; they are gentleman. Call his thing a penis to be on the safe side and tone down the above implications of sexual acrobatics.)

Analysis in brief.

In the above script I bombard the male brain over and over again with images and suggestions of amazing sexual success – it is really that simple. You don't need to do all of it. In fact I have a host of other things I can do with male sexual dysfunctions but this is a good addition to any hypnotist's toolbox. May it serve you well – I have found it to be 100% successful.

Case 13: Lie back and think of England – sexual dysfunction in women.

With ladies never be smutty or crude when it comes to sexual problems – ever! A women's sexual problem will almost always be based around relaxing enough to let go and experience a satisfying orgasm for one reason or another; unless of course her problem is her husband's premature ejaculation but that's another story! We are going to focus on the problem of a woman not achieving a satisfactory orgasm during sex.

WARNING! In the following process you are taking a lady through the experience of sexual bodily feelings. This must ONLY be done with the utmost tact and sense of decency. *Explain beforehand that all sexual arousal during the session is to be linked to her lover.* If she is uncomfortable with this – design a direct session where you describe what will happen when she makes love next (use the word 'will' a lot etc. suggesting 'in the future'). Lock it in with a post hypnotic etc.

Letting go into pure pleasure script.

(Deep hypnosis assumed)

'Thankfully all woman can **experience a deeply satisfying and blissful orgasm when appropriate*.** All you need do is **focus on the experience of blissful lovemaking** moment to moment. You know, really know the colour feeling of excitement, do you not? As you focus on that colour spreading all through you – let it emanate from within so that it fills every part of you...That's it.

When you **relax into sexual arousal at the right time,** it is usual to feel a warmth is it not? At times **certain blissful feelings can expand** all throughout your mind and body, is that not so? Have you ever been feeling so good that **wave after wave of wonderful feelings** washed through you and over you – again and again and again? Have you ever experienced a time when you could **feel those anticipatory butterflies in your tummy?** Good.

When the time is right, all you ever have to do is **relax into pleasure and forget the outcome** as you **be-cum absorbed** by other intensely pleasurable things. When **you are accessing your deepest states of sexual pleasure** all you need do is **let such feelings intensify naturally** without any effort. A deeper part of your mind controls such responses so that you can **simply focus on your growing pleasure.**

You can take any pleasurable feeling and watch it intensify all by itself in hypnosis and **you're experiencing deeply satisfying sex** is a type of hypnosis. You know how to **feel a warmth growing inside.** And that can spread all throughout your body all by itself because it knows how to do what it does as **you just come** along for such a thrilling ride. Feel that expand and radiate down to the extremities – to the tips of your toes, the tip of your nose and fingers even. That's the way. As you find your own way to **let this pleasure build, unconsciously,** notice that **that warmth turns into a more intense heat,** just when you need it to. If you **feel comfortable doing so,** let that happen now or save it for when **you make love in such a satisfying way** from this moment forth.

All human experiences of movement require a specific rhythm – when **you are sexually excited** you breathe a certain way, your

blood flow is altered, you move in *that* way.
You may notice **you are flushed.** Have you
ever done something so thrilling? Ever been
on a rollercoaster or just imagined doing so?
And as that experience progresses, as **your
feelings rise to a crest** you can **feel that
great excitement building,** more and more
and more. That's it! Have you ever had a
joyous experience when things just started to
heat up unexpectedly?

Some amusing rides are like that. As you
reach the peak of a particular amusement ride
you can heat up with excitement perhaps
there are awesome bursts of tingles of joyous
anticipation of what will soon be so. And as
you **reach the pinnacle of bliss so easily.**
You'll find that that **inner rapture and
extreme bliss can explode** at the high
point! And you can **know the
overwhelming absorption of letting go
into your most amazing orgasms over
and over,** at the right time with the right
person for you to share them with, now.

And when a mountain climber reaches the
peak of their quest, how much satisfaction can
they feel in the afterglow of the warmth of
intimate success alongside the power of
nature? They may be **throbbing or**

pulsating with such joy, wave after wave that they can bathe in and maybe the whole process can be repeated from the right set of tuned into rhythms over and over and over again when you **just relax into such heights of bliss** that delight you endlessly with your lover or on your own in differing ways of anyone **experiencing ecstasy...**There are times when doing nothing consciously is just the right thing to do. Is that not so?

So now you really know that when **you relax fully during lovemaking** blissful feelings can and do explode outwardly when that's right. There is a time to **let it all build and build from a warmth, to a heat, to a fire, to a climax of pure ecstasy!** That is overflowing and overwhelming you, now. And your unconscious knows when such a response is just right. And you can **bathe in feelings of delightful bliss** with your lover whenever you wish, you are a sensual woman, women do this, and **this is so.** Your instinctive templates of automatically and **fully experiencing sexual bliss** and union have been fully reconnected to, **now. That hit the spot,** did it not? And that's a nice thing to know, is it not?'

(*Sexual arousal in women can be triggered by the imagination just as it can in men – the difference being woman can powerfully orgasm due to it. This is why I use words like 'when' and 'appropriate' etc. so she doesn't link it to me!!! Give her time to process what you say before moving on.)

Case 14: Anger 'management'; impotent grief rage!

Anger is linked to anxiety: it's the fight response – the people who get 'anger problems' are those with balls (male and female) and those with a firm sense of injustice; often their needs aren't being met. Sexual frustration alone is a BIG source of anger! Anger can make you feel alive, energised and potent, tough if you like BUT it can be addictive and lead to health risks; including an increased risk of strokes – worse still, it can damage nearest and dearest relationships. Being around a permanently angry head is exhausting for all concerned!

Okay the process is part addiction control and part 'phobia removal'. Check out the script below which I used on a lady who watched her dad die of cancer; slowly, painfully. The person is 'ANGRY' (unspecified verb/trance word) they all want to be 'CALM' again. Unwanted state – wanted state.

RH PRO TIP: During the interview/pre-talk ask your client to name the unwanted state and the desired 'replacement' state: use their trance words to label the states in the session – these are their 'mind keys'.

Taming the anger beast script.

(Deep relaxing hypnosis assumed)

Part 1: Anger symbology flipping.

(NFH: use this with any low level state change work including phobias etc. If you prefer use the more complete version in the 'How to detraumatise anyone' script.)

'First thing to do – I now want your subconscious mind to give you a symbol that represents every aspect of that anger you had...whatever it offers you is right, just trust it's ability to process all that information that quickly. Whatever that symbol is, however it is symbolised is right for you – it may appear in your mind in any sensory modality and that's just fine too. I'll pause as it manifests... *(Give 'em 7-10 secs max.)*

Excellent. Now get to know that anger symbol – notice everything about it: colour, shape, distance, texture. You name it; get to know it intimately, objectively before we **change this state for good, now,** I'll be quiet for a while as you do that... *(Give 'em 10-15 secs max.)*

583

Good. Really pay attention to that thing...I want your your subconscious to change that symbol so that it completely represents X *(wanted state nominalisation etc. that you agreed upon in the interview – 'calm' etc.)* where you previously felt anger in certain times and places. Whatever those changes are, let them occur – trust them 100%! It's all in your mind...I'll be quiet so that you can **complete that process of symbolic change** to each and both of your satisfaction... *(10 secs max...)*

Brilliant! You are doing so well. We are nearly done. Next. Okay I want your subconscious mind to make any final and lasting changes to the new symbol so that it completely symbolises the feeling you want to feel to its utmost respect. If there are no more changes fine BUT if it now wants to **make any final changes for optimum success** please do so now, while I'm quiet. This is your opportunity to **take control of how you feel.** *(10 secs is usually enough – observe your client; get a feel...)*

Part 2: Installing the feeling of 'calmness in just the right place.'

Very good. Now you have this symbol and this new feeling of wonderful, safe and free calmness and it feels great. Okay, you recognise that this calmness is a feeling. Your new powerful symbol represents this resourceful state you desired and now have. And you also understand fully that all feelings belong somewhere very specific in the human body; that's their nature...That's how we experience them, how they make sense to us.

That being so, I know that you know exactly where this calmness/x belongs and feels most comfortable. This sense of ease and better responses, this feeling of being **secure inside, now.** This infinite ability to access **calmness as your base state – just locked in. Now,** you know where it needs to go inside that body. So simply move your empowering symbol, place it in the spot it needs to be in. Again I'll be quiet as you do a that *(10 secs should do it...)*

Fantastic! You are doing so well! Can you take

these wonderful set of feelings and responses which serve you so well and **let it expand and intensify now** extending powerfully and blissfully throughout mind and body! Let it flow all through you! Let it radiate beyond! Let it reach its most wonderful pitch of being! That's perfect! You can take this act as a sign and a signal that **you have that calmness fully locked in.** You are filled with this state – this is your new reality. Fully realise at all levels that **the changes have been made permanently.**

Calm responses.

That which made you lose your cool before is now - **no problem whatsoever** - situation, person, place or space: no event or occasion bother you that much from now on. **You are in control of all your emotional responses.** Save anger for when it's genuinely and appropriately needed. You walk through this world with a sense of deep and profound calmness that guides all you do. As this is true, you can **calmly think things through** whenever you need. And this is so.

(NFH: NEVER TRY TO REMOVE AN EMOTION!!! Now that has already solved the problem; if in a hurry you could leave it there but I never do; I whack 'em with an addiction busting module next...)

Dissociating from the 'anger addiction'.

Stage 1: Building in a better response.

Okay. Good. Now the interesting thing about anger is that as you learn **to control it, unconsciously,** and notice how much more comfortable you feel in so many situations that used to upset you, I'd simply like you to picture a time when you might have been tempted in the past to feel an excessive supply of that old emotional response before **you automatically respond differently, now.** So just imagine you're in that time and you are a bit pissed off/annoyed and that old feeling of anger is beginning to rise and - float right out of that time and see yourself over there and I want you to **objectively look at that** old anger response in a calm way and ponder any conclusions that you draw from this perspective. From this new vantage point new ideas and approaches will come to mind as you **resolve never to unnecessarily loose it** that way again. Take the time to **process that** while I am quiet for 10 seconds or so *(15 secs max....)*

Good. Now I know you learnt some things about yourself from that. But the good thing is you are not a robot. You do not have do what you sometimes did. What if you could **be automatically creative and flexible** at such times with certain people **keeping your sense of humour and a bigger, broader perspective** at all times, now?

And for a moment realise how entirely relaxed you can be as you **reset an instinctive calming response** into the deepest part of your mind. You **feel at ease** and it feels wonderful to **have a genuine sense of real self-control.**

Stage 2: Rehearsing objectivity at times of stress.

Can you once more picture a time that may have led to that old unwanted response......? Good. Notice it's that type of time or person that would have pissed you off and led you to get annoyed perhaps then increasingly angry. And before it gets too much you simply – float out of that time and watch yourself over there so that **unconsciously you can calm down at such times instantly** as you **teach yourself restraint.**

Notice how that you over there is far calmer as a result and how much more relaxed they look in all ways; notice how you **feel calm and soothed inside.** There is not always a battle to be fought. Sometimes there are better choices than fighting and you can **find better choices, now** and your creative part will help. As this happens and it will, you'll notice that a bigger space for calmness develops in your life and as a result you **feel calmer and happier overall.** And that's a nice thing to know isn't it?

(Get the client to practise this with two more examples as per stage 2 above; this will drive the changes in and create the needed re-association at such times in waking life...)

Stage 3: Associated rehearsal.

Excellent. Now you've taken the time to **learn**

some new things, I would like you to keep these amazing feelings of calm and simply float into yourself in various situations that would have triggered an excessive response and just become increasingly aware that as you practise being in those times you can **feel the deep reservoirs of calm control within.** Feel how much better you feel. No matter what others do. No matter what thing occurred that used to trouble you. How much better is it to be able to **think calmly no matter what** is going on? Knowing that toddlers can throw their teddy bear out of the cot and that's fine but **in maturity, now** we, as adults, can **find new and more enjoyably appropriate ways to respond** to any situation whilst we are in it. Take all the time you need in the next whole minute to go through as many situations as you please to **rehearse precisely the responses you really desire, now.** *(Shhh as indicated...)*

That's it. It is so simple to know that **regaining control is pleasurable,** wasn't it? You have a calm and clear mind that reflects reality as it is.

Direct suggestions for change.

In the past your subconscious responded in ways that were positive in intent but

counterproductive when applied to inappropriate contexts. In some situations *that* would be exactly the response to have to protect yourself physically or perhaps your integrity. You need anger so that people don't walk all over you. Anger can set limits beyond which others know they shouldn't tread. It can let others know how frustrated you were in response to certain events often beyond your control. Whatever that positive, protective response was, I would like to thank your subconscious for doing all that on your behalf. You did it automatically and exceptionally well.

But this person thinks and feels that **better generalisations can be made now.** They have had enough of that. From now on, in situations that triggered that old response you can **feel so much more calm and in control automatically.** You have unconscious mechanisms for cooling heat, for returning to calm after an upset and a whole host of other processes that return you to a feeling of healthy, optimum, long-term functioning – your base state you might say. But I want your subconscious mind to promise that that potential for anger will be there if

you should ever really need it. You can find so many more ways to respond to any kind of stimulus – you are not a knee that got hit by a doctor's hammer. You no longer fly off at the handle because you **handle things in a different way,** do you not? There may be a time to be more diplomatic, there may be a time when a joke would relieve the tension, there may be a time when you just need to refocus somehow on what you really want and what's really important. There are long-term consequences to actions. You can see beyond the old anger tunnel when you decide to **feel differently about a whole host of things, unconsciously.** And remember to relax knowing that your creative subconscious is aiding you in reaching your goals and ambitions, guiding you in a new flexible approach to the game of living. Now that we are quite done you can feel a knowing feeling that **profound change has occurred** (?). Attitudes, behaviours, feelings, re-associations of several appropriate subconscious structures have shifted on your behalf while you had a nice rest.'

(Exduction etc. There are a billion differing approaches folks – get knowledgeable, get creative. Make shit up on the fly! Therapy is a creative art form, a skilled game not a science.)

Case 15: Low-self-esteem + anxiety caused by job loss.

In the following script I (in part) used the NLP-esque hypnosis script that follows. I also used a version of my confidence boosting script which can be found in book 3, 'Powerful hypnosis'. I will not reiterate the latter here as it will just make this book too big.

I had a lady client come to visit me complaining of 'low-self-esteem'. What low self-esteem meant to her specifically was this: she had lost a job she really liked. This had been caused by the fact that she had exchanged a private email at her workplace making a joke about her boss/manager. In a gross invasion of privacy this manager had accessed her emails (spied on her) and found the 'offending' email. He was so incensed that he fired her: she lost a job she had worked at for over two decades. She lost her pension and she was nearing retirement age. But the main thing that was troubling her was the persistent intrusive image of this man discovering her 'treasonous' email. This image, entirely a product of her own imagination made her visibly flinch, moan out loud and physically crumple! *The image, not the event was the problem* – in a way it was a legacy of the very real trauma that she had experienced of losing her job. What follows is a section of the session as I said, it is really an involved NLP swish pattern with some added extras; some call it the 'Quick self-esteem fix pattern' but RH has improved it. My version is called...

<u>'The Rogue Hypnotist's traumatic image swish script.'</u>

(Deep hypnosis assumed – this module came first, the coup de grace was the confidence boost 'directly indirect' script. I start the script by eliciting the troubling image – it will cause a mild emotional reaction: her mind cannot escape it because she's in trance. Although I would probably use the 'how to de-traumatise anyone script' now, sometimes it can be good to try out different techniques. Look, the image doesn't evoke a really bad 'abreaction' a la psychoanalysis. She needs to know that it is just an image – it's the meaning she gives it symbolically that is the problem. Notes and step by step analysis for the hypnotist are in brackets.)

Getting a sense of how you 'do' self-esteem: submodality play.

'Okay. Now in a moment I am going to ask you to look at that image but only for a very short time before we **change that old reaction forever, now,** you ready?
(She winces and looks tense...)

Think of that time we discussed that made you feel bad about yourself. A time you perceived certain thoughts, images, feelings were in the forefront of your mind before we **change this for good.**

(I elicit the image. She gasps and whines, starts to curl up...)

Okay this won't last long I promise – here we go! See what you saw, hear what you heard, feel what you felt. Perhaps remember that time – that reaction your old boss had *(you can say - '...a time someone was rude/you were insulted/others negativity infected your self-esteem etc.')* Where are those feelings located? Notice their shape, size and anything else that is relevant. Good. You are doing really well.

(She is forced to confront this image – by

doing so you are already helping her. When you look at an image that seems scary over and over it loses its power through desensitisation. She trusts me, we have established a good working relationship – 'rapport' – she has told me she thinks I am a gifted therapist etc. She knows I won't leave her here...)

Notice any images that arise. Whatever image most symbolises that old response is now what we'll call your 'trigger image' *(cue image etc.)*. We'll use this to **change things.** Notice any sounds or other sensory modalities/qualities etc. *(smells, sounds etc.)* that you associated with that.

(Already the meaning is changing. I tell her that the problem is part of the solution. We are taking that trigger/cue that was associated to 'pain', we are going to link the old neural pathway to pleasure instead – watch...)

Okay, now step right out of that experience! Good.

(Her emotions subside – she is dissociated: remember if you've read my other books – dissociate clients from negative states.)

Just imagine a blank piece of paper. Recall and think of a nice pleasant time and let **these nice feelings fill you now.**

(The blank piece of paper evokes a neutral emotional state. I then evoke a nice one and tell her to think about it. If she is thinking about something, she cannot be so emotional. I am already screwing up the old linkages. She is being led quickly and elegantly in steps thus: pain – neutral – pleasure. I am training her that she can control her states far more than she believed. In trance the change is instant. In waking states emotions can be 'muddy'; in hypnosis they are discreet and pliable. I am in control of them. I am directionalising her brain. Now we start building in real power and resourcefulness...)

Now *(client's name)* you are going to **build in some power...**I want you to create a compelling image that truly represents the strong, resourceful and **positive self-esteem, now,** that you are about to own! Imagine seeing yourself in a bright, big, bold and colourful image with **great, profound, permanent self-esteem and total self-worth.** An image of a person with **total self-belief** too. Excellent! How much better does that feel already?

(At this point, as they view their nice, shiny self-worth image they'll look calmer, more confident: they may be smiling. Their chest may be uplifted with good feelings and the head may tip back as the good feelings shoot from the solar plexus up to the top of the head! This is a good 'ideomotor' signal that you are doing good work! She is also viewing how she wants to be in a dissociated way: this protects her from the past hurt and says, 'Brain, go toward this!' All NLP swish patterns say, 'Not that, this!')

How are you standing? What is your facial expression? Notice your body language! Be aware of that new attitude that you are oozing! How do you sound now? How would others **respond differently,** react, as they too are really enjoying being around your pure self-esteem? Because when you **feel really good,** others will too.

(Here we are simply designing in – leaving sufficient vagueness for it all to come from the client as to 'how' they would 'do' self-esteem...This is a form of modelling.)

Imagine yourself in a situation just propelled with **this healthy sense of self-esteem, now.** Notice how stimulating and genuinely motivating it is to be in this place. Somehow add in a real sense that this 100% new reality is in your future! This act simply removes/dissolves the effects of any past slurs, insults, comments, unfair criticism, hurts, past caring about all those unjustified attacks on your self-worth. This new image will allow you to **create your bright future, now,** responding to everything so much more positively.

(Here you are locking in the changes and giving post-hypnotics that they manifest upon awakening. I use the term 'healthy' self-esteem. I used to say 'high' but in some people this may create narcissism or arrogance – remember that psychopaths have off the charts self-esteem, they worship themselves. I don't want to create any more assholes in this world; it's already overpopulated with 'em!)

Okay, you are doing really well! Can you just turn up those colours, the brightness, contrasts, saturate that wonderful life-affirming image of who you really are with bold Technicolor! That's it! Make it very big in your mind! Attractive and irresistibly compelling! Turn up any sounds – make them surround sound stereo! Let the fantastic feelings grow in intensity now! That's it! More and more and more! Become fully aware of your greater sense of choice, support and self-reliance, your **creativity boosted, now.** All your attitudes, thoughts, perspectives, beliefs are becoming congruent, aligned and much more positive than ever before! It feels great doesn't it!

(Notice my tone and languaging is very enthusiastic and positively compelling throughout; who wants to resist that? I am simply amplifying the response using bog-standard NLP amplifying procedures using submodalities of amplification.)

Notice how this image and state are really attractive – something that entices you to really want to **make this change a part of your life. Now,** Connect to this state becoming more and more drawn to it. Feel an inner attitude that you need this and must have it! Experience your sense of all the possibilities of it. The ways that it already feels real for you. Put a cheeky, knowing, perhaps mysterious smile on that image of your true self – that's it! Imagine you can hear them think, 'It feels good to be me!' And they mean it! Make this voice attractive and resonant; like someone that you believe, in a really positive and supportive tone. Great! That tone allows you to **enjoy and appreciate the gift of being YOU!** Add anything at all you wish to make this image even better! *(Pause for 5 secs or so.)* Puurr-fect!

(Again we are enhancing the image using all sensory modalities. The more rich and vivid the description the easier it is for the unconscious to know exactly what to do. Next up – things start to get interesting...)

When **you're happy with the changes,** put a beautiful frame around that healthy self-esteem image. Shrink it so that it becomes a tiny dot in that space ahead of you. Make it sparkle at you magically!

Very quickly take that dot and jump it back to its previous size and aliveness! Add in the 'It feels so good to me me!' attitude and hear that convincing voice. Think of a sheet of white paper...Good. Now see that healthy self-esteem image again. Shrink it again to a dot. Take it back to full size. Think of a white sheet of paper... Shrink it to a dot once more. Take it back to full size. Great. Just take a rest.

(What we are doing here is changing the way

this client codes her concept of self-esteem at a deep neurological level. I am teaching her that the way her brain codes a concept like 'self-esteem' is plastic. It can be changed and played with like a toy. I do this submodality work briskly; I don't rush it but I ensure I am guiding the mind so it can't wander off and do weird shit. I elicit white paper and ask them to think not feel about it because I am giving their brain a rest: submodality work is tiring – it's odd. I don't want to overload her/him. Okay what follows next is the most important bit. I have numbered the parts 1 and 2: repeat stages 1 and 2 - 3 times!!! The brain works fast – say the following energetically! Up your tempo! Be definite: 'positively authoritative'! Don't ask – tell!)

Swish change process.

1. Okay...Shrink down the healthy self-esteem image and put it in the middle of the old, unpleasant image, the one you first thought about.

2. Now – saying the word **SWISH!** as you do – rapidly and simultaneously shrink the unpleasant image into a small grey dot and quickly blow up the other tiny dot into your full-sized fantastic self-esteem image so that it

covers the old one completely! Make the image even bigger, brighter, more colourful, compelling and attractive! Move it closer to you! Hear the sounds: amplify them! Hear that voice – 'It feels so good to be me!' and it feels even better! Now, let **these amazing feelings wash over you and flow through you powerfully!** Add in positive emotion, joyous enthusiasm and total determination! Lock in the changes, all the good feelings, keep them permanently! *(A beat.)* Now think of a blank piece of paper...That's it!

(When you swish you start from the old place – the old image and swish to the new. What this does is neurologically link the old associations to new responses; it is a quick and powerful form of a visual suggestion, saying, in effect, 'Brain, do this now!' It overlays the old neural networks with the new response very quickly. The repetition strengthens the new neural growth fast and stabilises it. The more we use a new neural path or an old one – the quicker it is wired in and becomes part of the brain's permanent architectonics. You are 'snapping' old connections to create new ones. This is why you must be careful with NLP. Very careful. Most people have no idea how powerful visualisations can be.)

Surrounded by positive self-esteem visualisation.

Let's **powerfully reinforce the work** we've done, now. Your new positive self-esteem will enhance every part of your life and make it more and more enjoyable. More pleasurable than ever before. Let your new sense of healthy and accepting self-esteem affect every single area of your life, now. Reach out and grab that image of that strong, solid self-worth as if it were a mirror and notice something new and uplifting about it. That's it! There are in fact thousands of these healthy self-esteem images behind it! These images are of you being realistically successful in so many things you do in life. You are strong, committed, powerful, happy, thrilled, excited and **feeling such pleasure** – as much as you can, **now.**

As you lift that image, all the other ones are elevated with it! Smile deep inside yourself and throw it high above you! Everything spreads out in the air above you. A split second later and all the images fall all around you, surrounding you! In front of you are thousands of future images covering the space ahead. To your sides – thousands of opportunities in life to seize! You can and will.

Behind you – thousands more showing you valuable energies and learnings from the past that lead to the myriad sparkling points along your past timeline! Imagine them each framed with a blinking, shiny frame yelling for your attention.

Get in touch with your growing state of confidence in facing any and all challenges, your new responses powerfully enhanced – **feel that abundant confidence** flowing through you, **now!** This resourceful state is supported by memories of your power. Send any remaining images of the former you that are negative behind the bigger positive ones so that – **you can't see them...any...more, now.** Have the positive ones so intense in their very many attractive qualities and any other added elements of positivity blinking and winking with brightness yelling for your attention, unconsciously. That's right! They now fully command your attention away from that past negativity. These empowering images continue to interrupt any negative wandering thoughts with a, 'Look at me! I feel good being me!'

Future pace: Dissociated.

Imagine waking up tomorrow finding that all

these images are still around you blinking and yelling for attention. See yourself with a mysterious smile. Imagine people really enjoying these vitally attractive qualities that you fully own – notice how they just seem to magically affect so many people in positive ways. Knowing too that you can **be comfortable with not pleasing everyone,** which is impossible and undesirable. You now have a fresh, eager readiness for the rest of your day and evening – **your energy is aligned and purposeful!**

When any negative things arise their power over you has gone, diminished considerably. Notice over the coming days, weeks, months and years to come the incredibly positive affects of your improved self-esteem – **you have worth, you have self-belief, you have all the poise you need** and your subconscious is backing you up in every effort and it feels great to know it! Many people will react in far better ways: you will **feel more positive and optimistic than ever.** It can mean being **more content, now,** at **peace inside** and **realistic** about negative people, situations, challenges and much **more creative in finding solutions, now.**

Future pace: Associated.

Now float into a future time that will confirm **this has worked wonderfully** – see what you'll see, hear what you'll hear – feel how good that calm, accepting confidence feels. Imagine from your own point of view everything working out great, handling challenges that arise more easily and calmly than ever: **your self-worth is stubbornly strong** even in the face of obstacles. As this is just the background of who you are now you can **fully focus on creating the kind of life and relationships you want, now.** You feel motivated and keen – full of zest! I'll be silent for a full minute while you **rehearse and lock in this change,** at a deep neurological level, **now.** *(Do so...)*

And that as they say is that! That's right! You can take this act as a sign and a signal that **these new responses occur automatically** as you fully accept and understand that – **these changes have been made, now.'**

(Add in other change work or throw in your exduction of choice. An exduction is provided in the appendices.)

Analysis.

This elegant piece of rapid change work takes place in the following way structurally:

- **Teach the client how to manipulate the submodalities of an image. This primes them that change is practically possible in real time experience.**

- **Do the swish work – repeat and stabilise. This is the 'symbology flipping' stage.**

- **Conclude with a bunch of helpful suggestions (verbal and visual) that back up the work you did.**

- **Future pace/mental rehearsal of new abilities etc.**

That is almost the end of the hypno-scripts, not quite but almost. It's time to wrap this book and its themes up.

Case 16: Getting rid of GAD – 'Generalised Anxiety Disorder'/free floating fear script.

First up: there is often trauma with GAD – do the 'How to detraumatise anyone' script if you deem it necessary (recall that the detraumatisation pattern gets rid of *any* unwanted feeling) then say this...Oh by the way we are teaching the client how to stop doing the patterns of anxiety and directionalising them to do the 'patterns of calm' instead.

Soothing the constantly anxious mind script.

(Deep hypnosis assumed)

'Up until now you had been anxious and worried – of themselves they are quite normal in response to certain events, situations, stimulus and episodes but sometimes that fear, anxiety and worry became excessive, had they not? It is now time to begin to calm right down by **slowing - certain - unconscious - processes - all the way down - now.**

Good, and as you begin to **relax even more deeply** in this place of deep calm, in whichever way best suits your purpose and intent. Because sometimes we worry about yesterday today, sometimes we worry about tomorrow yesterday and sometimes we don't even know why we are worrying and we worry about that but here it's time to **set those old processes aside** even though we and each and both of you fully respect that positive intent but the creative you knows **there are far better ways** to accomplish goals and needs. During this hypnotic process don't be too surprised if **insights arise from a relaxed mind, now.** Funnily enough you'll find **that old tension releases its grip.**

Step 1: Relaxed breathing.

(I am now going to model the internal processes of 'calmness' for my client... we start with calm breathing patterns.)

The good thing about you're own process of relaxation is that it involves a particular way of breathing. We all have differing patterns of breathing for differing emotional states and I know that your unconscious mind knows how to **habitually do calm breathing.** It breathed for you the very moment you came into this world. It has all the templates of **you're calmer breathing, now.** As all the tension leaves your body only to be replaced by deep reservoirs of essential calm and peace of mind you'll notice that we only **breathe so comfortably** then. When you **breathe this way** don't be too surprised to find that **excessive worry becomes quite impossible.** Wouldn't you like to drift off further and further into this pleasantly absorbed state as you simply take in information that aids you profoundly without effort and as you do **your habitual relaxation levels can only increase, now.** Remember to use the calm breathing patterns I taught you in the pre-talk whenever you need.

(NFH: see the appropriate section in this book for breathing patterns that actually do induce calm.)

Step 2: Noticing the world around you.

When we fret we fail to **really notice the nature of the reality around you.** Imagine you are going on a stroll through a beautiful place with your mind so calm and content that **you feel safe** enough to **look at the beauty and uniqueness of all this world about you** – you might notice people, plants, buildings, animals, the cloud patterns in the sky, so that in this place, in this outer state of absorption **that old worry habit becomes quite impossible.** Qualities of light and sounds, tastes and smells tempt your awareness externally so that **you find it so easy to gently focus.**

Step 3: Mickey mousing that worried voice.

Research has shown that when anyone worries, the reason it worries us is that we speak to ourselves in a certain unhelpful way in that mind of ours. That pitch might be too high and strained. It might just be too fast to process calmly. It might be too loud and that can make us feel a bit tense BUT the good thing is you can **alter that inner voice** so that – you speak more softly, deeper, calmer and slower to yourself and when you do that the message that you sent to the past over active worrying bit of your mind is **there is no danger** and so **you worry much less** and **feel much better on the inside.**

One thing you can do is something I learned from NLP – I call it 'Mickey Mousing a voice'. What do I mean? Imagine saying anything at all worrying in the voice of Mickey Mouse and find that it sounds funny so that it feels funny so that **you take worrying thoughts far less seriously than before, now.**

Whenever a worry pops into your head Mickey Mouse it and **smile and sigh contently inside** knowing **all is well, you are deeply safe.**

Step 4: Dissociating worried noises and pictures.

Another thing that your unconscious can do is **take those old worries and push them far away** so that they sound far off, dim and distant so that **you can barely hear them in future.** You might find that as they are unnecessary, **they just float off into the far distance, now.**

And sometimes people are more than capable of scaring themselves with big pictures that are moving, bright, colourful and bold with amped up sound about things that could go wrong. We call this a misuse of the imagination. But you can **halt that process** by making such pictures still, black and white, far away, humorously framed, in a different place and so tiny as to be barely perceptible – from that vantage point they seem so much less pressing and important, allowing you to **see beyond old black and white thinking.** As you learn to do all this very rapidly here and as your unconscious mind helps, you can take comfort in knowing that **you are taking firm control of that imaginative process** and the creative part of you only wants to help, always, now.

From now on **focus on what you want** to happen. And the consequence of such changes? You can **feel so much more assured inside.**

Step 5: Relaxing the mind and body profoundly.

As the body and mind are interconnected we know that if **that body is very relaxed** then so too follows the mind. So let's take a bit more time for you to **permanently reset the reality of a relaxed body.** Have you ever visited a place that made you **feel such deep peace of mind?** Not now but soon enough I am going to simply mention the names of various parts of your body...after which I will pause for a while...and when I do you will **feel a wave of such blissful relaxation** spread through that body part so that **your entire nervous system is profoundly calmed, now.** And as that relaxation only becomes more and more obvious you can go 10 times deeper and deeper into trance and into hypnosis with each body part I mention.

Okay? *(Rhetorical – move on...)* Ready?
(Ditto..) Head *(Pause for 7 seconds after each body part...)*...Neck...Shoulders...Chest...Upper arms...Forearms...Hands...Palms...Fingers... Finger tips...Tummy...Upper back...Lower back...Waist...Thighs...Shins...Calves...Ankles ...Feet...Soul/Sole...Tips of those toes...That's right; that much **more relaxed** and that **much more absorbed** by this pleasurable process.

Take this act as a sign and a signal that you can **conserve energy for when you really need it, now.** That's perfect...

Step 6 Getting essential needs met.

In order to **feel habitually relaxed** everyone needs certain essential needs to be met that are universal to all humans. The first plank of **your calm mind and body** is the reality that you must **eat healthy food on a regular basis.** A calm person gets all of their nutritional needs met as best they can. I would like you to imagine now just how you'll **fulfil this need in such satisfying ways** as I pause for a while *(30 secs...)*

Good. As you do this notice that you **feel so**

much more energetic. Your unconscious mind can take care of all your needs. It knows what all your needs are and don't be too surprised as a result of this process to find that **you are getting your needs met unconsciously** as part of your new lifestyle which supports these changes. And more importantly **listen keenly to messages from your subconscious in future.** Take action to live the kind of life you really desire.

Step 7: Losing the fear of fear.

Another thing you need to do is **lose that old fear of fear.** Fear is an alarm signal that prepares your muscles to take action. Most of the time in life **it is far better to remain calm** – fear is for physical emergencies only. If anxiety or fear ever begin to arise simply know that it was your fear of fear that used to make the fear worse; fear is your friend, it is only trying to protect you. If you **leave that old fear in the past** you'll realise almost magically that **that fear of fear cycle ends, now** and you'll **feel so much more calm deep inside.** You can even say to yourself – 'Go on fear do your worst!' and guess what? That old fear reaction subsides to much more manageable levels. And this is so.

Step 8: Dissociation from fearful thoughts.

It is possible to **dissociate from certain thoughts** that occasionally pass through anyone's mind. Old **worries can simply drift far away** – not a part of you. You can **observe them calmly** as they drift off. As this occurs you'll **feel much more peace of mind** in the face of any thought that once troubled or bothered you. You are not your passing commentary. You are you. You **no longer let that old absurd worry drag you along** like an out of control water skier. It's completely outside of anything normal or real to you – it won't happen.

Step 9: Taking time to rest and relax.

In order to **recover energy** after activity we need to **rest** now and again, vary our activity. You need to **sleep so well at night** as **this healing process removes old anxieties, now.** Here, you can reconnect to your natural recuperative powers. Here, you can get in tune with your body's natural rhythms of **rest** and alertness: we all need some rest time from time to time. Just enough to **feel good again.** Like recharging a battery I suppose. Know that **few things in life require a stressful response.** I wonder just how relaxed you will be in mind and body as a result of these many changes? You'll notice you **have more mental clarity.** That your body feels as flexible as your approach to practical problem solving, that unconscious insights, intuitions and hunches will come to your aid just when needed because **you are a much more relaxed person, now.**

Step 10: Putting an end to disaster thinking – a humorous metaphor.

(A prominent mental pattern of more 'severe' anxiety disorders is what you might call 'disaster thinking'; over dramatising and always imagining the worst...)

And all this talk reminds me of a certain story...

The story of the silly squirrel.

A long time ago in those days there lived a very silly squirrel in the depths of a deep dark forest. He had a certain habit of imagining disasters. One day he feared the world would end. Another he imagined was what would happen if the sun never came back out after nighttime. His frightened little brain would whirr on and on about the worst things that

619

could never come to be.

It was autumn, the changing season. Whilst out gathering nuts in preparation for his long hibernation he heard the weirdest sound ever. Things were falling deep in the wood. What things could they be? They sounded big and scary – he imagined that a great monster, a dragon was marching through the wood and the sounds were the sounds of its footfall. The silly squirrel ran through the wood yelling, 'The monster is coming! Run for your lives!' The badger and fox and deer and elk and moose and wolf and mountain lion all heard his cries and as he sounded so convinced they believed him and began to panic too! Soon all the animals in the deep dark wood were running around like headless chickens.

But thankfully, high up in the treetops was the great eagle who watched the goings on down below. He did not panic but he did become curious. Up there observing the goings on in a calmly detached way he smiled to himself and seeing from his vantage point that the silly squirrel was the source of the problem he flew all...the...way...down to investigate. He landed just behind the squirrel who jumped in fright. 'You startled me!' said the squirrel.

'Yes. I thought I might. I hear that you have seen a dragon,' said the eagle **calmly** with a little twinkle in his eye.

'No! But I heard it! Fly off eagle – take me with you somewhere safe. Fly me to a safe wood if you would,' begged the squirrel.

'But there might be a dragon there too. You can never be too sure these days,' said the eagle.

'That's true. I never thought of that!' gasped the squirrel, 'What'll we do?'

'Perhaps and its just a suggestion, perhaps we should go and spy on the dragon and tell everyone where he is so that they can escape!?' said the eagle.

'Good idea!' said the squirrel.

So at the eagle's invitation he hopped on the great bird's back and off and up they flew. High up as they were they could **see the forest for the trees** and from this new perspective even the squirrel began to **calm right down** and notice there was no sign of a dragon anywhere in the wood.

621

'I cannot see your dragon. Where do you imagine he is?' asked the eagle.

'I heard him marching through the apple trees!' squealed the squirrel.

'Well then,' said the eagle, 'Let's go take a look.'

Down they flew amongst the apple trees. As they stood there amongst the shadows as the sunlight pierced the canopy in shimmering shards a series of thuds – thud, thud, thud seemed to hit the ground nearby. The squirrel cried,

'The dragon eagle!!!'

'I see neither a dragon nor an eagle, save myself, ' laughed the wiser bird, **'Calm down and simply look!'**

As the squirrel did so he noticed apples falling from the trees. One after another. The squirrel began to see. He slowed down and looked around himself at all the apples that had fallen. Then he remembered it was autumn. Then he thought with crystal clarity that he had never actually seen even one tiny baby dragon. He had simply heard a noise from the depths of the woods and then...he began to laugh!

'I had better tell the others hadn't I?' said the squirrel to the eagle.

'Now that IS a good idea,' said the eagle.

And soon enough the deep dark wood was **all at peace once more.** And that's all I'll tell you because that's all I know.

Conclusion: Taming the imagination etc.

The wonderful thing about being human is the ability to **be purposefully creative.** We can imagine things that haven't happened. We can invent things. The problem is some people took those imaginings without a sense of humour.

Just because we can imagine something doesn't mean we should believe in it. I had a lady client who imagined the worst things possible and then thought it was real because she imagined it. That is an example of taking a great tool or asset and using it in a very silly way. So I taught her to see all those IFS for what they are – those pictures are just IFS and an IF is not a so. What she needed to do was **calm that imagination right down.** When anyone does, they get to **see reality as it is.** They get to **reflect on certain things in a much more pleasant way.**

You could create disasters that never happened but that would just be an unproductive waste of time and energy: by itself it solves nothing. We can't know the future in entirety but you can **easily relax with that.** Speculations can be interesting but sometimes we simply have to wait until a situation clarifies itself over time as evidence and genuine information emerges and you can **relax with that fact too.** 'What if, what if, what if??!' might be better off as 'So what!?' when appropriate. We are all capable of **living calmly with the certainty of uncertainty, now.**

As you go far deeper inside a state of incredible relaxation you'll find that what is certain is that from now on you'll be able to **step aside and view things in a more appropriately calm way.** Slow things down and certainly anticipate problems that may emerge and take precautions and relevant actions BUT remember that you need evidence, you need to **focus on good things too,** you need to **control those images,** you need to **trust a part that knows,** really knows, beyond, above, beneath and over it all that **all is really well** with you and **whatever happens you'll handle it.**

All appropriate adjustments occur. Shifts in patterns and structures. Feelings, perspectives, behaviours and values can and do **improve measurably.** So many positive alterations have occurred so that you **feel great** without quite knowing why. Because it's the knowing there's an unconscious how that is of major importance, is there not? *(Confusing language.)* Exactly. **Keep these changes with you,** emerging fully calm, wonderfully alert and totally confident on my count of 1 – 10 **feeling awesome** etc. You **control your energy unconsciously, now.'**

(Throw in a future pace if you wish – you know how to do it now right? - then you wrap up, do other change work, exduction etc. That's one way to do it – next we will look at how to help someone who didn't 'de-stress' and stop worrying early enough: they have reached their 'breaking point'; a hypnotist can help such a person recover with relative ease. See how all anxiety problems have very similar structural features and so solutions? Mix and match all the patterns in this book as

needed. When you can do that you will have achieved Mastery!)

Case 17: Relax, rest and recover from a 'nervous breakdown'.

Subconscious warning signal were ignored. The tipping point had been crossed. The person's immediate needs are to rest and recuperate their shattered energy levels: hypnosis helps like nothing else and it's natural. Nervous breakdowns aren't half as bad as they seem – simply; the mind and body must be calmed, now! The brain must be redirectionalised toward the fundamentals of good healthy living. The person was trying to put a circle through a square peg. No doubt the following will only play a part in a larger solution matrix grid.

Getting back on track: post nervous breakdown renergised relaxation script.

(Create a very powerful mentally and physically relaxed state of very deep hypnosis – take your time; the thoroughness of the induction is part of the treatment: you are reactivating natural rest and alertness cycles.)

'Up until now you had been ignoring certain inner and outer realities. You had refused to **pay attention to signals from the subconscious** that were telling you, in their own way that you must **live a different kind of life, now,** I understand why you did that, we discussed this - however it is now time to **make radical changes,** at just the right rate and speed, as we have both agreed.

Throughout your life your wholly benevolent subconscious has been protecting you in so many ways that I cannot even list them all now. It would take too much time – I would like to thank your subconscious for doing all those jobs so marvellously and elegantly for you. When you set a course in life your subconscious lets you know if it is the right one by communicating to you. And now it is time for you to **listen to its wise advice.** I know you had certain feelings and intuitions. I know you may even have had dreams, ideas and images. Thoughts that popped into your head saying **STOP! It's time to change track** and follow your true destiny in this life. Imagine you didn't have this protection mechanism – this feedback loop. What if you were heading toward a cliff but instead of listening to those uncomfortable feelings you overrode things and carried straight ahead regardless? Not such a good idea.

You have been dishonest with yourself, a far deeper part of yourself in fact which knows who you really are, so that you cannot lie to it because it knows more about you than you do. So as you **relax to such profound levels** where you can **easily absorb these learnings** you can know that when your conscious mind and your unconscious mind work together you are powerful.

Some times you need to stand up for yourself and what is right. There is no point banging your head against a brick wall. Some situations must be avoided if you are to **remain happy and healthy;** and some must be sought to **give yourself the deepest feelings of purposeful satisfaction.** There is a way you must live this life and express who you really are, appropriately. When you follow that path **there is no inner conflict –** everything just flows. Obstacles becomes ways to overcome challenges and **develop more mature responses and flexibilities.**

When you felt too tense, when you felt too overloaded – all you had to do was **take a break from the way things were –** for a while to **re-charge your batteries, here**. Imagine now a colour of **total energy, full rest and recuperation** filling your entire body...mind...and soul! That's right! Let that healing and restorative energy spread and grow as it glows more powerfully and intensely. You are re-filling with your core energy to do what must be done to not just survive but **thrive in this world** with so many abundant **pleasures, now!** Isn't it time you choose to **live zestfully**? Isn't it time to realise your true potentials? Isn't it time to **embrace who you truly deeply are with confidence** that it will all work out in the end? All you need do is take one step in the right direction and **this positive momentum simply builds.**

Your good health also requires the right fuel and exercise. It requires that you **find a balance between all your needs** as a unique individual living this life. Everyday you find ways to **satisfy all the needs you have** that we discussed. And the best part is that it is all effortless as the creative part works 24/7 to ensure this is so, while you are just getting on with the daily process of **simply enjoying living.** Each moment never to be repeated. Each moment has something to learn from. Each experience teaches us at least one more new thing. And you have been graced with the opportunity to **begin again in a way that suits your genuine nature, now.** And that's a good thing is it not?

Coping and thriving future pace: dissociated.

(Each ... = a 5-7 second pause.)

I want you to **have a vision** of the new you in just the right context – you are more than just coping – **you are thriving, now...**See how relaxed and at ease that you is...See how they take so many things in their stride...How they are handling things quite differently...See how much **more energy you have...**Notice how they are **taking care of all your needs...**What daily pleasures are they involved in? How does that increasing sense of satisfaction manifest itself exactly?...How precisely are you taking care of yourself better?...See how that you can **pay attention to any manner of signals from your subconscious** that serve as feedback with regards to your ongoing, lifelong progress through this adventure – your quest, the stages of living. Some signals are GO signs that you are definitely on the right track – such as when **you feel good and are fully aligned and congruent.** Other signals are STOP signs saying that you need to **change course appropriately, creatively, now.** Take a whole minute and a half to **learn some new things** that help. In trance. As you do, very many re-associations have already occurred, wasn't it? *(Pause as promised...)*

Associated integration of learnings.

As **you have 100% chosen this new path now,** I simply want you to drift into a time in your future that confirms **all this worked.** See through those clear-minded, relaxed eyes. Hear through those ears that have grown wiser. **Feel the confidence, energy, motivation and new direction flowing through you** in some situations that proves **amazing changes have occurred, now.** Feel how it feels to **respond more honestly yet resourcefully.** Feel how it feels to **be flexible and creative** throughout life. There is always more than one way to overcome anything at all. How does it feel to **have all that energy and calm locked in, permanently** (?) How do you recognise the improvements in the smallest and biggest of things? Be aware of the way others respond to you more positively. You are getting more done. You **feel great.** You **feel well** and most important of all – **you have the hope of the healthy, now.** Again – take this time in trance to **go through an amazing learning process** that benefits every cell and fibre of who you really are in incredible ways!

Only in the ways that are safest at all times. That's it.' *(Give 'em another 60 seconds...)*

Continue with the solution matrix interventions – stress management + worry modules are usual; even some form of drug or coping mechanism may have to be taken care of. Or just begin the arousal protocol. Scripts are as short or long as they need to be.

Case 18: Getting a good night's sleep without sleeping pills.

Okay, in this penultimate 'case' I am going to show you how to make insomnia a thing of the past. As always you may well have to tackle other parts of a problem matrix first. Once you've done that this script should take care of all possible forms of insomnia: difficulty falling asleep, getting back to sleep after waking up during the night, waking up too early in the morning etc. Insomnia is caused by background fear and worry; often multiple needs are unmet. Get the person to relax at night and victory is assured. Insomnia doesn't solve problems it compounds them. By the way, pretty much all the scripts in this book are too long – this is for training purposes. I always give too much and leave you, the hypnotist to tailor it to the individual you're assisting. Again, separate modules within scripts can obviously be used, with a bit of adaptation, for other problems. Without further ado...

Sleeping well without sleeping pills script.
Part 1: The essential structure of falling sleep.

(Very deep hypnosis assumed – note: make your voice tone slow and sleepy, throw in a few yawns etc.)

'The good thing about hypnosis _(client's name)_ is that it can really help you **sleep so much easier...Now,** you'll find as a result of this deep...hypnotic...sleep that **your sleep is so much more satisfying,** you'll awaken after this session and after **a good night's sleep every night** feeling so deeply satisfied, so deeply rested. Your body and mind deeply relaxed and calm. In order to **slide gently into perfect sleep** at night you need to begin to turn your **focus inside and ignore the irrelevant, now.**

With your eyes closed you are sending a message to your deeper mind that at this time of sleep, nothing out there is more important than this process. Sounds of any kind only help soothe and calm you – they are somehow comforting and cosy. They are just sounds that one might hear any night, background sounds that allow you to **sleep so soundly** and sooner than you know, you have fallen asleep so easily. It just happens, does it not? Things can just pass through awareness fleetingly on your way to restful sleep. Just because something is there doesn't mean it is of importance – the subconscious knows what is really important and can reconnect to those needs now.

Yawning and so tired...and so sleepy...inner voice sleepier and sleepier...dream fragments may occupy you on your way down...and it all starts with **a very deep level of pure physical and mental relaxation** that you possess. That's right. What if you could know, really know that at night time, when the time is right, nothing is more fascinating than sleep – at the appropriate time, you **become comfortingly absorbed by sleep at night-time.**

At night there's nothing else you need do but **sleep well.** Your mind can grow quiet and quieter still. Your body only grows more and more cosy and comfortable. You **become so relaxed, so calm** at night. And so you become sleepier and sleepier at just the right time. Sleeping well is a part of you. You were born with that ability that requires no effort, quite the reverse. A **peace of mind develops –** an attitude of gratitude for the day gone by, a nice sense of pleasurable

636

anticipation for the day ahead. And the time to talk to yourself is not just before falling asleep. Solve challenges during the day and leave the subconscious to do the rest while you sleep and unconsciously utilise your creative problem solving abilities. Don't be too surprised when solutions just pop into your mind when you **let go and relax into sleep** every night.

Silent...restful...slumber...that's the way. All the way down.

Part 2: Refocusing the mind inside - imagination training.

Imagine now – in your quietening mind, because there are appropriate times for conversations, are there not? Picture images of things you associate with sleep...whatever you subjectively associate with **good sleep** are the right ones...perhaps just one in particular...Let these images, and just the sense of them is more than enough: might even be a visual symbol. Whatever you like that helps **fascinate you inside** while I'm quiet for a bit... *(Give 'em 10 seconds or so...)*

Okay, now you've done that allow a sense of some sound or sounds, inside your mind to come to mind that you associate with sleep, might be a piece of music. I don't know – you do. Become absorbed by focusing intently upon that noise or noises that you associate with very good sleep – it might be the noise of silence. Might be a symbolic noise – whatever pops into the attention of your inner ear is just right. Trust the process. I will make no verbal noise while you experience this. *(Shhh – 10 secs etc.)*

Good. Now I'd like you to imagine what it would feel like to feel a texture that you associate with a great night's sleep. Something you could gently place on your cheek perhaps? Snuggle into or against. Something you might just place you hand on. Really feel that texture of that sleepy surface. Again it can be a symbolic texture – something that you feel is associated with sleep. That's it... *(Quiet 10 secs – they'll get the idea that silence = them having to work alone for a bit; after a while you won't have to keep saying why.)*

And could you now imagine a smell or smells that you associate with **a nice restful sleep** (?) That's the way. Anything at all that has meaning and positive associations with sleep. And smell is so important because we associate it to many deep memories instantly. That's it... *(10 sec pause...)*

Very good. What you have been doing is revivifying things you **associate with good sleep,** this begins the process, this ongoing process of you're connecting to memories, learnings, experiences and understandings of the deep/intrinsic knowledge of a good night's sleep. You have so many inner abilities to help you **do so, now.** Your unconscious was born with a blueprint if you like of **a good night's sleep,** an inner template of how to **effortlessly do it** *(hypnotic code).* It knows the many psychological and physiological component parts of **you're sleeping well again** and can put them into nightly unconscious practise, now. Integrate these learnings experientially. Thaaaa-aaat's it.

Part 3: Turning off the 'negative TV' at night.

The good thing about sleep is that it can be trying to try, the reality is by **doing nothing** and letting it occur naturally **your unconscious mind can lead you off into a deep, restful sleep night after night** after night and on and on and on. That's it. In the realm of sleep **your mind and body will rest and recover completely.** Your energy levels will be effortlessly boosted, **all anxiety is washed away, now.** You'll just drift off into the deepest layers of sleep and when you need to you'll **dream** all the right dreams.

Now what if you begin to think of worries a bit like TV news that appear on the TV screen in the mind's eye – when you focus on them they seem so pressing and 'real' but then you look outside and all is calm. There is no present danger. The sky is as blue as ever. It is as quiet as it ever was. I bet you'd gain great relief because **you're unconscious will switch off that inner TV at bed-time.** If you must do anything at night, before sleep you can calmly go over times when things went well for you, nice things that happened during the day. For you have succeeded at far more than you can consciously recall and this reality can make you **feel more secure** about so many things. And you can relax knowing that **you can handle any and all challenges in life.** As a result of these changes **the default setting of your whole mind is calm, now.**

Part 4: Taking control of the inner voice at night.

Some people like to talk to themselves at

bedtime and that's fine: but it is really very soothing to realise that you can slowly **turn down the rate, pitch and volume of that voice.** Slow it right...down......to...quiet. You might pleasantly talk to yourself in almost a pre-sleep whisper of sorts. And what might that sound like as you practise the right inner tone that you associate with falling to sleep easily as you have on many previous occasions? You may barely be able to hear something that quiet or perhaps that seemingly far... away. It can **become wonderfully quiet inside** that head. Some people think of nothing or think they think of nothing BUT they **really focus on simple things at bedtime.** So simple that those things may as well be nothing at all; and doesn't that, just somehow make sense, unconsciously? Of course it does. Now.

Some people tend to **drift off to a wonderful place of perfect peace** inside, using their creativity to go there now or later. Others recall pleasant places that they only associate with all the best feelings one can feel. Others have mental habits that are so boring, repetitive or mundane that they drift off easily at night as a baby does, after all that learning. Some recall times with the most loved ones. Silly and monotonous things help some AND your unconscious knows what things will be best, ideally suited to you...that's right.

At some level you'll better focus your thoughts at that time – what will relax you at that time? What makes you **feel as good as if you received a treat**? You are a deeply relaxed person and such people can order and direct their thoughts with total freedom that comes from the deepest sources of calmness within. I want you to **enjoy this freedom nightly** – night after night and on and on and on. You can trust that you do have and always had a very powerful mechanism that allows you to **switch off worry at night.** Perfect.

Part 5: The freedom to do nothing.

What do you suppose it would be like if you could 'think' about that kind of nothing that is really something soothing? You might develop your very own **images of comfort, sounds of comfort, feelings of comfort,** belief that comfort is possible, **now.** Fragrances, themes even, that help you **feel so calm, relaxed and comfortable** inside and out. Drifting off to sleep with all that freedom in your mind. At the right time you'll **effortlessly become absorbed by falling asleep and sleep.** All the freedom you need is within. So free to relax, not having to think – feeling quite free to drift off somewhat slowly yet surely or instantly. You do not desire to do that which you can't make happen. You cannot wish you were taller than you are and by wishing to make it so. Certain things you just allow to happen. So relaxed a mind and body that your thoughts are led by the state of **profound relaxation now.** Towards a place where wonderful, tranquil, restorative sleep occurs. And so where might you be, or not be at all, right now?

Where aren't you now? Some-place? No place? The middle of...nowhere in particular or not? You don't need to think here or there. No need for any kind of talking or commentary or unnecessary analysis at such times. You **only analyse and plan during the day.** No place in particular perhaps, now – the middle of somewhere that is nowhere. You don't have to think at all about that which requires no thinking, no need to chat away at that time, at just the right time and place, now. A place where **that body just rests** comfortably. That's it. Where you may **become absorbed by the real pleasure,** certain natural rhythms reconnected to. The rise and fall of that tummy. A breathing pattern – slowly,

slowly and more sleepily, now. Perhaps an awareness or no awareness takes place where you recognise that you aren't really thinking about anything specific at that time. **Your focus stays within an appropriate framework** of that which is helpful, useful, relevant to that process. Safety and pleasure only at that time. The sensations of that bed **softening** you nicely. You associate your bed with sleep, comfort, relaxation, making love, pleasant associations only can and will be located there, now. **Feel the nice sleepy feelings** that arise in that body as you drift off and **sleep soundly** at night. Resting body and mind to far deeper levels as you **rise in the morning refreshed,** well, clear headed, live your amazing life in better moods. **Confidence restored** in so many areas of life. But at night **you relax so deeply,** wind right down, all the way down and **sleep so soundly** and you will, will you not? Will you not?

Part 6: The sensations of sleep.

How much more comfortable can that body really become at that time? How much pleasure do you notice developing? And in this place, time, that body can feel as if its very, very heavy, some say it feels like you are melting into the bed. Some say that they feel very light almost floaty and weightless. A cloud drifting in dark, peaceful skies. As you certainly have many instinctive learnings of that which you wish, you can **re-access that ability now,** in this healing place. Drifting like a free floating twig - downstream. And I am curious, wondering, which parts of that body drifts off first? You need no awareness of that while you sleep nor of other things at that irrelevant time until they become relevant again. The river of life flows ever onward. Which parts are lightest? Heaviest? It just seems that at a certain time it would just take too much effort to move. So don't. Just **do nothing at the right time** and you will **sink down into peaceful sleep at night.**

Part 7: The breathing patterns of sleep.

Your breathing, you'll notice, is slowing down into sleepy breathing patterns because for every state, every altered state, now, that breathing pattern changes. There is a dreaming pattern of breathing. A falling asleep easily pattern of breathing. A **falling back to sleep easily** pattern and your wise unconscious mind knows what these patterns are, so that you don't have to do anything. **The autopilot of sleep is reset.** There is also **a calm pattern of breathing during waking consciousness** that you reconnect to, now. My voice, any voice can grow quieter and quieter still. Ever...quieter...A person can you know **feel wonderful** to be drifting off so easily and effortlessly and it's interesting that as you **drift off blissfully** you might find yourself in a middle place, in between states – not really awake, not yet fully asleep. But it is nice to know how **you have the support you need, inside and out.** You need not linger too long anywhere as you drift and drift, sensations of a kind might pass through awareness in passing – all are **calming, snuggling, soothing** – more perfect than ever before. That's right.

Part 8: Daily positivity.

During the day you will continue to **be the kind of person who succeeds.** A person who can easily **notice every opportunity** for your progress. There is a powerful force of energy within so you **feel determined** to carry on. Glowing from inside tangibly with a force of **pure positivity and self-belief** that is stronger than ever to endure, surpass and go beyond those former illusions. What if you could believe now that you will **radiate this positive energy**? See the colour of that flowing through you - head to toe **feeling awesome!** That's the way! A connection to the source of all your **patience helps.** Get a sense now of your more positive future and what you'll be doing in that with all this new power while I'm quiet – **dream a positive dream** of your future that can inspire you, now! *(Shhh for 20 seconds or so.)*

Tonight your dreams will help profoundly **integrate these learnings** into the depths of your neurology. Good. With your new positive attitude and feeling toward living you know that **excellent sleep is just an instinctive part of who you are.** And all you do now is nothing except **trust the unconscious** to guide you all the way down into the deepest restorative levels of sleep when you need to, now. You can easily connect to that deep slow wave sleep that heals, cures, relaxes and repairs amongst other things each and every night.

Part 9: The rules of good sleep.

Its best to avoid shift work, watching TV or using the Internet just before bed. To remove all electrical appliances from the bedroom. Avoid all tea and coffee, all caffeine, chocolate late at night when **your body needs to**

wind down physically. Do not exercise just before bed. A nice bath or shower can help anyone **unwind.** Do not sleep or catnap during the day – **save sleep for night-time.** Keep your bedroom as dark as possible at bedtime. Only go to bed when you are genuinely sleepy. When you **do all these things** you'll find that as you **lie down to sleep, you will feel so calm.** You will rest and snuggle into those sheets, the duvet and the mattress. Just enjoy that wonderful pre-sleep time of sweet pleasure and comfort because **the deepest part of you is so sure** with total confident security, in the way you know your own name, that deep refreshing sleep approaches every night. And this is so – trust the process. Your powerful subconscious, **unconscious mind, now,** helps you in all your efforts and that's nice to know, is it not? Deep sleep, deep sleep – deep...hypnotic...sleep!

Part 10: Future pace.

Imagine now a you over there preparing to **sleep so well at night...**See how calm and comfortable you look...**Feelings of sleepiness** already taking hold...Maybe you yawn, that's it...You go through your pre-bed routine, whatever that is for you...…You climb into bed...you snuggle down...your head lying on that pillow that whole mind and body so relaxed...and sooner than you know it – they are asleep. Out like a light! Just happens. See that person **sleep through the night** so peacefully...That's the way. At some point they may have to get up to relieve themselves but as soon as they return to bed they **fall back to sleep again with ease.** Perfect. In the morning they awaken feeling amazing, so calm and clear-headed, totally refreshed, at peace, re-energised, full of zest and motivation.

And now...go back to the beginning of that inner movie but experience it first hand – float into that you who is **sleepy** and about to go to bed. That's it. Now, go through that entire beautiful, pleasant process, the process of **you're sleeping well every night** and I'll be quiet for a full minute while you do so... *(Shhh.)*

Good.

Part 11: Final suggestions wrap up.

In each of these soothing experiences of many awarenesses it can **feel so nice** to be nowhere, yet somewhere, a special place for drifting off into **a deep peaceful sleep every night.** A place that allows you to **sleep all through the night very well** indeed. Thoughts not needed then, so you can feel **free to sleep safely** and calmly, focusing on sleep, only. Didn't you? Your body is so comfortable and that feeling remains with you. Underneath any passing tension it is there. All that matters is that **you can sleep** – going off somewhere, nowhere, anywhere nice, the place of just the right dreams, **deep physical rest and recuperation.** Peaceful, relaxed – SLEEP! Wrapped up cosily in the very core of who you truly, deeply are. And most important of all **having that deep faith,** that confidence in the deepest part of you that you notice your mind and body drifting...drifting like a leaf downstream...meandering on a sunny day through the dappled light...through the budding branches high above...into dreams...places...people...images you had - half unremembered...creations you never created – consciously...fantasticals of the imagination...just passing through some...or maybe that leaf just carries on down and down – stream to dream, now. Into the night, the enveloping night. The blanket of night blue. Knowing that the stars know how and when to shine in the great vault of the sky, while the world just sleeps. And anyone can **enter the vast oneness** of an ocean within of many various possibilities, haven't you? Whispering kind words and their fragments and fragments of fragments – sounds – words that **heal and sooth…**Some things to **stop trying** and **let it happen naturally**…because it really does know more than you…Anyone can allow themselves the exquisite luxury of being in this peaceful, sleepy state of mind, comfortable body for as long as is needed at that level…a long restful time when you **drift off to sleep far sooner than you expected,** hadn't you?

Sleep soundly, sleep soundly – see the opportunity to **sleep through the night** and when you wake up after the natural magic of this deep and restful sleep many hours later, you will **feel naturally rested** without any external aids, now. **Feel that energy** in your body. You feel so much better! **At that time there is nothing significant to think of** before you don't, for a while, wasn't it? But you can **drift off into a deep, peaceful slumber** as a consequence of all the myriad changes that were made, unconsciously, now. It is such a joy for anyone to learn, **really learn** that you can sleep, **sleep so deeply** and so you can accept the comforting sense of

651

peacefulness of that fact. You have a knowing feeling that this is so. And you **carry this within you** as you sleep, sleep, sleep – somehow, without knowing how because it's time to drift off pleasantly tonight and every night – **sleep so well, now!'**

(The only advise I can give the hypnotist is try to adopt a rhythmical speaking pattern suggestive of sleep, falling to sleep etc. Put on your actor's hat. For the low down on the very real power of hypnotic rhythms see my tenth and final book, 'Weirdnosis'.)

As an additional bonus tip – if you have a client who snores hypnotise 'em to sleep on their side. That should fix it.

Case 19: Detwitching a nervous twitch.

Although every NT (nervous twitch) client will differ I can tell you in my experience that there is a lot more work to do than the average stop smoking session etc. The problem matrix involved in a what we nominally call a 'nervous twitch' is the tip of the iceberg! The twitch is merely the matrices most obvious manifestation. Firstly do the 'How to detraumatise' anyone pattern; with severe NTs this may have to be repeated at least twice over 2 consecutive sessions. Each time the 'background trauma' levels will be reduced. You want it down to zero. Nothing less will do. Once you have done this you can start layering in suggestions to remove the twitch and rebuild the shattered ego underneath, for mark my words that is what you are dealing with – someone who has been treated like shit their whole lives; usually by one parent or both. These people often have multiple phobias etc., etc. – the lot! Imagine being trapped with bastards and never being able to escape.

There are lower level 'twitches' etc. If you have a young boy who plays too long on his computer etc. that is the problem – boys especially are playing too long and too often

on those things at an early age. The young
brain is not equipped to handle the artificial
info and the stress levels created by computer
gaming. This can then generalise out into a
stress reaction which can include making
noises when concentrating or when the child
is worried, stressed or anxious. Young children
should not be playing any computer games
until the age of at least 5 if not older in my
opinion. This problem affects boys worse than
girls. When I first started studying this I found
lots of mum's/mom's websites talking about
their sons developing twitches after computer
game exposure. These boys often become
addicted to the audio-visual stimulation so
that prying that hand held device out of their
hand is like trying to borrow Sauron's Ring
from Gollum! In these cases the solution is
obvious – cut down or cut out use entirely
until they are older. Use Skinnerian
conditioning (rewards) every time the boy
stays cold turkey for a week etc. Get him out
doing real world activities etc. Get him in the
woods making bows and arrows like our
grandfathers used to do! However most
children will simply grow out of the twitch - a
young developing brain is a funny thing!

I am only going to be able to give you so
much in the way of scripts for NTs of the more

severe variety. That will still be a lot however. The first script is a direct twitch removal script. It is very powerful and with fully motivated clients it'll work a treat, perhaps needing some reinforcement once or twice in the motivated.

Note: NTs must want to let go of all 'symptoms'; forget 'secondary gain' some use their twitches to manipulate people because they are nasty people – the abuse has scarred them and they too have become abusive in new and perverse ways. Such creatures cannot be helped unless they develop awareness of these manipulative patterns – I will show you how to help the ones that do have some insight. For this you need to tackle their 'dark side'; as they label it themselves. Additionally both NT sufferers and stammer/stutter plagued folk need help in overcoming their learned 'inferiority complex'. The following scripts are for a person who twitches around the eye area. You can alter the wording as required using your common sense.

PRO TIP: caffeine drinks and sodas, fizzy drinks etc. can make twitches worse. As can E numbers in children's candy/sweets etc. Cut them out entirely – AGAIN: think of all input including food and drink as information. All information affects a given system. Including a human nervous system.

NT Script 1: Direct suggestions for removal.

(Deep hypnosis assumed...This is a highly successful script – I invented it without any influence from others...)

Step 1. Pace the problem – thank the subconscious for creating it.

'I am now speaking to the deepest parts of your mind. You are in charge of this entire process. You are the source that has spawned those old unhelpful problems this person has had up until this moment - certain feelings, sensations, emotions, behaviours, perceptions, movements, beliefs, attitudes in the past. When you first originated these patterns – **that old problem matrix, now,** you had a whole host of very good unconscious judgments, a particular logic in doing so that were of sound mind, benevolently intended and positively purposeful with the understandings you had at that age of what the best responses would be to certain things. For bringing into existence that old twitch, excessive nerves, unnecessary movement of any kind, any fear of some situations, a lack of confidence, poor self image, self-consciousness and more besides back then. Perhaps the desire to avoid situations, perhaps certain people, you've had those reasons for organising and designing-in those previous subconscious structures...You could not have done it any better. I'd like to really thank you for all you've done to **look after and protect x** *(client's name)* **optimally, now.** Times change – this person has changed since then, their life has changed since then. With this in mind...

Step 2: Design-in the desired responses that the client now wishes to manifest.

Now you fully appreciate that the set of unwanted patterns – what I call the 'problem matrix' is no longer justifiable as the best option. This person wants better responses than that and you are capable of producing all of them. Because the potential you were born with is far greater and more powerful than that. I am going to give you some new information that you can use to **invent a far better system of appropriate responses** that will make each and both of you **feel amazing** about the whole process of positive change. Some change can be gloriously uplifting and inspiring.

It's time to acknowledge once and for all that all those former, unwanted, unpleasant, side-effect prone outcomes need to **be altered permanently** to this person's benefit at this time in their life allowing them to **gain total satisfaction** in each and every area of their life. Is that not so? *(Pause a beat...)* Good!

Our ancestors, we are told used to use stone tools and now we can fly into outer space. What if a new 'logic' began to function, unconsciously, now? In fact I know there is a very specific part of you that wisely created this problem with express intentions and I'd like your powerful creative part to start to **generate better solutions** to **fulfil those intentions maturely and appropriately, now,** in this profoundly relaxed place, that are acceptable to all parts of you, so that you can **let go of the old responses**

completely, now.

I know you now realise that what is far better, safer, healthier and most appropriate for x *(client's name)* is to **be totally, supremely confident in any and all situations,** calm, relaxed all over, in just the right way, focused when she/he needs to be, stress-free and in control in her/his daily life, wherever and whenever she/he needs to be automatically. Those old ways are unnecessary now. That entire face *(part of body experiencing twitch etc.)* can **completely relax** and you can **feel such comfort there -** past tension - fading - away for good, now. She/he is now totally confident in any and all situations, no matter how small or large, whoever or not it is, her/his **eyelids are so relaxed and functioning normally,** no matter where she/he is, who she/he's with, totally relaxed, comfortable, at ease now. She/he experiences only abundant, soothing confidence, calm and control in any situation, with any person that used to bother her/him previously and this is so.

And because **she/he is so relaxed and**

confident and always much calmer and in control overall, there are **no excess nerves at all,** and there never will be - **no excessive blinking,** no unfounded fears, no purposeless worry, or self-consciousness - gone for good. Nervousness and fear is for nervous and fearful people and you know and manifest the fact that **this person is a supremely confident person** whenever she/he need to be, automatically. Those old uncomfortable feelings, sensations, movements, those old behaviours and attitudes just aren't needed anymore. This woman/man is incredibly confident and calm and in control, she/he has total confidence in her/his abilities, identity; the normal, healthy functioning of all her/his body, the way she/he moves and speaks, posture and gestures, **a normal, healthy blink rate,** a confident tone and quality of voice, the way she/he thinks is filled with confidence. It just seems to radiate from them, now. And you have a knowing feeling that **things have shifted for the better.**

She/he is filled with confidence just for being who he/she is. And that is good enough for anybody worthwhile. A deep calmness can grow from this new reality and spread to all the body parts that need it. There is **no need for any excess tension there** anymore – let it go, leave it behind you, relax and notice all the things that make you smile more. Her/his self-image is strong yet completely realistic. As a result there are **no twitches,** and you know that there will be **no nerves of any kind...**you only **feel comfort - just there.** What colour is comfort for you? Imagine the colour of comfort soothing that past area of tension. Seeping deep into the muscles and nerves and the signals that go to that part of your brain and simply infusing the whole process with calm just as you knew as a tiny baby. Those potentials for **relaxing body parts** are still there so deep within the subconscious structures of your neurology. Reconnect to genuine, healthy potentialities, now.

This person is comfortable with authority, with the realistic degree of control and power, the resourcefulness they have. What if you began to realise that your new experience of everyday living is that you **have a**

completely calm face (?) Because, again the unwanted, ways were and are for nervous people – whoever they are? And since no one is actually a nervous person because nervousness is a feeling not an identity, therefore this person can't be what isn't. A supremely confident and very calm person would **have muscles that are perfectly relaxed, soothed, eased in just the right way;** a much more easy-going person in general. They **experience a pleasant warmth,** feelings of only growing contentment for your own unconscious reasons. Former unhelpful feelings are simply overwhelmed by the reality that you **experience an inner cheerfulness.** There is simply **a sense of relief now,** certain parts need a rest, they had been working too hard for no real good reason. You are **not at war** with yourself. Feelings of plenty, gratitude, well being and **deep satisfaction, inside now.** You will find that the reality is that **you solve problems better** when you **have such a feeling of peacefulness inside.** That is all over now. Long, long ago. **Let it all go.** The past is over – it isn't what you deserved, it wasn't your fault, it is just what happened. See so many things with a calmer, more objective point of view. When you **change your perspective** you'll find **you cannot retain those past patterns** that once held you back.

Who invents a forest path? I mean you go for walks and there are paths there, trodden into the ground over years and years of people simply following the same old paths but there is no reason why you always should; sometimes we need to **start to create better pathways.** In time these too seem as if **they have always been there.**

What if **you feel competence and total safety** in those settings which used to trouble her/him? In those over and done with times. Peace of mind. **Peace of face.** Piece of cake. **Now,** that's simply her/his new 100% total reality. That's who they are, what they now do, feel and live. They can **use common sense, intuition and intelligence** at all times. When **you are relaxed and focused** you can **easily access your essential creativity.**

As you find it **so easy to concentrate externally** when you need to, there are **no worries,** nor **no stress,** neither **no nerves,** definitely **no twitches** or excessive blinking, no fear of past imaginings which you no longer have to believe in any way – that old trance can be awakened from, now. None of that of any kind whatsoever. No silly or ridiculous thoughts and there never will be because such is really not the way of a totally confident person who is free to go anywhere that they wish on this earth **feeling total comfort,** meeting anyone and everyone that they wish feeling so good about themselves...knowing **no one is better than you.** *(Client's name)* is the equal of any. Comparing them only positively with others. Past images of this or that unrealistic comparisons simply fade away like shadows in the bright sunlight. It's impossible to compare unreasonably inside if you **solely focus attention on others socially.** Now, trust that everything else that truly matters will be spontaneously good. Who have you ever met that was totally perfect? Who has the right to demand perfection from anybody? What does anyone mean by 'perfect' anyway? I am quite sure it's not desirable to aim for the impossible. You can only expect from those that which they may realistically give.

The majority of **your thoughts are more positive,** you **feel positive feelings** about so many appropriate things from this moment on. As the inner environment has positively altered it must be the case that the outer manifestations reflect this, wasn't it? That's it. What if you came to believe that you **have more emotional control** than you consciously know? You **have more control of your self,** you can take tangible steps to **purposefully direct your destiny,** this life, any event, any space, location or personality is merely another opportunity to take things in your stride and **lighten up,** connect to your resources and thrive, here and now; anything you encounter can be a time to simply **be a relaxed individual.** Of course anyone might need an umbrella when it's raining but when the sun comes out you just enjoy the sunshine. It was necessary that you did those things and it is important that you now **change*.**

(*NFH: You can compare what <u>was</u> 'necessary' to what <u>is</u> 'important' when creating change work suggestions...)

Have you ever wondered how an artist views the world? They must study nature closely and **see the world as it is.** They must train themselves to notice how clouds often form cloud caravans that trail off into the distance. They must **notice the realities** of perspective. And this can only occur when **you're so calm.** The artist notices how light hits each leaf in a unique way. The artist sees the variety of colours and hues. The artist knows how to represent a more realistic approximation of Nature/Creation in all their works. Nature and natural forms and ways are so soothing anyway. Commune with nature often. The musical artist can notice qualities of sound that others can't. **Your power of discernment improves.** You also discover that **you are more creative** than you know. There are better ways than automatic – black and white can be replaced by a whole host of choices; as if there was only ever one; such a naive view, is it not? With all these new learnings and re-discoveries in mind surely –

there is **no real need anymore to twitch** (?) Find your own unconscious reasons to make all this so and **stubbornly stick to the new ways of being.** Deep serenity, deep serenity, deep serenity – **be yourself, like yourself, NOOOOW!**

Step 3: Generalised ego-boost suggestions etc.

This person has the mental toughness of a top athlete, determined and motivated to succeed in all they do, living up to their highest values, knowing they deserve the best, knowing what's truly important to them, accepting **this person is good enough** just as they are. A woman/man that is confident and totally in control of her/himself and her/his feelings at all times. Achieving worthy, deeply desired goals as easily as is possible. X *(client's name)* is a real winner. Someone who handles anything that life throws at them. Able to adjust their behaviour flexibly in just the right way. Safe within and so without: going about their business as freely as they wish. No matter how things, settings, situations, people change and they do and will.

(NFH: NT clients are like stammer/stutter clients in that they find it difficult to talk to new people or people they perceive 'out rank' them; have 'higher' social status etc. This being so I add a module that is very similar if not identical to a public speaking phobia.)

A confident public speaker: this woman/man is persuasive, able to **talk to anyone with confidence, throat and vocal apparatus calm and relaxed** as if you were speaking to a best friend. Blinking at the right rate and speed to keep the eyes healthy and safe. **Feeling so confident** makes others **relax deeply, inside, now.** Knowing what x *(client's name)* has to say is as important as anyone else, enjoying the spotlight, knowing that **others wish you well,** excited positively at the prospect of **speaking fluently to others** no matter how many, with enough energy to **perform well,** taking it in their stride, liking that others are looking at them, comfortable with it, amusing even, interesting, compelling, expressive and this is so. People may well comment on **this new calm, control and poise** and effortless self-assurance. **Speaking smoothly and freely – any old blockages GONE!;** communicate with ease. It all goes swimmingly. Gone are the old negative responses and unhelpful thoughts and beliefs of the past. No longer true about them in any way. **Holding eye contact** when appropriate. Trusting each body part, nerve and fibre to play its part: relaxed. Relaxed down to the cellular level. This person has an amazing ability to **remain calm in any and all situations** that once would have bothered them; this only makes you laugh now, amuses you: this certain success will surprise and delight them.

They totally trust this native ability, this person trusts you the subconscious to **protect x *(client's name)* sensibly,** keeping them safe from real danger, no longer fearing fear, any old perceptions of embarrassments, shame or self-effacement gone - calm and alert when she/he needs to be and indeed and allowing her/him to **feel wonderful more and more,** whenever she/he needs from **now** on. Happier than ever and deep pervasive happiness growing, spreading, **reaching out effortlessly,** share it with others too, they'll like it. In touch with innate feminine/masculine power:

oestrogen/testosterone levels boosted. Being born a woman/man is a gift.

Stable, trust-worthy confidence – in all the senses of that word that have positive meaning for x *(etc.)*. All the same, is it not, in this persons mind? She/He is her/his own comfort zone wherever she/he goes - freely. Old, unhelpful ways gone forever. They just can't bother this confident woman/man in any way...No fear, only courage, increased bravery, total positivity, the confidence to **take wise risks.** Keeps this **rock solid confidence always** – a rock in a crisis, maintaining poise, composure, control, calmness, resourcefulness, femininity/masculinity, an infinite capacity to learn worthwhile things, the ability to **react calmly and reasonably,** you're **feeling great, feeling 100% safe** enjoying this life fully.

They can handle anything or anyone with ease. If she/he is around a particular type of person or situation that would have troubled her/him, it won't fluster or disturb her/him, she'll/he'll actually enjoy it, **look forward to it** positively. Handling it with ease and humour; tough, assertive when needed, it just doesn't bother them anymore, in any way shape or form - she/he can even **laugh, joke and express yourself** just as she/he wishes if this person wants because that's simply who she/he is...confidently. Their innate power, unending **patience and understanding that others differ,** inventiveness, tolerance, wisdom, analytical ability, enterprising and original - always. Thinking for her/himself. It just doesn't matter what anyone else is doing, saying or where they are, in any position. Those old behaviours and feelings are not something that X *(client's name)* does any longer. Frankly, it's not a set of behaviours you choose. **No nerves, no fear, no twitches,** no excess, misdirected energy - no problem whatsoever. Her/His **energy is focused and it flows as it should** - it will seems like the most unbelievable thought in the universe; to feel any unnecessary fear in any situation???!! What a strange idea! And when **unneeded fear goes** only profound levels of relaxation and even **a sense of fun and playfulness remain.** You can **go with the flow of life.**

Appropriate, sensible levels of emotion.

Childlike unwanted, notions, superstitions and nonsense of a younger self doing its best: gone. As a child we believed many things to be true that just weren't and then in time folly, innocence turned to wisdom, experience and deeper knowledge, from girl/boyhood to wo/manhood. Leave behind the fearful ideas. Stop, unhelpful processes, update with better ones for that one. You experientially understand the power of stillness. It is so calm – there. There are no obsessive thoughts of the past, no avoidance, she/he avoids unnecessary avoidance, no fear of sensations, no silly phobias of any kind whatsoever. No past, imagined fear, **sensibly fearless, now.**

The very thought of any former negativity just seems absurd and ridiculous. Better ways of being, responding without knowing how – the seeds are planted and will bear fruit just as you wish...the past is the past, learnt from, then move on – **the sparkle and zest return, now** – because the old approaches are something that just wouldn't and couldn't happen in this person's life...it's completely outside of anything typical or actual; in fact **that won't happen**. Others are entitled to, can do what they want, they can think what they think, it doesn't matter where she/he is, X *(client's name)* will **always feel confident.** Perhaps there are times when being indifferent or unreactive would be appropriate: and you'll just know when, unconsciously. And no matter what happens during the ups and down of life it will seem the most natural thing in the world just to let this individual **feel great, totally confident, calm, composed, totally rational** and in charge of all of these new healthy responses, patterns, processes, attitudes and behaviours. Just a part of their ongoing reality. When that happens and it will, you the subconscious mind can allow this person to **feel a marvelous sense of inner strength and purpose,** a good feeling supporting these inner changes and the outer manifestations of them. **Keeping this certain progress** for the rest of her/his amazing, joy filled life.

Super command for the suggestions to be integrated now.

It is now time to **finalise this work.** Without delay – appropriately, safely fine tune and modify, adjust this person's energy levels, access to confidence, concentration and focus, normal muscular activity and blink rate *(etc.)*, wiring and rewiring, connections, neural circuitry now working perfectly, allowing them to connect to their true potentials. Determination and motivation to succeed boosted. Complete resourcefulness available whenever needed. Alertness and relaxation fully available. Feelings altered, thinking patterns improved, overall mindset and frame of mind suitably enhanced, ways of life and habits far better than ever, a world view that has expanded past the limitations of the old black and white thinking. **Do this** and transform anything else at all that you know, really know needs **a good trance-formation, now** to get this woman/man exactly what she/he wants here today, so that they **have a very calm face.** Complete the process, making these timely, incredible, healthy, sound advances and innovations. Subconscious restructuring of appropriate associations occurs right noooooooooww!

Just deeply know with a comforting knowing feeling that **these changes have been**

made.

The story of the bee.

Just the other day a honey bee thought it was trapped in my kitchen, even though the door was wide open; it was so scared about what might happen it flew back and forth in just one path, back and forth even though their was no exit that way. As the fear within subsided it rested and began to **calm all the way down** I guess and as it did so it must have noticed that all it ever had to do was simply fly to the right path and there lay its freedom.

Future pace variant: True reflections – dissociated.

(Simply using the word – 'that' dissociates someone in this context...)

Look into some device that reflects your new reality...That's it. That person you see has **no twitch at all.** Their face is calm and relaxed and behaves completely normally. That individual you see can fully recognise their worth. That person can **feel satisfaction and contentment.** They have a great many strengths which can be drawn upon. They are appropriately compassionate and likeable and you just get a natural sense of that inside you now.

That new you is cheerful and vigorous, you can see just how much they really **feel so good.** You just know that such a person can **feel okay, feel good** enough just as they are. Their confidence is always there, they possess a great self-image, they are creative, filled with curiosity, fluent, competent, composed and purposeful anywhere the go. They can maintain such qualities despite fluctuations in energy levels throughout a given day. See that person interacting with others in significantly enriched ways that please you... *(10 secs to process...)*

Good. You know that you can always count on their self belief. They **have a particular bearing that emanates self composure and dignity.** Others **feel this instinctively** in your presence. They **have mettle and self-reliance.** They have a certainty and pluck that is highly appealing. That person can totally trust their abilities. You know, really know that they know that they trust this powerful confidence is forever within them, and that **this is all deserved,** whenever she/he needs it, permanently. She/he has 100% total faith in you, the powerful subconscious mind to backup, assist and reinforce all their efforts.

No matter what the opinions of others are, good or bad – this is so. You can never please everyone – so don't bother trying. The one and only, never to be repeated again you, who knows who they truly are and what is really important and valued by them. And that is what ultimately counts. **Your mind is free.** You are fully free to **think for yourself.** That's right. Take 20 seconds to fully process these learnings in the silence... *(Shhh etc.)*

Associated integration.

('You' reassociates someone etc.)

Excellent! Now drift into that new you and **feel how calm that face feels;** a strong minded woman/man like that can face anything, anyone. You only **feel a sense of deep rooted security.** Take a colour that represents that and let it fill you head to toe with amplified levels of these gorgeous feeling that are yours to keep. That's the way...Let it expand and get bigger and bigger and bigger! That's it! Till every cell of yours is filled with this powerful feeling of security. She/He who has health has hope and she/he who has hope has everything!

Go through a situation in your mind, from your point of view that confirms **this worked powerfully for you,** wasn't it? You are that calm woman/man you always wanted to be and are way deep down inside. From this advantageous position you know you are a person of deep, genuine worth. You have very many attractive qualities. You **feel such calm in that place -** in body and mind. Things just working out very well for some reason, just not taking them or that seriously anymore. You deserve to **feel relaxed right there –** it's your birthright, alone and with any person known or yet to be known. A person who receives compliments but isn't dependent on them, learns from mistakes easily, forgiving of themselves and others who deserve it...grounded and focused. You **feel fantastic,** always calm and in control, a deep capacity to **rest and relax** when needed. Someone who takes their time. Does one thing at a time. Who moves through this world with purpose. Sometimes it can be best to **slow things down - comfortably.** Things knowing their proper function. A person whose imagination works for them. Visualises successful outcomes. Achieves goals. Takes risks when appropriate. Is **comfortable with uncertainty** if it arises. Enjoys challenges, knowing that they bring out the best in us. Do what you can, accept what you can't. Confident around anyone. Knows they are important, deserve success, the best. Funny and fun. Better company. Spontaneous and playful, more and more and more. **Sleep well at night awakening refreshed and relaxed** the next morning. Good company. You **tend to look on the bright side,** no matter what: a realistic optimist. You see problems as opportunities. There to be solved, now...You are able to **face up to reality with real strength and**

genuine hope. These new learnings, understandings and relevant perspectives give you enormous peace of mind, now. You simply have everything you need to **thrive** at a deep unconscious level.

(Did you notice the use of face metaphors above?)

Generalised positive suggestions for any client.

You can do what has to be done to allow you to **achieve your goals,** with the knowledge that all your actions are moving you forward and allowing you to progress toward your ongoing destiny. Enjoy the journey as much as the destination. You are responsible for making the kind of life that you want. You **make things happen**. You are a doer, you **connect easily with others.** Trust your intuition. You are the master of your fate. You fully believe in that place where you believe things most of all that **you are a fully confident person** and this is so. Your imagination works for you. You **use your imagination constructively and**

680

positively to allow you to **achieve your goals** on a daily basis.

Unnecessary fear based doubts and past hesitations no longer hold you back. Gone for good. You are happy, optimistic, well, healthy from this moment forward, you **feel really good,** you **focus on joy, pleasure and happiness,** you set and achieve goals effortlessly more and more, you **solve problems easily,** you live a confident, relaxed, optimistic, positive, stress free lifestyle. Your patience, love and appropriate trust are increased. You are flexible, adaptable; you **learn from feedback calmly, objectively** and move on. You handle any and all setbacks with ease. There are many ways around obstacles and you can consider many ways when appropriate. Your energy levels conserved and boosted when appropriate. You are a highly attractive person inside and out, everyone can find the good and pleasant in themselves, you realise that you are a ray of sunshine in so many people's lives. Great fun to be with, funny, a pleasure to be around. You feel good, so others do too. Friendly and approachable when appropriate,

assertive when needed. You can protect yourself. You know what your boundaries are and you guard them and expect others to respect them.

Any old, fearful limiting beliefs you had are gone, no ifs or buts. **Focus on what you want to happen.** When you see opportunities you go for it, without hesitation. Plan your successes; give yourself the right amount of time to do what you need. There is a time to be relentless and a time to let things that aren't worth your effort go. You **have unlimited patience and determination**. Real fear is an acceptable emotion, it cannot harm you. Process it, observe it without resistance: let it pass. All your emotions are acceptable. Fear allows you to pay attention and then it passes. You **feel such calm and peace of mind** from now on. Remember to get enough **rest** and to exercise, perhaps pamper or spoil yourself from time to time. Be kind, generous, caring and supportive of yourself. There exists for you **deep muscular relaxation at exactly the right times and places:** this is yours to own. Excelling at all you do well.

Images that used to bother you shrinking, in black and white, smaller and smaller, further away, vanishing. Old fears/phobias/worries melting away. **Your inner voice confident, kind, supportive** at all times. My helpful words, glued, locked, cemented permanently in place. You have regained all your inner strength. Seek out your own path. All this only makes you calmer still. You **have all the essential self-belief you need** to do what you want to do. Out with unwanted tension. You breathe in calmness, now...

You regard yourself realistically and positively; your self-esteem is from this moment on like an impregnable fortress. You are like a rock, solid, powerful, no matter how the world changes about you; your deepest values, sense of who you truly are, strength and poise remain forever. **Keep these changes with you.** You are free from those problems you had had, now...And you remember, your mind is your mind. You have achieved everything you wanted out of this session without knowing how. Just before we successfully conclude this session you can **reinforce every positive belief, idea and notion you've ever had about yourself, now.** You can allow yourself to **experience peace of mind,** knowing **the changes have been made.** Enjoy the process of becoming who you truly are and throw in a giggle or two after all laughter is THE best medicine. Remember we are all most attractive when we are enjoying ourselves, when we **laugh and smile and just enjoy living.** The world is such a beautiful place. Notice colours, sounds, sensations, **pleasurable feelings only increasing, intensifying deeply.** Profound moments of bliss! You magnetically **attract positivity into your life.** Positive, pleasant people, experiences. You are descended from generations of survivors: this knowledge gives you strength. Embrace the abundance of this world. There is beauty, kindness, love around you: natural things are beautiful. You are free, really free. Forget to remember these commands and instructions: allow them to work for you unconsciously, now, but allow the fruit that grows from these seeds to surprise and delight you...That's riiiight!

Final wrap up.

(We know that when you tell a client a session is nearly over that they go deeper – so bash in some more helpful suggestions...Dumb ideas have been swimming around in that brain for years, a good bit of repetition can bash 'em out fast.) We are almost done. Realising now as you **relax even deeper** that from this moment forward you find and get the greatest pleasure from making yourself and deserving others happy in life-affirming, appropriate and mutually beneficial ways, from making yourself and deserving others **feel loved, cared for, wanted, needed and appreciated** in all that they say and do and that from this moment forward you no longer need, want, crave or desire any manner of uncomfortable situation or that old behaviour which is no longer true about you; instead **focusing your powerful mind on total health** in your life as you continue to be the magnificently strong and confident, happy, healthy, calm, relaxed and loving person that you have now become and will continue to be every day in every way. **Making others**

happy makes you happy remember what you give out is often that which you have reflected back to you. You find a way to **express your generosity** in the right way for you. You **think, feel, act, imagine confidently.** You enthusiastically and easily **make the changes** that lead to certain success. You move towards many appropriate pleasures in healthy new ways. The mouse is now a lion, the seasons change, you explore your world boldly with childlike joy and enthusiasm, unbounded curiosity. You **no longer hide,** you take your rightful, place in this world, now...If you were to try in vain to go back to how you were, you could only fail, and who wants to succeed at failure!??? You only **move forward to certain success.** Trust the process. Trust all the deepest parts of you. That's right etc.'

Okay Padawan. That's a good foundation to build on. Other modules and tricks that help NT sufferers follow.

Additional NT modules 1: Negotiating with a NT client's 'dark side'.

(You can use patterns for negotiation with subconscious 'parts' that I gave away in previous books; the most powerful are found in book 8, 'Hypnotically deprogramming addiction'. However the following rather direct negotiation may also help. Client's often link unwanted habits to 'dark sides'; these are really protective parts which get nasty when needed. Something everyone needs actually but it can be set off too readily and worst of all with loved ones: not a good idea. Save it for muggers etc.)

Tales from the dark side.

(Deep hypnosis assumed...)

'So far you've been causing X *(client's name)* to overreact to certain stimulus, to get angry, moody, withdrawn, overly defensive, to say nasty things to the people this person loves most of all. You also caused him to do x, y and z *(list of unwanted behaviours linked to this part by client)*. And I understand you've

687

had 100% valid reasons for doing that and you've been performing those varied functions to satisfy that intent very well but from now on that is not what is wisest, ideal or even most advantageous for this person in any area of life at all. The time for that service has now passed for good. **Enough is enough.** What is most excellent, the best way to provide security and optimum health all round at this point in their life is for X *(client)* is to **accept one's inherent self-worth** as a unique individual, to **listen calmly to loved ones' points of views,** to **trust those that deserve your trust,** to perhaps **laugh more,** to **see the funny side,** to **feel confident** and **be in a good mood** in most situations, like water off a duck's back, to **stop doing behaviours x, y, z, now.** There are better options and choices whose appropriate utilisation improves all areas of life tangibly. And you know what they are far better than me. You have choice now; especially in this place.

Enlist the creative part's help.

In fact while you are this relaxed, I would like

your creative part now to generate, at an unconscious level, a number of better, more appropriate responses in those situations and times inappropriately pattern matched to back then – to **create ideas, feelings, behaviours that support and enrich X's *(client)* life,** their most important and cherished relationships, now. These will effortlessly manifest in daily life. So many different possibilities of responses available and won't it be interesting to discover what they'll be? People in your life now aren't responsible for what someone else did at times back then. You fully understand this now in meaningful ways. **You are safe** in this world now, many people love and appreciate you and so **your focus can change;** you can **find better ways to protect yourself optimally.** You could even **notice all the proof that others love and like you,** respect you deeply, only want what is best for you. Once and for all – it's time to move **past all that stuff,** is it not? You can keep going on and on around that roundabout/traffic circle or deeply acknowledge it's time to **move on.** That's right.

Finalise process.

So complete this changing process now at the unconscious levels of processing – you, the subconscious processes are going to **make whatever changes are necessary** in X's behaviours, emotional responses to certain social cues, ideas, attitudes and more as rapidly, as securely as possible in the next few seconds to allow this person to be who they really are. Needed **re-associations occurring, now.** To really **be that kinder, more open, loving, fun loving, joy filled person** that you truly deeply are – and can be. And that's that.'

NT additions 2: Redeveloping deep muscular relaxation.

(Deep hypnosis assumed...)

'As you **relax even more deeply** I want you to realise that in this place, **in that place there is no pressure** one way or another. You are more relaxed at an unconscious level – this is so whoever you are with. There is no need for that. When you are finished with any device you **switch that old mechanism off,** do you not? What if you re-access such deep levels of unconscious relaxation here that **that old pressure* simply fails to build again.** You have no need of that.

(*NT client's complain of a building pressure...)

<u>Resting and stillness.</u>

What does anyone do when **a muscle group is no longer required to work**? That's right. You **rest that part,** don't you? When the wind blows through the wood, the moment the wind had blown on through and passed, the whole surface of the trees are still. There is **no unnecessary movement.** What if that kind of **stillness** could be a soothing colour which massages itself so deeply into just the right place that you can **feel wonderful peace in that place, now.** Or will you just **feel the relief** of making no unneeded effort anywhere at all? Have you ever been near a lake or the sea when **there is matchless stillness there** (?) You just sit down and the calmness of the sea or any body of water seems to spread into you just by watching calmness, in nature you **feel so calm all over.** That's it.

Control panels in the mind.

(As you can see, I'm quite fond of these; they are a good construct to play with in any hypnosis work...)

As you know, at least at a deeper level, your deeper minds control so many things for you, on your behalf, way in there, beyond anyone's awareness. But it is nice to know that **that part can do things for you. Right now,** just imagine a control room in your mind. That's it. Notice a **control** panel in that room in your own way which is the instrument for **full unconscious control over the movements in that place. Now,** just adjust that so that **everything works as it should, effortlessly.** I don't know exactly how you need to do that but you do. As you correct it in the right way, notice how you **feel an increasing sublime sensation of serenity in that place.** And as a consequence of you knowing experientially that **you have**

692

regained control, on a sigh inside or outside you can **let go** to far deeper levels of hypnotic healing, now. I'll be silent for 10 seconds so you can **complete this transformation...** *(Do so.)*

Brief dissociated future pace.

Just how much more comfort do you feel there? How much more comfortable can it become? Now, focus on the new feelings of inner satin smoothness. Feel the softening as if **a tight knot has been finally untied.** Whenever you need this level of relaxation in any situation, with any person known or yet to be known you will **only feel this relaxed there.** Picture going through several situations **keeping this easy pleasure freely available** in all your muscles. Good.' *(Give 'em a minute or so...)*

NT additions 3: End spasms.

(Believe it or not hypnosis can treat muscle spasms; the following can help with NT client's too...)

'If you are going to do something **you must finish it properly so that you feel satisfied.** So all I want you to do now is to simply imagine, as many times as you want in the next minute, tensing that muscle system where you experienced that x *(twitch/tic etc.)* Just imagine tensing it fully and completely and then **letting the whole system rest.** That's right. Go ahead and do that as another listens to the importance of what I say...From now on, once **that process is entirely done** you can **let go and relax.** Once something is done properly **you have no need to do it again** and again. And what if **you didn't even need to do it** visibly? You can do it in your mind. Just as smokers can **gain satisfaction** by having an imaginary cigarette. You can **simply imagine carrying out that process** of **using that muscle system once and then letting it rest in entirety.** You can practise rehearsing **this feeling of satisfaction** just by using your ability to visualise. Why? Because the same neural networks are activated through the mind's eye as are activated in real use. So there is no difference. You may even **do this unconsciously** so that you can **relax and**

finish all the interesting things that absorb and relax you throughout the day; after all there are **far more interesting things to focus on** in life, are they not? Wasn't it? That's it!

Go ahead and find your own appropriate way to **make this work** for you as I am quiet for a whole minute. And when your deepest mind knows that **things have changed for the better** it will send you a knowing feeling of profoundest satisfaction that what need be done was done. *(Shhh...)* Excellent! You are doing so well!'

NT bonus tip – the toe press:

Some therapists train their clients to relax and dissociate from the urge to twitch by pressing down a big toe. Why the toe and not the hand I have no idea – perhaps it works for some by being oddly distracting? This is in effect a post hypnotic trigger to calm down. NLP calls it 'anchoring'; it's just Pavlovian training. In it's original form (the way I was first taught it) I have found it never works; not once! But I included a revamped version (mine!) just in case you can make it work. **I prefer the desired state/behaviour to be available instantly and unconsciously to clients without gimmicks.** The process itself may have use in other contexts: can't hurt to learn it!

Toe/finger press association process.

Step 1: Link a dissociated relaxed image and a movement.

'Imagine now a very relaxed and easy going you who is **twitch free.** See that relaxed body and face. So **calm. No tension. No pressure.** See them over there on some kind of screen that suits you best. Notice on that you – **there is no twitch/tic.** See how comfortable that you feels. As you look at that image of **deepest peace of mind and body** simply press a preferred big toe/forefinger and thumb/tongue to the roof of your mouth etc. nice and softly. As you do that **your deepest unconscious can make a powerful link** between that relaxed vision of you and that movement you just made......

Good. Just release that now. **Relax that area** once more. Okay, I will be quiet for a whole minute and I want you to keep watching the calmest you, inside and when you are ready, at least two more times, make your own private movement so as to **strengthen that association.** Make sure you **rest that part**

in between making the movement you chose. That's it. I'll be silent a whole minute as you **form new pathways inside.** *(Shhh...)*

Good. You can take this new training of your own mind by you as a signal that as soon as you **make that connection** in future, as soon as you might have a certain urge, **that old urge to twitch is pleasantly swamped and smothered** by the **new feelings of total peace of mind** and only the urge to **let go into peace** remains. It need last only a few moments – only doing this when it's safe and appropriate. Feel a foretaste of the satisfaction as **those old associations are gone.**

Step 2: Dream future pace.

Can you **dream** having all the calm you need

and using this link whenever needed while I'm quiet a bit longer, really **making this new calm a part of your deepest neurology**(?) And sooner or later you will have practised this unconsciously so much that the **new neural pathways and connections are just there** so that **you need not make any unnecessary movements** – peace can be a

permanent part of that part. Even when it needs genuine use. Nooooow! That's a nice thing to know is it not? Take this act as a sign and a signal that **all changes have been made.** That's right.'

Part 2 b: The end of anxiety?

In a wider sense – you wish but...

'Anxiety' is not set in stone for life.

Let's recoup. You and your clients are not defined by any one emotional response. Crippling anxiety is not part of anyone's identity. Freud was an insane idiot. His tangled, octopus-limb like handwriting at his life's end shows he totally lost his marbles. Not that he had many left to lose. There was only chaos left in him. His theories about the creation of personality in childhood circumstances are so much demented waffle; personality is present at birth, it is genetic – it can only be supported in its healthy expression or hindered. Excessive anxiety is not an inherent part of anyone's personality but rather a sign that things must change for the better. ***Positive change can occur at any point in our life when we take the responsibility to create the change we desire as individuals.***

The fact is we don't want to get rid of anxiety, any more than we want to get rid of pain, any more than we want to get rid of our sense of touch; we just need to listen to what it is telling us; we need to pay attention to our intuition, hunches and ideas that spontaneously pop into our head, we also need to listen to our conscience. An additional insight is this: all but the genetic psychopath, and they exist, know the difference from right and wrong; we don't learn morality but we can unlearn it; it is in fact hardwired into the very fabric of our souls. An anxiety code fact is:

When we <u>do</u> good, we feel less anxious.

However realistically, as Western society becomes more and more narcissistic, insane and chaotic anxiety levels *will* hugely increase. And so I hope that this book has convinced you that...

There is no such thing as an 'anxious person'.

Anxiety is a much needed response that has been demonised. Normal responses to stressors, often caused by a simple lack of satisfaction are not pathological – the normal has been labelled 'abnormal' and the truly abnormal 'normal' ever since the madman

Freud began spouting his quasi Gnostic doctrine of self-obsession and perversion. His widely accepted irrationalisms were merely clear markers that Western civilisation had begin the process of collapse. Widespread belief in the irrational is a key indicator of a civilisation in decay. The West is dying. No one is doing anything to stop this.

There is no such thing as a 'neurotic', no such thing as a 'nervous person' no more than there is no such thing as a 'drug addict' or 'addict' – processes have been neuro-linguistically transformed into 'personality traits'; all of these things are nominalisations/reifications of complex verbs – things we do, often just for a while when life is going a bit shitty, as it does for everyone. If you are anxious you are not 'maladjusted' (to what? According to whom? On what basis/criteria?) – you are just a bit unhappy or very unhappy: once your brain calms down and you start getting your needs met and so feel genuine daily pleasures, you'll feel good again. Honestly. None of this stuff is rocket science, **_modern humans need to get back in touch with what it truly means to be a natural human being._** Humans are naturally wild and not domesticated at all. I thought you might like the next script...

701

The 'How to come off of anti-depressants – safely' script.

Warning: anti-depressants (ADs) of various kinds can create some very nasty 'withdrawal symptoms'. If you are taking them or your clients are – you must come off them in a controlled manner. If you have a good doctor they'll help you find the appropriate rate of cutting down on the 'medication' (legal drugs in this instance). Various types of ADs are highly physically addictive: all this must be understood and a sensible plan for a gradual reduction must be developed – your health, safety and sanity are of the utmost importance at all times. Some people are so hooked that they have to cut down very gradually – sometimes as long as you've been on them you have to take that amount of time to get off them. Others have no problems at all. It all depends on the individual. All drugs taken long-term have side-effects (consequences). ADs should only be used when a serious crisis has developed. *Changes in lifestyle and other habits that maintain good health as outlined in this book must be met and committed to for life.* They are not just part of 'getting better', they are essential patterns for healthy and happier living. Now let me show you how hypnosis can help those who want to quit these nasty drugs.

Rebalancing the brain script.

(Deep hypnosis assumed etc.)

'Now the fact is pills don't make anyone happy. The only thing that can make y**ou feel good and happy** is to stick to your commitment to **change in all the ways you need to.** We discussed the importance of **you're eating good quality food.** You know you need to **maintain an enjoyable exercise program** that is just right for you. But the main thing that gives anyone **a sense of deep meaning and purpose** which in turn is the real root of your sense of **deep inner security, now,** is to **find your life's purpose.** It is unique to everyone – no two people can have the same one; it's as special as the uniqueness of your fingerprints and your DNA. You have been born with special talents – when **you connect with these talents** you will find the source of the wellsprings of zest and joy for you in this world. When you **find ways to express those talents** your life is enriched more than you know and you can **really know this, now.** When you discover your own way to **connect to your purpose and talents** a

703

process of discovering why you are here will unfold that will surprise and delight you, nooooo-ooow!

You see as a child you were born with **a sense of optimism.** You were able to **feel a joy at the simplest of things** in which was contained a wondrous glory. You instinctively knew how to feel about various things. You knew how to **feel a sense of happy anticipation** before doing certain things, learning certain things. You knew and know that you also need to **feel calm and so relaxed** to work at your best. You knew that you had this ability called 'the imagination' – it is connected to your problem solving creativity and also works best when **you relax about the process and essential challenge of living.** You innately knew and know that when you **feel this special form of relaxation** in mind and body that all of your resources are available for you to handle any eventuality well. Because **you are a relaxed, happier, more resourceful person** as a consequence of all the work we've done. That's how you were and are meant to be in this reality. It's just a part of who you are and such people can leave any kind of crutches far behind them because you don't need any drugs to **feel good naturally.** That's it.

The power of your brain and its healing and detoxification abilities are not even understood by science. The brain is such a sophisticated piece of biological 'machinery' if I can put it that way. It knows, really knows how to govern a process of **healing change. Now,** it is more than capable of making new pathways, new learnings, new healings and helpings, new associations, re-associations of so many unconscious structures that aid and assist you in all those efforts, wasn't it? That's right.

Did you know, consciously, that **change can happen so quickly** with appropriate, connected physical changes. The brain, your brain is capable of astounding feats of healthy readjustment and it already knows how to do it, it always has. Your brain knows how to make you **feel, really feel so optimistic** about your far better future by making plans consciously and *unconsciously* to **create a far better life for yourself.** It knows how to make adjustments so that you relate more comfortably with others and it knows how to make you **feel that sense of your inner strength and fortitude** when you need it most. You **have more inner flexibility** than you know. You **have more courage** to **see beyond the present problems** to the better times ahead by **taking action daily to do things you enjoy.** Which people will you be spending more time with? Others less or not at all? Your brain knows how to adjust the process of **healthily rebalancing your brain chemistry** as you **come off of that medication so easily,** safely and only at the right rate and speed; and your unconscious mind knows precisely what that is. Trust it, **trust yourself** in all the relevant ways. Now, every process can only occur optimally at a certain speed - respect that reality fully. I'd like you to see a good feeling colour spread through your mind and body when a significant part of you agrees that **this essential healing process is already well under way.** Won't it be fun to **just add another success** to your collection? You need not be a chemist to know that your brain can **make the right alterations in certain manufacturing processes** so that you **feel good and healthy** through this adjustment phase. Your level of **even deeper relaxation and calm** than ever before makes it all so much more easy.

In this place – rediscover how to live your life better than ever. I'll be silent for a full minute as your brain makes some important revelations available to you that help this change along. Ideas, insights, images, plans and visions all your own and private can and will become known to you that allow you to **succeed in this.** *(Keep your promise...)*

Great! Finally, I'd like you to simply imagine how this process occurs in reality. How you go about doing it. What help you need. Information gathered. New habits sustained. See that you looking much happier and healthier as all **those neurotransmitters adjust perfectly.** That's it. Look at that you **leaving those unneeded drugs behind you** and learning to do it all on your own as you **have self-reliance, now.** You always did, did you not? Deep down, underneath the illusions of former unhelpful beliefs and tensions. All you need is already within. Powerfully! And now...I will be silent again and in that time, anything else that needs to happen to **fix this success in your mind** does so. For two whole minutes as you finalise this process for yourself, in all the ways and pathways you need, now. Learn from yourself how you did it all already. What **meaningful goals lie ahead of you**? That's the way...'

(Silence and then wrap up...)

What recurring themes occur with anxiety and its cessation?

A brief series of overall conclusions follow.

- *The importance of laughter and a sense of humour.* I don't care how bad things are – **NEVER LOSE YOUR SENSE OF HUMOUR.** If you do, you are in big trouble.
- *The importance of 'strategic flexibility'.* When we relax our brain's ACC can generate new solutions to problems. There is never only 1 way to solve any problem. Think of an obstacle: create as many ways to get over, under, above, through, around it etc.
- *The stronger your sense of reality the better.* **Those who are most in touch with reality as it is are the strong and sane ones:** delude yourself, stick your head in the sand, believe various irrationalisms and sooner or later fear and anxiety will get you. The more accurate your map – the saner you'll be.
- *Anxiety, arousal and heightened performance.* A wee bit of performance nerves does you good; in fact we know it improves performance. It is part of

knowing you are alive!

- *How to become 'immune' to anxiety.*
Eat properly, live a fulfilled life, meet
supportive people who enrich you daily,
keep yourself fit and well, avoid
unnecessary medicines, don't drink too
much booze or ingest too many
stimulants, make sure you have enough
money, balance work and having a real
life, be fascinated by reality and keep in
touch with it etc. **EVERY DAY - DO
THINGS THAT MAKE YOU
FEEL GOOD, NOW!**

- *The no-ghost in the machine.* The aim
of psychiatry is to kill off the ghost in
the machine – your soul! They use
drugs, electro-convulsive torture and
other forms of abusive mind control:
this they call a 'profession'.

- *The future of anxiety?* The constant
change of the permanent revolution of
Globalisation will lead to widespread
nervous and psychotic mental
disorders. The process is in full swing
BUT you can survive the madness. The
antidote to the post-modern millennial
hysterically narcissistic mind set is good
old fashioned **STOICISM!** Not the
philosophy, no but good old fashioned
level-headedness in a crisis.

- *Reclaiming total confidence!* Nervous energy is provided for dangerous situations – when you realise that, as long as you use your wisdom and common sense that any situation can be survived and learnt from you will grow in confidence; anxiety is a test. If you heed its lessons and alter various responses you will mature more than you know. A truly satisfied mind is impregnable. Bar the end of the world.

Appendix 1: Extra RH NLP-esque patterns that might help.

If you have read my books you'll know I'm not a big fan of NLP, though sometimes it has its uses. Below I have included two NLPesque patterns with my own Rogue Hypnotist improvements. They can both be used to help resolve *mild* 'trauma' from the past. The first which I simply call the 'Reframe past experiences pattern' can be used when a client has had lots of small but mild unpleasant experiences, the consequences of which are still holding them back in the now. You cannot change what happened in the past but you can change how it is interpreted. Often a child, young adult or adult has no caring, supportive person to whom they can turn for wise advice and support in times of stress, strain, upset or crisis. In the first pattern you can get a person to be their own supportive 'guardian' who can give their younger self some helpful pearls of wisdom. Read it through – its intent is quite self-explanatory.

WARNING: Do not use these 2 patterns on people with severe trauma; use the how to traumatise

anyone patterns first then do use them if you feel it's needed! If you don't you might get a bad 'abreaction' – a bad thing! Always play safe!

<u>RH anti-anxiety pattern 1: Reframe past experiences.</u>

(Deep hypnosis assumed – don't say the numbers, they are for your ease of learning.)

1. 'Feeling wonderfully relaxed, I want you to **imagine** a TV screen in your mind. Now, dissociated, see a still, black and white image of a younger you in a time when you were in a situation that you wished had gone differently. A time when you could have used, when you needed support and encouragement. *(Give 'em 5-7 secs, it doesn't take long...)*

2. Okay...when you have that experience – float, step, **drift** into that image, that time and see your younger self. Go over and greet them. Tell them that you are from the future,

tell them that they get through this time, tell

them that they have many pleasant and amazing experiences yet to come. Tell them that they are worthwhile, good and loved just as they are, that they learnt from this time and moved on, tell that younger you anything that you think you needed to know that would have helped them...I'll wait while you do that now. *(Pause for 10 - 15 seconds to allow processing...)*

3. Very good. Once you have done that I want you to hug the younger you, give him/her a kind fatherly/motherly kiss and then wave goodbye with both of you **feeling good and supported, inside...** *(5-7 sec pause)* When you are back looking at that TV having made those changes, we'll do that for two more old memories in which you needed more support and encouragement, times when you needed a kind, supportive word or friend. Notice already that **you feel much better, now.**

4. Excellent – you are doing really well x *(client's name)*! I want you to imagine a TV screen in your mind. Now, dissociated, see a

713

still, black and white image of a younger you in a time when you were in a situation that you wished had gone differently. A time when you could have used, when you needed support and encouragement. *(5-7 etc.)*

5. Now, when you have that experience – float, step, **drift into that** image, that time and see your younger self. Go over and greet them. Tell them that you are from the future, tell them that they get through this time, tell them that they have many pleasant and amazing experiences yet to come. Tell them that they worthwhile, good, loved and accepted just as they are, that they learnt from this time and moved on, tell that younger you anything that you think you needed to know that would have helped them...I'll wait while you do that now. *(10-15 seconds pause – you'll get a feel for when the right time to proceed is with experience; look at your client!)*

6. Good. Once you have done that I want you to hug the younger you, give him/her a kind fatherly/motherly kiss and then wave goodbye, both of you **feeling good,**

supported, so much <u>more secure,</u> inside, now... When you are back looking at that TV having made even more of those changes, we'll do that for one more old memory in which you needed more support and encouragement, times when you needed a kind, supportive word or friend. Notice how **you feel even better than before, now.**

7. I want you to imagine a TV screen in your mind. Now, dissociated, see a still, black and white image of a younger you in a time when you were in a situation that you wished had gone differently. A time when you could have used, when you needed support and encouragement. *(5-7 etc.)*

8. Now when you have that experience – float, step, **drift into that** image, that time and see your younger self. Go over and greet them. Tell them that you are from the future, tell them that they get through this time, tell them that they have many pleasant and amazing experiences yet to come. Tell them that they are worthwhile, good and loved, totally accepted for who they truly are, in all expressions of that uniqueness and their

715

wonderful radiant individuality, that they learnt from this time and moved on, tell that younger you anything that you think you needed to know that would have helped them...I'll wait while you do that now. *(10-15 secs...)*

9. Once you have done that I want you to hug the younger you, give him/her a kind fatherly/motherly kiss and then wave goodbye both of you **feeling good and supported, with a sense of profound security, a new bubbling up of only blissful and joyous feelings, now...**When you are back looking at that TV having made even more changes, and while I am so quiet for a whole minute, I want your unconscious mind at an unconscious level only to go through any memories like this, in which you needed more support and encouragement, times when you needed a kind, supportive word or friend, now. Recoding, reframing and **learning from those experiences** in ways that only make you **feel better, more worthy and confident,** more forgiving of those who deserve it, knowing almost everyone is doing the best that they can with the resources they

have, now...Meanings, feelings, associations, the way you processed certain information can and do **alter profoundly, permanently, now.** Wise learnings can occur very rapidly in that powerful brain of yours. Thaa-aats right!' *(Give 1 whole minute of silence.)*

The next pattern I call the 'drop-down through pattern'. It is useful for dissociating people out of resourceful states and associating them into really good and powerful ones. It is quite an odd pattern but clients often wake up after and say, 'Wow! That was amazing!' or words to that affect. Again use on low level upset, mild unpleasant stuff. You are saying to the mind – leave that state in the past and do this instead. It utilises spatial predicates, for in fact you can send a human brain up, down, sideways – you name it!

The Drop-Down through Pattern.

(Deep hypnosis assumed)

'As you rest so deeply here I want you to notice...

Phase 1: Identify the experience and emotion you want to transform.

1. What emotion, feeling, memory or experience would you like to transform so that it enhances your life? Are there any emotions or experiences that undermine your success _(that you associate with problem x – public speaking/stuttering/nervous twitch etc.)_ that you would like to eliminate? Which emotion have you predominantly associated with x in the past? Can you name it in your own mind and to your own satisfaction, now? _(7-10 secs to process etc.)_

Phase 2: Step into that experience.

1. For the purposes of your helpful transformation, can you simply recall that experience and step into it so that you see what you saw, hear what you heard, and fully feel what you felt. Be there again. _(5-7 seconds processing...)_ Good.

2. Where do you feel that in your body? Can you specifically locate it now? What does it feel like exactly? How intense are you

718

experiencing *that* emotion? As you anticipate the possibility of x where had you felt that? *('That' not 'this' = dissociate. See book 2, 'Mastering hypnotic language'. Give the client about 10 seconds to process this.)*

3. Good, just be there with it for a moment, noticing...just noticing it fully...really knowing that **it is just an emotion** and that **you are so much more than any emotion...Now,** what does that mean to you? What meaning had you associated to that past experience before we **go beyond it altogether**? *(Pause 7 secs...)*

Phase 3: Drop down through the experience.

1. This may seem or feel strange, but you do know what it feels like when you drop? Course you do...With that in mind and feeling that feeling of dropping, just drop down through that experience until you drop down underneath that feeling...Plop! That's it. Great! Amazing isn't it!

2. What feeling or emotion lies underneath that emotion? *(5 seconds pause only – push*

on...)

3. And now just imagine dropping down through that feeling. *(Note: as always use the personal languaging, the 'trance words' that the client gives you. See 'Powerful hypnosis'. People code their own experience in the unique way THEY use words; it may well differ greatly from yours.)*

4. Great. You are doing so well! And what feeling comes to you as you imagine yourself dropping down through that one?

(Their facial expressions will almost always tell you all you need to know, they might nod or smile etc. All you do is just keep repeating this dropping-down through process until the person comes to 'nothing...' That is, to no feelings, to a feeling of a 'void/ emptiness' I do it this way...)

5. Now, all I want you to do is keep on dropping down through those old, formerly unresourceful states until you reach a place where **you have gone beyond all that permanently** and feel nothing, a void if you

like. This is a sign and a signal that **you are past all that, now.** And after that comes the best bit where we fill you up with all the amazing and powerful resources that you need and can re-access in the state of hypnosis. *(This makes the client feel safe that you aren't going to leave them in the void!)* I will be silent until you wiggle a finger, nod your head or somehow let me know you're done. I will be silent a whole minute, which is easily enough time to **complete the process** or until you let me know you're done...*(Do so...)*

Phase 4: Acknowledge the temporary void.

1. Very good! So for a moment only just experience that 'nothingness' or 'void'; choose you own label for that oblivion. *(5 sec pause is enough – move on...)* Excellent Good. **You have finally gone beyond all of that, forever!**

2. Now let that nothingness open up and imagine yourself dropping through and out the other side of the nothingness. You are going to **start to access all your powerful**

and pleasant states beyond what wasn't really true anyway. Good, if it helps just imagine opening the earth up if you have to and dropping down through that, do anything you need to. It's time to **access your power!** 3. What amazing things are you experiencing when you come out the other side of the nothingness? What positive state or states have you found to make a part of who you really, truly are? Do you see or hear anything unique or helpful in this place? **Keep that powerful state within you** from now on as a gift.

(NFH: Repeat stage 3 several times; continue till you have a minimum of 4-5 powerful resource states. I do it this way...)

4. Okay that's good. Now, what amazing feeling or emotion lies underneath that emotion? Access and **fully experience that incredible feeling** inside you now. Feel how good that feels! *(7-10 seconds to wallow in it!)* And that just feels better, better, even better! **Lock that feeling in** too and keep it as a permanent part of your total self... *(Pause a beat)* And now just imagine dropping

down through into 3 more wonderful feelings that create such **a real sense of strength and security inside** of you. As you do that, whilst I am quiet for a full minute and a half, notice these feelings are always just as good or even more powerful, pleasant and helpful in all appropriate ways than the ones before. They build upon one another, mingle and forge a new, powerful state within. It remains with you. Building **a solid foundation of core strength within!** So go ahead and drop down through and beyond past imagined limitations into your most amazingly powerful states of mind and body that maintain a new, resourceful mega-state – where **all of these feelings form one coalesced whole inside, now.** *(Shhh for as long as you promised; again you can set up a finger wiggle* or a time frame in which the task is completed etc. Use your judgement. After a reasonable time proceed onward anyway...NOTE: *The finger wiggle is not necessarily an ideomotor signal. I let the conscious mind wiggle to me to in hypnosis. It's watching to 'one side' as it were.)*

Phase 5: 'Meta-state' the past problem situations.

(NFH: Use each resource state to 'meta-state' each old problem/trigger situations. This means you are linking the experience of feeling good when they once felt rotten etc. in those times. You create a link by getting them to feel the new positive emotion gestalt and imagine being in a past trigger situation.)

1. And so, when you **really feel these good, resourceful states and experiences inside** about that old problem situation, in the past, because now **it's just a situation,** how does that positively transform things? And when you even more fully **feel these amazing states radiate from your core,** what other positive, empowering transformations occur? How good does it feel to **know this is so**? The **old feeling are forever gone,** smothered by the complete power of the new!

2. Just **stay right here in this wonderful set of feelings** and as you **experience it fully,** what happens to the way you now

consider that old situation that used to bother you? You **feel different** don't you? How much better do you feel from here? From this advantageous perspective?

3. When you **feel this amazing state intensify,** I want you to **feel these wonderful feelings of - warmth, freedom, confidence, power, fluency, calm** *(etc.)* What else shifts tangibly with regard to how you feel about being in those sorts of situations? How much have things improved for you?

4. *(Setting up post hypnotic work...)* From this new place, perspective, learning, understanding and great set of zestful, **positive, empowering feelings that only lie within you, always, now,** again what do you truly feel and hear? What sums up this state new state of core strength for you? Can you put it into one phrase or word? *(A beat...)* Now, automatically **whenever you feel or sense that you might have experienced x (unwanted behaviour) you will instantly go into this new state again** at just the right time – just recall that phrase consciously

or unconsciously now and you will find you will **always be in total control over that old challenge** that you once had, and you can, can you not? Don't be too surprised and delighted at how confident, fluent, calm, happy and relaxed you are as you **react so much more happily in those situations, now,** and in your wonderful future...

Phase 6: Test your work!

1. Let's see what now happens when you *try,* and I want you to really *try* to see if you can get back the problem state that we started with. When you **try to do that,** what happens? **It's gone or altered significantly,** has it not? You like this new, more empowering experience, don't you? This is a much better place to act and live from. *(Let them try for 3-5 secs max!)*

2. You can take this act as a sign and a signal that you can **take this power into your future.** Into all of your tomorrows and into all your relationships, into any and all challenges? Get a sense of whizzing through time, **feeling new feelings then,** through many situations

that confirm **this has really worked.** *(10 second pause.)* That's it. Great! You can even take it for granted that you can **do what others do easily,** it's simply what you now do too, confidently, powerfully with anyone and everyone, any time, any place - and this is so.'

(If the client person still has some 'negative' emotions after you have taken him or her through the process, then simply repeat the process. That is, recycle through those feelings as you did with the first negative feeling. You may have to do this two or three times. Do it until the person does not experience any negative feelings. <u>End note: some NLP types promote a variant of the above as a 'cure' for stammering/stuttering – if only it were that simple!!!</u>)

Appendix 2: Pertaining to Pan – fear in lonely places!

The mystery of 'Pan-ic'. It is the 1920's, The New Forest, England. The last recorded case of death by panic. The corpse was found crouched against a tree, the mouth showing the bared teeth of the utterly terrified. It is a fact that people in lonely places out in nature can be overwhelmed by a sudden onslaught of irrational panic. Panic is derived from the Greek god Pan; the Christian equivalent is Lucifer. Pan personified nature – grottos, caves, dark woods and dells were his haunt. He was said to shout out at the lost wayfarer in the woods. Fords, bridges and sea shores represented the threshold between the land of the little people, fairies, elves, the Tuatha DuDanann or Sidhe who might abduct children and ruin crops for a trespass onto their realms. Apparently it was always worse if they saw you first! This is known as 'getting the spooks'.

In the 1920's again, two young men in their 30's were found dead in the Cairngorms (Scottish mountain range); they were completely healthy but their hearts had stopped – the doctor recorded 'heart failure' but privately he reported they had died of fright; both were found face down as if running from 'something'. He had never seen such healthy corpses.

The ancients believed nature to be populated by all manner of 'entities'. Those who worked alone in nature often 'worshipped' Pan (bribed by offerings) such as fisherman, hunters, shepherds etc. The author of '39 steps', John Buchan told how he and his huntsman guide in Bavaria had been struck by irrational panic which made them flee for their lives in the Alps; both gripped by a wild surge of pure unexplainable terror!

Makes ya think!

Appendix 3: 50+ Anxiety Code maxims.

1. Fear is the mind killer. (Yes, I was one of those few who watched David Lynch's 'Dune' all the way through!)

2. Anxiety is brain pain – it's the signal saying, 'Hey STOOPID! Something is wrong! I am scared about the way things are going! Change course or I'll make you feel worse!'

3. All behaviour is positively intended. No matter how odd it appears.

4. A fear-soaked brain is not working properly. In fact the entire front thinking part shuts down. If we are very afraid we are in state of pathological waking trance. Extreme emotions = hypnosis! Fear = executive function conscious mind activities are offline! If you aren't thinking you are reacting.

5. The worst cases of anxiety based problems will *usually* be found amongst the victims of the 'drama of the family'.

6. Anxiety is caused and 'cured' by specific things in the real world.

7. In order to fulfil needs you must take action.

8. A brain that is not overly aroused is a healing and an efficiently working brain.

9. Continual hyper-vigilance and false pattern matching creates paranoia.

10. Anxiety does not make us safer, it makes

us unable to think clearly. We are therefore more likely to be endangered by it.

11. You can't remain on a war footing forever!

12. Keep calm and carry on.

13. Keep both good and bad stress within manageable limits.

14. When we are heavily stressed our body acts as if it is under physical attack.

15. There is an optimum way to respond to challenge and a lousy way!

16. The roots of fear are perceived <u>immediate</u> threats to the person that are risky to survival for which heightened vigilance is required.

17. 99.9% of worry is a huge waste of time and energy that changes nothing; it turns molehills into mountains.

18. Do courage to get courage.

19. All worry is an upside down positive intent in disguise.

20. Worry is a form of mental attack or torture that we perform upon ourselves!!! We wring worries to death, turning them over and over – thereby we strangle all the joy out of our lives.

21. It is when extreme worry persists chronically and obsesses us that we can get serious health problems; physical and psychological.

22. You must be comfortable with uncertainty.

23. The more you try to suppress or ignore

something the more intense and explosive the eventual reaction will be.

24. To get rid of fear lose your fear of fear.

25. You can only take so much shit and something is going to give.

26. A good night's sleep keeps anxiety at bay and/or a good night's sleep is Mother Nature's anxiety annihilator par excellence!

27. In a fearful state we are highly programmable. Learnings however daft can be swiftly imprinted at the unconscious levels in such states.

28. Young mammals learn what is dangerous and safe by monitoring their parents' /caregivers' reactions.

29. The technical definition of what we call 'learned helplessness' is a habitual behavioural response pattern wherein any organism that is forced to 'endure aversive, painful or otherwise unpleasant stimuli' and thus, as a consequence becomes 'unable or unwilling to avoid subsequent encounters with those stimuli, *even if they are escapable'.*

30. As an adult you always have a degree of influence. If you do nothing, you are choosing to do nothing!

31. Trauma is so emotionally destabilising because it represents a violation of our right and universal human need to have a sense of safety and security that is 100% inviolable.

32. The separate traumatic memories are not the point – it is the emotions associated to them that are the problem; once you decouple the emotional trauma safely the old memories are processed as normal unpleasant memories that we all have. A rule for therapy and life is: you should only experience a trauma once!!!!

33. A detraumatised mind can heal spontaneously.

34. To be anxiety free you need good quality relationships or cut the shits out of your life and bring in all the life-affirming positive people you can!

35. To be anxiety free you need to live your life with self-generated meaning.

36. To be anxiety free you must choose to be free to choose. Calmness requires a degree of self-determination and self-reliance. Humans need to have a degree of control over the outcomes they seek; if they do not have this they become anxious in proportion to which their sense of control diminishes.

37. Human love soothes the human soul.

38. Secure individuals are best found in large, involved and extended family groups.

39. If you want to stay calm eat a healthy organic diet as much as humanly possible.

40. A relaxed brain can solve problems easily. We have a need to be calm to perform at our best 99% of the time.

41. Rest, recover and kiss anxiety goodbye.

42. In order to feel happy and calm mankind needs to feel there is more to existence than the mere struggle to survive; when this is replaced by materialistic nihilism he sickens.

43. In order to feel secure and calm you need to have a firm grasp of reality as it is, not as you wish it were.

44. A satisfied mind is not anxious. Anxiety is triggered by a lack of satisfaction.

45. If you want to avoid anxiety seek daily satisfactions or if you want to be anxiety free do things that give you pleasure daily!

46. In order to beat anxiety for good you must have a relaxed yet alert base state.

47. We need both REM sleep and deep physical restorative sleep to feel calm daily.

48. People project their own limitations onto reality, that's why most people live boring, pointless lives; you need to live this life as the adventure it is!!!

49. You cannot laugh and be anxious at the same time! Usually!!!

50. To halt anxiety in its tracks you must interrupt its usual activation process.

51. When we do good, we feel less anxious.

52. NEVER LOSE YOUR SENSE OF HUMOUR.

53. Those who are most in touch with reality as it is are the strong and sane ones.

Appendix 4: Worry loops diagram.

The following illustration is more of a metaphor than a scientific reality, however a client once 'described' her worries by making a looping gesture with her hand and finger, perhaps this is the origin of the term 'loopy'?

The worry loops diagram.

Appendix 5: Genuine human needs - advanced model.

The following has the most advanced model of human needs I have yet collated. It takes into account meta-levels of human needs. Needs are both necessary and important. The necessary is often not important till it is threatened or missing. In no particular order...

Genuine human needs hierarchy.

'Animal' level:

1. **Physical survival:** oxygen, time and space, food, sunlight, water, shelter, working senses and body etc.
2. **Security:** the absence of threat. In platitudes known as 'peace'. Military defence is a part of this as is 'border control', true social cohesion provided *only* by shared ethnicity, a fixed language, customs and spiritual responses etc. If a society lacks these essential security concerns it collapses: no ifs or buts. It is just a matter of time.
3. **Economic:** specific ways in which to take action to preserve and expand one's survival needs beyond

subsistence level. This leads to leisure, thought, high culture, technology etc.

4. **Sex and reproduction:** bonding, natural pleasure and *vitally* procreation.

Human level.

- **Gregariousness/companionship:** we have a need for others; they provide satisfaction via stimulation, care, love, protection, esteem (sense of importance), admiration, wisdom, models of imitation, learning opportunities, structure, the human need to talk etc.

- **Meaning and purpose:** why am I here? What is the point of existence? What role am I to play in reality? One's sense of having a super-objective: the source of all human motivation. Dissatisfaction of this need = 'alienation'. Contains a 'spiritual component'. My little nephew once said to me, 'Why am I here?' I didn't tell him as that is for all of us to discover as individuals *if you are capable of it.*

- **Explanation:** we have a need to know in order to enhance survival and joy. This is why all children are curious about reality. We have a hard-wired drive to seek truth; until family, school and the media brainwash us – we can exist with a false framework for some time in a controlled environment; think 'The Truman show'. The fulfilment of this need protects us from psychosis; 'functional' or otherwise. Civilisations in the past 6000 years have required functional psychosis in order to exist.

At any one time we fractionate between each need's satisfaction: this we call living. They all interrelate. ***Again note: the necessary is taken for granted till it is missing. Then it becomes (temporarily?) important.*** This I call 'the matrix of the natural order'. It _cannot_ be circumvented; ever. Human nature is no abstraction it is very real.

The following 40 or so questions, originally published in full in book 5 in the series, 'Wizards of trance' (I've added some new ones) can be used by any 'therapist' to help clients focus on need satisfaction. You do not have to ask all of them: In therapy sessions I usually focus on 12 or so that seem pertinent to the client before me. Clients will tell you if they do not care about certain 'needs' being met. _Listen to them!_ Just because YOU value something doesn't mean THEY do! You are treating an individual not a statistic.

Questions to ascertain degree to which universal human needs are being met NOW.

Underlying presupposition – *what is missing in this person's life?*

- **Are you eating healthily?**
- **Are you exercising regularly?**
- **Do you feel isolated and if so is that a problem?**
- **Do you have enough friends?**
- **Do you have a good social life?**
- **Do you receive enough positive attention from others?**
- **Do you feel psychologically secure?**
- **Do you broadly speaking feel physically safe?**
- **Are you financially secure?**
- **Are you secure at home/in closest relationships?**
- **Is your work/job fulfilling?**
- **Is your work/life balance as you wish it to be?**
- **Do you spend enough time with your family?**

- **Do you feel you have enough time?**
- **Do you feel you give enough good quality attention to others?**
- **Do you feel you help other people enough?**
- **Do you feel you have enough space or too little space around you? Is the lack etc. stressful?**
- **Are you overly bored?**
- **Are you overstressed/overloaded?**
- **Are you loved, appreciated for the totality of who you are, in all ways, unconditionally or otherwise by at least one person?**
- **Do you feel connected to something 'bigger' than yourself? Group? Cause? Religion? Politics etc.?**
- **Do you feel you have sufficient control/influence in your life?**
- **Are you honestly able to get privacy when needed?**
- **Do you have at least one genuinely close friend?**
- **Do you feel an emotional connection in your life to enough people in ways that satisfy you?**
- **Is your social status/role/s important to you and if so is it**

appreciated and acknowledged? (This can be son, daughter, wife, dad etc. as well as a work role.)

- **Do you feel admired?**
- **Do you feel valued as a family member?**
- **Do you feel valued at work?**
- **Do you feel able/talented/competent in at least one if not more areas of life?**
- **Are you mentally and physically stretched in ways you find meaningful?**
- **Do you treat yourself often enough?**
- **Do you get enough fresh air and sunshine?**
- **Do you get out into the country often enough?**
- **Is there something missing from your life?**
- **Do you experience sufficient natural pleasures in daily, day to day living?**
- **Is your sense of curiosity about the world around you satisfied?**
- **Do you feel you have sufficient knowledge to solve problems/this problem?**

- **Do you feel you have room to develop and 'grow' as an individual?**
- **Is your sex life satisfying? (May not be best to ask during therapy. Note it for yourself as you talk to a client. Are they getting enough?)**
- **Do you feel enough other people find you attractive?**
- **What would you do with your life if you knew you could only succeed?**
- **What are you most passionate about and does your day to day life genuinely reflect that?**
- **If you could wave a magic wand and everything was how you want it; how would it be different? (This question is twee but reveals dissatisfactions and goals.)**
- **Do you think you have found your life's mission or purpose? Have you answered: why am I here?**

NOTE: you may not need to ask them all. Where appropriate get the client to rate the fulfilment from 0-10. 0 = no fulfilment. 10 = total fulfilment. A rating of less than 3 can, in some people, be enough to trigger anxiety or depression.

NOTE: humans do have 'spiritual' needs; this is well understood. However such concerns are not the field of the therapist. Stick to material needs. This being said modern man's 'spiritual poverty' is at the heart of the 'Western' mental health crisis. Over the coming decades this will only intensify. However, this matter is far beyond the scope of this book.

Appendix 6: Why you are better off self-medicating with alcohol than taking Big Pharma drugs.

Pills or booze? Consider the following. Psychiatric drugs cause the deaths of over 500,000 (that's a massacre!!!?) people aged 65 and over YEARLY in the West. Are we actually seeing a form of covert euthanasia posing as treatment? My answer is yes.

A Danish scientist Professor Peter Gøtzsche, research director at Denmark's Nordic Cochrane Centre said in a recent article in the British Medical Journal that the use of most antidepressants and dementia drugs could be halted without inflicting harm on patients. He further stated that the benefits of these pills were 'minimal', and had in fact have been overstated vastly.

So why do I say booze is better than pills to manage anxiety? Let me explain myself. I am not advocating drinking all day to calm nerves like some kind of Oliver Reed, Richard Burton hybrid. I am saying that when tense or bit stressed it won't kill you at the end of a day to have a wee dram or two of your favourite pleasure. Moderate alcohol consumption is in fact linked to longevity, a healthier brain in later life (Alzeimers sufferers are often teetotallers), lower blood pressure and decreased anxiety. Booze has a bad wrap. Humans have used it for eons. Just use it wisely. Make sure the quality of the product is very good. Alcohol is information. Surprised? I am the *Rogue* Hypnotist!

Appendix 7: 'Codex Traumatica!' The detraumatisation formula.

Here is the core structure of 'how to detraumatise anyone'; once you know it you can play around with it and create your own wordings.

The detraumatisation process.

WARNING! THE FOLLOWING CAN BE USED TO ALTER ANY EMOTION/STATE – ONLY USE ETHICALLY!!!

Step 1: Decluttering residual negativity phase.

1. Haunted house metaphor.
2. Elicit 'place of perfect peace'.
3. Visualise placing all negative internal processes into a container symbol.
4. Shoot symbol off into the distance (dissociate negative emotions phase – proximity and association are linked in the brain's internal representation codings; we even have this in our langauging – 'Out of sight out of mind' etc.).
5. Elicit symbol of positive potential.
6. Fill symbol with positive internal processes.
7. Associate client into a positive self filled

with the new resources.
8. Future pace changes (association to positive emotions phase).

This part of the process clears away any unforeseen obstacles to the head on trauma removal – the client will now have sufficient ego-strength to complete the vital second phase of changework. This incorporates RH's principle of 'loading the dice in your favour'.

Step 2: Trauma symbology transformation phase.

(Before doing anything get the client's trance words for the unwanted *and* desired states.)

1. Induce deep hypnosis.
2. Elicit a symbol that represents the specific unwanted emotional state etc.
3. Client rates the strength of the feeling subjectively.
4. Client examines symbol.
5. Client changes symbol into one that represents the opposite desired state.
6. Get them to make one final set of changes so that the process is totally complete.
7. Place the new symbol in the body where it feels right.

8. Expand the feelings in intensity.
9. Take client to a 'safe place'.
10. Locate a feelings container.
11. Place as much of the new state in the container as is required.
12. Leave safe place.
13. Rate new state's strength.
14. Intensify it even more.
15. Exit.

Very simple, highly effective and adaptable to a whole host of 'issues'.

Appendix 8: The 4 basic patterns of 'depression' - the worry trance feedback loop exposed.

Depression is a pathological trance; it is created and maintained the following way.

1. Human needs go unmet – loss: insufficient pleasure and satisfaction result.
2. Person worries about unmet needs but does not take action to solve them - rumination.
3. Daily anxieties exhaust brains dreaming-out capacities. Over dreaming and poor sleep leads to exhaustion.
4. Exhaustion leads to 'bad mornings' and lethargy, lack of motivation etc. Tiredness etc. prevents one from getting needs met and creates more anxiety.

Ad infinitum.

Appendix 9: 'Depression' case; an undiagnosed form of 'ego state disorder'.

The following represents a case whereby I was presented with a client who was varyingly diagnosed as having, 'Schizophrenia', 'Bi-polar disorder', 'Depression', 'Psychotic depression'. None were correct. She had been left on powerful antidepressants and anti-psychotics for 30 plus years. What was the real problem and how might one go about helping such an individual? See my notes below...

Suspected 'ego states': mild MPD/DID Ego state disorder matrix.

Note: each persona/ego state had its own 'voice'.

- **The rebel:** voice of a teenage girl. Sassy. Sticks up for self. Anti-authority. Contradictory for the sake of it. Smugly self-satisfied. Ignorant. Emotive. Attracted to leftist political extremes. Her mother, her tormentor was attracted to violent extremist political philosophies. Was she really seeking to rebel or to forge a link with her abuser through faking a similar doctrine?

- **The bully:** in traditional ego state therapy this would have been called 'the protector'. That was its function. Its tone was unpleasant, domineering, almost barking. It was very nasty and vindictive. Its post hypnotic trigger was any form of perceived 'criticism'. It was always angry. It called people nasty names and found their vulnerabilities and exploited them. It liked to order others around; this often took a covert form through nagging.

- **The introjected mother:** this was a clone of the mother's persona. It involved dressing like her. It spoke in its mother's accent not its own.

- **The victim:** 'poor me' its sad tone seemed to say. This self, wallowed in self-pity of the most maudlin kind. It alone worried about other's opinions, often obsessing over them in trance loops. It was hypersensitive and impressionable to the point of instant somnambulism. It took on every opinion offered.

- **The mature self:** the wise one. This

self was a caricature of a wise, balanced and compassionate person. Its tone was slow and 'hippyish'.

- **The carer:** this part was capable of deep caring and enjoyed children. Its voice was high pitched and sentimental.

- **The hypochondriac:** this spoke in a rushed voice as it was often seeking to justify itself. Note: This was the crux of the matrix; _**the client's mother only gave her positive attention when she was ill.**_ She had operant conditioned her child to become ill or fake illness to receive love and attention. Did her mother 'have' Münchhausen's syndrome by proxy? Who knows! She could have just been evil. 'Illness' and love became associated in this woman's mind as a young girl. This prevented her from recovering. Recovering = no love!

- **The playful one:** this was one of my favourites. It was fun, liked being silly and laughing. It was always in a good mood but could be annoying. It was childlike and joyous. Thing was it was in a 62 year old woman's body.

Conclusions:

- The intent of each part was positive.
- The strategies used by each part were rigid, inflexible, robot like and often awful. Goals were often not achieved satisfactorily and this led to increased stress as even basic emotional needs for intimacy were not met.
- She had been so mercilessly criticised as a child in a concerted attempt to break her spirit that 1. It created the 'alters'/ego states. 2. It left her selves in a perpetual feedback loop. Unable to change so as to protect its core self from splitting. It had become an entrenched survival mechanism.
- The individual had a pattern of constant lying to others and more importantly its selves.

Solution matrix plan.

- Hypnotise subject very deeply.

- Elicit each part in the imagination.

- Find out its role.

- Detraumatise all parts in one go or one at a time.

- Accept all parts underlying intent.

- Ask it if each part would keep the intent but with the creative part's help find better strategies to achieve goals that helped it meet its needs/functions.

- Remove destructive strategies from the behavioural repertoire.

- Put the new strategies on a list of to dos.

- Integrate all parts.

- Stop worry.

- Build in a coping with 'criticism' ability.

- Collapse external cue associations that triggered personas.

- Fix sleep problems.

- Exduction.

- Extra note: during the interview stage I may make possible use of analysing the client's 'speech reversals' to discover underlying (hidden) 'factors'. Advanced therapy model – beyond this book.

Appendix 10: Some random tips and facts!

Before we end our little journey together I thought I'd sling out some random facts, perspectives that you might find interesting.

Paranoia vs 'Pronoia' – why paranoia ain't all bad!

There are times when you should be paranoid! Paranoia has a bad rap. Imagine you are considering entering a dangerous neighbourhood? Should you be all deluded and go 'pronoia' (the retarded idea that everything will *always* go well and turn out right!) like Pollyanna and think: 'Bad stuff never happens to me! Just those TV people!' ??? Or maybe should you be a wee bit paranoid and not go there at all? I leave the answer to you Sherlock. Remember New Age cults promoted the idea of 'positive thinking' no matter what; or as I call it being completely MAD!

What was Soma?

Soma was actually an unknown drug, probably derived from plants or a plant that was used in Ancient India by the high ranking

Aryan priesthood and aristocracy during certain religious rites; this is what Aldous Huxley used for his model in 'Brave New World'. Remember 'happy pills' don't really solve a thing!

The strange obsessions of psychiatry.

Did you know that all the originators of that psuedo-subjectivist 'science' called psychiatry were all obsessed by the occult? They said professionally that all mental illness had nothing to do with spirits and demons but at the same time they were all into that shit???! Nuts. Check out my last book 'Weirdnosis' for the low down on even weirder stuff! There's nothing out there like it!

The hidden need – on the need to be an individual.

The political extremes of 'left' and 'right' are really identical: each denigrates the importance of the individual – the individual and his and her inalienable rights are sacrosanct. Societies that violate this core principle experience mental health catastrophes as the Western world is now experiencing. Everyone has the right to differ. Differences of opinion lead to real progress.

This is the traditional way of the West. Everyone sees the world in a slightly differing way. Their bodies, brains and nervous systems differ. The genders differ. ***Individuality is built into the very matrix of being human.*** Socialist societies seek to wreck this reality by producing conformity of human outcome: i.e. a sub-human 'product'; more on this in the final book.

Chemically induced depression, obesity and autism.

Many forms of so-called 'illnesses' are simply the result of being poisoned. 'Depression' can be caused by the consumption of too many pesticides etc. in the diet. Books alone could be written about this. You may have to advise clients to go completely organic. The more natural all forms of information received by the body are – the better for overall health. Yes food is a type of information and poisons like glycophosphates are too. This topic is TOO big to expand on further here.

Appendix 11: Shutting down the experience.

After you induce trance you 'shut down the experience'; I have written about this in other works but to make this book complete I have added a variation to the one I used in my last book, 'Hypnotically deprogramming anxiety' here.

Shut down the experience script.

(Add this in after several deepeners. Say with authority and expect 'magic' to happen!)

From this very second on...all sounds...all voices...inside and out...create an ease in your **focus on my voice, now!** at some level or just **drift off somewhere** nice...You follow meaningful words...ideas that help only more easily...Nothing that happens, that I do, bother you in any way, shape or form... **Whatever I say can** promptly occur, can exclusively **become your new total reality** no matter if it sounds funny, brand new, or very different! You can experientially know what I say! You can **think what I suggest** you do! You can **believe what I tell you** to believe! And you can **feel that which I suggest** powerfully with every part of your being! When I say **you can do it,** whatever it is, you can **do it** and you can know that you can know you can. Only with regards to the matters we are working with obviously*.

And now...everything that occurs merely takes you deeper and deeper...Bodily changes and actions...sensations and awarenesses...You can **go deeper and deeper** than ever before, now!

(This section is an indirect super-command-suggestion, saying in effect – 1. Anything from now on is defined as 'hypnotic'. 2. Think, feel, believe, act and know what I suggest to you from this instant on.

**This phrase may get resistance BUT I follow it up with a safety feature suggestion which says, only do as I say with regards to the hypnotherapy problems etc. Thus they are ensured they won't become my mind control bitch!)*

Appendix 12: A trusty exduction.

If nothing more new scripts can stave off boredom. I created this little exduction for you Padawan. It will work fine with all the anxiety scripts within. It is a variation on an old theme...

A trusty exduction script.

Part 1: Places in the mind and amnesia module.

All these positive ideas and changes have been placed in that place within where you know things to be true. Things like the sun sets, that you know how to breathe. Those old, outdated ways have gone to that place where you place things that were true but no longer are – you knew certain people, you went to school and then **it all changed.**

The certainty of your success is permanently stored in that place where you know, really know that **amazing changes have already occurred, now...**You don't have to remember, the important things is to **have certain experiences naturally recorded in**

your mind. Their presence has been and will be of service to you. It's nice to know **they are there, unconsciously, now...**

Part 2: Post hypnotics.

(These just save you time so I advise you use 'em.)

If you ever want me to help you in the future all I will have to say is **'PURE PEACE!'** *(etc.)* Only within the context of a hypnosis session obviously and **you will instantly re-enter a state of trance and hypnosis 50 times deeper** than the one you have experienced easily and quickly. Almost done...

Part 3: Awakening process.

Okay, I am now going to count from 1 – 5 and on 5 everything relevant I have said in this hypnotic session will remain with you at a subconscious level...Only growing stronger every second of each day of your amazing, more fun-filled life! Enabling you to continue being the happier, healthier, **more relaxed, satisfied, confident** and loving, calm person who is free and **100% feeling normal** *(etc.)* with precisely the right mindset, now, to **achieve your positive, healthy and realistic goals by taking action.** Your subconscious aids you in all your efforts. Your poise is good, sense of self-worth returned. That fully resourceful person you have now become, and always really were deep inside, and will **continue to be** from this moment forward – only building on your secure foundation of success.

On 1 – Realising now that you will awaken every morning and after this session with an inner warm glow of confidence, a renewed optimism for life that just radiates from you and others notice it! **Keep just the right level of relaxed alertness** that you need.

On 2 – Noticing how much better you feel, how proud you feel about yourself for allowing yourself to **overcome challenges** that you once had that now no longer bother you – it's as if your mind and body have been magically purified! And your conscious self can relax in the trusting knowledge that these new habits operate automatically and unconsciously, now.

Remember: a relaxed mind is creative.

3 – All unnecessary relaxation now leaving the body! Lighter and brighter! Almost as though you now **realise that a huge weight has been lifted from your shoulders!** You **feel completely free!** When you **wake up** in a few moments time you will have an overwhelming feeling of being very happy, **super calm – and that's your new normal,** feeling alert and full of vitality and energy that you'll want to express! You **feel incredibly motivated** and full of zest for life! Every day there is more to learn and do!

4 – **More aware** of your body and room around you, aware of noises – **normal waking feelings now** returning to every muscle group and cell that needs to **feel wide awake!** You can forget to remember what you can remember to forget! **All changes made** and locked in! Your breathing **returns to normal waking** breathing! You feel clear and fresh throughout mind and body! Totally re-energised! Ready to get on with all the fun things in life! So much has improved!

763

Feeling secure, open your eyes on **'5'!** *(Voice building to climax!)* That's it, you're done.

(Which is a suggestion. The rule of hypnosis exductions is, broadly speaking is – the longer in the longer out; especially for first sessions...)

<u>*A brief note on anxiety session 'After care'.*</u>

This is how you address that topic...

- Let anxiety clients know you are always available if they need help.
- Tell them to see what happens – if the effects last for 2-3 weeks that usually means that they are doing fine and dandy. Only a life stressor might derail things, not always, but if it does tell the client not to blame themselves.
- Say, 'If I don't hear from you I'll assume you're fine.' Never pre-book another appointment for them – this presupposes failure! If they need more help they can contact you. This builds

trust. _Beware doing otherwise: you will 'subcommunicate' dishonesty._

That's all the aftercare I ever give! For greater details of my therapy approach in general – see 'Powerful hypnosis'.

Appendix 13: Skin and stress.

I thought I'd leave you with an interesting insight. I have come to the conclusion through direct experience that a great deal of the time skin problems are actually caused by stress. I have written about this in previous books but let me give you a very clear example: A lady came to see me for depression, anxiety, confidence etc. She had quite bad psoriasis. We tried to treat it: didn't work. 4 years later I get an email from her; she had retired from a retail job she hated. In fact she had hated every job she ever did in her life. She was really enjoying retirement and her psoriasis had completely vanished! Doctors had given her every cream and potion available to no avail. It was all about stress.

The skin is a stress barometer: it lets you know what is going on inside. The skin may well be the window on the soul more than the eyes. Other things being equal what factors would make skin disorders worse?

- An urban environment.
- A crap job.
- A violent environment.
- An unpredictable environment.
- A high level of pollution.

- Bad food.
- Overcrowding.
- A 'culture' of rudeness, intimidation bullying.
- Family/relationship stress.

Conclusion: anxiety and stress create skin problems. If you have skin problems and are in a 'stressful environment': get out of it!!!

Appendix 14: The REAL socio-historical environment in which you practise 'therapy'.

As I have explicitly and implicitly said in my books, the social context in which a 'client' (suffering human being) is living and experiencing their day to day social reality affects them deeply, unsurprisingly. Your clients are witnessing, experiencing the total collapse of Western Civilisation. It is any wonder so many people are 'mentally ill'. They are in fact not remotely 'ill', they are reacting quite normally to all the chaos going on around them. The social environment in which we exist shapes our human potential. A human society = humans + culture. Western culture is being systematically dismantled. An example of this would be the fact that 'modern' (contemporary) Britain is now almost 100% a parasitical rather than a producing society. Another defining characteristic of a collapsing society is the increasing power of 'vested interests groups'. Rampant self-indulgence and non-productive ego satisfaction for example in ostentatious displays of wealth yet another indicator.
So what are the key indicators of a civilisation's collapse? Western society is in what is known as Stage 4 to 7 of a collapsing

civilisation marked out by:

1. **A declining rate of economic expansion in the core area.** Outsourcing, mass capital movements to India and China etc.

2. **Growing social tension and class conflicts** (increasingly bitter and dangerous); this also includes racial conflict (divide and conquer).

3. **Increasingly frequent and increasingly violent imperialistic wars.** Oops.

4. **Growing pessimism and irrationalities,** belief in otherworldly superstitions and mass drug taking (see below).

5. **A rise is 'irrational activism'** – especially in the realm of politics – this is expressed in 'mainstream' extremist fanaticisms; for example Marxism, Fascism, Feminism, Corporatism, Gnostic New Age etc., the rise of cults.

6. **The rise of 'socialism'.** Unable to get needs met through economic means people seek a beggar thy neighbour policy in order to make ends meet. This creates an irresponsible dependency and entitlement culture.

7. **Irrational coping mechanisms.** Gambling, increased use of drugs (20th century smoking epidemic was the first sign), obsessions with sex and sexual perversions

(as seen in animals in zoos).

8. **Increased crime.** Thank God that's not happening! England is now more violent that ANY US state. 'Crime' also becomes 'legal' for Elites.

9. **Mental health catastrophe.** Mass outbreaks of 'neurosis' and 'psychosis'. Obsession with death and an afterlife etc. One of the main indicators of mental collapse in the West is the plague of pathological narcissism across all social classes, genders and races. Bizarrely this was predicted in the Bible as a sign of the End Times!??!

10. **Invasion.** This has already begun – the existing populous is replaced. This is the final stage of the collapse process; in our time this is seen as mass, uncontrolled 'immigration' to the Western nations. This mimics the same process begun by Rome after 200 BC and its victory in the Punic wars: Italians were 'deported' to the new provinces of North Africa/the Levant etc. for the benefit of the Roman establishment as troops and replaced on their landholdings by cheap, foreign slaves.

That ought to cheer you up! And you wonder people are 'crazy'? When psychopaths rule - chaos reigns. Yes folks, this is a book for grown ups. Interested readers can look at: **Carrol Quigley's 'The evolution of**

Civilisations'. By the way if you think any of the above is a sign of 'progress' you are de facto psychotic.

Finally? Not yet...

Almost there...one last book in the Rogue Hypnotist project to go! And it's gonna be really weird: that's why I called it –
'WEIRDNOSIS! Astounding confessions of a Rogue Hypnotist!' Lots of new stuff that no one else is telling you about; discover Sithnosis, 21st century trance, Psychopolitics or Neo Hypnosis of the Bolsheviks and Nazis, Martian invasion hypnosis, learn 'SCSS' (you'll have to buy it to find out what this stands for – hint: it has to do with creating a willing sex slave!), how to create trance using hypnotic poetry; known as – hypno-poetics, a full study on the *real* subjectivity of the creative imagination, an intensive study of the mechanics of hypnotic eye power and the evil eye, covert idea implantation and New Age/Gnostic social subversion in romance novels, advanced level cold reading formulas, how to do hobo-hypnosis (my term for 'street' hypnosis), a full script for 'resisters', how to spot a somnambulist from their handwriting (no joke!) and much, much more: told of course in my inimitable and meek fashion.

Look out for it on Amazon...I'm going out in style baby! We're almost done Padawan! You've almost graduated as a Rogue-notist!!!

R.H. November 2015.

Made in the USA
Monee, IL
28 June 2020

34911685R00424